ADVANCE PRAISE FOR LESSONS FOR A WARMING PLANET

"Provides an expansive treatment of the impact of environmental law in its broadest sense on our nation's lands, resources, and peoples. In doing so, it offers a valuable perspective on our present-day contestations over natural resource extraction, climate, equity, and environmental protection.

—Alexandra B. Klass, James G. Degnan Professor of Law,
University of Michigan Law School

"Professors Camacho and Daniels provide an engaging history of U.S. environmental and natural resources laws, and a fresh framework for understanding what features and challenges have emerged and endured in our laws over the past 250 years. Their insights into law, history, and culture provide important lessons for the future of U.S. environmental law."

—Sean Hecht, Managing Attorney, California
Regional Office, Earthjustice

"This book appears at a time when the United States Government seems determined to abandon or reverse any energy and environmental policy that mitigates global warming and it could not be more needed. Examining American legal history from the earliest impact of European settlement to the present, the authors explore the broad array of policies that have been adopted both to encourage and rein in the impacts of economic exploitation on nature. The results of this unusually deep assessment of the evolution of environmental law take us well beyond the march of legislation and litigation and inspire new thinking about how to address the current crisis."

—Mary Nichols, Distinguished Counsel for the Emmett Institute
on Climate Change and the Environment, UCLA School of Law,
former California Air Resources Board Chair (1979–1983, 2007–20)
and California Natural Resources Agency Secretary (1999–2003).

LESSONS FOR A WARMING PLANET

LESSONS FOR A WARMING PLANET

A VITAL HISTORY OF US ENVIRONMENTAL LAW

ALEJANDRO E. CAMACHO and BRIGHAM DANIELS

New York

NEW YORK UNIVERSITY PRESS
New York
www.nyupress.org

Library of Congress Cataloging-in-Publication Data
Names: Camacho, Alejandro E. author | Daniels, Brigham author
Title: Lessons for a warming planet : a vital history of US environmental law / Alejandro E. Camacho and Brigham Daniels.
Description: New York : New York University Press, 2026. | Includes bibliographical references and index.
Identifiers: LCCN 2025042971 (print) | LCCN 2025042972 (ebook) | ISBN 9781479802814 hardcover | ISBN 9781479802852 ebook | ISBN 9781479802838 ebook other
Subjects: LCSH: Environmental law—United States—History | Environmental law—Social aspects—United States | Environmental law—Political aspects—United States | Environmental law—Economic aspects—United States
Classification: LCC KF3817.C36 2026 (print) | LCC KF3817 (ebook)
LC record available at https://lccn.loc.gov/2025042971
LC ebook record available at https://lccn.loc.gov/2025042972

This book is printed on acid-free paper, and its binding materials are chosen for strength and durability. We strive to use environmentally responsible suppliers and materials to the greatest extent possible in publishing our books.

The manufacturer's authorized representative in the EU for product safety is Mare Nostrum Group B.V., Doelen 72, 4831 GR Breda, The Netherlands. Email: gpsr@mare-nostrum.co.uk.

The cover art visually represents annual global mean temperature data from 1850 to 2024 as colored tree ring stripes. Tree ring design: igreen/Jonathan Fieber ©. Climate Stripes: Professor Ed Hawkins and the University of Reading (https://showyourstripes.info) and used under a CC 4.0 license.

Manufactured in the United States of America

10 9 8 7 6 5 4 3 2 1

Also available as an ebook

To Kathleen, Santiago, Nicolas, and Elisa

A.E.C.

To Kellie, Abigail, Grant, and Elizabeth

B.D.

CONTENTS

LIST OF FIGURES

INTRODUCTION

We begin our story—the history of and lessons from U.S. environmental law—on the shores of the iconic Boston Harbor. Long before American Revolutionaries hurled chests of tea into the harbor in protest of British taxes, norms and later on laws managing use of Boston Harbor played an important role in the lives of inhabitants and in their relationship with their surrounding environment.[1] For millennia, the harbor had brought Native Americans to its shores.[2] These cultures subsisted on wildlife from the area's forests, planted and harvested agricultural products, and enjoyed Boston Harbor's bounty of striped bass, flounder, and shellfish. They adopted management strategies such as controlled burns of forests, crop rotations, and fish weirs that all enabled sustainable harvests.[3]

The Massachusett tribe occupied the harbor when the first English colonists arrived.[4] The British Crown, using the Massachusetts Bay Colony charter of 1629, sanctioned Puritans to settle Boston.[5] As settlers came, they not only pushed out Massachusett and then Wampanoag, Pequot, Nipmuc, and other Indigenous communities from the area, but also they brought with them diseases that tore through the local tribes.[6] The harbor was deep enough for shipping boats and had an archipelago to shelter Boston's shores from winds and waves, making it an ideal port.

For at least the first two centuries under both British rule and then as part of the United States, the relationship between European settlers and the harbor and its shoreline relied on a legal and economic system that sanctioned divvying up the spoils without much thought about the effect on the environment. Boston's growing fishing industry hauled in seafood. Like many early American cities, settlers were allowed to fill Boston's surrounding shallows as they saw fit. In most instances, the law encouraged this: When individuals salvaged undevelopable wetlands by filling them, in return they gained legal title to new valuable properties.

Small projects by landowners and large-scale, public projects (like rail lines connecting Boston's ports to its commercial center) consumed ecologically important wetlands. [7]

In the mid-1800s, the City of Boston put into place some of the nation's first-documented wetland legal protections—not for environmental but rather economic purposes.[8] Locals worried that filling the shallows might compromise the harbor's depth and thereby thwart local commerce fueled by Boston's ports. The city eroded these legal protections, however, bit by bit, project by project, so that Boston's total landmass grew through the filling of wetlands by a land area of about one-sixth.[9] With the Industrial Revolution sweeping through Boston into the rest of the United States, more than rocks and fill dirt made it into the once pristine harbor.

Even as Henry David Thoreau warned against materialism and extolled the many virtues of conserving nature along Walden Pond just twenty miles away,[10] in meaningful ways Boston became an unregulated common dump. Raw sewage was the most controversial aspect of Boston's water pollution problems. Enabled by public laws and institutions, in the 1800s, the harbor became a collective sewer once Bostonians began adopting indoor plumbing.[11] In fact, the word *sewer* came from the notion that the contents in the sewer traveled *seaward*.[12] Characteristic of cities of the time, stormwater runoff carrying waste from industry, commerce, transportation, and residences added to the city's pollution problems.

The first government attempts to do anything other than facilitate the delivery of raw sewage to the shallows of the harbor came not with regulation but with infrastructure. Both to deal with pipe blockages and to extend pipe distances, in the 1870s, Boston extended the sewage drainage pipes miles through the harbor and over islands.[13] Well into the 1900s, the government continued to build and extend pipes. Still, the growing length of the pipe was far from enough to stem the unintended consequences of sewage and often flatly ignored industrial pollution. Though miles offshore, if the tide or winds shifted disadvantageously, raw sewage made it back to the coast. Disgusting, unsanitary pollution was simply an ordinary part of life.

At the turn of the twentieth century, the Progressive Era brought unprecedented public health and conservation reforms across the country, and Boston was no exception. While many reforms focused on addressing the harsh conditions of the city's tenement housing,[14] Fredrick Olmstead's influence and public support for more open spaces led to the creation of the nation's first regional park system, much of which sat along the city's rivers and coastline.[15]

Despite these efforts to preserve some urban greenways, Boston continued to grow, and so did its effects on the harbor. "Modernization" brought with it industrialization, chemicalization, and suburbanization, introducing a whole suite of stressors to Boston's waterways.[16] In 1938, still in the throes of the Great Depression, the Massachusetts legislature commissioned a study of the harbor, which resulted in a report recommending treatment of Boston's sewage due to challenges including "grease balls on the beaches, floating matter, and foul odors in Boston Harbor."[17] While resisting full treatment, the city took some steps to treat its sewage to rid it of some of its most blatant public health risks. However, scientific studies continued to show pollution levels more than a thousand times worse than those deemed safe by other states at the time, with underprivileged individuals exposed disproportionately.[18]

The United States began to awaken to an era of environmental protection in the 1960s and 1970s. In Boston, like other cities, community groups and chapters of national organizations sprouted up and raised health and environmental concerns.[19] This burgeoning environmental movement successfully pushed in the 1960s for designation of portions of Cape Cod's shoreline as protected National Seashores.[20] Yet the countercurrents of powerful industry and at best indifferent policymakers[21] allowed the pollution problems of Boston Harbor to continue to worsen. In 1972, Congress passed the landmark Clean Water Act and, despite the dictates of the enactment, Massachusetts lawmakers balked at the cost of treating sewage before releasing it into Boston Harbor.[22] Even during the nation's most prolific period of environmental protection legislation, Boston lagged most other cities in treating sewage effluent. By the 1980s, the harbor was known as "America's dirtiest harbor."[23]

After running along the beach only to find himself plodding through human sewage washed ashore, William Golden, not only an avid runner but also an environmental lawyer, decided to sue the city to force action. In 1985, a Massachusetts district court held that Boston needed to act.[24] Finally, Boston began treating sewage before releasing it in the harbor.

State and federal regulations remediated contaminants in Boston Harbor while more rigorous implementation and enforcement of the Clean Water Act further reduced direct and indirect discharges.[25]

Boston Harbor still faces significant pollution challenges—effluent from the surrounding city; overfishing; invasive species; and most ominously, the foreseeable effects arising from climate change, such as sea level rise.[26] And like virtually every other metropolitan area, marginalized communities in Boston continue to bear the brunt of environmental harm.[27] Legal doctrines, processes, and structures enabled Boston Harbor's extensive environmental damage; nonetheless, over the past few decades, they also ensured that, despite the difficulties that persist and loom large, Boston Harbor is cleaner than it has been for centuries.[28] And the law will indelibly shape its future as well.

PAST AS PROLOGUE

The story of Boston Harbor is an account that could have been told a million ways, about a million places, across the United States. The stories of the places around the country are inextricably tied to laws that exploit and those that protect the environment. The history of environmental law in the United States—the ebb and flow of legal doctrines, processes, and institutions that have enabled consumption and conservation, all accompanied with undercurrents repeatedly pulling against the tide—plays a central role in the broader narrative of U.S. history and the environmental health of not only the nation, but also the planet.

Indeed, the United States has played an outsized role in creating the global environmental threats of the twenty-first century. At the same time, in the twentieth century, it repeatedly pioneered most of the important legal innovations designed to protect the environment.

Is its legal system on the brink of Charles Dickens' "spring of hope" or "winter of despair"?[29] It is hard to say, because these questions will be decided by a collective story the country has yet to write. Despite the enormity of the environmental challenges we face, previous generations of Americans have faced comparable questions; this book examines some of their stories and scours them for applicable lessons to apply to our current challenges.

In broad terms, this book endeavors to explore how the United States has found itself with such a fraught relationship with the environment as a way of better understanding how this relationship can be improved. As authors, our interest is not an impartial one; our careers in studying the law inevitably have shaped the way that we size up the fundamental challenges currently facing the planet, particularly climate change. Our desire to author this book is deeply rooted in our shared belief that there is not only a great need for legal change to protect the environment, but also that this change is possible.

Our conviction stems, at least in part, from the legal changes and innovations—both incremental and radical—adopted in the past, despite considerable economic, social, and political forces to the contrary. It undoubtedly is true that one must take great care not to draw too many inferences about what might occur from a review of historical events and movements[30]—particularly for what is likely to be a no-analog climactic future.[31] Notwithstanding this axiom, the history of environmental law in the United States is one of the only repositories of information relevant to understanding potential avenues for meaningful legal reforms today. As such, this book is not just an accounting of *what* happened, but also an exploration of *why* it happened, as a way of distilling possible lessons for those willing to consider *how* to navigate the challenges of our times.

FIVE INSIGHTS FROM U.S. ENVIRONMENTAL LAW'S HISTORY

THE IMPORTANCE OF LAW IN SHAPING OUR ENVIRONMENT

The first and perhaps most simple insight is that law has virtually always been at the center of environmental protection and degradation in the United States. The book situates the narrative of the evolution of environmental law into a broader U.S. environmental history. It engages with important historical figures and ideas that changed the nation's approach to the environment, as well as the social, political, and economic factors that contributed to environmental challenges and the law's ability to address them.

The book asserts that a thorough comprehension of the law and legal developments is fundamental to an understanding of the relationship between the peoples of the United States and its environment. The law has been central to debates about the ways and the extent to which public health, environmental conservation, and social justice concerns can and should prevail over other public and private interests. The law was, is, and will almost certainly always be central to any attempt to use or protect the greater environment.

THE LAW OF PROTECTION *AND* EXPLOITATION

Second, we assert that consideration of the laws that have allowed for and even facilitated environmental harm is central to comprehending and devising laws that might serve to repair or prevent future harm. Indeed, looking only at environmental protection laws is like only picking up one side of a coin. As such, our analytical lens is much broader than the lens most have used to investigate the development of environmental law in the United States. Rather than focusing solely on legal developments that have led to environmental protection, we also trace the development of major legal drivers of environmental degradation.

The analytical implications of this insight are threefold. Temporally, while most analyses only reach back to the adoption of federal pollution control law in the 1970s, or to the complicated natural resource legacies of progressive reformers like President Theodore Roosevelt, our discussion traces legal developments back to precolonial history that preceded formation of the United States. Second, rather than an exclusive focus on federal policy, this book draws on state and local legal developments, as well as their interplay with federal law. Finally, as environmental degradation and protection have been facilitated through developments in a wide range of legal fields—such as property, administrative, corporate, and consumer protection—the book's examination extends into these fields as well. We posit that this wider lens helps in understanding not only how we got to where we find ourselves but also how we might best navigate a productive way forward.

OSCILLATIONS AND UNDERCURRENTS

Descriptively, legal change related to the environment in the United States has typically been characterized by eras of ebbs and flows.

Generally, each era's currents take the form of either exploitation or conservation. Nonetheless, each era included undercurrents —social, political, and legal critiques or resistance—that that defied major currents of the day. These frequently gain enough momentum and become major currents in subsequent periods. The ushering in of a new era frequently is premised on a course change in which prior undercurrents gain ascendancy, in part as a reaction to long unaddressed harms or prior legal change and to undo incentives created in the past. These new prevailing waves often have grown out of unsuccessful resistance in prior eras, with new events and incentives changing the state of play later. Our current era, what we call the "Contested Era," may be uniquely described as involving turbulence—incremental ebbs and flows both in terms of the time elapsed and extent of legal change—rather than a single dominant current and undercurrent.

More normatively, overwhelming existing scientific evidence suggests that the United States will have another substantial course correction on the environment. The problems of the emerging Anthropocene—climate change; unparalleled emerging technologies; unprecedented disparities in wealth; and increasing unwillingness or inability to govern through compromise, to maintain fundamentals of democratic republicanism, to recognize facts, and even to recognize the core problems facing the planet—at least suggest the potential for a new era. Whether such an era will primarily promote democracy and conservation or not remains uncertain.

ACCRETIONS, EROSIONS, AND AVULSIONS

In many circumstances, the law of the environment in the United States developed slowly, through incremental accretion or erosion of legal protections, perhaps inventing new tools that tweak existing law at the edges. However, other legal innovations have come in episodic floods that institute fundamentally new legal paradigms.

Whether an incremental change or avulsion, these changes in the law can be categorized as substantive, procedural, or structural in character. *Substantive* legal changes include new goals that supplemented or replaced prior objectives, as well as the regulatory or management strategies for achieving such goals. Beyond broader goals of efficiency (administrative and/or market), fairness, and legitimacy, the four most prominent environmental protection goals frequently were—and continue to be—lumped together. These include the following.

- *Nonintervention* stresses shielding nature from active human intervention, thus keeping ecological systems in (or returning them to) a "natural" state.[32] The federal Wilderness Act epitomizes such an approach.[33] This approach also draws on perspectives on the spiritual, psychic, and existence values of the natural.
- *Historical preservation* seeks to ground preservation and restoration to a historical baseline.[34] Many existing legal goals focus on promoting ecological inertia or restoration of an ecological system to an earlier state. Natural resource managers also regularly focus on promoting the preservation or restoration of existing or past ecological conditions.
- *Sustained yield* focuses on maximizing productivity of a particular resource or resources for the purposes of human use or consumption, something common in many laws governing the extraction of resources ranging from timber to fisheries.
- *Promoting health*, the basis of most U.S. pollution control laws, primarily seeks to protect people from environmental risks. Similarly, though rarely passed in law, we frequently find rhetoric and science focusing on protecting or promoting ecological health.

Legal mechanisms and innovations for achieving such goals included, for example, property rights, new common law doctrines, and a wide array of prescriptive and market-enlisting administrative regulations.

However, accretions and avulsions also occurred in legal *process*. Initially, such procedural mechanisms were legislative and judicial, but they increasingly have included administrative processes conducted by management or regulatory agencies.[35] More recent forms have included the authorization of citizen administrative lawsuits, environmental impact assessment processes, adaptive management, and collaborative governance processes.[36]

Structural legal developments consist of changes in legal institutional arrangements, including the relationship between institutions. Early forms of structural governance in the United States, for instance, include constitutional separation of powers and federalism doctrines that delegate certain constitutional authority to particular institutions.[37] Subsequent forms have included the proliferation of federal, state, and local administrative agencies with overlapping and distinct jurisdiction, as well as the development of various forms of intergovernmental coordination.[38]

LEGAL EXPERIMENTATION AND IMAGINATION

The final crosscutting theme of the book considers numerous factors that have catalyzed legal change, especially to manage overlooked or emerging environmental risks. The book explores the roles of leadership; social movements, coalition building, and interest convergence; and information and technology in advancing legal change.

Ideas

A particular subtheme is how ideas about conservation and environmentalism have emerged and developed over time. Gifford Pinchot studied forestry in Europe decades before refining and then implementing pioneering ideas about sustainable resource management.[39] John Muir conceived of a wilderness preservation ethos in 1890; it was almost seventy-five years before the Wilderness Act instantiating this conservation goal was adopted.[40] The book seeks to better understand how knowledge creation has translated into legal change. Relatedly, it considers how developments in other knowledge fields—such as environmental economics, environmental politics, environmental ethics, environmental science and ecology, and sociological theories of race and race relations—have catalyzed the development of environmental law.

Experimentation

Another subtheme focuses on how ideas germinate, sprout, and pollinate through legal experimentation. In many circumstances, novel legal theories, strategies, or programs adopted by one jurisdiction—such as park designation and preservation, air regulation, or environmental risk assessment and disclosure—are met with skepticism or resistance, prove successful, and then are emulated by others. We see how change can happen through the iterative interplay between multiple levels of governance, with change at one level often altering the state of play at other levels.

Idealism Versus Pragmatism

Relatedly, the book considers the important roles throughout U.S. environmental legal history of both forcefully idealistic and incrementally pragmatic strategies for managing environmental problems. Idealists are purists who have sought to fundamentally transform, and even revolutionize, the political, economic, and legal system to advance conservation and safeguard public health. On the other side of the ledger, we find pragmatists who have identified environmental protection or conservation as important goals, but either identify other social objectives as similarly important or compromise their environmental goals for more realistic aims. Rather than a simplistic dichotomy, we learn how this tension between pragmatist and purist impulses exists in the hearts of many individuals in the environmental legal movement.

Adaptive Governance

More normatively, the book considers how political, social, and legal institutions have and have not invested in legal imagination to address environmental problems. Undoubtedly, complexity shapes and inhibits laws related to the environment. Because the environment is complex, it is important to understand not just the state of the law and its potential to address environmental problems, but also the adaptive capacity of legal doctrines, processes, and structures to accommodate change.

Notwithstanding periods of adaptation, the law has conventionally been oriented toward promoting certainty, rigidity, and resisting change.[41] This orientation has at times limited the effectiveness of legal tools employed to manage complex and dynamic ecological phenomena. A similar thread emphasizes the lag in environmental law. Certain initial premises of most U.S. law furthering environmental protection have been based on limited understanding of other complex systems (e.g., ecological processes or markets), and these laws persist as foundations of the legal system despite having been later proven to be outmoded.

A ROADMAP

In this book, we highlight five major eras, each one the focus of one of the five core chapters. Below, we lay out a road map of the book while illustrating the broad arc of the ebb and flow of development of law to address environmental problems.

The first of these eras, explored in Chapter 1, runs from precolonial North America through 1890—what we call the "Allocation Era." We note that this period is frequently overlooked in histories relating to U.S. legal development and the environment. But this era is critical in laying the country's legal foundation for massive resource development and the emergence of environmentalism and early legal restrictions designed to mitigate harm from resource exploitation. During this era, legal doctrines made resource ownership possible for the masses of primarily European immigrants, even as African Americans were savagely brought and kept in bondage and Native Americans were cruelly and repeatedly ejected from their ancestral homes under color of law, often through force and violence. The private property rules embraced during this period sought to promote acquisition, development, and use by offering clear rights that provide certainty and resist change.

This era has a long shadow, establishing enduring rules governing resources like water, oil and gas, and wildlife that mainly promote consumption and typically ignore values rooted in conservation or preservation. During this time, the federal government often assumed control of the division and allocation of land to promote settlement and facilitated the exploitation of natural resources by settlers and industry, including railroad and mining interests. As the wild American frontier closed, pressure grew to override preexisting Latine ownership and further expropriate Native American land and resources—even those expressly reserved for tribes in treaties with the federal government.

While less dominant, this era inaugurated environmentalism as well as a degree of environmental protection through the law. There were modest checks on widespread resource exploitation and the most egregious forms of pollution. Most notably, the era saw legal innovations that resulted in the first efforts to preserve and protect public lands through the creation of not just our first state and national parks but the first of such parklands anywhere.[42]

Chapter 2 then turns to the crucible of environmental protection in the Progressive Era (from 1890 to 1920), a time when localities, states, and the federal government enacted an array of health and conservation laws in significant part as a reaction to the closing of the frontier and the perceived excesses of the time. During this era, emerging debates and legal change in pollution abatement, food safety, and land and resource conservation evolved in tandem with labor, temperance, and antitrust reforms. This progressive movement relied in part on a growing (albeit incomplete) understanding of ecological and environmental science, including extending some of these insights to infamous principles of social Darwinism and the explicit exclusion of non–Western European immigrants, people of color, and women.

During the Progressive Era, laws related to the environment deeply restructured American life, despite dogged backlash particularly in regions where supersized industry was frequently left to dominate, unchecked by a laissez-faire governing philosophy. The U.S. Supreme Court committed lands underlying navigable water bodies into the hands of the states with a charge to conserve them for the good of their publics. The U.S. Congress passed legislation that attempted to limit pollution and promote public health through reform legislation, such as the Rivers and Harbors Act[43] and the Federal Meat Inspection Act.[44] Likewise, Congress passed the Migratory Bird Treaty[45] as a response to the enormous pressure on migratory birds from hunting. Finally, perhaps the most significant and lasting legal innovation of this era was the large-scale establishment of public land conservation areas and dueling attempts by pragmatic conservationists and idealist preservationists to create national parks, forests, wildlife refuges, and monuments.

In Chapter 3, the book surveys how, from 1920 to 1960, the law reflected significant social and political changes in which conservation largely waned in its influence in favor of development, allowing the United States to emerge as not just a global superpower but also a super polluter. The New Deal initiated transformative legal change, including unprecedented investments in infrastructure and public works to manage economic and other hardships that emerged during the Great Depression and World War II. In the "Modernization Era," the proliferation of the federal bureaucracy and public regulation, governed by a new field of administrative law, initiated the modern administrative state that in later decades served as the foundation for modern environmental law. Laws in the postwar boom of the 1950s also promoted rapid land development and resource use.

While public recreation opportunities continued to grow through the federal land reserve system, state land development policies and local zoning, ostensibly enacted to protect community health, safety, and welfare, hastened urban sprawl, pollution, habitat loss, and racial and socioeconomic segregation. Federal loan subsidies and tax breaks for home ownership and investments in an interstate highway system helped center the suburb at the core of the "American Dream"—an aspiration mostly only within reach of non-Latine whites.

Federal laws investing in energy generation infrastructure led to a rapid proliferation of coal, hydroelectric, nuclear, and oil extraction and production, each creating unique environmental challenges. Legal rules that more generally promoted resource extraction and overlooked the negative by-products from industrial mass production of consumer goods, such as air conditioning and the automobile, contributed to a paradigm shift in the rate and direction of growth while accelerating pollution and ecological degradation. Even among all the government policies to promote economic growth, the era also witnessed an undercurrent of modest federal legislation trying to stem pollution through regulation and funding, serving as valuable experiments providing lessons for those pressing for reforms that would eventually come.

In Chapter 4, the book turns to the "Environmental Era" of the 1960s and 1970s—the defining decades for federal environmental legislation thus far in the United States. Events in the 1960s—mounting evidence from writers like Rachel Carson,[46] public outcry about nuclear fallout, and disasters like the Santa Barbara oil spill[47]—built momentum toward the modern legal infrastructure of environmental protection through political mobilization, charismatic leaders, and unlikely coalitions. Legislation in this decade highlighted rival modes of thinking about federal land management—maximizing yield, historical preservation, and natural preservation (the last epitomized by the Wilderness Act, the most aggressive law in the United States aimed at preventing human intrusion on federal lands).

The shortcomings of federal attempts to enlist states to reign in pollution in the 1960s, however, led Congress during the 1970s to pass a remarkable cascade of unprecedented federal legislative innovation mandating states to address water, land, and air pollution. The era not only saw the creation of the core statutes that make up modern environmental law but also the founding of and growth of many federal environmental agencies and nonprofit organizations. The era culminated with the establishment of a pioneering legal regime that completely changed longstanding liability rules and procedures to push the cleanup of dangerous hazardous waste sites.

Despite this unparalleled growth in public environmental legal infrastructure, inevitably the rapid adoption of experimental legal approaches led to a range of deficiencies in standard setting, implementation, and enforcement. Meanwhile, persistent political resistance from regulated industries and other interest groups allowed prominent environmental issues (such as energy policy and environmental justice) to be ignored or at best only partially addressed.

Buildout, backlash, contestation, and polarization have become the dominant themes of the "Contested Era" explored in Chapter 5, as environmental law has evolved turbulently from 1980 to the present day. Presidential administrations have undone and redone, continually reinventing administrative agencies and reinterpreting rules. An era typified by divided government, Congress routinely has undercut presidential administrations and exerted constant pressure on existing statutes. Federal and state courts pushed in different directions. Indicative of the increased polarization, what has become increasingly identified as "red" states sued the federal government during "blue" administrations, while "blue" states sued the federal government in "red" ones. Interest groups of various stripes have found ways to promote their agenda and influence policymakers at all levels.

This era is marked by legal evolution, primarily through regulatory and judicial interpretation, with increasingly sporadic Congressional adjustments and innovations. This buildout of U.S. environmental law started with the Reagan revolution and a significant deregulatory, anti-environmentalist reaction to the prior era—including program defunding and obstruction in implementation of statutory regimes. The remainder of the millennium was characterized by pragmatism and conciliation, fueled in significant part by increasing partisan rancor mollified through the tenuous and uneasy success of moderating policymakers. The proliferation of significant policy experimentation (such as emissions trading and negotiated regulation) was borne out of inventive attempts to reconcile competing aims and increased awareness of the complexity of environmental problems.

The new millennium, meanwhile, has seen the ascendancy of more immoderate influences and significant battles in the courts and legislatures accompanied by incremental policy advances. Polarization has reached a new level with the advent of the first Trump administration and its protectionist, anti-regulation, and anti-science agenda, largely held in check by a battery of successful lawsuits challenging regulatory rollbacks in a wide range of subfields. Yet reflexive partisanship ensures that fundamental environmental challenges, such as farm and urban runoff and environmental injustice, remain inadequately addressed. Most prominently, amid Alaska and Gulf of Mexico oil spill disasters and conflicts over pipelines, fracking, and other fossil fuel development, global anthropogenic climate change has received limited policy attention except through interstate greenhouse gas mitigation collaborations, adaptation planning, and the unprecedented investments in green infrastructure during the Biden administration. The second Trump administration's rejection of bedrock environmental legal protections, attacks on environmental justice, hostility to clean energy, and flouting of the rule of law, however, has supercharged the turbulence of the era.

The book concludes with our attempt to connect the themes of the book and elaborate on the lessons for what we anticipate will become the next era of U.S. environmental law—one in which the country grapples with previously unattended and new environmental problems. Climate change looms large, exacerbated by fossil fuel dependency and depletion; sprawl; resource overuse and scarcity; water, air, and land pollution; habitat fragmentation and biodiversity loss. As in other eras, emerging technologies offer unprecedented opportunities and risks that might help address these many challenges—or, left unchecked, intensify and expand harms.

We argue that the history of U.S. environmental law provides essential information about what may be to come. Just as the country has endeavored to meet seemingly insurmountable challenges in the past, a new era of environmental lawmaking—shaped by economic, scientific, and ethical forces, and formed in the crucible of key political moments—is certainly possible.

Can and will the United States reclaim a leadership role in addressing the pressing environmental problems that confront the world? Will it mainly be remembered for its contributions to global environmental problems, despite its many innovations and contributions to environmental law? It remains unclear whether the American public and its various private and public institutions are up to the task of shifting governance toward promoting long-term ecological health; to fostering informed public deliberation about the immense, enduring value of ecological resources; and to conserving them for future generations. Yet this was also the case before each of the other major turning points in U.S. environmental history. We provide insights into what the roadmap to change may include and what lessons the past holds.

It is often said that those who do not understand history are doomed to repeat it.[48] Not only due to our desire to clearly avoid follies of the past but also to find solutions for the future, we argue we need to understand the history of environmental exploitation and protection. It is not just a look backward but a roadmap for the future as we search for a pathway to the planet's much-needed legal changes.

1

THE ALLOCATION ERA

EXPLOITING A NEW COUNTRY (PRECOLONIAL-1890)

INTRODUCTION

In the 1830s, coming off an unsuccessful run for the presidency, Senator Henry Clay played a critical role using his power as a lawmaker to chart the new nation's course. Clay, both an ardent slave abolitionist and slave owner, was much like his young country—full of lofty ideals but frequently struggling to live up to them.[1] One place where he did not conjure contradictions, however, was in his lifelong support for America's economic expansion. As a senator, he called for and worked toward the "transformation of the condition of the country from gloom and distress to brightness and prosperity."[2] But what would bring the change? In Clay's mind, it was "mainly the work of American legislation, fostering American industry."[3]

Legal innovations did much more to change the environment than anything else written at the time, including the still admired words of proto-environmental advocates like the Transcendentalists Emerson and Thoreau.[4] The most impactful laws on the environment, however, found roots in exploiting the environment, not protecting it. For Clay, like many at the time, *progress* meant something much more specific—*economic progress of European settlers.*

It is a fair argument that the seeds of environmental protection law were planted in response to such "progress." Environmental exploitation, unsanitary conditions, and westward expansion were pervasive enough during this era that, like Emerson and Thoreau, many began to understand the stakes of environmental protection by witnessing some of what was already lost. While little about Clay conjures the environment, other than perhaps his crane-like build and features, he played a central role in shaping the relationship of the country to the environment. Tracing his legislative legacy in many ways illustrates how his desire for economic progress resulted not only in environmental problems but also went so far to feed the country's political appetite to reverse course.

In the story of the law's relationship with the environment, we find much in the first centuries of European settlement that many legal environmental histories overlook: the driving forces such as colonization aimed at exploiting resources and people; the creation and territorial expansion of the United States itself; the building of railroads, steamships, and roads; the clearing of forests for farming; the transformation of rural communities into cities; the development of mechanized industry; the mining of coal; the building of dams; the exploitation of slaves and immigrants; and a genocide of Native Americans and the attempted destruction of Native American culture. Just as Clay called for, many early innovations—including legal innovations—particularly worked to the advantage of American industry. Exploiting the American continent's resources—frequently through the suppression and disregard of those not protected by the American legal system—is the prominent theme we find in looking at the interaction of American settlers with the environment.

The period of American history covered in this chapter, which begins just prior to European colonization and ends in 1890, frequently illustrates how the law facilitated allocation and use of natural resources, as well as the ways that it prioritized economic gain and resource allocation and use over other values. More specifically, we see that the law established and legitimized rights to the continent's resources, promoted their exploitation, and allowed the harms from such actions to be borne by others without any legal recourse. The story we tell reaches back before the early colonists began settling and European leaders made empire building in North America an ambition. We highlight the ways that the colonists originally relied on Europe's legal traditions to shape the relationship between people and the environment, and how different levels of government restructured that law to serve the ends of development, ranging from laws establishing private ownership (including slave property) and actively promoting such ownership (such as relinquishing federal lands for homesteaders and restructuring water law).

While far from the dominant narrative of the era, we also find a burgeoning appreciation and concern for the environment reflected not only in literature and society but also in law. Limited legal efforts sprouted up to protect wildlife, public lands, and public health. Though in many ways these laws just foreshadowed things to come, these shadows were cast from something that even today we would consider environmental protections.

NATIVE AMERICAN LIFE, DEATH, AND IMPACT ON COLONIAL NORTH AMERICA (PRIOR TO RECORDED HISTORY–1600S)

At least ten thousand years before Christopher Columbus's crew spotted North America inching onto the horizon, and perhaps much earlier, Indigenous peoples began inhabiting what is now the United States.[5] Millions (and most likely tens of millions) of thriving Native Americans lived on the continent.[6] Long before the emergence of the U.S. legal system—from which U.S. environmental protection would grow—colonization brought about raw devastation of life and radical changes to North America's environment.

Much of the lore around the constellation of Native American cultures that thrived before Europeans arrived frequently fails to capture the complexities and diversity of these societies. When it comes to the environment, Native American societies have frequently been depicted as living in complete harmony with nature.[7] While many of these cultures were sustainable—as the longevity of their ways of life attest—treating Native societies as enlightened environmentalists gives both too much and too little credit to these societies, ignoring the significant effects Native people had in shaping their environment while also overlooking ingenious methods that Native Americans used to work and inhabit the North American continent.[8]

European settlers had different views on how to work the land, and at least the historical narrative often has failed to appreciate what Native American communities were doing or how they did it. Instead of using shovels, hoes, and plows, tribes often used fire to clear large swaths of land.[9] Fire-cleared land proved essential to agriculture. Native people often planted and scattered seeds in one season and, when they returned, vegetables of all different sorts were there for the harvest. Fires also proved helpful for hunting by reducing the underbrush where game could hide. Most of the populations of Native Americans were nomadic, though some large ancient cities could be found, particularly near modern-day St. Louis[10] and Mexico City.[11] And smaller communities thrived in particularly advantageous tracts of land in the harsher terrain of the arid West.[12]

While fire proved advantageous to Native American communities, it also reshaped the landscape.[13] Fields replaced forests along much of the eastern coastline and from the Gulf of Mexico up the coast; the same is true of the west coastline. Fires were also regularly set through much of the grasslands of the Great Plains and the arid regions of the Interior West. Fire also reordered the dominance of species. For example, along the east coast, trees like maple and chestnut were replaced with trees that would germinate seeds when fires burned, such as the loblolly pine. Populations of animals and plants that thrived in denser forests were diminished and pushed out of large swaths of the landscape. In places with challenging terrain or particularly robust forests, fires failed to prevail: Ancient forests continued to grow along the northern coastlines of the west and east coasts and in the Great Lakes region.[14]

Much of the early recorded history of the interactions between the Americas' native people and Europeans tells of abuse, subjection, and violence.[15] While such direct harms were devastating to be sure, the most destructive and life-threatening result of these early interactions was the introduction of diseases to native populations brought across the Atlantic. Native Americans' immune systems were completely unprepared for the respiratory diseases that would hit them, particularly smallpox and to a lesser extent influenza, measles, and tuberculosis.[16] Within a few generations, largely due to the spread of disease, native populations crashed. Historians frequently estimate the killing off an estimated 90 percent of the original inhabitants of North America.[17]

As populations of Native Americans crashed, the use of fire on the land also nearly disappeared. Just as fire had shaped landscapes, the lack of fire did the same.[18] Forests reclaimed fields. Loblolly pine lost ground to maple and chestnut. Ecosystems adjusted or crashed and were replaced. So great was the impact on the land that some modern climate scientists hypothesize that a period of global cooling—sometimes referred to as the little ice age—was set off by the decrease of greenhouse gases on the planet as new forests in the Americas sucked up carbon dioxide.[19] The decimation of Native Americans dramatically changed the land during the period of colonization and illustrates the impact that humans have had on the environment long before the more obvious impacts that came with colonization and then industrialization.

To various degrees, most Western European countries jockeyed for wealth and power by exploiting peoples and resources in North America. However, three countries in particular—Spain, France, and Britain—played the dominant roles. The continent's Indigenous people suffered as these countries contended for resources and land, either through enslavement, removal from desirable lands, or introduction of European diseases that would ravage Native Americans.

While much of this suffering is beyond this book's scope, European efforts to claim lands and exploit resources reflect a relationship with the environment and Native Americans that defined the era. After Columbus, waves of Spanish conquistadores seized lands, including parts of what are now the American South and West. Meanwhile, Spanish authorities worked with the Roman Catholic Church's attempts to build missions across the continent to convert Indigenous people.[20]

In its own attempt to lay some claim on what is now the United States, France established colonies and forts on the states bordering the Great Lakes and the Mississippi River.[21] While French authorities attempted to ally themselves with Native Americans, these efforts focused on tapping into natural resources—particularly fish and furs. In other places, like the Caribbean and South America, French settlers also sought to establish agricultural products, particularly rice, spices, and sugar.[22]

As British colonies grew into major population centers along the east coast, they claimed special importance in the history of the U.S. environment. Their drastic impact was partially because they fought, displaced, and pushed out Native Americans; captured and assimilated the Dutch colonists in what is now New York; resisted, tamped down, and divided Spanish and French attempts to colonize; and, as detailed next, frequently made headway in developing legal institutions and doctrines even where more forceful methods failed to bear fruit.[23]

THE PERSISTENCE OF COLONIAL LAW AFTER INDEPENDENCE (1780s–1850s)

Aside from the settlers themselves and the physical infrastructure they built up, the most enduring legacy left by European colonists was their legal structure. The colonies imported legal traditions from the countries from which they came, and these legal traditions were largely retained even after the Revolutionary War was fought to cut ties with the European governments. This is particularly the case for judge-made precedents—generally referred to as common law.[24] Common law, particularly laws surrounding resources, unsurprisingly, largely protected the interests of white colonial settlers and helped settlers resolve conflicts among themselves. In this common law, we find some of the seeds that would grow into environmental law.[25]

The imprint of English law was particularly important. Imported law used in this period controlled access and clarified rights to scarce resources.[26] Rules, most notably those governing private property ownership, sought to promote resource use by offering clear rights that would ostensibly provide certainty and resist change. While these laws undoubtedly advanced the overriding commitment to incentivizing the acquisition and settlement of territory and the development of agriculture and mineral extraction, the devotion to expansion and resource use would become problematic in the coming decades.

British common law, particularly, dictated natural resources allocation. While environmental law in centuries to come would increasingly become more of a focus of federal policy, in the decades following the ratification of the U.S. Constitution, it was common law that structured the legal resolution of most conflicts over the environment.[27] Many inherited legal doctrines of the English common law that would later become the line of first defense in the hands of environmental advocates—most notably, nuisance, trespass, and the public trust doctrine—were both applicable and widely influential in resource management in most states at the nation's founding.

Illustrative of the law of the time and still, even centuries later, one of the most frequently studied opinions in American law schools is the case of *Pierson v. Post*.[28] The setting for the case was the turn of the nineteenth century on New York's Long Island, along Southampton's undeveloped coast. More specifically, actions giving rise to the lawsuit occurred in what Judge Daniel Thompkins, writing for the majority, described as an "uninhabited, unpossessed and waste land, called the beach." The conflict between Lodowich Post and Jesse Pierson concerned the taxidermized remains of what the court referred to as "one of those noxious beasts called a fox." More specifically, Pierson had spent a day "hunting, chasing and pursuing the same with his dogs and hounds." Then, with Pierson hot on the heels of the fox, the fox ran by Post on the beach, and Post shot and killed the fox.

The question raised in *Pierson v. Post* is, who gets the fox? Should it be Pierson, who had spent his day chasing the fox with his dogs? Or, should it be Post, who happened to be on the beach when the fox came charging along the coast?

How the case was decided also provides a fitting example of how common law was used and evolved to account for new fact patterns. At that time in New York, it was settled law that if wildlife was killed on private property, it would belong to the landowner regardless of who fired the shot.[29] *Pierson v. Post* raised a novel question to New York courts: What happened if wildlife was shot somewhere other than private property, such as an uninhabited, unpossessed beach?

To reach its decision, a dissenting judge would have delved into the norms of hunters in the area. But in delivering the opinion of the court, Judge Thompkins relied on centuries of precedent from outside New York and even the United States, leaning on European jurists like Bynkershoek from the Netherlands, Puffendorf from Germany, the great Roman legal scholar Justinian, and Fleta from England. It is one of many decisions that would rely on common law to resolve disputes in the newly formed nation. Specifically, while the court praised Pierson for his effort, the court also noted that when Post shot the fox Pierson's "stratagems and strength were nearly exhausted." Therefore, despite referring to Post as "a saucy intruder, who had not shared in the honours or labours of the chase," the court determined that Post (sauciness aside) could keep possession of the fox.

This result serves as an early American application of the rule of capture—the hunter that first shoots the "wild and noxious beast" takes it home. The influential rule is no stranger to natural resource allocation. During the eighteenth and nineteenth centuries, judges often resorted to the rule of capture when asked to resolve disputes involving resources with fur, fins, or feathers.[30] Relying on capture created clear rules to resolve disputes and, perhaps more importantly, provided powerful incentives to pursue and exploit resources. Legal innovators drew on this rule of capture in natural resource contexts well beyond rights to wildlife, including water, oil, and gas, largely promoting consumption and use over conservation or preservation.[31]

NEW SETTLEMENTS AND EVICTIONS FROM ANCESTRAL HOMELANDS (1700s–1800s)

As settlers came to North America and elbowed their way west, spreading across the original states of the Union and beyond, conflicts between Native Americans and settlers became increasingly common over land.[32] Well before the formation of the United States, securing land meant incrementally displacing Native Americans from their ancestral homelands. Once this land was taken, it regularly would be distributed under norms and rules established by immigrant settlers.[33] After the United States became a country, one question that had to be addressed was who owned all the land under the new government's jurisdiction that was not in private hands—ranging from the wildlands deep in the frontier to unclaimed lands on the perimeter of existing communities.

The newly formed government took the position that any land not owned by white settlers at the time the country was formed belonged to the government, despite the history that Native Americans had with the land for tens of thousands of years prior. This position was tested in a case that made it to the Supreme Court of the United States called *Johnson v. M'Intosh*.[34] In 1775, Thomas Johnson purchased land in Virginia from members of the Piankashaw Indian tribe. Though he would become a prominent U.S. politician after the American Revolution, Johnson was still a British subject at the time of this purchase. Johnson died in 1819 and tried to leave what he believed was his land to his heirs. Though Johnson did not know it, in 1818, William M'Intosh struck a deal with the newly formed U.S. Congress to purchase eleven thousand acres of the same land that Johnson had ostensibly purchased earlier.

Figure 1.1 *Ni-a-có-mo, Fix With the Foot, a Brave* (1830) by George Catlin, depicts a member of the Piankashaw tribe, around the time of *Johnson v. M'Intosh.*

The question before the Supreme Court was simply, given these two purchases, who owned the disputed eleven thousand acres?

In a unanimous decision, the Court determined that M'Intosh owned the land. The reasoning provided a foundational precedent that bound up notions of ownership along racial lines—privileging the settlers over Native Americans.[35] Specifically, Marshall found that Native American land rights were not transferable because the Native Americans had been conquered, but he conceded that Native Americans had the right of occupancy so long as the federal government permitted them to remain. With reasoning that may be both surprisingly frank and offensive to a modern reader, Chief Justice John Marshall justified the decision with a clear mindset of the colonizer:

> On the discovery of this immense continent, the great nations of Europe were eager to appropriate to themselves so much of it as they could respectively acquire. Its vast extent offered an ample field to the ambition and enterprise of all; and the character and religion of its inhabitants afforded an apology for considering them as a people over whom the superior genius of Europe might claim an ascendency. The potentates of the old world found no difficulty in convincing themselves that they made ample compensation to the inhabitants of the new, by bestowing on them civilization and Christianity, in exchange for unlimited independence. . . .
>
> We will not enter into the controversy, whether agriculturists, merchants, and manufacturers, have a right, on abstract principles, to expel hunters from the territory they possess, or to contract their limits. Conquest gives a title which the Courts of the conqueror cannot deny, whatever the private and speculative opinions of individuals may be, respecting the original justice of the claim which has been successfully asserted. . . .
>
> But the tribes of Indians inhabiting this country were fierce savages, whose occupation was war, and whose subsistence was drawn chiefly from the forest. To leave them in possession of their country, was to leave the country a wilderness; to govern them as a distinct people, was impossible.[36]

The upshot of the ruling meant at least two things. First, it meant that Native Americans were deprived of the right to sell property to individuals without the authorization of the U.S. government. To this day, the federal government serves as the trustee for any lands held by American Indian tribes.[37] Second, it meant that the unoccupied land dispossessed from Native Americans not owned by settlers automatically belonged to the federal government.[38] With that federal ownership came federal land management.

The prevalence of *unclaimed* lands in the possession of the federal government increased the further west one went. *Johnson v. M'Intosh* focused on lands in the Midwest that the Northwest Ordinance had brought into the Union.[39] Similarly, the Louisiana Purchase had already extended the country from the Louisiana's coastlands to the mountains of Montana.[40] All these lands would be added to unclaimed lands in other western states as the nineteenth century rolled on. Particularly as relatively unpopulated new states were added to the Union, thus adding vast tracks to lands owned by the federal government, the power of the federal government to manage, lease, or permanently transfer land grew in importance.

As for the Native Americans, the Court in *Johnson v. M'Intosh* gave tribes very few political alternatives other than ineffectual redress to Congress, which at this time was no redress at all.[41] Two major themes emerged in Congress's interactions with the tribes. As a starting point, many of the treaties attempted to assimilate Native Americans by transforming them into farmers.[42] With authorities relying on the premise that Native Americans themselves needed to be tamed, they promoted a narrative that Native Americans could and should learn how to farm and participate in the taming of the American wilderness.[43]

The misunderstanding that Native Americans did not know about agriculture is in some ways surprising. After all, it is well documented that the European settlers frequently relied on agricultural practices developed by certain tribes.[44] This reality, in fact, is the basis of the first Thanksgiving.[45] Such reliance continued well into the nineteenth century—sustaining the fur traders on excursions into the frontier.[46] Yet, despite this history, many treaties stubbornly insisted that Native Americans were all hunters who needed to become farmers. For example, a treaty with the Creek Indians in Georgia promised the tribe "useful domestic animals and implements of husbandry."[47] After the turn of the nineteenth century, treaties frequently promised tribes training in agriculture. One summary of such programs concluded, "Often government farmers knew less of farming in the wilderness than the people they were sent to instruct."[48]

A second recurring theme was the persistent breach by Congress of promises to tribal authorities, particularly when settlers desired the land and resources provided to Indigenous peoples in treaties. Because of these breaches, tribes often were forcibly removed or "resettled" from one part of federal land to another.[49] It is noteworthy that some of the bloodiest interactions between settlers and tribes occurred in places where Native Americans had embraced the agrarian life that treaties with the tribes frequently demanded.

For example, in Alabama, North Carolina, Tennessee, Florida, and Georgia, attempts to convert Native Americans to Christianity, to teach them English, and to adopt land ownership in many ways were effective with the Choctaw, Cherokee, Seminole, Chickasaw, and Creek Indians.[50] As settlers attempted to grow cotton on increasing amounts of land, particularly after the invention of the cotton gin had made the South's cotton crop internationally important, the land of these tribes became desirable to settlers. Southern state governments added to the pressure by passing laws aimed at driving out Native Americans by trying to abolish the rights of tribes to govern themselves while at the same time creating a process to take tribal lands and redistribute it to white Georgians. The Supreme Court reviewed these state laws in *Worcester v. Georgia* and held that these laws could "have no force."[51] But the states did not relent, and President Andrew Jackson refused to enforce the Court's holding, calling the decision "still born."[52] Shortly thereafter, in 1830, Congress passed the Indian Removal Act, which gave President Jackson power to negotiate with tribes in the South to remove them from their ancestral lands and relocate them west of the Mississippi River.[53]

This resulted in what became infamously known as the Trail of Tears, a forced mass exodus of Native people from Georgia deep into the frontier in what is now Oklahoma.[54] The expulsion resulted in the near decimation of those making the trip.[55] While the process of resettlement was often nothing less than settlers taking over desirable tribal lands and pushing the tribes to undesirable federal lands, the creation of federal Indian reservations had a lasting impact not only on the lives of native communities but also on the U.S. landscape and environmental conflicts to come.

FOLLOWING GOD AND PLOWS (1600s–1800s)

While certainly a number of those who moved west did so by calculating whether they would be better off, getting the numbers to make sense became much harder to justify in the arid West. Many of those who made the move did so based on commitments of faith. Many believed that God wanted them to move west, and like the captive Israelites in the Bible, they would trust in their faith and wander in the desert until they made it to the Promised Land.[56]

The first to make the journey into the deserts of the West were the Catholic missionaries, who started colonizing and developing the West even before the United States was a country. These missionaries began settlements that ended up serving as the foundations of a number of cities in the West, many of which would place extensive pressure on resources, particularly water.[57] Spanish missions not only included the presence of missionaries but also the construction of churches; the forced resettlement and abuse of native tribes, as well as the building of communities for converts, frequently followed.[58] The first Spanish missions in the West were in New Mexico and Texas and included the beginnings of the cities of Santa Fe, El Paso, and San Antonio.[59] In the 1680s, Father Junípero Serra helped start California's first mission in San Diego. By the 1760s, the last of the more than twenty California missions was being constructed in San Francisco. Other missions were established between those two locations, primarily along the West Coast.[60]

Many decades later, in 1845, a journalist named John O'Sullivan coined the term *manifest destiny*.[61] Included in the idea was the notion that the expansion of the country was God's will due to the moral superiority of the young democratic United States over both the preceding native tribes and the monarchies of Europe.[62] As O'Sullivan put it, "And that claim is by the right of our manifest destiny to overspread and to possess the whole of the continent which Providence has given us for the development of the great experiment of liberty and federated self-government entrusted to us."[63] Though labeled a century-and-a-half in, "manifest destiny" provided divine pretext for the era's predominant values—allocation and development.

Two years after O'Sullivan first wrote about manifest destiny, Mormon settlers made their way to find a home in the valleys of the Rocky

Mountains and stopped in Salt Lake City, Utah.[64] Over the last half of the nineteenth century, the Mormons founded about five hundred settlements from today's Mexico to Canada, including Las Vegas and as far west as California. Whereas many settlers frequently prided themselves on their independence, the Mormons eked out a life in the desert through extensive cooperation.[65]

Others, such as California's mining 49ers and those who followed the Oregon Trail, also found their way to the West.[66] The completion of the transcontinental railroad in 1869 made not only travel possible but the transportation of goods and resources to and from the West as well. This opened the West to broader development and lured many into the West particularly where economic opportunities cropped up. This resulted in increased urbanization in those outposts particularly accessible by train—where trains already stopped, or rails crossed. It also resulted in increased rural settlement not only in the resource and water rich parts of California, Oregon, and Washington, but also in other rural areas of the Interior West particularly suited for grazing and agriculture.[67]

EXPROPRIATION, SUBJUGATION, AND ALLOCATION OF PROPERTY (1700s–1850s)

The promotion of development occurred not only through common law allocation of property rights but also through more direct laws and governmental sponsorship of entrepreneurial capitalism, as advanced by a contemporary of the time, British economist Adam Smith.[68] This economic system was decidedly not, as sometimes championed, laissez-faire (i.e., free from governmental intervention). Governmental support for development was intentional, traceable to the Constitutional Convention, at which the Founding Fathers voiced robust support for governmental subsidy and regulation that boosted resource exploitation.[69] Establishment of (1) a federal bank to promote the stability of the banking system through regulation;[70] (2) private patent protections to stimulate inventions;[71] and (3) expeditions (such as Lewis and Clark's) to survey the unchartered (and untapped) western continent (followed by apportionment of such lands) all serve as examples of indirect and direct government aid for private development.[72]

Some of the most important and frequently troubling national policies related to land had direct connections to the disparate way diverse groups of people were treated under the law. This is most clearly reflected in the use of land being used to lure immigrants from Western Europe. Beginning with the Naturalization Act of 1790 and for almost a century that followed, the federal government did not place significant restrictions on European immigration.[73] Lax immigration laws and the policy of westward expansion frequently went hand in hand.

The story for non-European people was very different. The distinctions made between national origin and race was not at all subtle; citizenship in this era was explicitly limited to "white persons."[74] Despite inequality of the law, up until the closing of the frontier, the great abundance and seemingly wild character of much of the land in the United States were cause for a radical re-conception of natural resources at least for European settlers. In the Old World, ownership of sizable plots of land was mostly attainable only for royalty and the aristocracy. In the United States, however, land ownership was now conceivably an obtainable dream, at least for the masses of qualifying "white persons" wishing to immigrate.[75]

The federal government also tried to draw immigrants and their posterity into the frontier using appropriated federal lands legitimized under *Johnson v. M'Intosh*. The decisions made during this formative period about federal land management would have lasting implications. For the first century or so, the government's role in *governing* those lands was in many ways limited to disposal. Initially, much of this was done bit by bit, as parcels of land were in one form or another either sold or given to private individuals and corporations. To facilitate this, for decades, the federal government had land offices throughout the frontier to dispose of land to those who were willing to work the land. Congress set up the General Land Office, an agency many consider a predecessor of the Bureau of Land Management (BLM).[76] The General Land Office sat within the Department of the Treasury, and the major role of the office was to dispose of lands and keep records of who received the lands from the government. Once lands were distributed in an area, offices in that area would close and frequently relocate to unsettled areas to the west.[77] Thus, a key function of federal law was to promote the allocation, development, and exploitation of land and its natural resources.[78]

While the Supreme Court sanctioned wholesale federal actions to expropriate property from Native Americans, the Constitution explicitly allowed for Black people to be treated *as* property.[79] As a result, the economic system that grew out of the South came to increasingly rely on slave labor. While not every white household in the South enslaved people, the most successful agricultural operations in the South did.[80] Throughout the early history of the United States, and particularly in the South, most Americans in every state lived rural lives and relied on agriculture for their livelihoods. Thomas Jefferson—the face of the agrarian ideal—evangelized, "[a]griculture is our wisest pursuit, because it will in the end contribute most to real wealth, good morals, and happiness."[81] In the case of Jefferson's *wisest pursuit* in the fields and gardens of Monticello, he relied substantially on the toil of enslaved people.[82]

While the brutality of American slavery is hard to encapsulate, it brought millions of trafficked people to the United States. As the states in the North prohibited slavery, the Southern states became increasingly reliant on it. Tobacco farming and the booming cotton industry were both propped up by the work of enslaved people. The work of enslaved people not only carried the Southern economy, but also transformed the landscape, clearing large tracts of land and decimating many ecosystems.[83]

In 1862, Congress passed the Homestead Act and established a more defined policy of land disposal.[84] Before this time, federal lands disposed of by the government were generally transferred in enormous tracts and often to land speculators. The Homestead Act opened the possibility of securing federal lands to citizens of every stripe—including immigrants, former enslaved people, and the working poor. The country adopted an official policy of enticing non-Latine settlers deeper into the interior of the nation.[85] Most of the transfers of federal lands through the Homestead Act happened in the 1800s, though they continued to trickle in until the 1930s.[86]

Under the Homestead Act, the federal government transferred about 270 million acres to homesteaders, which amounts to more than 10 percent of all the land now in the United States.[87] As a general rule, the further east the available land was, the more likely that homesteaders took possession of it. In some places, particularly throughout the Great Plains, virtually no federal lands remained.[88] As new rail lines made their way into the frontier, homesteaders were sure to follow. A century after the passage of the Homestead Act, President John F. Kennedy would aptly label the Homestead Act "probably the single greatest stimulus to national development ever enacted."[89]

TRANSPORTATION INNOVATIONS AND WESTWARD MIGRATION (1800s)

Advancements in transportation made many things much easier, such as getting agricultural goods to market and making immigration and emigration increasingly more manageable.[90] Government policies contributed greatly to transportation innovations and were frequently justified on the basis of spurring natural resource use and development (particularly the settling of the expansive Western Frontier). Furthermore, the federal government leveraged government funding and especially apportionment of its land holdings to spur investment in transportation.

Before the Civil War, to facilitate westward expansion, Congress funded the building of a single road in Ohio dubbed the "National Road."[91] Yet it was typical for state governments to fund such transportation projects rather than the federal government.

Probably the most significant governmental commitment that altered the young country's transportation system was the decision to build the Erie Canal. Even from today's perspective, the idea of the Canal is ambitious: The Canal would span a distance over 350 miles, and it would require a series of locks that allowed boats to climb six hundred feet in elevation.[92] And while the Canal would only be four feet deep, it was forty feet wide; at times this required cutting into limestone and construction done by hand or with the help of animals.[93] Upon hearing the proposal, President Thomas Jefferson rejected the idea outright, calling the Canal "little short of madness."[94]

As federal funding for the project failed to materialize, the State of New York, under the leadership of Governor DeWitt Clinton, decided to pay for the project. While politically risky at the time, Clinton convinced the New York legislature to spend $7 million (about the equivalent of $115 million today).[95] Subsidizing the Canal made the Great Lakes (as well as the Mississippi River) accessible from New York Harbor and made

New York an internationally important shipping city—dramatically decreasing transportation costs, frequently in excess of 90 percent.[96] In this way, New York City began its growth that would result in it becoming one of the United States' megacities. It drew many new settlers deep into what was then a wilderness to grow grain out on the then-prairie and clear lumber, shipping both by barges to the New York Harbor.[97] It also unleashed a sort of environmental devastation—certainly unbeknownst to those using the Canal at the time: The connection of these previously unconnected water bodies created a highway of invasive species that still complicates ecosystems of the Midwest today.[98] The great success of the Canal as a tool of economic development may make Jefferson's resistance seem foolish and the Governor the wit, though perhaps such an assessment may be tempered by the substantial destruction of forests and plains that accompanied the Canal's development.

Federal resistance to funding transportation projects broke down during the Civil War. During the war, the federal government proved much more willing to fund transportation and significantly directed the country's expansion of rail lines. The Union Army built rail to connect its troops to critical supplies.[99] This is just one example of many that provided the North a technological advantage over the South.

Beyond the rail built for the Civil War, private industry—spurred by government incentives—pushed rail projects across the continent. Specifically, in 1862, Congress passed the Pacific Railroad Act, which tasked the Union Pacific and Central Pacific Railroads to do this work.[100] In the West, this meant the Central Pacific would start out in Sacramento, California, and wind its way through the steep climbs of the Sierra Nevadas. Eastern rail had already made it to Omaha, Nebraska, so the Union Pacific Railroad would start out on the banks of the Missouri River and the gentle terrain of the Midwest. For each mile of rail built, the enactment promised to transfer large tracts of federal public lands (initially 6,400 acres and later twice that much) along with $48,000 in government bonds.[101]

President Abraham Lincoln reported to Congress in 1864 on the nation's efforts despite difficulties created by the Civil War: "The great enterprise of connecting the Atlantic with the Pacific States by railways and telegraph lines has been entered upon with a vigor that gives assurance of success, notwithstanding the embarrassments arising from the prevailing high prices of materials and labor."[102] While the Central Pacific started in earnest once the enactment was passed, the Union Pacific would not see its completion until after the Civil War ended. This network of railroads meant that trips that would have taken more than a month of strife in previous decades now could be completed in days in comfort. While the first part of the 1860s saw a country torn asunder by civil war, as the decade ended, the railroad had joined the country together.

While the transcontinental railroad was the most significant transportation innovation of the country's first hundred years, it was just one of many lines built around this time. Each time rail was laid, so too were opportunities for development that were previously unthinkable. As incentives to build railroad lines, the federal government gave railroad companies a total of 185,000,000 acres of land during the last half of the nineteenth century.[103] As the federal government coaxed the railroads west, rail companies, in turn, leveraged impoverished minorities, particularly poor immigrants from China, to make unsettled lands more accessible to the heavily populated Eastern United States.[104] Other lands were entrusted to newly minted States with the intent of providing them some resources of their own to exploit and generate a revenue stream to build schools, universities, and hospitals.[105]

WATER LAW MEETS AMERICAN INNOVATION AND WESTWARD EXPANSION (1800–1880)

While land laws were instrumental at enticing settlers to pursue agriculture, the first half of the nineteenth century also saw profound changes to water law that similarly facilitated economic growth. Rather than focusing on accommodating agriculture, however, these changes mainly came about to accommodate additional pursuits, ranging from mining to new innovations in industry. The water law imported from English common law allowed those who had land abutting water bodies (riparian landowners) to take modest amounts of water for domestic use; it mainly worked to protect the natural flow of water bodies instead of its consumption.[106] Specifically, it forbade those with riparian rights to interfere with a waterbody's "natural current, without diminution or obstruction."[107] Exceptions to natural flow included rights of riparians to dock boats on the banks and to otherwise use the surface of the water.[108]

However, *Tyler v. Wilkinson*[109] reinvented riparianism. Written by the celebrated jurist Joseph Story before he was named to the Supreme Court, the case focused on the Pawtucket River, which flows between Massachusetts and Rhode Island. The river had a small waterfall, and below it a dam had been built that allowed some water to pool. Along the river's banks, textilists had built mills to take advantage of the water's force. The water flowed through a ditch, which was originally dug in a failed attempt to help fish spawn, and later dammed by the mill owners to power water turbines.

The very nature of harnessing the power of the river required obstructing the river's "natural current," which contradicted a faithful application of riparianism as it had evolved over centuries in British courts and had lived on in the United States. In considering the demands on the Pawtucket River, Judge Story found that the law should give way to the demands of industry, concluding that applying the rules applied for centuries "would be to deny any valuable use of it."[110] Instead of demanding no diminution, Story instead resolved, "There may be, and there must be allowed of that, which is common to all, a reasonable use."[111] This reasonable use requirement that Story first articulated in the context of riparian water rights in Massachusetts would spread over the next few decades and find footing in courts in every state at the time.

However, water rights as we think of them today—the right to use water for consumptive purposes like agriculture, mining, industry, and residential purposes—in many ways received very little consideration in the early history of the United States. The reason for this is that the location of the original colonies and the states that became settled during this period were in the East, where water from rainfall was plentiful and generally enough to serve agricultural purposes.

As drier states began to join the Union (such as Texas joining in 1845 and California in 1850),[112] riparianism proved to be a poor fit for the needs of settlers and development, despite these states' sparse populations. The value that riparianism maximized was flexibility to accommodate many uses—including new and changing uses. But these new arid states craved certainty, not flexibility. These settlers wanted to make sure that, if they were willing to try living in an arid land, the water they relied upon would be theirs going forward.

The first case that recognized water rights that differed from riparianism was a case before the California Supreme Court in 1855, *Irwin v. Phillips*.[113] In that case, the California Court considered a water dispute that arose among miners who came to the state as part of the California Gold Rush. Had the rules of riparian water law applied to this case, the court would have found that none of the parties had rights to the water for a very simple reason—the miners were on federal lands, which meant that neither of them owned riparian land and therefore neither had riparian water rights. Instead, the court recognized a new basis for establishing water rights, at least between those without riparian rights: something the court referred to as *prior appropriation*.[114] By this, the court meant that those who first diverted waters from a stream or river would have a superior right to those who came later and wanted to do the same.

While the miners followed this rule informally, the court's judgment provided a greater degree of certainty. The California Court noted explicitly that it wanted to provide an incentive to promote mining. Specifically, it wrote that the miners "have taken the waters from their natural beds, and by costly artificial works have conducted them for miles over mountains and ravines, to supply the necessities of gold diggers, and without which the most important interests of the mineral region would remain without development."[115] While it would take decades, by the turn of the twentieth century all of the states in the West would supplant riparianism with some variation of prior appropriation as their primary water rights regime.[116]

Even as Western states reshaped water law, visionary thinking about the importance of water policy went unheeded. As context, the deeper settlers pushed into the arid West, the more water became an important factor in settlement decisions. Often the viability of settlements in the West came down to a central challenge: water scarcity. As both the footprint of development and actual borders of the United States expanded across the continent during the nineteenth century, legal systems developed to foster the rapid investment in and allocation, use, and development of resources—highlighting, if not exacerbating, clashes over such resources that linger even today.

By the end of the 1860s, exploration of what would become the United States was quickly becoming outdated. Much of the land now included settlements connected by a seemingly ever-expanding network of railroads and steamboats.[117] John Wesley Powell, however, in charting a trip along the Colorado River, found one of the few remaining opportunities to venture into what was considered by white settlers to be the unknown of the time.[118] While the river included extensive settlements of native peoples, this would not be marked—at least by him—despite whatever evidence that presented itself otherwise.

A gruff mountain man who lost much of his right arm as a Union soldier during the Civil War's Battle of Shiloh, Powell was tailor-made for a public yearning for tales of a wild, untamed frontier. The trip was paid for by the United States government, a commission meant to expand the country's insight into the Interior West.[119] During the trip, letters written by Powell and those in his crew were frequently published in newspapers around the country.

The trip that began in Utah's Green River and then continued to the Colorado River did little to dispel the idea that the stretch of river was "unconquerable." At the outset, Powell and his crew faced setbacks. The party, who traveled in four boats, lost the first boat shortly after starting the trip. Papers around the country reported that the now-renowned boat called "The No Name," plunged over a series of waterfalls. After falling "twenty to thirty feet, crashing into a rock, rebounding and filling with water, then smacking broadside against another rock," the boat "cracked in two, and the men were thrown into the foaming avalanche, passing from sight."[120] Despite the public acclaim, the trip proved too much for some of Powell's co-travelers. He lost another crew member a month in and, three more just days before the trip ended in an encounter with Native Americans.

Along with his new-found fame, Powell also found himself providing innovative recommendations to Congress about the future of the West. His report to Congress was not issued until a decade after his trip ended and recommended a daring reimagination of the rapidly growing West—one that not only recognized but was even built around a recognition of water scarcity. Powell's proposals included drawing states along water basins, slowing migration, and rethinking resettlement of the most arid parts of the Interior West.[121]

Powell's proposal, while noteworthy, did little to reshape the arid West. Rather, development in these areas followed a pathway that frequently both ignored water scarcity at critical junctures while at the same time frequently finding other opportunities to make it the source of conflict. Considering this scarcity, Mark Twain was purported to aptly diagnose the problem simply: "Whiskey is for drinking, water is for fighting!"[122]

UNPRECEDENT PRESSURE ON WILDLIFE AND SOME EARLY PROTECTIONS (1800s)

Like the innovations of water law in the West to accommodate settlement and those in the East to accommodate industrialization,[123] the law changed to make way for exploitation of wildlife resources. At the state level, the era saw the development of legal doctrines to incentivize hunting of wildlife that built on the English common law's rule of capture as exemplified in *Pierson v. Post*. Transportation innovations and easier access to firearms that followed on the heels of the Civil War put unprecedented pressure on American wildlife. In some instances, market pressures added to the rush to kill wildlife, even to the point that it threatened the survival of some species.

Yet it is worth noting that the era also saw a countervailing trend—one that recognized the need for some wildlife protections and limits to the general rule of capture. The earliest laws, dating back to before the formation of the United States, put numerical limits to the number of deer a person could hunt, particularly in pursuit of only deer skins, along with establishing hunting seasons.[124] Similar regulations were passed in several places protecting waterfowl and fish, including take limits, hunting and fishing methods, and season limitations.[125] Even though these laws did not dominate the era, their existence is among the very earliest uses of laws in the United States to facilitate a degree of environmental protection.

Still, these inroads were modest. The law more generally, not only permitted but even encouraged hunting without limits.[126] Perhaps the starkest example involved the law promoting hunting of bison herds during the 1800s. Before Europeans came to North America, the continent had an estimated thirty million bison.[127] Bison, although common, were majestic; these enormous creatures became emblematic of the continent itself, particularly of the remaining frontier found in the American West.[128] As represented perfectly in the images found on buffalo nickels circulated at the turn of the twentieth century, the plight of the bison themselves is only one side of the coin. On the other side of the coin, we find the plight of the Native Americans who had for recorded history relied on bison as a major food source.[129] The rule of capture and direct U.S. government action promoted the wasteful and even spiteful killing of bison.[130] While some bison hides were brought to market, most of the bison killed were not. Rather, hunters and even the U.S. military systematically slaughtered millions of bison—all with the goal of depriving tribes who depended on them of bison and forcing them to abandon

Figure 1.2 This photograph of two men with a mountain of bison skulls (taken in the 1890s) in Michigan vividly highlights the scale of the destruction of the herds.

lives of hunters and gatherers.[131] At the close of the 1800s, it is estimated that fewer than a thousand bison remained.[132]

Bison were not the only species pushed to the brink, or even beyond. The passenger pigeon went the way of . . . well, the passenger pigeon. While the species would not be gone until the beginning of the twentieth century, the extent of the loss was breathtaking. Consider this recorded memory:

> In May 1850, a 20-year-old Potawatomi tribal leader named Simon Pokagon was camping at the headwaters of Michigan's Manistee River during trapping season when a far-off gurgling sound startled him. It seemed as if "an army of horses laden with sleigh bells was advancing through the deep forests towards me," he later wrote. "As I listened more intently, I concluded that instead of the tramping of horses it was distant thunder; and yet the morning was clear, calm, and beautiful." The mysterious sound came "nearer and nearer," until Pokagon deduced its source: "While I gazed in wonder and astonishment, I beheld moving toward me in an unbroken front of millions of pigeons, the first I had seen that season."[133]

Indeed, passenger pigeons were once the most common bird in North America. Passing of a flock could take days and leave substantial guano in its wake.[134] Again, the rule of capture and the absence of hunting regulations combined with a perception by some of passenger pigeons as an interminable pestilence led to the acceptance if not the encouragement of indiscriminate killing.[135] It is reported that in one hunting competition of these birds, the winner of the contest shot a staggering thirty thousand birds.[136] Although there is some evidence that passenger pigeons were in decline even before the colonization of the Americas, there is no doubt that the pressure put on these birds hurried their decline.[137] This loss was particularly hard on Native Americans: While a kill of bison could provide a feast, the abundance of pigeons sustained subsistence lifestyles.[138]

Very rarely would the law divert away from the direction of rule of capture since it worked to facilitate resource consumption, but a couple of exceptions to this characterization are noteworthy. The most serious limits occurred on species that were both particularly sought after and easy to track. Laws were put into place to protect the interests of oyster harvesters by granting each harvester the vested right to the resource.[139] Of course, oysters do not move far, and seabeds where they flourish could reasonably be split up. Giving particular harvesters rights to collect specific oysters created the incentive to take actions to prevent overexploitation of the resource, i.e., a "tragedy of a commons."[140]

Whaling was also limited. Particularly during the first half of the 1800s, blubber from whales was used as an energy source though for most people unaffordable. Logic suggests that the size of whales made it difficult to over harvest them without being detected. There were other more minor efforts made from time to time, including some ineffective efforts to slow salmon harvesting[141]—something that would prove increasingly necessary over time. Just prior to the Civil War, whaling became less and less common and was replaced by kerosene and petroleum oil.[142] While future eras would witness whale conservation protections decoupled solely from sustaining yield, a property rights regime founded on unfettered slaughter carried the day during the Allocation Era.

THE CIVIL WAR'S EFFECTS ON THE ENVIRONMENT AND ITS PROTECTION (1860s–1880s)

Given the stakes of the Civil War, which resulted in the loss of over 750,000 soldiers and countless civilians[143] and eventual emancipation of 3.5 million enslaved people, it is admittedly awkward to focus on the ways that the war affected the nonhuman environment and the laws associated with it; however, both were impacted by the war. These include significant effects not only on the physical environment but also human health.

GEOPHYSICAL AND INDUSTRIAL CHANGE

The most obvious direct effect on the environment was seen wherever the Civil War was fought. It was not just a war among soldiers; rather, the Civil War included "violence against civilians, cities, farms, animals, the landscape itself."[144] Of course, the environment is often harmed by wars, but the Civil War's effects were particularly stark. One of the critical strategies of both sides was to not only strategically fortify places to secure food for one's own hungry army, but also to deprive those on the opposite side the same by burning crops, cutting down trees, and releasing animals.[145] Because the armies did not have much in the way of provisions and relied on pillaging wherever the armies moved—one historian memorably labeled this grim aspect of the war the "great food fight."[146] As a microcosm that was playing in many places during the war, consider the on-the-ground report from U.S. Captain Theodore, writing about the Union's preparations for the battle in Virginia: "[I]t is wonderful how the whole country round here is literally stripped of its timber. Woods which, when we came here, were so thick that we could not get through them any way are now entirely cleared."[147]

The long-term impact on the environment went well beyond the physical changes that occurred during the war on various battlefields. The North already had several economic and societal advantages over the South at the beginning of the war, such as increased industrialization, more established rail lines, a larger population, and more food crops.[148] The Civil War further intensified government and private industry investments and the growth of railroads, particularly in the North. Where rail lines were found and particularly where they merged, development spurred by market forces often followed.[149] Much of this investment in industrialization relied on coal for energy.[150]

While some of the costs would have been obvious at the time, it is hard to imagine that anyone involved in these investments would understand the implications of such investments either on the United States' economic trajectory or on the natural environment. An immediate consequence of this increased urbanization and more intensive industry was increased air and water pollution. In many ways, the Civil War ushered in the United States' longstanding bet on fossil fuels that would cause traumatic shifts in the global climate.

Because industry was so vital to the war effort first and to the growing cities later, it was common for such increases in pollution to result in little political response in cities.[151] Courts too, recognizing the importance of growing industries, were recalcitrant in the early phases of industrialization to apply common law causes of action, like nuisance law, to the problems resulting from industrialization.[152]

A major change hurried along by the Civil War was an increased dependence on coal. Coal, particularly bituminous coal that burns hotter than other coals, had already been identified as necessary for iron ore smelting in the early 1800s.[153] At the turn of the century, hydraulic turbines powered industry, but during the 1840s, hydraulic power began to be replaced with steam power.[154] Steam required heat, and heat required fuel—either from wood or coal.

The Civil War dramatically increased reliance on coal, as the country increasingly relied on ironworks.[155] Iron was useful in war, and the industrial processes relied upon to smelt iron, relied on coal. The demand for iron and reliance on coal did not end with the Civil War. Rather, once the iron and coal were not used for the war, together they hurled ahead industrialization in the United States.

The demand for coal and iron pushed ahead coal mining in the United States. For the most part, in the name of progress government policy combined with a private property rights regime to endorse coal mining—and with it, the contamination and destruction of many landscapes and natural resources.

There are a couple of notable deviations from this theme, however. First, in some instances laws were given force to limit excesses found in mining at the time. Due to extensive use and abuse of animals—particularly horses and mules—both in mining operations and society more generally, some states responded with laws prohibiting inhumane cruelty toward horses and other domesticated animals.[156] In addition, by the end of the Allocation Era, we begin to see some states pushing ahead with laws to monitor coal mines, particularly for worker safety. Pennsylvania was the first state to pass such legislation, as the state was a leader in coal mining and had also suffered a mine fire in the Avondale Colliery that killed 108 coal miners.[157]

CHANGES IN PUBLIC AND SOLDIER HEALTH

With the Civil War came not only environmental destruction and increased industrialization but also early environmental regulation. This represents another major departure from the Allocation Era's overwhelming extractive relationship with the environment. In many ways, however, this represented less of a value change than one that the country's circumstances required. Stunningly, about two-thirds of the soldiers who lost their lives in the war died not from rounds of mortar but rather disease.[158] Troops on both sides frequently found themselves in crowded conditions in hot, humid climates, and subject to poor management of human waste and garbage—breeding grounds for insects, poor sanitation, and the spread of disease. While these environmental risks may seem obvious to those with today's sensibilities, it took a great deal of effort and genius at the time to see the connection and minimize the risk.

While study and protection of public health had been gaining ground since the 1600s, it made giant strides in the 1800s. War precipitated much of this, but it also grew out of advancements in science. Importantly, just years before the Civil War started, John Snow brought the emerging discipline of public health—and particularly the study of environmental hazards—a scientific rigor it had previously lacked.[159] Snow, a doctor in London, noticed that a cholera outbreak was focused on a certain part of the city. In 1854, he investigated an outbreak that had hit part of Broad Street particularly hard. Trying to find commonalities among those hit by the outbreak, he zeroed in on water used by some Londoners as a major risk factor and traced which wells and pumps drew water from a particular aquifer. By comparing death rates among people relying on different water sources, he found that water companies that drew water upstream from environmental risks correlated with no deaths, while those who drew downstream were associated with high death rates. He was able to show through this exercise that cholera was a waterborne disease associated with pollution. In making a report to the British Parliament, the coverage of his findings pushed the field of public health forward and highlighted that disease could be addressed by focusing on reducing environmental contamination.[160]

With these advances in human understanding, it is little surprise that as military leaders began to focus on the problem of preventing the loss of troops due to illness, public health regulation increasingly played a role in military camps. The U.S. military looked for contaminants causing health risks, and even took it one step further, following Snow's method of collecting and analyzing information that led to substantial improvements.[161] Camps came to understand risks, assigned soldiers to help with monitoring, and then worked to eliminate dangerous conditions. Military hierarchy and discipline resulted in the training of sanitary policing for officers. Among the Union armies, the U.S.

Sanitary Commission assumed responsibility for this role, becoming a proto-federal environmental health department.[162] Health specialists not only relied on expertise from the battlefield, but also leaned on the lessons learned in similar settings, such as the work of the nurses working with Florence Nightingale during the Crimean War.[163]

As the Civil War ended, health specialists saw similar failings in health and sanitation back home, particularly in the urban areas that grew along with industry during the war.[164] These health specialists helped identify ways to apply the lessons learned from the war to improve urban conditions. Soon public health departments began appearing around the country—the first and one of the most sophisticated was founded in New York City.[165] Early public health laws establishing public health departments were among the most meaningful early environmental laws. As it became understood that sanitation measures could help with deadly outbreaks of typhoid and cholera, a number of Northern cities, including Chicago and New York, passed laws and began to build some early sewage systems to rid city streets of human waste and garbage—a problem that was typically pronounced in poor parts of growing cities.[166] Public health laws began to lay a groundwork that policymakers would revisit many times when dealing with the relationship between people and the environment—care for the environment is important because human health depends on it.[167]

MANUFACTURING NATURE IN GROWING CITIES, AND EDEN IN THE FRONTIER (1850–1880)

Industrialization drew more people from the countryside, and urban areas grew as a result. By the end of the nineteenth century, the United States was no longer a rural country; for some individual states, this transition occurred by the time of the Civil War.[168] Adding people into urban areas exacerbated problems of pollution, garbage, and sewage disposal. Perhaps it was the crowding, or maybe it was the longing for greenspaces left in the countryside; regardless, the mid-1800s saw notable efforts to protect and reclaim natural spaces. This represented yet another undercurrent that differed from those grappling with the limits of wildlife populations and managing public health risk, but it nonetheless was an important step forward in using law to protect the environment.

Some cities had included greenspaces to be used for commercial spaces (e.g., outdoor markets) and public grazing into their design almost from the beginning, most notably the Boston Common. However, other cities needed to act to salvage *natural* spaces within areas that had already begun to urbanize. The most notable of these efforts kicked off in 1853, when the New York legislature gave the City of New York the power of eminent domain to secure more than seven hundred acres for Central Park.[169] By the 1860s, the park had expanded by another 150 acres. Using the power of the state to condemn the land, New York City secured land that was in large part undeveloped grazing lands. Still, securing the sizable park resulted in the displacement of 1,600 people, including an African American community and the homes and operations of immigrant farmers and pig ranchers.[170]

The designer of the park, Frederick Law Olmsted, curated landscapes and created a refuge from the bustling city. However, the park did much more than provide a place for recreation. In many ways, the park stood in a rebuke to the chaos of the time—a nation torn by a Civil War and a mass migration of people from the South to the North and from the countryside to growing cities. Olmstead's design took full advantage of the unique landscape—a rocky terrain with outcroppings and overlooks, which he complimented with greenspaces with manicured gardens, roads and trails, maintained fields, and occasional buildings that frequently mimicked those found on estates of European royalty. Everything was designed with the aspiration of providing a sense of peace and heightened civilization to all the city's residents.[171]

The popularity of Olmstead's creation sparked a movement. Olmstead himself would take on another five hundred or so projects in his life throughout the country but mainly in the Northeast. Some of his more well-known projects include others in New York, including Morningside and Riverside parks in New York City, Prospect Park in Brooklyn, and Delaware Park in Buffalo.[172] He also designed Fairmount Park in Philadelphia, South Park (later Washington and Jackson Parks) in Chicago, Belle Isle Park in Detroit, Cherokee Park in Louisville, the grounds of the U.S. Capitol, and the landscape of Stanford University.[173] Many other cities tried to mimic what Olmstead had created, and as the United States urbanized, more parks were developed all over the country. City parks, often considered the "lungs" of cities, were built in other eras as well, but their prevalence in many ways can be traced to the public investments made during this era. This is evident because not only were many parks created during this period, but so was the norm that parks would be found in suburban and urban areas.

While Olmstead tried to create the countryside in America's growing cities, the United States took on another sort of preservation project: protecting federal lands. It is hard to know whether preservation would have occurred without Olmstead, but it seems unlikely that the idea of a national *park* would have made much sense without the park movement Olmstead set off. It is also logical that the idea to set aside lands for recreation and preservation both in urban areas and in more-remote areas grew out of a time where many came to understand the cost of urbanization and the loss of nature as the frontier moved west.

Out of all this came what Wallace Stegner, one of the West's most celebrated writers, called "America's best idea": the world's first national park.[174] For decades, fur trappers and locals had reported the wonders of Yellowstone and were frequently met with disbelief. With the hopes of drawing attention to the area and thereby stimulating local economic interests, business and civic leaders from the area approached the federal government. In 1871, the government sent Ferdinand V. Hayden and a team of about fifty others to take on the first federally funded geological survey.[175]

Hayden not only accomplished the job, but he also came back with photographs, drawings, maps, stories, and zeal. Hayden found what might seem an unusual ally to protect Yellowstone: the railroad industry eager to publicize his findings as a strategy to drum up interest in transcontinental travel. The industry helped publicize Hayden's findings. Soon after returning, Hayden was exhibiting photographs and drawings in the U.S. Capitol building and proselytizing his message of preservation to all who would listen. Hayden coupled his exhibit with a warning that without protection, Yellowstone could suffer from overdevelopment.[176]

A core problem with this idea, encountered in Yellowstone and repeatedly thereafter, is that while national parks often project the ideal of "untouched" nature, the lands that became parks were frequently inhabited well before they were designated as such. Delivering on the vision of Yellowstone, Yosemite, and many other parks to come not only meant evicting local settlers but also forcibly removing Native Americans from

Figure 1.3 ***The Grand Canyon of the Yellowstone*** **(1872), painting by Thomas Moran.**

their traditional lands, and originally, it took the U.S. Army to impose park protections.[177] Although national park designation would promote preservation, their creation often resulted in immediate issues of social injustice. Additionally, as parks like Yellowstone got their footing, the influx of visitors began to build momentum for gateway communities just outside the parks' boundaries.[178] This is particularly true of park entrances, where trains would drop off tourists. As tourists increasingly made their way to the parks, parks needed management to ensure protection from their own visitors.

Yellowstone was the first attempt to set aside federal lands for preservation. It is noteworthy that the designation of Yellowstone came seven years after the federal government granted a request from California to transfer Yosemite to the state to set aside the land for preservation, dating back to 1864.[179] In many ways, however, it took a few decades before Yosemite would face the pressure from tourists that Yellowstone saw after its designation. Interestingly, as the State of California tried to chart a way forward for Yosemite, it commissioned several advisors, including Olmstead, for advice.[180] California did not accept all of Olmstead's recommendations. However, they remain important because within them we find not only the fundamental tension between protection and use but also the lens of the time that held out projects like Yosemite as somewhat of a rebuttal to the brutal nature of people exposed by the Civil War. In 1865, Olmstead wrote:

> It was during one of the darkest hours, before Sherman had begun the march upon Atlanta or Grant his terrible movement through the Wilderness, when the paintings of Bierstadt and the photographs of Watkins, both productions of the War time, had given to the people on the Atlantic some idea of the sublimity of the Yo Semite, and of the stateliness of the neighboring Sequoia grove, that consideration was first given to the danger that such scenes might become private property and . . . their value to posterity be injured. To secure them against this danger Congress passed an act providing that the premises should be segregated from the general domain of the public lands, and devoted forever to popular resort and recreation.[181]

* * *

From the moment of its independence (and indeed well before), the United States and the laws that shaped its environment focused almost exclusively on promoting allocation, exploitation, and development, all for almost the exclusive economic benefit of European settlers and their descendants. Near the end of the Allocation Era, it was not much different—even if the pickings were slimmer and (at least nominally) the tent of allowed participants had grown a bit larger. Legal regimes started to develop to reward mining and use of less obviously valuable lands,[182] and Congress passed laws to incentivize "improvement" of federal lands that homesteaders had passed by, such as "swamplands," "desertlands,"[183] or land dominated by timber or potential stone quarries.[184] In 1872, Congress passed the Mining Act to encourage converting unused federal lands for mining.[185] It provided retroactive protection for claims of western miners made as far back as the California Gold Rush, going to great lengths to protect property rights for those who provided evidence of minerals on federal lands.[186] Like virtually every other law in the Allocation Era, however, these laws favored some more than others in the development race. Because of the added expense of these types of developments and investments, these laws frequently proved more advantageous to the wealthy and corporate interests.

Environmentally, the longstanding theme of these and other laws in the Allocation Era, however, was that human and environmental health were barely an afterthought. Mining and other land laws incentivized the destruction of ecologically important landscapes, particularly as these developments frequently dovetailed with development of surrounding lands previously provided to homesteaders or railroads.[187] Mining laws did not account for their environmental consequences—let alone try to minimize them. Among other harms, abandoned mining claims would eventually grow to pose serious environmental problems in certain parts of the United States.[188]

The full severity of those consequences would not be understood for years to come. Despite some important countercurrents of the era rooted in other values seeking to facilitate environmental protection, near the end of the century, a prosperous but increasingly ailing nation sat at a precipice. It would soon see a powerful and sustained check on this prolonged era of unrestrained extraction, expansion, and disregard for human and environmental health. In comparison to the Allocation Era's focus on exploitation and at best modest gestures toward environmentalism, *progress* in the decades that immediately followed took on an entirely different meaning.

2

THE PROGRESSIVE ERA

FIGHTING EXCESS IN AN AGE OF EXCESSES (1890–1920)

INTRODUCTION

In 1893, Fredrick Jackson Turner captured the nation's attention through a most improbable method: publishing an academic paper focused on a finding buried in a Census Bureau report.[1] The finding signaled something significant—the end of the Allocation Era. "Up to and including 1880 the country had a frontier of settlement," he wrote, "but at present the unsettled area has been so broken into by isolated bodies of settlement that there can hardly be said to be a frontier line."[2] Leveraging numerous policy interventions to spur migration and investment, westward expansion had finally reached across the continent. "Up to our own day," Turner went on, "American history has been in a large degree the history of the colonization of the Great West."[3] Even if government policy afforded ample opportunities for American expansionism in the Pacific, Caribbean, and elsewhere,[4] the seemingly unceasing movement by American settlers to find an "unsettled" landscape as a new home in mainland United States was finished.

During the Allocation Era, pressures on natural resources had periodically captured the public's attention—such as the collapse of whale populations due to the pursuit of blubber, or the devastation of bison due to the pursuit of their skins.[5] The frontier, however, provided the nation plausible deniability for the need to conserve. Willfully blind to limits, federal and state law of that era focused instead on simply promoting development of the next horizon. Though it might require battling and displacing yet another population of Native Americans or overcoming the challenges of a new landscape, these hurdles were surmountable for the new nation. The frontier's line repeatedly shifted as settlers moved west, frequently along with government-facilitated transportation innovations like the Erie Canal or the transcontinental railroad. It seemed that nothing would stop it. No reckoning for exploitation loomed on the horizon. With little or no understanding that the jig was up, movement of the line of the frontier was halted as it ran into a serious geographic constraint—the beaches of the Pacific Coast. The closing of the frontier thus served as a symbolic, if not actual, poignant pivot in the relationship of the American polity to its resources.

The 1890 census included another important insight about American life at that time. While only 5 percent of Americans lived in urban areas at the first census in 1790, a hundred years later more than a third of Americans lived in cities.[6] The country had started to see the growth of industry in cities, reinforced, if not spurred in part, by the beginning of the Great Migration of African Americans from the American South to the North and from the East to the West.[7] Though these processes of migration, industrialization, and urbanization may have been provoked in part due to the absence of market restraints, unfettered markets also reflected a purposeful policy choice. Where the government did intervene, it almost always reinforced expansion, frequently at the cost of the environment.

By 1890, Chicago had become the country's second largest city, surpassing a million people.[8] Unlike other large cities in the United States—New York, Philadelphia, and Washington—Chicago was built almost entirely as a product of the forces of migration and industrialization. The rails built into the city, subsidized by federal and state legislation authorizing funding as well as liberal use of the eminent domain power,[9] brought a thousand trains in and out of the city a day.[10] Chicago had become the central place to trade the bounties of the frontier—such as lumber from the forests around the Great Lakes and the crops from the many farms including homesteaders.[11]

Turner's scholarship might have never received the attention it did if he had not delivered a speech at a convention held on the outskirts of the renowned 1893 World Fair in Chicago.[12] The 1893 Fair was the first large-scale elaboration of the "City Beautiful" movement and thus modern urban planning that sought to address poor living conditions by cultivating civic virtue through urban beautification and grand monuments.[13] The fair illustrated the possibilities of electrification, mesmerizing visitors through "the sheer beauty of seeing so many lights ignited in one place, at one time."[14] During the Progressive Era, such electrification would proliferate, fostered by government support,[15] and with it, the seeds of the nation's addiction to fossil fuels.

Like the lights of the World Fair, the Progressive Era represents a stark contrast from the nation's history that came before it. The Progressive Era represents the first elemental oscillation—a significant enough inversion in the goals, processes, and structures of law and the country's approach to human and environmental health to qualify as a new era and not just another countercurrent or accretion perceived only after much time had passed. This era ushered in fundamental changes that created and redefined entire areas of law. To help us understand what prompted the legal changes of the era, it is worth focusing at the outset on the nuance beyond the dominant value that emerged to define the era of government fighting business interests on behalf of ordinary people.

At a basic level, the Progressive Era was built on a simple principle—government should protect the public from the forces of industry. From trust busting to regulation of food and the creation of public lands—along with the establishment of many government institutions, new decision-making processes, and aggressive substantive standards—the new era represented the government standing up to industry excess that harmed the public. Yet the story is more nuanced.

Transformational environmental legal change came at least in part by blending business interests and the language of economics into Progressivism. For Progressives, natural resource conservation was fundamentally "good business."[16] For certain business interests it resonated,[17] they and their political representatives[18] embraced this approach to scientific, efficient resource management.[19] Some even suggest that during the Progressive Era, scientific management and organization efficiency were the primary motivators for the era's looming legal changes aimed at environmental conservation.[20]

Aside from the motivations of the Progressives themselves, the legal environmental protections arising from the era, in some sense, came in part because certain industry proponents leveraged reform for non-environmental interests.[21] The oil industry, for example, accepted (if not endorsed) Progressive federal and state regulation as a way to limit fluctuating supply and thus promote stability for the industry through resource conservation.[22] Some have gone as far to suggest that the federalization of conservation law can be understood primarily as a product of Eastern industrial interests exerting control over the development of Western natural resources.[23] Some Western industries resisted conservation,[24] in particular mining, lumber, and large cattle interests.[25] Even in these industries, there were "prominent leaders . . . who out of conviction or for partisan reasons were loyal supporters of Theodore Roosevelt and his policies."[26] Moreover, Western state leaders, conservation groups, and urban centers seeking protection of water and power resources were instrumental to the enactment of federal conservation programs,[27] as were populist agrarian allies.[28]

Leadership mattered here too. To some extent overcoming the powerful forces of industry and capitalist laissez-faire ideology[29] came about due to charismatic leaders such as Theodore Roosevelt, Gifford Pinchot,[30] or John Muir[31] wielding populist and Progressive arguments and scientific evidence about the many harms to the landscape and citizenry wrought by unregulated industry.[32] The three pillars of Theodore Roosevelt's "Square Deal" were at the heart of environmental law that grew out of Progressive Era: conserving natural resources; limiting corporate and plutocrat power; and protecting consumers.[33]

A key tenet of the time linking these three goals that redefined the relationship between people and the environment was recognition of the "harms of unregulated individual power,"[34] and the capacity to address such harms through the effective application of government through law—regulations, incentives, and punishments.[35] This included reigning in corporate excess and public harms through government regulation, but also other prominent social reforms like the imposition of federal income and corporate taxes[36] and prohibitions on the sale of liquor.[37] Another value rooted in the era, taken up by Louis Brandeis and Woodrow Wilson among others, emphasized promotion of societal efficiency by leveraging scientific expertise, professionalization, and public administration.[38] This emphasis on making government more efficient through the employment of technocratic experts in public administration was nonetheless in tension, if not conflict, with the Progressive movement's appeal to making the political system more democratic and inclusive.[39]

Key catalysts for change included the reporters who covered the Progressive agenda and the ills it aimed to address. The press's influence on these topics was by no means an innovation of the era. In fact, scholarly critiques and journalistic muckraking about the harms of industrial capitalism had been occurring for decades. For example, Henry George in his book *Progress and Poverty* famously brought to the public consciousness concerns regarding dangerous inequalities of wealth, arguing for the use of land taxation to capture the public interest in property.[40] The work of journalists and scholars focused on the negative effects of unrestrained capitalism and industrialization began to pile high, detailing harms such as rampant pollution, resource waste, unsafe products and working conditions, anticompetitive behavior, and political corruption.[41] Combined with the closing of the frontier, these accounts helped stoke both consciousness and the appetite for systemic action never seen before in the adolescent nation.

In addition to the inspiration of those leading the charge, it took the efforts of thousands of people to bring about these fundamental changes. Through a diverse—and sometimes discordant—coalition of social movements and the contributions of many, the Progressive Era saw American society deeply restructured. The restructuring, in significant part, came through the law at various scales of government, with many reforms beginning at the state or municipal level.[42] Reforms particularly occurred in regions where supersized industry was previously left to dominate unchecked by a laissez-faire governing philosophy, laying bare both the promises and challenges of the free market. Far removed from the formal levers of federal power, demands for change came from places as varied as Upton Sinclair's muckraking journalism depicting some of the horrors of industrialization and the need for worker and food safety,[43] as well as preservationists like the eccentric mountain dweller and Sierra Club founder John Muir.[44] It came from suffragettes who, through "women's clubs" and "settlement houses," advocated pollution control and public health as part of "municipal housekeeping," which included the installation of sewer systems, street sweeping, trash removal, and street lighting in urban environments.[45] The list, detailed further in this chapter, goes on and on.

The legal change of this era, as that of those that follow, needs to be understood in the context of the broader narrative and particularly the legacy of what came before it. Society was beginning to recognize the many costs of the Allocation Era, which included pillaging of natural resources along with unfettered industrialization. The Allocation Era included the neglect of and assault on public health and the physical environment. The mindset of the Progressive Era was in part a reckoning with that legacy. The demands for redefining changes too came from recognition that to get a foothold enough to start addressing these costs, it would take extensive action at various scales of government. The environmental laws that sprang out of this era were part of this national rejoinder to the closing of the frontier. Policymakers tapped into public sentiment to take on obvious and blatant overuse, and social discontent related to the increasing impacts of industrialization, urbanization, and perceived intemperance throughout American life. Nonetheless, in some instances laws, processes, and institutions created in the Allocation Era proved resilient and made it through the Progressive Era unchanged or only marginally so.

Though not the core story of this chapter, it is crucial to note that the Progressive Era's policies aimed at reducing corporate power and market excess were inextricably linked to suspect principles of social Darwinism and eugenics.[46] Perhaps unsurprisingly, the reforms sought were at times unambiguously advanced to the exclusion of non–Western European Protestant immigrants, people of color, and women.[47]

That is not to say that there were not important contributions made to environmental protection and justice for and often by those belonging to marginalized communities. Leading Black intellectuals Booker T. Washington[48] and W. E. B. Dubois,[49] for example, both esteemed the natural environment, whether for its spiritual or more utilitarian values.[50] Nonetheless, their focus on promoting environmental and public health was understandably eclipsed by more pressing and fundamental issues of civil rights that permeated the African American experience of the day—the oppression from Jim Crow laws, poll taxes, and literacy tests designed to disproportionately harm immigrant and Black Americans,[51] and the Supreme Court decision in *Plessy v. Ferguson* making "separate but equal" the law of the land.[52]

Moreover, the Progressive conservation movement certainly did not have uniform effects on all communities. For instance, poor rural communities often raised objections to conservation laws for criminalizing unauthorized poaching or timber cutting and clearing on public land.[53] Concerns about corruption and "purifying" the election process may have been operationalized through enfranchising women but also voter registration and literacy test requirements, largely disenfranchising Black voters in the process.[54] Perhaps most conspicuously, the establishment of public lands also continued the longstanding maltreatment of Indigenous populations. Several national forests, parks, and monuments that were established completely dispossessed tribal nations or excluded them from long-established uses for hunting, fishing, and gathering.[55] The sweeping legal changes fueled by Progressive environmentalism, indeed, were often far from just.

With all of that as background, this chapter tells the story of the profound changes that frequently reordered the relationship between people and the U.S. environment. It chronicles legal transformations in federal land and wildlife management, infrastructure planning, and public health and food and drug regulation. And it discusses the changes to American procedural and structural governance, including the ways in which the Progressive Era's commitment to expertise and science played out in early bureaucracies attempting to govern human interactions with each other and with the broader environment. Yet it also explores a steadfast undercurrent in which the extractive and exploitative values of the earlier Allocation Era persisted in certain policy arenas.

CONSERVATION AND PRESERVATION OF PUBLIC LANDS, CLASHING VALUES AND PROTECTED LANDS

Major changes related to the environment came in multiple forms during the Progressive Era. While Progressive environmental reforms frequently focused on promoting public health by curbing the excesses of large industries in America's cities,[56] the most consequential and lasting environmental legal changes of the era advanced various environmental goals in lands far away from these urban areas.

Though Theodore Roosevelt may have served as an important catalyst for this era's reforms more generally, there is little doubt that he was the primary spark for the many of the steps taken to establish, protect, and better manage the nation's public lands. In the White House, Roosevelt took advantage of powers previously delegated to the President by Congress to manage federal lands and also convinced Congress to authorize additional powers while in office. Roosevelt brokered a monumental shift in how the United States treated its massive portfolio of natural resources—setting them aside by law on behalf of the public and in service of a variety of public values, rather than promoting privatization of these lands to induce exploitation of resources therein.

It should be noted that the Progressive Era experienced notable progress in federal land conservation even before Roosevelt's presidency—though he still played a key role then too. Before becoming President in 1888, Benjamin Harrison had shown a real interest in protecting public lands as a U.S. Senator. He sponsored legislation in 1882 to make the Grand Canyon the nation's second national park. Harrison's efforts failed then because he could not find sufficient support to overcome resistance from industry forces and their supporters.

One notable example of such a supporter of industry was Secretary of the Interior Henry Teller, a politician from Colorado, who repeatedly opposed managing federal lands in ways that would interfere with their development.[57] Teller expressed open hostility to the budding conservation movement: "We could not have settled Colorado if we had this new-fangled notion of conservation."[58] His skepticism to relying on government to avert environmental harm—as he described it, "the theory that the people don't know enough to take care of their resources"[59]—is at once reminiscent of the prior Allocation Era and foreshadowing of the persistent counter to conservation for decades to come.

Once Harrison became president, however, he had more success. Theodore Roosevelt focused the Boone and Crockett Club—an exclusive club for wealthy men who loved hunting and the outdoors[60]—to lobby the Harrison administration for further protections of public lands. Harrison in turn persuaded Congress to provide increased authority to the President to set aside forestlands through the Forest Reserve Act.[61] To the dismay of land speculators and developers and to the ire of some in Congress, Harrison used this new-found authority to protect more than a dozen stretches of public lands throughout the West, including a large forest reserve near Yellowstone[62] and another encompassing the Grand Canyon—seen as a prime mining opportunity in Arizona and particularly criticized due to the lack of trees in the newly designated "forest."[63]

Under President Cleveland, beginning in 1893, Roosevelt joined the administration as U.S. Civil Service Commissioner.[64] Cleveland used Roosevelt to lobby Congress to enact the Lacey Act,[65] providing criminal penalties for poaching of wildlife and commissioned the U.S. Army to protect Yellowstone National Park from a wide range of threats ranging from mining to vandalism.[66] Roosevelt left the federal government after a couple of years and returned to New York to become New York's police commissioner, while Cleveland's administration continued to designate and expand the nation's forest reserves.[67] With fewer than two weeks in office, Cleveland designated "twenty-one million acres of new forest reserves, increasing the acreage by more than 150%."[68]

In the 1890s, even though Congress had passed legislation to create a few national parks, there nonetheless was a substantial political and social undercurrent resisting conservation.[69] Most prominently, a persistent Congressional delegation from Western states—where most federal lands were—was intensely interested in promoting consumption and development. They managed to attach a rider to an appropriations bill that would have eliminated all of the forest reserves.[70] Opposition to conservation took a variety of forms, including (1) localist claims that Western conservation strategies were primarily motivated by a desire to promote remote interests in the East, (2) antidemocratic allegations that Western states were not consulted before the creation of reserves, and (3) more direct consumptive objections from industry to "locking up" forests.[71] Rage from railroad and timber interests was particularly vociferous.[72] Cleveland was trying to decide how to handle the appropriations bill and its rider on his last few days of office and ultimately vetoed it by refusing to sign, throwing the pages of the bill to the White House floor in frustration as he left to attend the inauguration of his successor, President William McKinley.[73]

By leaving the scattered pages strewn across the floor, Cleveland also left the issue to McKinley. This time, Congress produced a compromise in the form of the Forest Service Organic Administration Act of 1897.[74] The bill melded ideas from both Cleveland's critics and conservationists, and it was inserted in an appropriations bill.[75]

On one hand, the enactment has elements that seem very much a part of the previous era. The bill clarified that the purpose of forests were mainly agricultural, treating the nation's forests as enormous federal tree farms.[76] Additionally, Congress limited the executive branch's discretion, requiring a finding that the land designated was land where the timber was "more valuable for the mineral therein."[77]

In the compromise, however, there were several features that sought to harmonize it with the Progressive Era. Designated forestlands were subject to Forest Service oversight "to improve and protect the forest within the boundaries, or for the purpose of securing favorable conditions of water flows, and to furnish a continuous supply of timber."[78] In doing so, the Organic Act embraced both the notion of using science to provide for a steady supply of timber along with the idea that any harvest should be effectively managed to avoid erosion and other adverse effects to the land.[79] This seems like a response from Gifford Pinchot, who advocated that resource extraction on public lands should be tempered with a "national policy and muscular enforcement," without which "the country's forests would soon be cleared, its mines exhausted, its soil barren, and its rivers clogged with the sediment of erosion."[80] Of course, oversight of the nation's far-flung land was no easy task, given the technology and administrative capacity at the time.[81]

While many in Congress expected Harrison's successor, McKinley, to pull back some of Harrison's designations, McKinley opted to leave them alone (though not adding designations of his own). The same would not be said of his Vice President and successor upon McKinley's assassination—Theodore Roosevelt.

Roosevelt worked with Gifford Pinchot to make and remake the Forest Service. His relationship with Pinchot began years earlier when Roosevelt was still governor in New York. In February of 1899, Pinchot paid a visit to Theodore Roosevelt.[82] Pinchot was by no means unknown to Roosevelt. In fact, a few years before this based on his reputation, Roosevelt had nominated Pinchot as a member of the Boone and Crockett Club. As an amateur but serious scientist, Roosevelt had published several books that melded his passion for hunting big game and environmental science.[83] For his part, Pinchot was likely the only professionally trained forester in the country. The son of a wealthy family, Pinchot had leveraged family fortune to study forestry in Germany. By 1899, Pinchot worked for President Grover Cleveland, mainly on landscaping issues in Washington, D.C.[84] The United States Forest Service had not been fully formed yet, something that Roosevelt and Pinchot would take care of together in later years. So, for the time being, Pinchot was a forester without a forest.

Pinchot and a friend had made their way to New York's capitol, Albany, enroute to the Adirondacks to summit a mountain in the middle of winter. The two stopped by to meet Roosevelt in person. Roosevelt and Pinchot began the evening by swapping stories of adventure and talking about the natural world. As time went on, Roosevelt could not resist the urge—well, of just being Roosevelt. He challenged Pinchot to a boxing match. (After getting elected, in a quintessential Roosevelt move, he had a boxing ring installed into the New York governor's mansion.)

The lanky Pinchot stood taller than the stocky Roosevelt, giving Pinchot the advantage of reach. Shortly after starting the bout, Pinchot jabbed Roosevelt, and Roosevelt fell to the ground. One can only imagine the thoughts of the invited guest watching the governor get up from the ground trying to clear his head.

Regardless of what was going through Pinchot's head, he probably did not expect Roosevelt to do what he did: challenge Pinchot to a wrestling contest. This time, Roosevelt ended up on top, literally—Pinchot pinned to the ground in defeat.[85]

These fights were but a precursor to what ended up becoming a long-term friendship and partnership. Probably more than any two other people, Roosevelt and Pinchot would fight against extractive industries to usher in the nation's conservation movement—from a lofty idea to reform the relationship of the American public with nature, into the reality of law and a new field of public administration. In the last half of the 1890s Pinchot worked in the Department of the Interior as an expert and evangelist for the country's forests, starting with President Cleveland.[86]

On balance, Pinchot embraced a utilitarian goal of maximizing yield, with a degree of Progressive Era antimonopolism thrown in for good measure: "Natural resources must be developed and preserved for the benefit of the many, and not merely for the profit of the few."[87] While monitoring the nation's forests amounted to an enormous task, Pinchot favored enough oversight to provide for pragmatic landscape management, rooted in science. He advocated for "wise use," which frequently meant maximizing present yields while embracing long-term sustainability, as the primary objective guiding America's resource management.[88] Under this paradigm, forest conservation was essentially congruent with an agriculturalist's approach to resource cultivation.[89]

One of the first meetings Roosevelt took after he was made president was with Pinchot, who pled his case to transfer the national forests from the Department of the Interior to the Department of Agriculture.[90] While it took years of advocating to Congress, mainly by Pinchot, it happened eventually, and Pinchot was then appointed to be the first Chief Forester to oversee the Forest Service.[91] Once Roosevelt had Pinchot in that position, the two worked to designate the vast majority of existing national forests (designating 150 in total) before Congress took away the power to unilaterally designate forests from Roosevelt and presidents to come.[92]

Yet the utilitarian, yield-maximization objective embodied by Pinchot's Forest Service was not the only strand of environmentalism blossoming in the United States. The most iconic meeting Roosevelt had on the environment occurred on the other side of the country, when Roosevelt camped in Yosemite with John Muir, probably the most memorable figure associated with the country's public lands other than Roosevelt. Far from the wise-use notion, Muir sought preservation of the "natural" world. He was a Romantic, who associated God in beautiful landscapes, particularly Yosemite.[93] Part scientist and part poet, he came to politics reluctantly as he was convinced that it might prove helpful in garnering protection for the wildlands he loved most. He came with an unflinching

Figure 2.1 Theodore Roosevelt (fifth from left), Gifford Pinchot (behind and to the right of Roosevelt), and John Muir (to Roosevelt's right) in a sequoia grove, Yosemite National Park, California, 1903.

will set on preserving public lands—particularly those he loved most in California—as a self-evident, if not holy, crusade.[94]

With considerable nudging from allies, Muir began a concerted public outreach campaign. Under President Harrison, Muir celebrated the designation of three new national parks, which in many ways served as a bridge between early efforts to designate parks as merely freaks of nature to implementation of something more than the wise-use conservation land ethic commonly found among Progressives.[95] Muir—frequently referred to as a preservationist—came to embody the idea that there was worth in preserving these lands, not for their use but for their beauty and power to heal the masses of a rapidly urbanizing country who were increasingly alienated from nature. He, the advocacy group he helped found—the Sierra Club—and this preservationist model emphasized resisting change by cordoning off landscapes in a supposedly historically pristine state. Perhaps because they were considered congruent, preservationists did not distinguish between maintaining preexisting conditions (what one might call *historical* preservation) from minimizing human intervention (what one might dub *natural* preservation).[96]

While not always due to direct lobbying from Muir, Roosevelt at times went to great lengths to implement the agenda of preservationists, as well as wise-use conservationists. Around the same time he camped with Muir, Roosevelt met with leaders of the Audubon Society.[97] He was told about challenges facing migratory birds—particularly egrets—which were in great demand by poachers who were responding to the demand for feathers to adorn hats fashionable at that time. Roosevelt learned about how this had particularly devastated Pelican Island in Florida. With a stroke of the pen, Roosevelt "so ordered" the island set aside for shore birds.[98] This was the first of fifty-one bird refuges and another four game refuges he would designate, eventually forming the basis for the National Wildlife Service to manage such areas.[99] Though the goals of each refuge varied, in large part they merged wise-use conservation with historical preservation by seeking to maintain viable native populations of valued species for hunting, fishing, and other recreational uses.[100] They would not, however, allow large-scale commercial harvesting of wildlife. Probably more than any other aspect of lands management, these efforts matched up with Roosevelt's lifelong passions, ranging from hunting, his own advocacy work with the Boone and Crockett Club, to his writings in conservation biology.

During Roosevelt's presidency, Congress passed the Antiquities Act,[101] thereby creating another tool Roosevelt (and future Presidents) could rely on to magnify public and private land conservation. The statute authorized the executive to preserve national monuments primarily for their historical value. Though management of each monument varies depending on the proclamation and management plan, designation as a monument has the practical effect of at least constraining if not entirely prohibiting development in a monument area.[102] Congressional debate focused on the appropriate purposes for designation, with some suggesting it should be limited to small, contained archeological sites or unusual natural features.[103] The broader political context of the time, however, suggests that not all legislators saw it that way, particularly the bill sponsor, John Lacey, who had worked with staff within the Department of the Interior to hone the sparse language of the bill.[104] In two sentences, the Act itself is quite capacious, allowing the setting aside of "historic landmarks, historic and prehistoric structures, and other objects of historic or scientific interest that are situated upon the lands owned or controlled by the Government of the United States."[105] Though he only had about eighteen months left in office, Roosevelt managed to set aside eighteen monuments, some in line with the more strict construction some in Congress envisioned—such as Petrified Forest in Arizona and Devil's Tower in Wyoming.[106] Before leaving office, however, he designated some sprawling, much more controversial monuments, most notably—and to the ire of Western extraction interests—the Grand Canyon.[107] Congress also passed legislation designating five national parks, which Roosevelt signed into law. To be sure, no other president during the Progressive Era—and arguably of any era—did as much as Roosevelt to reshape the nation's environmental policy.

An overlooked contribution of Theodore Roosevelt was getting Pinchot and Muir to work together despite their differences.[108] Many have suggested that the two had a relationship as irreconcilable as their guiding philosophies.[109] However, that case is frequently overstated, perhaps more than anything a reflection of how historians believed they *ought* to have felt about each other.[110] Their working relationship should not be surprising, as preservationists and conservationists were part of a much broader coalition of activists who entrusted government to not only check the private excess of prior eras but also affirmatively promote the public welfare for both current and future generations.

Perhaps nowhere does the tension between the philosophies of Muir and Pinchot play out more persistently than in Progressive legislation governing national parks. From the designation of Yellowstone in 1872 to 1916, the country's national parks were protected, if at all, through ad hoc decisions by the Department of the Interior, Department of War (U.S. military), and the Forest Service.[111] As the United States began to prepare for potential entry into World War I and with a country still largely committed to the ideals of the Progressive Era, Congress passed and President Woodrow Wilson signed legislation creating the National Park Service (Park Service System Organic Act).[112] The agency was charged to[113]

> promote and regulate the use of the Federal areas known as national parks, monuments and reservations . . . by such means and measures as conform to the fundamental purpose of the said parks, monuments and reservations, which purpose is to conserve the scenery and the natural and historic objects and the wildlife therein and to provide for the enjoyment of the same in such manner and by such means as will leave them unimpaired for the enjoyment of future generations.

At least as compared to other federal lands, the national parks emphasized maintenance of preexisting native conditions, though they also were secondarily concerned with minimizing management and promoting use.[114] Nonetheless, the charge that asks the Park Service to provide for both "use"—Pinchot's conservation—and leave the same lands "unimpaired"—Muir's preservation—is still a conflict that the Park Service struggles to straddle.[115]

The differences between the conservation philosophies of Pinchot and Muir were and remain real, brought into sharp relief in the fight about whether to dam the Hetch Hetchy River in Yosemite National Park. To Muir's dismay, he was unable to get Roosevelt to stop the dam before Roosevelt left office. In years that followed, Muir continued to lead the fight for conservation, arguing, "Dam Hetch Hetchy! As well dam for water-tanks the people's cathedrals and churches, for no holier temple has ever been consecrated by the heart of man."[116] While Pinchot was not central to the plans to dam the river, he nonetheless is remembered (often notoriously) for testifying in favor of damming the river before Congress:

> Now the fundamental principle of the whole conservation policy is that of use, to take every part of the land and its resources and put it to that use in which it will best serve the most people and I think there can be no question at all but that in this case we have an instance in which all weighty considerations demand passage of the bill. . . . If we had nothing else to consider than the delight of a few men and women who would yearly go into the Hetch Hetchy Valley then it should be left in its natural condition. But the considerations on the other side are simply overwhelming.[117]

While this episode is frequently remembered as Muir's last stand, as he died shortly thereafter, it is equally valid to remember it as the end of Pinchot's federal political career.[118]

WILDLIFE MANAGEMENT BEYOND FEDERAL LANDS (1890–1920)

Even as groundbreaking Progressive Era reforms found a welcome reception in Washington, D.C., more modest but nonetheless consequential developments in substantive legal doctrines and processes in state capitols across the country redefined the relationship between people and natural resources. Development pressures ensured that state laws would continue to support resource exploitation. Yet the emerging conservation ethic of the era—along with the developing emphasis on scientific expertise and professionalization of public administration—made states fertile ground for both the creation of natural resources management agencies and implementation of meaningful conservation measures.[119]

At the state level, perhaps the most forceful shift away from the Allocation Era and toward environmental protection was to regulate wildlife depletion—a move that largely grew out of a desire to meet the demand for hunting rather than a dedication to preservation. As the Progressive Era came into being, wildlife faced intense pressures. Beyond the indirect effects on wildlife from human settlement, access to guns, wealth in cities, and transportation innovations provided previously untapped hunting opportunities.[120] By the 1880s, every state had some form of hunting or fishing regulation, and during the 1890s—even as federal protections increased—state regulation became even more aggressive in regulating hunting and fishing and in staffing administrative agencies to oversee this regulation.[121] Frequently the voice for conservation came from wealthy Progressive hunters, epitomized by the Boone and Crocket Club. In an opinion that reflected the ethic of the Progressive Era, the Supreme Court rebuffed attempts to curtail state regulation of wildlife through litigation and held that states had a right "to control and regulate the common property in game . . . as a trust for the benefit of the people."[122]

While most hunting regulation happened at the state level, the federal government supplemented these efforts. Outside of designating federal lands for wildlife habitat, the most notable new federal wildlife management law was Congressional passage of the Lacey Act of 1900,[123] the oldest extant federal wildlife protection law. Though the law was primarily directed at preserving game and wild birds by making it a federal crime to hunt game with the intent of selling it in another state, it also enables the federal government to regulate the import of wildlife deemed "injurious to the health and welfare of humans, the interests of agriculture, horticulture or forestry, and the welfare and survival of wildlife resources of the U.S."[124] Even today, this provision remains the primary vehicle in federal law for preventing the introduction and spread of invasive species. Congress also enacted the Migratory Bird Treaty Act, implementing the Migratory Bird Treaty entered with Mexico and Canada,[125] which punishes the hunting and even selling of migratory bird species without a federal permit.[126]

It was not just the political mood of the Progressive Era that ushered along hunting regulation and wildlife protection more generally. State and federal management of wildlife grew concurrently with important scientific advancements in ecology, even if it did so imperfectly. The advent of modern ecological science in part was a reflection of the growing understanding of, and concern about, the interactions of organisms—particularly humans—and their environment.[127] Newly formed scientific management principles were applied by administrative agencies in service of promoting more efficient resource use.[128] For example, the Forest Service managed forestlands with the intent of improving timber health and ensuring a sustained and maximum yield of wood products.[129]

While this created opportunities to better manage wildlife and resources, sometimes a flawed understanding of this nascent science resulted in flawed management. Consider three examples where such an approach proved problematic. First, certain fire-suppression policies and techniques intended to minimize timber waste ended up permanently altering the dynamics of some forest ecosystems in ways that made them more susceptible to large-scale fires, disease, and infestation.[130] Second, some ostensibly scientific game management practices led managers to decimate predators as a way of cultivating robust game populations. Such strategies, however, caused some game populations to soar, overgraze, harm existing preserves, and ultimately collapse, exemplified by the popular example of overgrazing by the Kaibab deer herd in the Grand Canyon during the 1920s.[131] Lastly, game managers erected fences to retain populations of elk and bison but inadvertently threatened species survival.[132] Still, even if wildlife protection efforts had some unforeseeable negative consequences, attempts to manage wildlife using scientific management represented an important deviation from the past.

INFRASTRUCTURE AS A PUBLIC GOOD

The federal government's newly pursued protection of public lands advanced in parallel with legislative authorization of and massive appropriations for new forms of public infrastructure. While these infrastructure investments often yielded important public benefits, they also transformed physical landscapes and impaired ecosystems. Though narratives about the Progressive Era's environmental legacy often overlook harms inflicted by the Progressive agenda, it is hardly surprising that the story of the Progressive Era is more complicated.

The role of government in the Progressive Era was not simply to stand against laissez-faire capitalism; it was to facilitate development in many places as much as it was to restrain it in others. The Reclamation Act of 1902, for instance, authorized the federal government to commission water diversion, retention, and transmission projects in arid lands, particularly in the western United States.[133] President Roosevelt posited that lands should be usable and settled by farming families, and that it was wasteful to have water in western rivers not being used by people.[134] Over the next decades, the United States Reclamation Service, later renamed the Bureau of Reclamation, used the Reclamation Act to irrigate the West through a series of dams on waterways, often at a steep cost to the environment.[135]

The federal government began to play a larger role in providing and regulating transportation as well. In 1918, the U.S. Department of Agriculture formed the Bureau of Public Roads (BPR) from precursor units. A predecessor to the Federal Highway Administration, the BPR was charged with building roads in newly formed national parks and national forests; aiding states in road construction; and conducting transportation studies.[136]

Even the very first federal antipollution statute really focused more on facilitating transportation rather than avoiding contamination. The Rivers and Harbors Appropriations Act, also called the "Refuse Act," required permits "to throw, discharge, or deposit, or cause, suffer, or procure to be thrown, discharged, or deposited . . . from the shore . . . any refuse matter of any kind . . . other than that flowing from the streets and sewers . . . in a liquid state, into any navigable water."[137] Signed into law in 1899 by President McKinley, its focus was on keeping the primary thoroughfares of the nation at the time—navigable waterways—passable for commercial and military vessels. The law, however, was rarely employed until its sudden resurgence in the 1960s.[138]

SHORING UP BUT REGULATING PRIVATE RESOURCE RIGHTS THROUGH COURTS AND BUREAUCRACY

The changes between the Allocation and Progressive Eras were transformational but in no way absolute. While the federal government during the Progressive Era took several pioneering steps to promote conservation of lands and wildlife, it also took actions further locking in the Allocation Era's legal system of resource privatization and incentivized resource development.[139] For instance, while traditional homesteading was largely completed by the beginning of the era, the federal government passed legislation for existing homesteaders to enlarge their claims[140] and for some ranchers to stake homestead claims.[141] The federal government, by continuing to rely on the General Mining Act of 1872, also allowed miners to file claims locking up and profiting from mining vast areas of public lands.[142]

The Progressive conservation ethic also barely penetrated the substantive law on water rights initially formed in the Allocation Era. One important legal development in water law at the federal level was the Supreme Court's *Winters v. United States* decision.[143] The Court for the first time recognized that when the federal government establishes a Native reservation, it impliedly reserves sufficient water rights to support that reservation—meaning if a reservation is for the purpose of Native Americans settling land and farming it, water to accomplish the reservation's purposes are also set aside. Later case law would clarify that the same logic applies to any land reservation that contemplates water use as part of the reservation (such as a land reservation for a national wildlife refuge in significant part due to waterfowl).[144]

Moreover, even though the structural and procedural changes to water law bear the Progressive stamp through the bureaucratization of resource management, these changes also indirectly worked to solidify the Allocation Era's water law regime rooted in promoting private ownership and incentivizing development. In 1890, as it entered the Union, Wyoming became the first state to legislatively create water law and delegate administration of that law to an agency, the State Engineer.[145] Many other Western states facing water scarcity followed suit.[146] In creating administrative agencies, these states largely maintained the prior appropriation doctrine developed in the Allocation Era but transformed their procedural governance from one relying on court enforcement of common law to one dependent on a state bureaucracy to shore up property rights in water.[147] The laws did include elements that on their face seem consistent with the emerging Progressive Era's conservation ethic—such as the requirement that water be put to a "beneficial use" and that such use meets a "public interest" standard.[148] Over time, however, the agencies and courts put the most weight behind assuring that—at least for white settlers—private water rights were stable, crowding out and minimizing the most obvious conservation potential of Western water law.[149]

Even in the Progressive Era, it would take some time before the country would try to bring any semblance of a public conservation ethic, or even rationality, to what quickly became its most sought-after resource—oil. One vantage point for viewing what became the country's oil addiction is from the scheming in John D. Rockefeller's Standard Oil boardroom. Through business sense, ruthlessness, and monopoly power, Rockefeller became the world's richest person almost entirely through exploiting oil resources.[150] Though the Progressives took some time to focus on oil conservation, by no means did oil generally, or Rockefeller particularly, escape the notice of the era.

In fact, Standard Oil was seen as a textbook example of a business monopoly and received particular attention during the debate surrounding passage of the Sherman Anti-Trust Act of 1890. President Taft called for the passage of the Act to restrain what he called "the greatest monopoly and combination in restraint of trade in the world[,] . . . an octopus that held the trade in its tentacles, and the few actual independent concerns that kept alive were allowed to exist by sufferance merely to maintain an appearance of competition."[151] The Sherman Anti-Trust Act of 1890 authorized the Department of Justice to seek judicial limitation on monopolies and anticompetitive conduct, as well as private lawsuits by injured parties seeking compensation from such violations.[152] The Department of Justice under President Roosevelt brandished Roosevelt's reputation as a trust buster by moving to break up Standard Oil,[153] though by the time the case meandered through the courts all the way to the Supreme Court, Roosevelt was out of office.[154]

Beaumont, Texas provides a second illustration of the Progressive Era's insatiable quest for fossil fuels, as well as its initial failure to bring significant order to the nation's resource frenzy. This was the site of Spindletop, the nation's first gusher, "which spurted oil more than 100 feet high for over a week,"[155] spewing 800,000 barrels in that time.[156] It drew throngs of people who "press[ed] close enough to feel the black mist on their faces," and soon thereafter, "[d]rillers swarmed into the Beaumont area, leased every acre, including pig sties, drilled as many wells as they could squeeze on to each lease, and then produced oil at full flow in order to out-drain the rival operator next door."[157] With so many drilling and extracting—legally—as quickly as they could, only 5 percent of the field was extracted before the natural pressure of the field gave out.[158] While the chaos of Spindletop could have provided a rationale for government efforts to attempt to regulate oil extraction, oil production went hand in hand with the growth in consumer demand to buy it. Indeed, soaring production nationwide would bring life to the American auto industry,[159] and with it, automobile emissions as a major source of air quality problems.[160]

Slowly, and by no means uniformly, some Progressive attempts to reign in excess took root. State legislation, judicial application of common law, and exercise of regulatory authority served to both encourage oil production but also adopt rudimentary regulations to stem the most chaotic elements of the market, like well-spacing laws and protections for surrounding landowners from waste (e.g., if companies failed take simple precautions to protect the property interests of other producers or otherwise frustrate the societal interest in maximizing resource production).[161] An early case from Indiana exemplified this judicial effect and provided important precedent that in decades to come would claw back some of the intemperance and environmental damage promoted by the rule of capture—the Allocation Era's baseline rule in which ownership of a common or unowned resource is determined by first possession. Citing "great danger to life, and injury to persons and property,"[162] in 1893, the State of Indiana enacted a law attempting to regulate oil production.[163] An oil producer—Ohio Oil Co.—challenged an aspect of the law that required producers to channel any produced oil into a pipeline within two days to reduce both pollution problems and fire risks related to natural gas escaping into the air. By 1900, the case had made its way to the Supreme Court.

Ohio Oil claimed that the state's enforcement of this two-day requirement violated its constitutional rights by effectively taking its private property; it therefore demanded that the state provide it compensation for its losses. The company argued that it should be able to allow natural gas to escape from the oil indefinitely[164] and without regard to how the gas might affect neighbors or their properties. The Supreme Court sided with the state, noting that states could justify regulation to avoid waste or harm to neighboring people and property.[165] Incrementally, the foundational Progressive substantive objectives of conservation and public health would work in concert with procedural principles of administrative and judicial regulation to shape natural resources law.

THE EMERGING PUBLIC TRUST DOCTRINE

The relatively unknown but longstanding public trust doctrine that found its footing during this time has all the trappings of the Progressive Era. Specifically, Chicago's coastline on Lake Michigan served as an important catalyst both for regional growth and a fundamental judicially created canon for countering the excesses of that economic development. In the 1800s, the lakefront became increasingly important to Chicago's future growth, a future that was tied up with Chicago serving as a central hub for railroad spurs in the region. For decades beginning in the 1850s, the city of Chicago, the State of Illinois, and the federal government provided Illinois Central Railroad legal accommodations and grants of property that allowed it to develop along the shores of Lake Michigan.[166] Up until 1872, railroad infrastructure was positioned along the shore or by filling wetlands associated with the lake. The desire to fill and the materials to accomplish it grew dramatically, as fill became a way to discard refuse from the Great Chicago Fire,[167] a blaze that burned down eighteen thousand buildings and left more than one hundred thousand people homeless.[168]

In 1869, the Illinois legislature deeded additional property to the railroad that would allow the expansion of infrastructure though wharfs and piers out into the breakers of Lake Michigan.[169] While those with the Illinois Central Railroad worked hard to get the ability to expand out into the Lake, a great many Chicagoans and others from the area disapproved and even resented the doling out of the lake. This is perhaps seen most clearly in the *Chicago Evening Journal* imploring the public to act to prevent "The Great Swindle."[170]

By 1873, the economy of the Midwest had soured and helped foster popular resentment and movement against railroads in rural Illinois. The combination between those in Chicago who had fought and lost to keep Illinois Central from expanding into Lake Michigan and rural populism created a new politics.[171] In that year, the Illinois legislature passed legislation that reversed its own decision from just a few years earlier and barred the railroad from future expansion into the lake.[172]

Relying on a previous grant to use the bed of the lake and ignoring the subsequent legislation that forbade it, the railroad started building an expansion. Litigation promptly followed, and the case made its way up to the U.S. Supreme Court. The Court ruled in favor of the State of Illinois and against the railroad. In doing so, Justice Harlan, writing for the Court, articulated what became known as the public trust doctrine. Citing previous decisions from state courts as well as legal scholars, Harlan explained that beds and soils underlying navigable waters—like Lake Michigan—are held by state governments "in trust for the common use," which not only provided the public the right to use them in pursuit of commerce and travel but also forbade states from distributing these if such a transfer contravened the public trust.[173] Because Illinois's Central grant to the railroad disregarded the public trust, the Court deemed them void. The Court cited language suggesting that the public trust doctrine was part of the legal heritage provided to the United States when it adopted English common law,[174] and scholars since have traced to doctrine as far back as ancient Roman law.[175]

Despite its ties to much older history, it is important not to overlook the public trust doctrine's fit with the Progressive Era in which it was brought into United States jurisprudence. The notion that natural resources, like lake beds, had been too readily given away in the past and that legal protections were needed to protect the public good, particularly from well-financed interests like railroads, perfectly encapsulates the spirit of the era. While the public trust doctrine would grow into a mainstay of environmental protection in decades to come, it is also worth noting that at its inception within the United States, the doctrine had more to do with not allowing a state to fritter away the public's ability to use navigable waters for individual material gain—commerce, navigation, and fishing—than it had to do with safeguarding the environment more generally. It hardly seems an accident that the ability of the doctrine to find footing in U.S. law came in an era and within a set of facts that allowed the Court to push back against big business stripping away resources that previously served the broader public.

PROGRESSIVE ATTEMPTS TO ADAPT COMMON LAW TO ADDRESS POLLUTION (1890s–1910s)

Pollution had gone largely unchecked in the United States up to the Progressive Era, and the technological innovations that proliferated since the Civil War made for some truly repugnant circumstances. Upton Sinclair's muckraking masterpiece, *The Jungle*, provided a troubling window into how dire problems like water contamination from industrial activity had become by the turn of the twentieth century.[176]

> "Bubbly Creek" is an arm of the Chicago River, and forms the southern boundary of the Union Stock Yards; all the drainage of the square mile of packing-houses empties into it so that it is really a great open sewer a hundred or two feet wide. . . . The grease and chemicals that are poured into it undergo all sorts of strange transformations, which are the cause of its name. . . . Bubbles of carbonic gas will rise to the surface and burst, and make rings two or three feet wide. Here and there the grease and filth have caked solid, and the creek looks like a bed of lava; chickens walk about on it, feeding, and many times an unwary stranger has started to stroll across and vanished temporarily. The packers used to leave the creek that way, till every now and then the surface would catch on fire and burn furiously, and the fire department would have to come and put it out.[177]

Given these conditions, it is not surprising that we find the evolution of the common law doctrine of nuisance in many states during this period to help rein in some of the Progressive Era's biggest polluters. Two of the most notable decisions were suits decided by the U.S. Supreme Court.[178] The cases, taken together, highlight the limitations and potential of common law courts for addressing emerging environmental harms.

Missouri v. Illinois,[179] "the Supreme Court's first interstate pollution case,"[180] displayed several of the shortcomings. The suit focused on what was one of the greatest engineering feats of its time—Illinois had changed the direction of the Chicago River to shift away not only the industrial pollution Sinclair wrote about in *The Jungle*, but also the copious amounts of raw sewage Chicago had been dumping into Lake Michigan. With the river flowing the other direction, these contaminants now ran into the Desplaines River and then on to the Mississippi River. Missouri's suit alleged that by reversing the river, Chicago's sewage was now causing typhoid fever to spike in St. Louis. Missouri sought an injunction from Illinois for fouling the Mississippi River. Missouri rooted its legal claim in the common law tort of public nuisance.

After "hear[ing] from 350 witnesses, amass[ing] over 1,000 exhibits, and compiling a record in excess of 13,000 pages," the Court unanimously rejected Missouri's nuisance claim.[181] While Missouri's claim might have made logical sense, more than logic was needed. Nuisance claims required plaintiffs like Missouri to provide sufficient evidence that the actions of the defendant (Illinois) caused their harm, not just that it made sense that they did. The Court remarked that never "so remote a source" had previously been shown to cause a nuisance.[182] The Court noted that given that Chicago's muck had mixed so well into the Mississippi by the time it reach Missouri, showing that Illinois caused Missouri's typhoid outbreak would require "most ingenious experiments and . . . interpretation [of] the most subtle speculations, of modern science."[183] While the Court interpreted nuisance broadly enough to potentially include attenuated environmental harms from pollution, it nonetheless found that the judicial principle of *stare decisis* militated against extending nuisance to more remote harms in a rapidly industrializing world.[184] And the adversarial common law system continued to place the financial and technological burden on the plaintiff to marshal all the evidence of public harm.

Litigants fared better in the other Supreme Court case raising a public nuisance claim, *Georgia v. Tennessee Copper Co.*, as the Supreme Court recognized the potential to rely on flexible doctrines like nuisance law to address harm from newly emerging technologies. The State of Georgia brought a suit against a copper smelting company that operated across the border in Tennessee. The company burned organic material from rocks in an open-pit—the smoke from which was so noxious it caused "wholesale destruction of forests, orchards, and crops" in Georgia.[185] The Court found in favor of the state and enjoined the company from operating in this manner. Justice Holmes wrote of the pollution Georgia suffered:

> It is a fair and reasonable demand on the part of a sovereign that the air over its territory should not be polluted on a great scale by sulphurous acid gas, that the forests on its mountains . . . should not be further destroyed or threatened by the act of persons beyond its control, that the crops and orchards on its hills should not be endangered from the same source.[186]

The fact that the State of Georgia brought the suit played heavily in its favor in seeking injunctive relief, as private plaintiffs previously only had been able to obtain monetary damages for their troubles.[187]

Beyond the Supreme Court, many state courts considered nuisance liability for pollution from a range of sources indicative of the time. Examples of successful nuisance cases include a farmer suing a mill for the water pollution it introduced into a stream,[188] a neighbor suing a tannery due to the odor it emitted,[189] and residents suing a construction company for "dirt, dust, smoke, cinders," along with the "fine particles of cement and stone" of its machinery.[190] Though the common law's prototypical reliance on generalist judges to compensate (rather than prevent) private injuries was not tailor-made for addressing prospective public harms, some courts nonetheless found ways to adapt nuisance law to emerging environmental problems.

REGULATION FOR CONSUMER PROTECTION AND PUBLIC HEALTH (1900–1920)

Though litigants sought adaptations of the common law to redress the effects of industrial capitalism, the Progressive Era is more notable for the emergence of public regulation to try to restrain markets and protect the public. As this Progressive Era dawned, Congress established through the Interstate Commerce Act the first federal regulatory body, the Interstate Commerce Commission, to regulate railroad rates.[191] For the next several decades, prescriptive regulations became widely adopted in a wide range of contexts, such as the operation of elections,[192] banking,[193] and—perhaps most prominently—public health, including food safety.

Though Sinclair's *The Jungle* may also have depicted environmental horrors, it is primarily known for the abhorrent picture he portrayed of the meat packing industry at the time. Sinclair—a committed socialist—had meant to provide the nation with insight into the horrors of the industrial workplace and plight of the working class. The labor movement was undoubtedly aided by accounts like Sinclair's, with unions pushing for greater pay, safer working conditions, and less hours.[194] Many states established industrial commissions and labor departments, the first administrative agencies (which could issue and enforce worker health and safety regulations without having to go back to the legislature), and workers' compensation laws that displaced common law tort claims in exchange for an allegedly simplified administrative system of benefits for workers injured while working.[195] In 1913, Congress also established the Department of Labor (which from a health perspective initially focused mostly on women and children),[196] and in 1912, the Public Health Service was allocated authority to address occupation-related diseases.[197]

However, Sinclair's depictions of food adulteration were what caused widespread distress:

> Particularly disturbing were the accounts of the workers, sick with tuberculosis, spitting on the floor, then dragging butchered meat across it. There were tales of meat in storage rooms, rotting and covered with rat droppings, which was then made into sausage, detritus and all. There were even tales of workers who had fallen into the great acidic lard vat and become, after their bones had been fished out, a part of "Durham's Pure Leaf Lard."[198]

President Roosevelt, after hearing such reports, was so disgusted that he threw the sausage served to him that day out the window.[199] The country apparently felt similarly; within weeks of the release of Sinclair's book, meat consumption in the United States fell by half.[200] For his part, Sinclair lamented the book's inadvertent success, stating "I aimed at the public's heart, and by accident I hit it in the stomach."[201]

After Sinclair landed his gut punch, Roosevelt sprang into action. The allegations found in *The Jungle* were in many ways—even putting aside the public's demand for action—tailor-made for the President, who had made a career of hammering businesses for taking advantage of people.[202] After personally consulting with Sinclair, Roosevelt decided to launch an investigation to try to verify the claims made by the muckraker.[203] The report of the inspectors could not confirm the most troubling aspects of Sinclair's account, and some including Roosevelt have raised questions about the veracity of some of Sinclair's allegations.[204] Still, at least some of what Roosevelt's inspectors found, to use Roosevelt's words, was "revolting."[205]

In sending on the report, Roosevelt focused on the danger to public health posed by the conditions observed. He wrote, "The report shows that the stock yards and packing houses are not kept even reasonably clean, and that the method of handling and preparing food products is uncleanly and dangerous to health."[206] He also concluded that "[u]nder existing law the National Government has no power to enforce inspection of the many forms of prepared meat food products that are daily going from the packing houses into interstate commerce."[207]

The investigative report he provided to Congress provided its own shocking revelations related to food handling. The most explosive item in the report reads as follows:

> As an extreme example of the entire disregard on the part of the employees . . . we saw a hog that had just been killed, cleaned, washed, and started on its way to the cooling room fall from the sliding rail to a dirty wooden floor and slide part way into a filthy men's privy. It was picked up by two employees, . . . and hung up with other carcasses, no effort being made to clean it.[208]

Not surprisingly, these findings captured the attention of both Congress and the nation.[209] While limited forms of regulation had been in place beforehand, Congress passed the Federal Meat Inspection Act of 1906, which with some modification remains the core of meat processing regulation in the United States today.

In contrast to the retrospective, remedial, adversarial focus of the common law, this new public law approach relied heavily on a comprehensive prescriptive regulatory process. The Meat Inspection Act, for instance, included three major innovations. First, it delegated the power to a federal agency to set standards for facility sanitation operating procedures, food content, and labeling. Second, the new legislation required federal permits for facilities that process meat or poultry and then sold them out of state.[210] Third, it provided for enforcement through animal inspections by federal officials (carcass by carcass, before and after slaughter), labeling and certification monitoring, sporadic testing, and responding to contamination incidents.[211]

Taking a step away from the specifics, more broadly, the key elements of this new form of social regulation comprised of rules that govern private activity; standards that serve as benchmarks for determining compliance; penalties for those who did not comply; and an administrative agency charged with enforcement, including monitoring and levying sanctions.[212] Also, tied to the value of promoting public health and stemming excesses of businesses, the Pure Food and Drug Act of 1906 followed a similar public regulatory framework. The law prohibited the sale of adulterated or misbranded food and drugs in interstate commerce, primarily focused on ensuring accurate labeling. It recognized national standards for drugs, prescribed penalties, and led to the creation of the nation's first consumer protection agency, the Food and Drug Administration, to implement the law.[213] In addition to empowering federal inspectors, both of these laws include novel legal tools that require public disclosure of products and inspections as a way to, as the great Progressive Justice Brandeis put it, allow sunlight to act as "a disinfectant"[214]—something sorely needed in the food industry at the time.

Other laws followed a similar public regulatory blueprint and were tied to promoting public health. The Federal Insecticide Act of 1910,[215] for example, was the first federal pesticide legislation. It was primarily focused on promoting effective agriculture, rather than public health or environmental pollution concerns.[216] The act authorized the Department of Agriculture to set standards for the insecticide and fungicide manufacture, to require certain disclosures on product labels, and to inspect and remove from the market any products deemed "adulterated" or ineffective.[217]

It was not just Roosevelt and journalists who brought these laws to life. A movement of mostly wealthy and middle-class women was instrumental in building support for many of these social regulations. Though seeds had been planted earlier through antebellum organizations like the Woman's Christian Temperance Union (WCTU) and the Young Women's Christian Association (YWCA),[218] the Progressive Era saw a quantum leap in influence of civic institutions dedicated to "maternalist politics," in parallel and conjunction with a movement to establish women's suffrage. Maternalist politics involved activism appealing to women as mothers and wives and directed at issues for which women were identified by some as having a particular capacity to address.[219] These included a range of social reforms, such as improving public education,[220] revamping the juvenile justice system,[221] addressing labor conditions for women and children,[222] and otherwise promoting public health, such as through nationwide campaigns for public milk stations to reduce infant mortality and state aid to widowed mothers through "mothers' pension" programs.[223] Maternalism certainly was influential in the Progressive Era, the first fundamental transformation in the relationship of American law and government with health and the environment.

Yet, as with many other campaigns in this Progressive Era, these initiatives to promote social welfare often were conspicuous in their exclusion, particularly of the interests of people of color.[224] This exclusion, though not exclusive to environmental and health harms, undoubtedly

Figure 2.2 Women's Club visiting the Adirondacks (1898), photograph by Katherine Elizabeth McClellan.

had important implications on both people and the environment. For example, poorer communities of color were much more likely to face dire environmental exposure as workers or as residents near polluting industry, and these disparities actually increased despite efforts by some health activists.[225] Widespread discrimination and exclusion resulted in both some populations facing much more harmful environmental problems than others and the governmental disregard for those problems.

OVERCOMING THE FORCES OF DISCONTENT

The Progressive Era saw an unprecedented shift in the law and the relationship between government institutions, markets, and the environment—even if it was not conceived of to be environmental law at the time. These changes had their detractors though. Those resisting Progressive Era changes included a broad and ever-shifting coalition of charismatic policymakers, public health ideologues, scientists, advocates, and even business interests. Much of big industry and Wall Street found Roosevelt and conservation to be "dangerous,"[226] and sought to circumvent these fundamental changes in society. Extractive industries, food manufacturers, land speculators, railroad companies, and others sought to thwart federal management and regulation designed to reduce or prevent harm caused by self-interested activities.[227]

These forces were well represented in the political arena. For many issues, the face of the resistance within the government belonged to Secretary of the Interior Richard Ballinger, a well-known political rival who "objected to the Roosevelt/Pinchot program to preserve the western landscape."[228] Ballinger focused much of his efforts on assisting corporations, primarily in the coal-mining industry, whose interests were impacted by conservation efforts. Indeed, he locked horns with Pinchot numerous times, most famously regarding access to Alaskan lands.[229] Pinchot, who "abhorred giveaways of public land to miners, loggers, and corporations,"[230] considered the way Ballinger assisted corporations seeking access to coal lands in Alaska improper and unsustainable.

Other policymakers challenged the Roosevelt administration's drive to address market failures through robust federal authority. Most prominently, Senator Weldon Heyburn opposed Roosevelt's agenda, including expansion of the national forests, arguing that "no federal money should be spent on forests, that it was a violation of state's rights."[231] Similarly, Representative Frank Mondell was well known to be antagonistic toward conservation, opposing the repeal of the Desert Land Act of 1877 (which promoted desert development) and the Timber and Stone Act (which promoted timber and mining)[232] as well as the preservation of wildlands.[233]

These opponents had some success in curbing federal authority, often by limiting the resources provided—sometimes with devastating effect. Federal land management serves as a prime example. In 1910, there were only five hundred forest rangers employed to manage National Forestland nationwide; rangers in Montana and Idaho, for example, were responsible for monitoring almost two hundred square miles each.[234] In July, a violent lightning storm triggered nearly a thousand fires across twenty-two forests in the Northern Rockies.[235] A massive fire, which came to be known as the "Big Burn," tore through Idaho and Montana, consuming more than three million acres in thirty-six hours, killing at least seventy-eight men, including rangers and volunteers.[236] Pinchot estimated that $1 billion worth of timber had been lost in the Big Burn, and argued that the "fire was not inevitable . . . it was 'the ironbound reactionaries,' led by Senator Heyburn of Idaho, who had left the people's forest without adequate stewardship."[237] Such resistance continued into President Taft's administration: "[S]ome of the land that Roosevelt had set aside had been turned over to private interests by Taft. The big man talked of conservation, but his actions showed otherwise. And his Secretary of the Interior, Ballinger, the administration's advocate for letting corporations have their way again with public land, was still in charge."[238]

Yet during the Progressive Era, antiregulatory opposition was frequently quashed and overcome by public sentiment stoked by skilled and charismatic policymakers relying on effective documentation and communication about the harms of unfettered resource exploitation[239] and markets and the value of governmental authority to temper such forces. Indeed, in the aftermath of the Big Burn, an outpouring of public support helped push Congress to direct more funding and resources toward the Forest Service.[240] Efforts by land speculators to build railroads in Yellowstone were "effectively blocked on the grounds that it would be an infringement on the park's integrity."[241] And when Congress was less obliging, President Roosevelt used executive authority to adopt conservation measures, such as relying on the 1891 Forest Reserve Act and 1906 Antiquities Act to reserve areas like the Grand Canyon and Teton Mountains as national monuments.[242] Moreover, while the conflict between Muir's preservation ethic and Pinchot's conservationism at times led to conflict that might have obstructed further environmental reforms, some argue that their rivalry "offered different reasons to move beyond short-term exploitation" that led to "a productive expansion of the audience for their shared passion."[243] As such, this clash in ideas may have reached antiexploitation forces that either one of them would not have been able to mobilized individually.

* * *

Eventually, however, the protagonists of the Progressive Era, including progovernment conservationists, preservationists, and proto-environmentalists, lost the upper hand. By the end of the Progressive Era, the voracious desire by many institutions, policymakers, and citizens to expand and develop untapped and seemingly boundless resources, combined with an optimism and faith about the capacity of markets and technology to address human demands, seemed to gain again in ascendancy.

Indeed, a new era in U.S. environmental law had dawned. And, while the Progressive Era had created and reshaped important legal areas, it far from addressed every environmental or human health harm. While those who stood in opposition to the Progressive Era eventually built a coalition that helped put an end to it, many of the legal goals, processes, and institutions the era had built would prove difficult to dismantle.

3

THE MODERNIZATION ERA

THE GREAT ACCELERATION TO THE ANTHROPOCENE (1920–1960)

INTRODUCTION

Law in the Modernization Era transformed the United States. The era spans radically different moments in U.S. history—the Roaring 20s, Great Depression, New Deal, World War II, and the baby and economic boom of the Cold War. During the era, American life changed dramatically and purposefully into something much more recognizable to the present day. The legal system's approach to the environment also radically shifted, away from the Progressive Era's conservation and precaution toward treating the environment as an instrumentality for extracting economic growth and facilitating consumption.

The scope and scale of change that the country witnessed is hard to overstate. This is the era in which the American Dream—the aspiration (some would say illusion) of opportunity and upward mobility for all—was coined.[1] Automobiles, though initially only really available to the well-to-do, largely replaced streetcars and horse carriages in America's cities, while horse plows were supplanted by tractors on many American farms.[2] Fertilizers, insecticides, and engineered crops began increasing yields.[3] Televisions—not even invented at the beginning of the era—became commonplace, and telephones went from luxuries to a basic household need.[4] Air conditioning changed how and where Americans lived.[5] Expedient (and often dangerous) chemicals found their way into most households.[6] Plastics, rare at the beginning of the era, proliferated and were increasingly found in nearly everything.[7] Nuclear bombs, invented during and credited by some for ending World War II, hung over society as a sword of Damocles.[8] A country that in previous eras had migrated from farms into cities now followed new transportation infrastructure into a new form of American living—suburbia.[9] New cities took root, particularly in the arid American West.[10] After World War II and amid the Cold War, the United States took on the mantle of world superpower, from then on working from the assumption that its citizenry deserved the benefits of modernity.

The environmental fallout of the era was likewise severe and multifaceted. During the Modernization Era, the county became increasingly reliant on fossil fuels—oil and gas fueled the growth of the automobile market and coal facilitated electrification across the country. Suburban development gobbled up farms and forests. Hydrologic energy made by dams flooded plains, canyons, and obliterated ecosystems. Many of the risks, ranging from nuclear fallout to exposure to newly created chemicals, began to present novel and often poorly understood health risks.

Of course, legal strategies, processes, and institutions helped underwrite these changes. Lawmakers and the courts created the legal foundation for societal transformation. They adopted direct subsidies in a range of sectors to accelerate development and consumption. They created a large administrative bureaucracy, local ordinances, and administrative processes to facilitate development. They limited corporate liability[11] and regulations in a range of substantive areas that might have guarded against risks to health and the environment caused by these societal changes. Health and safety regulation, moderation to protect the public interest, and land and wildlife preservation did continue, but they most certainly were a countercurrent.

To illustrate the extent of change experienced during the Modernization Era, perhaps the construction of interstate highways provides a window into not only large-scale environmental and social transformation but also the government's role in facilitating this change. Before the 1950s, road development was at-best a regional matter and often local. Early innovations of public roadbuilding occurred mainly in the Northeast, frequently paid for by state and local governments and justified using tolls designed to help recoup public investment.[12]

Though its importance would not be understood for decades, the paradigm shift in transportation came through an experiment that began as the Progressive Era was ending. In 1919, the armed forces questioned as a matter of national security whether it was even possible to bring military equipment across the country. To answer that question, the military put together a convoy to traverse the U.S. mainland.[13] The limitations of the nation's roads soon were quite evident. With roads in many places consisting of no more than divots made by wagon wheels (or even less), the convoy's trip from Washington, D.C. to San Francisco ended up taking sixty-one days. Concerns about duration, however, were far surpassed by the truly harrowing nature of the trip. Not only did several of the convoy's vehicles fail to complete the journey; of the expedition's 258 enlisted soldiers, twenty-one of them died due to accidents and the harsh conditions they faced along the way.[14]

Nearly forty years later, as the Modernization Era ended, President Eisenhower—a participant and organizer of the 1919 convoy—would successfully call on Congress to build a federal interstate highway system.[15] This colossal government undertaking would help connect cities to previously distant countryside and make interstate travel commonplace. It would also help station the automobile—and belching pollution from combustion engines at virtually every street corner—at the core of twentieth-century American life.

"Modernization," like "allocation" in the nation's first era, profoundly changed virtually every aspect of American life. The law in this era fundamentally altered government, infrastructure, where people lived, energy production and use, Main Street and Wall Street, mass communication, and the natural environment. Indeed, modernization would come with human and environmental costs that would not be understood—let alone addressed—for decades. The current plight of the planet can be traced to many of the decisions made during the era. And legal decisions, processes, and institutions are repeatedly the catalysts of the era's most impactful changes.

A ROADBUILDING BOOM

It was not just highways that came to define the Modernization Era but roads more generally. The pursuit of roadbuilding in many ways provides insights into the values guiding change during the era. Specifically, during the era, public demand grew for a network of roads suitable for automobiles. More generally, the political and legal changes of this era had more to do with the judgments of white middle-class American voters and consumers about what would make life more convenient and help facilitate the growth of personal wealth and opportunity.

While the federal government played an enormous role in road modernization, the first federal efforts in the era were modest, though they provided important precedent in discussions of federal funding in the decades that followed. The Federal Aid Highway Act of 1921 was the first, providing federal matching funds for limited road construction and improvements.[16] More importantly, it also helped create a governmental consensus about the need for an interstate highway system and a planning process with states determining the routes the system would include.[17] In the Great Depression of the 1930s, federal funds (even matching funds for state projects) were harder to access, as the New Deal advanced by FDR diverted funds to other federal programs and projects.[18]

As federal efforts fizzled, state and local governments took the lead on road infrastructure. Of all these efforts, roadbuilding in New York City under the guidance of Robert Moses proved to be particularly aggressive. Moses showed great skill in harvesting financial resources in pursuit of goals to modernize New York, leveraging tolls from built projects and funding from New Deal programs to construct massive infrastructure projects, including the Triboro Bridge, the Hudson Bridge, the Queens Midtown Tunnel, and the Westside Highway.[19] Yet without federal support, most cities, let alone poorer rural areas, did little roadbuilding.

However, in the 1950s, through both serendipity and calculated scheming, those pushing for an interstate highway system saw a major payoff. President Eisenhower happened to be particularly convinced of the advantages of roadbuilding. To be sure, as the commander of Allied forces in Western Europe during World War II, Eisenhower understood the great importance the autobahn played in travel within Germany.[20] As alluded to above, Eisenhower helped lead the 1919 military convoy across mainland United States and even drafted the report detailing the harrowing journey.[21] Although initially ambivalent about a prominent federal government role on this issue,[22] Eisenhower soon made roadbuilding a top priority.

While Eisenhower played a pivotal role in creating change, it was not just Eisenhower that made highway expansion possible. The effort relied on the groundwork strategically laid by others with sway over the federal government that primed Washington for major highway building proposals. Within the government, leadership of Public Works Committees in both the U.S. Senate and House of Representatives had worked diligently with the Bureau of Public Roads (later to become the Federal Highway Administration) to push a cogent vision of roadbuilding waiting for its political moment.[23] Industry players cooperated with these efforts, ranging from road builders to vehicle manufacturers.[24]

More broadly, this episode provides an important case study about the power of leveraging aligned political and economic actors to secure change. The collaboration of these organizations serves as a key example of what is known as an "iron triangle"—a mutually beneficial relationship in which each entity cultivates political will to accomplish policy goals while standing to benefit personally by doing so.[25] In this case, elected officials amassed power by delivering district projects; agencies gained long-term relevancy and agency brass obtained a way to show leadership; private entities gained commercial opportunities; and all of these parties benefited from the revolving door between them. Often in the years that followed, those advocating for environmental change would find themselves at odds with economic interest groups and the politicians allied with them. In instances in which economic interests and environmental protection aligned, changes frequently came with much less effort.

In this case, Eisenhower leveraged a coalition of political and economic interests very effectively.[26] Leaning on both national security and economic justifications, he impaneled a commission of military experts, engineers, and state transportation officials to envision the ideal expansion of roads across the country.[27] This process resulted in a skeleton plan for the country to build forty thousand miles of roads that largely echoed and reinforced findings coming out of the Federal Highway Act of 1944. In 1955, Congress passed the Interstate Highways Act,[28] which provided a pathway for the federal government to underwrite most of the highway system through a federal gas tax, though it required some state matching funds.[29] This was the most expensive public works endeavor in American history through that time.[30] The road network combined with state-funded roadbuilding to fundamentally alter transportation in the United States, particularly for those working in American cities.

Building highways amounted to a colossal subsidy for the automobile industry. This not only proved to be a great expense of taxpayers' funds but also was to the detriment of other modes of transportation. Buoyed by such support, cars and highways supplanted other prevailing transit options, especially trolleys and streetcars. While transit trips grew from about fifteen million in 1920 to well more than twenty million a year in the 1940s, transit ridership shrank during the 1950s and by 1960 was only about ten million a year.[31] On the other hand, vehicle miles traveled continually grew during the Modernization Era, ending up more than fifteen times larger than where they began.[32]

Building roads also induced other investments. While suburbanization may not have been the explicit aim, the 1950s' roadbuilding boom certainly facilitated it. The decision to invest so heavily in roadbuilding increasingly made Americans much more dependent on vehicles and reduced the effectiveness of transit systems. In many places, the communities that boomed made owning a car a practical necessity[33] and led to yet another shift in the urban planning worldview—that cities should be designed and redesigned around the automobile.[34] It is no accident, then, that drive-in movies and drive-in restaurants became emblematic of the 1950s. And of course, increased suburbanization provided further momentum for the construction of even more roads still.

Even as highway building provided easier access from commuter towns to cities, these same highways were sometimes transposed on top of longstanding city neighborhoods. These new roads regularly had a disproportionate impact on communities of color—communities that found themselves on the losing end of "white flight."[35] Placement of these projects in communities of color was far from accidental.

> Often under the guise of "slum removal," federal and state officials purposely targeted Black communities to make way for massive highway projects. In states around the country, highways disproportionately displaced Black households and cut the heart and soul out of thriving Black communities as homes, churches, schools, and businesses were destroyed. In some cases, entire Black communities were leveled.[36]

Latine, Native American, and Asian communities also were intentionally targeted for such development.[37] Perhaps the most prominent example of discriminatory planning involves the influential planner Robert Moses, who led the design of New York's highway construction that not only destroyed communities of color but also designed highways to purposefully make it difficult for the populace to access public beaches with the aim of excluding the poor.[38] While a number of communities put up a fight—and in a few instances actually prevailed—for the most part these projects further marginalized people who were already struggling.[39]

In essence, federal, state, and local governments were directing public dollars to buy the land of poor and minority landowners to subsidize the automobile industry and promote automobile access for budding, mostly white, suburban communities. Beyond the demolition and division of communities with deep historical ties, roadbuilding also led to localized air pollution that disproportionately harmed the remaining residents of poor and marginalized neighborhoods.[40] Pollution from cars left a lasting legacy of health impacts on society—increased premature mortality, cardiovascular and respiratory problems, increased incidence of cancer, and developmental problems in children.[41]

Expansion of highways, however, was only one of several important government policies that led to suburbanization.

POLICIES DESIGNED TO PROMOTE SUBURBANIZATION

The archetypal community in the United States began as rural and agricultural in the Allocation Era. This shifted to urban during the Progressive Era, spurred by mass migration into growing cities. In fact, at the dawn of the Modernization Era, more people resided in urban areas than outside of them.[42]

Particularly after the Industrial Revolution and growth of urban industry in the Progressive Era, cities were difficult to live in especially for the poor, despite the job opportunities. Economic growth had been built on technologies that caused serious local pollution problems for communities near factories. Pollutants spewing from growing industry reliant on combustion engines combined with increased automobile pollution, burning coal for power, burning trash for disposal, overcrowding, and concentrated poverty combined to spur health and other social problems.[43]

When the Great Depression first hit in the summer of 1929, however, this trend toward urbanization abruptly reversed, and the difficult situations found in urban areas multiplied. The economy plummeted, businesses failed, and jobs evaporated. Poverty and lack of opportunities made cities difficult places to live. As the Depression wore on, many of the remaining businesses and the jobs began to migrate out of cities, leading many to move to rural areas to farm, causing growth in the West and South—much less populated areas of the country.[44] As job opportunities continued to dry up in urban areas, even more people left cities to search for jobs, including to streetcar suburbs.[45]

During World War II, United States industry ramped up to meet wartime manufacturing needs, boosting the appeal of cities. But as the war ended, the country began an urban exodus to newly built suburbs, using new roads and cars built by industries looking to pivot after the end of World War II. This trend continued—and accelerated—throughout the remainder of the Modernization Era.[46]

As with other pervasive societal changes in prior eras, suburbanization involved more than just aggregate social choices and preferences. Rather, policy and legal changes like local zoning ordinances and federal housing policies fueled the growth of sprawling suburbia. Undoubtedly, many suburban residents considered such living the idyllic manifestation of the American Dream. Yet it was also true that suburban life was built through various policies that allowed for (if not encouraged) suburban communities to ignore many negative environmental and social harms.

PROLIFERATION OF LOCAL GOVERNMENT ZONING, SPRAWL, AND SEGREGATION

While zoning law's roots reached firmly into the Progressive Era, the rapid proliferation of local land use zoning in the Modernization Era undoubtedly was a key legal factor in advancing suburban sprawl growth. Like most other forms of governmental intervention in the Progressive and Modernization Eras, including the rise of administrative law and the administrative state more generally, the underlying premise of zoning was a reliance on professional expertise to define the public interest—trusting expert urban planners to guide land development and minimize conflicting land uses.[47] The first municipal zoning codes were enacted as early as 1908.[48] However, municipal zoning only began to substantially proliferate at the advent of the Modernization Era, with public land use regulation mushrooming for the next century.[49]

An important impetus for the rise of zoning was the U.S. Supreme Court's decision upholding its constitutionality in *Euclid v. Ambler Realty*.[50] In the 1920s, the village of Euclid sat on the outskirts of Cleveland on the banks of Lake Erie. Euclid was among the first local governments to experiment with zoning. The village council adopted simple zoning regulations, which established three height districts (setting maximum building heights) and four area districts (providing minimum lot sizes).[51] It also established numerous use districts seeking to separate industrial from residential uses, restrict the most intensive industrial uses to properties near the rail line that went through the village, limit commercial uses to lands a bit further from the rail, and only allow residential uses on the land furthest from the rail line.[52] Ambler Realty, a land speculator who saw its land value plummet due to Euclid's zoning restrictions, sued the village, claiming that its land use restrictions were unconstitutional.

In *Euclid*, the Court focused on the reach of state authority to regulate private land use decisions. Unlike the federal government, which derives its power from the enumerated powers found in the U.S. Constitution, local jurisdictions rely on the "police power"—a general authority to govern held by U.S. states (and habitually delegated to local governments) to protect public health, public welfare, public safety, and public morals.[53]

The case had three major impacts on American land use law and the American landscape. First, the Court held that local governments acting under delegated state police power could regulate land uses quite extensively. The Court allowed Euclid to impose a range of height, area, use, and other restrictions on private lands, in what became known (and widely adopted) as "Euclidian Zoning." The Court saw the advantage of zoning. "A nuisance may be merely a right thing in the wrong place—like a pig in the parlor instead of the barnyard,"[54] the Court reasoned.

Unlike common law causes of action like nuisance, which generally only allow a claimant to sue in court after a harm has occurred, separating land uses (like factories and residential areas) allowed the government to avoid foreseeable land use conflicts and prevent the proverbial pig from going in the parlor. In this regard, zoning was one of the earliest forms of public environmental regulation; it sought to avoid the most harmful effects of private land use through prospective standards and permitting.[55]

As the Modernization Era progressed, zoning "quickly became the dominant means of land use regulation" in the United States.[56] Following the lead in *Euclid* and relying on the Standard State Zoning Enabling Act created by the U.S. Department of Commerce in 1922 to promote local zoning restrictions, every state empowered communities to embrace this new paradigm of largely decentralized public land use regulation.[57] In addition to embracing *Euclid*'s vision of zoning as providing for more orderly development and reducing conflicts between land uses, urban planners extolled it as a tool to assist urban areas mitigate poverty, address inadequate housing options, and create more effective infrastructure and public spaces.[58] These planners grew in their sophistication and created "almost scientific policy documents" meant to guide "officials through their development decisions."[59]

Second, increased reliance on zoning by local governments had important consequences that frequently worked to facilitate suburbanization.[60] Widespread adoption of area districts requiring minimum lot sizes decreased land densities, which made communities less walkable and conducive to mass transit. Furthermore, separating uses meant more distance between homes and places of work. Separating commercial uses in turn frequently meant also planning to facilitate cars through adequate parking. Unsurprisingly, as communities adopted zoning codes, much of the growth that followed required suburban growth not just due to market demands but to zoning's limitations on land.

Third, zoning frequently was deployed to do more than just separate types of land uses: It often worked, sometimes explicitly, to separate types of people. This was present in zoning discussions from the beginning. In fact, *Euclid* dealt with this issue directly. The Village of Euclid not only sought to separate residential uses from commercial and industrial uses; it also sought to separate multifamily apartment units from

Figure 3.1 Aerial photograph of suburban sprawl, 1949.

single-family homes. Yet the *Euclid* Court upheld such segregation, concluding that an apartment building often was a "mere parasite" to single-family home communities that could destroy their residential character, create hazards, and limit their attractiveness.[61]

Of course, some land use regulation was explicitly, and later implicitly, directed at excluding people not only based on income, but also race and ethnicity.[62] Some of the earliest kinds of zoning divided people according to their race, such as white neighborhoods and Black neighborhoods.[63] Zoning was (and is still) frequently critiqued for leading to both intentional and unintentional racial and socioeconomic segregation.[64]

Even if cities like Euclid did not intend to divide people, the effect of Euclidean zoning was to separate residents according to their incomes.[65] While explicit racial zoning has been unconstitutional for over a century, fiscal zoning laws adopted to promote uses that increase local tax revenue or reduce public service demands (such as single-family homes or commercial uses) remain commonplace and legal—not just throughout the Modernization Era, but today.[66] Indeed, zoning is regularly characterized with frequent racial undercurrents as a tool for NIMBYs ("Not-In-My-Backyard," i.e., people advocating against locally unwanted but often regionally valuable land uses), particularly when it comes to the location of apartment building and affordable housing.[67] While the Supreme Court may have expressly banned intentional discrimination prior to this era, exclusionary zoning laws undoubtedly provided an abundance of avenues not only for promoting sprawl but also economic and racial segregation.[68]

FEDERAL HOUSING POLICY BUILT SUBURBS AND INCREASED SEGREGATION

In addition to investing in sprawling highways and upholding local zoning, the federal government also worked to facilitate suburbanization and segregation indirectly through racist federal laws and policies. To be sure, market forces and private choices played a significant role, as non-white urban immigration in the 1950s triggered emigration by waves of wealthier white Americans to new, largely white suburbs.[69] Yet certain federal housing authorities actively worked to promote segregation in the process of incentivizing homeownership only by white Americans.

The story of "white flight"[70] is frequently told with federal law playing a prominent role in resisting segregation through the landmark case of *Brown v. Board of Education*.[71] *Brown*'s required school integration resulted in a backlash from many white parents who not only opted not to send their children to a desegregated school, but also moved to suburbs in pursuit of racial homogeneity.[72] Well after *Brown*, those fighting segregation would have to grapple with the fact "that many [white people] react[ed] to the dismantling of that segregated system by attempting to flee to the suburbs."[73]

Yet *Brown* and its legacy are only part of the story of the federal government's role related to segregation. Both before and after *Brown* legally mandated school desegregation, the U.S. government took many steps that facilitated housing segregation. Some government policies just tolerated private racism, failing to intervene as landowners openly discriminated in real estate transactions, private banks "redlined" non-white customers to keep them out of perceived white neighborhoods, and real estate brokers steered potential buyers to neighborhoods that fit clients' racial profiles.[74]

Yet the federal government also played an active role in promoting segregation. Consistent with the federal government's interventionist approach to markets during the New Deal, active involvement in segregation ramped up considerably, with numerous federal programs designed to help segregate American neighborhoods, particularly the suburbs. The Public Works Administration, for instance, built low-income housing stock that divided people into segregated housing developments and introduced segregation to places where it had not existed before.[75]

After World War II, the Federal Housing Administration (FHA) focused on building large suburban developments to house white, non-Latine residents. There was nothing subtle about the racial nature of the government's efforts. In fact, the FHA went so far as to require that new white owners purchase such housing subject to legally enforceable restrictive covenants mandating that owners and their successors in perpetuity promise to sell only to white purchasers.[76] The FHA, which offered favorable insurance for mortgages, also encouraged segregation by lowering assessed risks for properties that included these racially restrictive covenants and providing high ratings for applications in neighborhoods where there were no people of color.[77]

Even as the U.S. Supreme Court marched forward on reversing segregation and discrimination, the federal bureaucracy and Congress marched unflinchingly in the opposite direction. In 1948, for instance, the Supreme Court in *Shelley v. Kraemer* would finally overrule precedent that allowed racially restrictive covenants.[78] Even so, the FHA evaded and subverted the ruling for a decade, refusing to change its rules and procedures even after the Solicitor General directed them to do so.[79]

Furthermore, when the country welcomed home World War II veterans who served in the racially integrated military, the G.I. Bill only allotted its full set of benefits to white, non-Latine veterans and the Veterans Administration tied the benefit of financing a new home to the FHA's racially biased regulations. As such, non-white and Latine veterans were not allowed to access the loans necessary to purchase these suburban homes.[80] This meant the Leavittowns on the East Coast or California's Daly City that became the suburban housing stock for many veterans

Figure 3.2 **The Shelley family.**

due to FHA loans would not be available to many Americans. Taken together, these structural advantages created or allowed by governments not only supercharged the growth of the suburbs but also meant that their growth was overwhelmingly white and non-Latine.

For those who qualified for government-built housing or relied on government loans, perhaps the primary embodiment of the American Dream was realized—stability of home ownership situated in the suburbs. Very frequently, such housing was accessed through new roads and highways also built during the Modernization Era.

In years that followed, these homes became a major vehicle to create generational wealth. However, because the federal government obstructed similar opportunities for people of color, the government's exclusionary policies had significant effects on the ability of those excluded to create generational wealth. This induced wealth gap continued to have an echo effect that frequently played out in ways that exacerbated inequality and continues to hinder mobility and opportunity for marginalized populations today.

Yet it was not just unequal access to the benefits of the suburbs but also unequal exposure to pollution that further hindered mobility, even as they devastated local environments. Some of these harms were apparent immediately, and some of these costs have emerged with time passing.

THE ENVIRONMENTAL HARM OF SUBURBANIZATION

The opportunity for convenient home and land ownership, buffered from the disadvantages of both urban and rural life, appealed to countless Americans and became a reality for many at the time. Still, suburban growth—spurred on by law, policy, and government investment—came at a considerable environmental cost.

Some of these effects could have been noticeable to even a casual observer at the time. Places that once were fields or forests became a new development or a shopping center,[81] frequently and unapologetically named after the place plowed over to build it: Deer Meadows, Springfield, or The Orchards.

Other impacts were less obvious. Laws in the Modernization Era established the trajectory of extensive land, water, air, and ecological harm driven by suburbanization for the decades to come. While increased open space and lower property costs, traffic, and pollution served as key inducements for the suburban migration, laws encouraging such development induced a range of environmental harms regionally. Suburban development introduced new pollutants to water resources: oil from vehicles and machinery, road salts, chemicals used in households and businesses, fertilizers, and litter.[82] It also converted ecologically productive wildlife habitat into a less productive alternative and resulted in habitat fragmentation.[83] And laws subsidizing automobile travel helped degrade air quality.[84]

Of course, Modernization Era policy choices promoting suburbanization resulted in environmental effects in deserted urban centers as well. One of these was the heat island, increasingly important as our planet warms.[85] A direct consequence of urban flight for those left behind was the loss of resources to address a slew of social problems, including among other things investment in urban greenspaces. The lack of trees made urban microclimates appreciably hotter, sometimes to such a degree to make them health hazards. Water, air, and solid waste pollution also became even worse as urban cores hollowed out, with communities of color and the impoverished particularly forsaken and exposed.[86]

DAMMING AND REPLUMBING THE NATION'S WATERS

Beyond a massive interstate highway system and suburban development, laws in the Modernization Era provided significant federal funding and facilitated private investment in infrastructure focused on dams, hydropower, and water use. Like other infrastructure investments of the time, it came at a significant cost to the environment.

The ecological harms were not the most controversial feature of dams for that era, however. The public safety risks of water storage (which increased with a project's size) were already well known for decades, following a major dam failure in the 1890s in Pennsylvania that took more than two thousand lives.[87] Nevertheless, for decades water infrastructure developers continued to be subject to minimal safety oversight. Lack of attention to the potential of dam failure was perhaps best exemplified by the St. Francis Dam and its aftermath. Los Angeles built this dam as part of the controversial Owens Valley water project, and it catastrophically collapsed in 1928 (killing over five hundred people downstream).[88]

To address concerns about public safety risks, in 1929, California passed some of the first dam safety legislation requiring state safety reviews, eliminating conspicuous exemptions for municipalities with engineering departments, and creating a licensure program for civil engineers.[89] Yet like other dam safety regulation for decades that followed, the legislation completely ignored ecological effects of damming rivers, creating lakes, and rerouting water through extensive pipelines.

The federal role in water infrastructure began with the Federal Power Act of 1920 (FPA),[90] which straddled the Progressive and Modernization Eras. Before the FPA, the federal government did not play a role in regulating hydroelectric power; to the extent that regulation occurred, it came from the states. The enactment primarily attempted to promote hydroelectricity development through Progressive-style regulation of the wholesale markets, assuring market power was not abused.[91] Under the FPA, the federal government asserted authority over the regulatory gap that had developed between state Public Utility Commissions (PUCs) and those who bought and sold power across state lines—a gap that existed because state PUCs were constitutionally forbidden from regulating power transactions that involved parties across state lines.[92] To address this gap, the FPA created and conferred licensing authority to the Federal Power Commission[93] (a predecessor to the Federal Energy Regulatory Commission in the 1970s) for hydroelectric plants on navigable waters in the United States, essentially authorizing the coordination and development of federal hydroelectric projects.[94]

In the years that followed, Congress set off in earnest a period of mammoth dam construction. Unlike preceding federal dams, many of the new dams were designed to serve multiple uses—adding power production and municipal water delivery to the core goal of providing water to agricultural beneficiaries.[95] As Professor Dan Tarlock has aptly explained:

> [Dam building and hydroelectricity] developed in an era of almost absolute faith in the ability of technology to promote progress and the efficient use of natural resources. . . . The major issue was not whether rivers should be dammed for multiple uses including hydro, but whether this resource should be developed by governments or by the private sector.[96]

The heavy reliance on dam-generated energy during World War II only solidified the foothold of dam development on the country's rivers.[97]

Beyond damming many of the nation's rivers (sometimes in multiple locations), the Modernization Era also saw extensive public funding for channelization of waterways. While canal systems in the early 1800s facilitated transportation and by the late 1800s also enabled agriculture, the Modernization Era saw canals developed in conjunction with dams and pipelines to promote electricity generation and to facilitate metropolitan growth, particularly in the western United States.[98] While a few of these projects received state funding, like the (in)famous Mono Lake aqueducts,[99] most of these projects were federally funded, including the damming of Hetch Hetchy—a place John Muir compared to Yosemite—to provide San Francisco water.

Perhaps the most notable example of the new federal involvement in water resource provision was its facilitation of the damming of the mighty Colorado River at Boulder Canyon, at the border of Arizona and Nevada thirty miles south of what was then just a small gambling outpost in an expansive desert—Las Vegas. Development of the Colorado River caused consternation from states with an interest in the river, particularly those upstream of the proposed dam. Would the "lower basin" states (Arizona, Nevada, and California) find a way to capture the Colorado River the same way Los Angeles was gobbling up water resources within California? The federal government attempted to quell the high-stakes controversy. Over eleven months of negotiations, then-Secretary of State Herbert Hoover brokered a deal among the states on the Colorado River. Ultimately, in 1922, the "upper basin" states (Wyoming, Utah, Colorado, and New Mexico) and the lower basin states agreed that each basin would get 7.5 million-acre feet of water, and that the states in each basin would in turn negotiate how to split up their respective allocations.[100] "The big thing about the Colorado River Compact [was] that it [broke] the blockade on development of the whole river," wrote Hoover.[101]

While the 1922 Compact quelled the immediate conflict, it also had several flaws that set the West on a collision course with water scarcity for the next century and beyond. First, the Compact included a wildly optimistic assumption of the amount of water that could be appropriated. The Colorado River in ordinary times did not have fifteen million acre-feet to go around, which was not obvious at the time because the negotiations occurred when the river was unusually full. Second, the Compact neglected to factor in what adjustments would occur in times of drought—a particular problem in the arid West where variation of water is common from year to year. Third, the Compact did not foresee anthropogenic climate change and the tremendous extent to which it would squeeze water resources. Despite the negotiated results' shortcomings, this agreement paved the way for negotiations that would result in Congress pursuing the colossal Hoover Dam in 1928,[102] which used as much concrete as "would pave a standard highway 16 feet wide, from San Francisco to New York City."[103]

Shortly after the Hoover Dam was authorized, the Great Depression hit, and FDR became president. As the country tried to weather the financial downturn, water projects saw a construction boom, not a bust. For FDR, Western water projects became a mechanism to spur job and economic growth—whether they offered significant energy output or not. Dozens of dams and other infrastructure (such as the Central Valley Project in California, which replumbed an entire region)[104] were authorized and built under the New Deal's Works Progress Administration[105] and other emergency funding authorized by Congress designed

Figure 3.3 Photograph of the Hoover Dam (1935) near completion, taken just two days before the concrete was finished being poured.

to stimulate the economy, again with little regard to their environmental effects.[106]

Like the federal interstate highway system that was backed by powerful corporate interests, water projects became the subject of important political spoils. The noted environmental historian, Marc Reisner, said, "Congress without water projects would be like an engine without oil; it would simply seize up."[107] Objecting to a water project was a surefire way for a Congreeperson to lose support for water projects in one's home district.[108]

Nonetheless, not all these projects were without controversy, and these controversies gave voice to some of the most prominent social, political, and legal countercurrents in the Modernization Era. Intense debates within the State of Washington, for example, focused on the wisdom of constructing the Grand Coulee Dam (though much of the objections focused on the economic viability of the project rather than the environmental impact).[109] In a few cases, objections—frequently from those outside of Congress—put an end to projects. In 1945, for instance, the United States Army Corps of Engineers abandoned a dam on the Potomac River after substantial protest about the environmental effects of the proposed dam from conservationists from the Izaak Walton League, the National Parks Association, and various garden clubs.[110] In 1956, the Sierra Club—again largely for environmental reasons—protested construction of the Echo Park Dam in Dinosaur National Monument in Utah and eventually led to Congress removing the Echo Park Dam from the Colorado River project.[111] The Sierra Club similarly opposed other such projects with some success, such as the proposed Bridge Canyon Dam in the 1950s, which would have backed up the waters of the Colorado River into the Grand Canyon National Park.[112] Many other projects, however, went forward despite protests. Like the damming of the Hetch Hetchy, often the desired benefits of the projects (in Hetch Hetchy's case, drinking water for San Francisco) won the day.

It should be noted that the (largely unheeded) concerns raised at the time about government funding and/or approval of dam development were largely focused on public safety, not ecological effects. As would be understood decades later, this slew of water infrastructure projects would dramatically change the purposes, morphology, hydrology, and ecology of many of the nation's rivers.[113] Said one later commentator of the replumbing of the western landscape of the era:

> It had made rivers run uphill, . . . and celebrated the achievement in brilliant neon colors playing over casinos, corporate offices, [and] shopping malls . . . It had turned an austere wilderness into sparkling serpentine seas where fleets of motorized houseboats circled under hot cloudless skies . . . Then it had taken that same water and raised cotton with it, filled city pools with it, thrown it in the air with fountains and let it blow away.[114]

By funding, approving, and building pipelines and canals along with the dams, the law essentially turned deserts into farms, satisfied metropolitan thirst (for a time), and generated substantial amounts of electricity. But these laws also fundamentally altered and eventually impoverished riparian ecosystems that had existed for centuries.

Water infrastructure development and policy was also far from immune from the racism that afflicted other federal legislation of the era.

Native American tribal communities were at best disregarded in such development, if not directly targeted.[115] While many dam projects were designed to provide an economic boost to rural communities, rarely did tribes share in the benefit despite the fact that many tribes had signed treaties that envisioned tribal members farming arid reservations. Moreover, Congress authorized the Bureau of Reclamation to use Japanese American internment camp prisoners for labor to build dams, which the agency did to help construct Anderson Ranch Dam on Idaho's Boise River, for example.[116] To make way for dam development, human and ecological communities were bulldozed for decades in the name of modernization.

THE UNITED STATES GETS ADDICTED TO OIL AND GAS

Along with the proliferation of the combustion engine, the United States' addiction to oil and gas—key contributors to land, water, and air pollution (including greenhouse gases) for the next century—became deeply entrenched during the Modernization Era. In 1920, oil production was 1.2 million barrels a day; it grew to more than 7 million barrels by 1960.[117] Natural gas production grew by more than fifteen times during the era.[118]

Not surprisingly given this growth, policy innovations of the time arose out of the desire to promote oil and gas production. For example, in 1954, following years of private offshore oil exploration,[119] President Harry Truman cleared the way for offshore oil drilling by issuing a Proclamation on the Continental Shelf.[120] In 1958, the United States played a critical role in convening and drafting the convention for the United Nations Conference on the Law of the Sea, seeking to constrain and provide some equity to resource access on the continental shelf[121] The United States ultimately did not sign the global treaty, though it largely chose to abide to the treaty's terms.[122]

In a related strategy, federal tax incentives proved to be impactful legal tools for stimulating oil and gas development. The first major tax break for development was adopted in 1913, allowing oil producers to write off up to 80 percent of the costs of the first year of an oil exploration project, and a second write off was added in 1926 that allowed oil companies to deduct their taxable income by 27.5 percent. "We could have taken a 5 or 10 percent figure, but we grabbed 27.5 percent because we were not only hogs but the odd figure made it appear as though it was scientifically arrived at," said the tax break sponsor, Senator Tom Connally, later in life.[123] While the first tax incentive was important, the second allowed even enormously productive oil companies to shield large profits from the federal government. These incentives continue (albeit in a less lucrative form) to this day.

Many states also enacted laws governing oil and gas extraction designed to spur on the oil industry.[124] These regulations clarified ownership rights, most notably for resource pools sitting under contiguous properties, to expedite production, limit resource waste, and provide for equitable division of profits. Requirements that oil producers equitably share profits with all those with property interests in an oil field created clear incentives for *unitization* or *pooling*—drilling only as many wells as is optimal for production rather than as many wells as possible.[125] To jumpstart these sorts of reforms, FDR convened an advisory committee that facilitated negotiations among oil-producing states and focused resources in creating a workable regulatory regime. Ultimately, Congress adopted this framework in 1935 as an interstate compact.[126]

However, there were some, albeit limited, blows to the all-out exploitation machine of the Modernization Era. First, albeit only in the 1950s, most states did adopt basic pooling and conservation measures called for in the interstate compact.[127] Second, scandals like the high-profile 1924 Teapot Dome scandal, involving illicit loans to Secretary of the Interior Albert Fall from companies given leases to government oil fields, certainly brought to the public's and policymakers' attention the many opportunities for corruption and grift related to the booming fossil fuel industries.[128] Third, the seeds of natural resource and conservation science and management that initially sprouted in the Progressive Era continued to grow, even if only weakly. A 1952 presidential commission chaired by William Paley established Resources for the Future (an organization dedicated to independent environmental research)[129] and released a report detailing the perils associated with increasing dependence on foreign natural resources and the need to transition to renewable energy.[130] These legal, political, and scientific undercurrents lingered despite the predominant current that defined progress as maximizing development.

EXPERIMENTING WITH NUCLEAR ENERGY

Nuclear fission power also controversially arose in the latter decades of the Modernization Era as an outgrowth of the invention of the atomic bomb.[131] A year after the dropping of two atomic bombs that completely annihilated Hiroshima and Nagasaki and essentially ended World War II, Congress passed the Atomic Energy Act of 1946, which established the Atomic Energy Commission as a civilian authority for controlling and managing nuclear technology—an authority that ultimately eclipsed in virtually every way state power to regulate nuclear technologies and waste.[132] In the Atomic Age that followed, nuclear fission technology served not only as the basis for Cold War weapons of global destruction but also as a potential source of energy, and was encouraged by Congress "to the maximum extent consistent with the common defense and security and with the health and safety of the public."[133] A revision of the Atomic Energy Act in 1954 allowed the federal government to provide private companies access to restricted technical information about nuclear energy and fissile material production, paving the way for development of a civilian nuclear power industry.[134] Moreover, the Price–Anderson Act in 1957 significantly subsidized the private nuclear power industry by limiting the liability of nuclear utilities and contractors of potential nuclear power plant accidents.[135]

Nonetheless, in no small part due to the perceived risks of nuclear energy, throughout the era, proposed nuclear power plants remained the subject of public controversy and lawsuits. In 1956, for example, the United Auto Workers president sued to halt the construction of a proposed nuclear reactor in Laguna Beach, Michigan.[136] Despite resistance and controversy, the first nuclear power plant in the United States went online at Shippingport, Pennsylvania in 1957.[137]

While much of the public surmised the existential threat of nuclear war, few at the time were aware of the significant health and environmental harms produced in the mining, refining, testing, and manufacture of nuclear material. For example, top secret plutonium manufacturing in Hanford, Washington produced nuclear material for the Manhattan Project and later most of the U.S. nuclear arsenal, but also massive harms to the surrounding towns, tribes, rivers, and ecological communities that were only later disclosed and even today remain unremediated.[138] Similarly, the 1945 Trinity test in Alamogordo, New Mexico that marked the first atomic weapon explosion led to a wide range of human and ecological harms that were only fully understood decades later.[139] Even as nuclear technology continued to develop, the effects of testing became increasingly manifest by increased incidence of serious illnesses by those exposed to radioactive fallout, including increased heart disease and various cancers, including leukemia.[140] The environmental costs of modernization were indeed percolating, even if covert and poorly understood.

Despite widespread obliviousness about the true risks of nuclear harm, in retrospect the rhetoric and concerns about nuclear risks in the era were proto-environmental in significant ways. Testing of nuclear bombs had decimated several places on the planet, forcing evacuations (for example on the Bikini Atoll of the Marshall Islands) and caused radiation sickness due to nuclear fallout in people a hundred miles away from testing sites. Even in the 1950s and before most environmental issues came to the fore in the United States, survey data showed that half of Americans saw nuclear fallout as a "real danger" to the planet.[141] The budding awareness and organizing in the Modernization Era served as templates for the public advocacy that would become mainstays of the environmental activism in decades to come. Those sounding warnings were rarely on the prevailing side during the era, but their concerns certainly entered the public consciousness, with fallout from nuclear tests becoming "the first environmental pollutant to take on the dimensions of a global threat."[142]

CHEMICAL ENGINEERING CHANGES AMERICAN LIFE

The Modernization Era also experienced a rapid proliferation of new chemicals, largely for industrial use, with little public oversight of their safety (or the safety of their waste by-products). The first major push for new chemicals and compounds grew out of military demands during World War II and the willingness of the federal government to procure a range of products and advancements to further the war effort.[143] For instance, while World War I witnessed large-scale chemical weapon deployment, the United States and its Allies rarely deployed these weapons during World War II despite extensive investments.[144] The demand for explosives, however, led to massive increases in nitrogen development as well as the accidental discovery of Teflon.[145] Though invented decades earlier, production of synthetic rubber ramped up substantially, as most natural rubber was in Japanese-controlled Southeast Asia.[146] Similarly, synthetic fibers (like nylon) and plastics made it easier to make supplies like parachutes and parts for weapons and vehicles.[147] The synthetic insecticide DDT was funded in part by the desire to protect soldiers from insect-borne diseases like malaria and typhus.[148]

Postwar manufacturers took these innovations and applied them to a multitude of commercial uses. DuPont, for example, used nylon for stockings, Teflon for a wide range of products, and found various commercial uses for rayon and x-ray pigments.[149] Plastics soon served as a cheap substitute for innumerable products.[150] Postwar agricultural production included widespread use of pesticides like DDT and synthetic fertilizers (which got a boost from wartime nitrogen factories).[151]

A key accompaniment of the chemicalization of modern American life was the development of a mass production, mass consumption cultural ethic. Rampant consumer demand—a long standing driver to a host of environmental problems—was not only normalized but encouraged in this period.

> World War II stimulated technological innovation and provided Americans with exciting new consumer products. These products soon became broadly available on a much larger scale to meet the consumer demand. . . . Air conditioners, televisions, processed and packaged foods, and automobiles dramatically changed the American lifestyle.[152]

For virtually all these products, thousands of workers, day-in and day-out, were exposed during manufacturing to toxic and hazardous risks. Some particularly tragic aspects of the stories stand out, such as the exposure of workers to radium or nuclear fallout.[153] Yet there were many more but less sensational risk exposures, ranging from long-used chemicals (like lead) to synthetic compounds with unknown risk profiles (like DDT and polychlorinated biphenyls). For every story told there were many more concealed or ignored. Additionally, because many were not just ingredients of products themselves (like asbestos) but used in production processes, worker exposures were especially high. Yet the law did very little to regulate exposure, even if some particularly acute cases might have provided a basis to seek legal redress through common law or Progressive Era workers' compensation laws.[154]

Moreover, during World War II and the decades that followed, very little effort was made to safeguard public health or the environment from the known and unknown risks of the use, production, disposal, and by-products of these now abundant and diverse new chemicals, even though scientists like William Vogt sounded the alarm bells (though at times it must have felt like shouting in the wind).[155] Disposal practices were often reckless, with toxic waste sites emerging in waters and lands around the country.[156] And perhaps predictably in concert with zoning practices, manufacturing and disposal sites were regularly located close to or in low-income neighborhoods and communities of color.[157]

SCIENTIFIC EXPERTISE, BUREAUCRACY, AND THE SCAFFOLD OF ADMINISTRATIVE LAW

As opposed to highway building and other government actions that resulted in immediate and profound environmental effects, perhaps the most consequential legal change in the Modernization Era that affected human and environmental health was the rise of the administrative state. Efforts to build the administrative state during the era arose in significant part from a more broadly embraced effort to proliferate, diversify, and rely on scientific expertise. Disciplines dedicated to the study and/or development of human and natural systems, for example, developed and matured over these four decades, including public health, ecology, environmental chemistry, geoscience, and atmospheric science.[158] In government operations, growing reliance on these disciplines built on trust in and dependence on science and professionalism from the Progressive Era. Relatedly, efforts to professionalize public management that started in the Progressive Era further took hold, with fields like public administration and urban planning gaining widespread recognition in universities and governments at every scale.[159]

The federal government played a crucial role in the development and legitimization of science and engineering far outside the walls of government offices, most directly by serving as a key funder of scientific research. During World War II, the federal government provided significant funding for industrial and university research, particularly related to promoting military capabilities (such as the Manhattan Project, which invented the nuclear bomb).[160] Creation of the National Science Foundation in the post–World War II years and steadily increasing appropriations to promote U.S. competitiveness deepened the support for and trust in scientific expertise in government.[161]

In terms of changes that took hold within the government itself, over the course of the era's four decades, federal legislation played the pivotal role in integrating science and evidentiary decision making into an expanded and influential administrative state. The Great Depression of the 1930s resulted in widespread economic collapse and a popular desire for the government to intervene to stabilize the economy and reduce rampant poverty. As President, FDR responded with the New Deal, an unprecedented massive governmental expansion involving public investments, financial reforms, regulation of previously unfettered markets, and the creation of many new administrative agencies and programs.[162] Administrative agencies, legitimized by understood professional expertise and political accountability, were increasingly empowered to guard against economic harm and strengthen the social safety net. Like much of government, agencies charged with overseeing natural resources deepened their expertise and capacity to govern. The Bureau of Land Management, for instance, was established in 1946[163] through a merger of the General Land Office (which oversaw the disposition of ceded and acquired lands) and the U.S. Grazing Service.[164]

The proliferation of this expansive federal bureaucracy necessitated a redefinition of and guardrails for the role, powers, and responsibilities of administrative agencies. In 1946, Congress provided the contours of this through the Administrative Procedure Act (APA), which provided a comprehensive default set of procedural rules articulating and governing the promulgation of legally binding regulations (regulations) to agency decisions applying rules to a particular circumstance (adjudications), providing for a degree of government transparency and requirements for public participation.[165] In addition to the political checks available to Congress and the President, the APA provided affected parties opportunities for judicial review and possible invalidation of agency decisions if, depending on the type of decision, the court deemed it arbitrary or not in accordance with the law.[166] These checks by each branch of government serve to balance deference to recognized agency expertise with some accountability to the law and constitutionally recognized democratic institutions. Yet, at least in the Modernization Era, agencies maintained broad discretion to "modernize" as they saw fit.

The growth of the administrative state not only had important implications in the development and form of government in the Modernization Era. It also had momentous echo effects on environmental laws that later followed. Increasingly, the role of federal and state governments changed. In the Allocation Era, management largely focused on enabling resource exploitation; in the Progressive Era, utilization was moderated by public health and resource protection mandates. Administrative law developed in the Modernization Era, however, served as fundamental procedural mechanisms for the three branches of government to serve as democratic restraints on bureaucratic expertise. This procedural governance would serve as the scaffolding upon which public environmental law would be built in the next eras.

LIMITED CORPORATE LIABILITY AND STOCK MARKET REGULATION

Innovations in corporate law also had important implications on the environment and facilitated the Modernization Era. Neither new regulations of Wall Street nor longstanding common law liability doctrines served as meaningful avenues for limiting these harms to human and environmental health. While the Progressive Era, through antitrust and health and safety laws, saw the most aggressive limitations placed on industry and commerce up to that point in U.S. history,[167] in significant ways, the Modernization Era pushed in the opposite direction. These legal innovations not only had important implications in the marketplace but also for the environment.

As the era got underway, the United States' superpowered economic engine continued to trust heavily in the limited liability corporate form and markets more generally. In fact, before 1930, the trust in corporations was so great that the federal government did not regulate securities markets at all.[168] After World War I, a surge in stock market activity occurred, with new securities offered to investors and banks investing great sums in the stock market.[169] Half of these stocks became worthless after the 1929 stock market crash and a "run on the banks" that helped launch the Great Depression.[170]

In response, Congress passed two statutes that still serve as the bedrock of securities regulation today. While both enactments provided important safeguards to protect investors, neither of these worked in any meaningful way to stem the impact of corporations on the environment. The Securities Act of 1933 required investors to receive significant information about securities being offered for public sale through a registration process and prohibited fraud in the sale of securities.[171] The Securities Exchange Act of 1934 established the Securities and Exchange Commission (SEC) and gave it broad powers over the securities industry, required public companies to provide periodic reporting about business risks and operations, and prohibited insider trading.[172]

While these laws constituted the most significant restrictions on Wall Street ever,[173] they are premised largely on the assumption that markets will be efficient and manage risk as long as investors have sufficient information about the risks of investment.[174] However, environmental risks—such as the externalities caused by manufacturing, industrial processes, and products—were only ever tangentially a consideration in this regulatory regime.[175] Relatedly, the common law tort system—and its reliance on plaintiff litigation, retrospective and remedial orientation, and generalist judges—remained very much an imperfect check as well.[176] The public and environment thus continued to bear the brunt of the more latent, diffuse, uncertain, and collective risks of modernization.[177] And even in those circumstances when regulatory action or litigation were successful, the limited liability corporate form could serve as a key escape valve that left the public and environment bearing these same risks.[178]

COMMUNICATION REVOLUTIONS PROMOTING MODERNIZATION

While the implications to the environment—and for that matter governance of many kinds—were in many ways unknowable during the Modernization Era, the proliferation of radio and later television technologies fundamentally destabilized mass communication in the Modernization Era.

Regulations lagged behind these technologies but eventually were enacted to at least partially adapt to the ways broadcast media affected the transmission of information. A notable unforeseen effect of these regulatory changes, however, was to induce an oligopoly of private communication outlets that promoted consumerism and development and indirectly stifled the dissemination of information about modernization's harms.

Commercial radio and then television destabilized and then dominated communication in this era. After the first commercial radio broadcast in 1920,[179] for the greater part of that decade radio broadcasting remained unregulated and largely chaotic.[180] The Radio Act of 1927 eventually required broadcasters to become licensed and serve the public interest, and in turn, provided stability in the use of the radio spectrum.[181] Television use mushroomed well after the first one was invented in 1927—with less than ten thousand U.S. households having television sets in the mid-1940s to almost forty-six million by 1960.[182] In 1934, Congress established the Federal Communications Commission (FCC)[183] to reinforce a duty in broadcasting to act "in the public interest, convenience and necessity."[184] By the late 1940s, radio and television broadcasting licenses were scarce and operated under strict governmental control.[185] The FCC reinforced government control of both radio and television in 1949 through the Fairness Doctrine, which required broadcasters to devote airtime and contrasting views to controversial matters of public interest.[186]

Despite the Fairness Doctrine's intent to curb undue market concentration,[187] a handful of radio and television broadcasters soon emerged as the primary mainstream sources.[188] These few key players overwhelmingly reflected, if not championed, core tenets of modernization, including industrialization, consumerism, and resource development.[189] Though the regulatory framework would be minimally refined in later decades,[190] it nonetheless would prove to be even more inadequate for dealing with the explosive technological advancements of later eras.

RESOURCE ACCESS, OVERUSE, AND SOME PROTECTION

FEDERAL LAND RESOURCE EXTRACTION AND ACCESS

With some safety rails intact from the Progressive Era, in dealing with natural resources, the Modernization Era largely returned to the extractive mindset of the Allocation Era. In the Modernization Era, however, the search for resources was bundled up with the country's push toward its broader project of reconfiguring the way the country lived and worked. All this pressure on the country's natural resources faced some pushback from a concerned minority, including to some extent by Native American tribes.

New roads providing unprecedented access to forests and markets, combined with the invention and advancement of motorized equipment increased timber harvesting both in pace and geographic scope. Particularly as the suburbs swelled after World War II, timber harvesting on Western federal lands and Eastern private forests faced intense pressure. Clear cutting of entire sections of forests became common.[191] In the 1930s, the harvest from the national forests amounted to about a billion board feet a year; by 1940, that number had doubled, and during World War II, four billion board feet a year was harvested.[192] Demand for wood shot up even further after the war, mainly due to the housing boom, so that annual timber harvests on federal lands were around twelve billion board feet by 1960.[193]

Illustrating the durability of legal changes, the General Mining Law of 1872 remained untouched despite the Progressive Era's other checks on industry, providing extensive mining access to federal land for fees close to free for almost half a century. Yet during the Modernization Era, easier access—due to mining technology and transportation improvements—and growth in demand for coal, gravel for paved roads, and phosphates for fertilizers increased interest in resources on federal lands that previously were less valuable.[194]

In response, Congress passed the Mineral Leasing Act of 1920, which allowed land managers to restrict free prospecting of minerals on federal lands, authorized leasing of federal lands for minerals not governed by the General Mining Law, and maintained federal government royalties for mineral extraction.[195] As investment in expensive equipment became almost mandatory to compete, mining operations largely transitioned to gigantic corporate operations.[196] The Indian Reorganization Act of 1934[197] restored to Indian tribes the management of land and mineral rights on their lands,[198] even if its focus ostensibly was on reversing prior cultural assimilationist policies toward Native Americans.[199] These modest federal efforts to impose order on mining activities, however, did little to reduce the damage from these increasingly in-demand resources and prolific mining technologies.[200]

New conservation legislation over grazing on federal land provided a key win for detractors pushing against the grain of facilitating resource exploitation during the Modernization Era. How these reforms actually played out, however, provided much more mixed results. While calls for grazing reform were common during the Progressive Era,[201] Congress did not act until it faced increased grazing pressures during the Great Depression, leading to the Taylor Grazing Act of 1934.[202] The Act put an end to open grazing on public rangelands,[203] authorizing a new Division of Grazing in the Department of the Interior to administer a permitting system for allocating such grazing.[204] The agency came to oversee fifty-nine grazing districts, which soon encompassed around 170 million acres of federal land.[205]

Despite the ambitions of the law, the Taylor Grazing Act failed to bring about sweeping conservation changes on the ground, fundamentally because the legal changes did not sufficiently constrain the incentives of grazers. Perhaps the most important manifestation of this played out in the new law's creation of local grazing districts and advisory boards for each of the districts, which provided a platform and mechanism to extract the spoils of newly found political advantages for local grazers.[206] Rather than merely advising, the grazing boards became power brokers, often with an outsized influence on local land managers, frequently convincing managers to protect and enhance the ability of grazers to access public lands.[207]

Finally, recreational use of the nation's public lands spiked considerably, in concert with the emergence of both the automobile and a democratic ethic in public lands management. As automobile access increased,[208] visitation grew rapidly, particularly among non-Latine whites.[209] Though it took decades to build out, beginning in the 1920s, public land management emphasized the need to make recreational access to certain components easy, while maintaining others as more remote. Particularly in National Parks, *front-country tourism*—development of roads, trails, campgrounds, and facilities,[210] all with the aim of increasing access by vehicle and day users—became a core goal,[211] and remains so today.[212] Paradoxically, such management often presented protected lands as pristine and undisturbed by human activity, despite the longstanding history of close tribal connection and (often unsuccessful) tribal attempts to retain or restore access to such lands and resources.[213] As tourism to federal lands grew, so too did the beginnings of many gateway communities near the most visited public lands, which would eventually themselves grow into major constituents of national parks and cheerleaders for visitor growth.[214]

A COUNTERCURRENT OF RESOURCE PROTECTION

Preservation of Some Public Lands

While policy and legal innovation in the Modernization Era frequently diminished environmental concerns for the sake of economic development, natural resources during the era also experienced a protective undercurrent that broke through enough to create some significant strides in conservation. Some of these protections might have been at least in part based on reckoning with practical limitations of the nation's natural resources, but in important instances laws and policymakers took significant steps to safeguard resources out of immediate harm's way.

When the country went beyond the mark, frequently the common denominator was the involvement of Harold Ickes, FDR's Secretary of the Interior. Fashioned in many ways in John Muir's tradition of environmental preservation, Ickes stood in the way of many development schemes, including hydropower development. He helped establish national monuments that would mature into treasured national parks (including the Everglades (Florida), Jackson Hole (Wyoming), and Joshua Tree (California)) and the Cape Hatteras National Seashore (North Carolina). He even helped create national demand for Kings Canyon National Park in California by pitching the idea to the Sierra Club.[215] During his time with FDR, Ickes helped usher in a wide range of conservation programs and projects and an agency to oversee wildlife reserves, many of which dated back to the Progressive Era.

A New Take on Livelihoods and Conservation

A consistent objection to conservation efforts across our nation's history has been that conservation results in lost jobs and economic opportunities. At least to some extent, the New Deal's Civilian Conservation Corps (CCC)—an outgrowth of Emergency Conservation Work Act of 1933[216]—brought the reach of that perceived trade-off into question. The popular program provided many jobs related to conservation and development of natural resources and focused on increasing rural livelihoods and quality of life: At its height, it provided as many as a half-million people working in racially segregated work camps focused on conservation and natural resources development, primarily in national forests.[217] Prominent projects included reforestation of federal lands (via planting of an estimated two billion trees)[218] and building infrastructure like roads, trails, and terraces to increase forest accessibility.[219] By the time the CCC program ended in 1942, it had employed more than 2.5 million people.[220]

Wildlife Conservation

The Modernization Era experienced intense habitat modification, loss, and fragmentation, with prior pressures on ecosystems compounded by those from automobile use, roads, suburbs, and dams. Given these mounting ecological harms, it may not be a surprise that the field of ecology surged in this period. Eugene Odum released in 1953 what many consider the founding textbook of the field, *Fundamentals of Ecology*.[221] Scientists began to try to understand not just how ecosystems worked—which had been of interest for centuries and topics of serious study in the 1800s by the likes of Charles Darwin and Alexander von Humboldt—but also how human interactions complicated these systems.[222]

Some legal responses fueling the countercurrent of wildlife destruction provided federal funds for states willing to invest in protecting wildlife. Building on a legacy of hunters as conservationists that flourished in the Progressive Era, the Pittman–Robertson Act of 1937 (also called the Federal Aid in Wildlife Restoration Act)[223] provided a tax on sporting firearms, ammunition, and bows to create a fund for states to help with wildlife restoration efforts. The state programs funded with the excise tax included acquiring and improving wildlife habitat, introducing wildlife into suitable habitat, researching into wildlife problems, surveying wildlife problems, acquiring and developing access facilities for public use, and hunter education programs. Similarly, in response to declining waterfowl, Congress passed the Migratory Bird Hunting Stamp Act of

1934,[224] which funded migratory bird refuges by requiring hunters of waterfowl to buy a "duck stamp." Based on the success of these programs and the desire to protect fisheries, Congress passed the Dingell–Johnson Act of 1952,[225] which established an excise tax on fishing tackle used to fund conservation projects for aquatic species.

In keeping with the era's increased reliance on bureaucratic expertise, Congress also established and funded new federal agencies to avert harm to certain valued species. The Migratory Bird Conservation Act of 1929 established the Migratory Bird Conservation Commission to review and approve land acquisitions for waterfowl refuges,[226] leading to the creation of more than one hundred protected wildlife sanctuaries.[227] The Fish and Wildlife Coordination Act of 1934[228] and amendments in 1946[229] required federal agencies to consult with a newly created Fish and Wildlife Service on impacts of proposed water infrastructure projects on fish and wildlife.[230] Fisheries and marine resources nonetheless faced mounting pressure fueled by changing American diets that included fish and increasing commodification of fishery resources.[231] Congress also passed the Bald Eagle Preservation Act in 1940, prohibiting sale, killing, or possession of the iconic national bird.[232]

* * *

In the four decades of the Modernization Era, law had profoundly shaped the trajectory of the human and nonhuman environment of the United States in at least four fundamental ways. First, keeping in mind that the relationships between law and the environment are broad, law had created and fortified a local, state, and federal bureaucracy understood as experts in managing a broad spectrum of human activity and environments and in carrying out some of the legislative, executive, and judicial functions of government.[233] Second, a legal infrastructure had built a physical infrastructure that was the backbone for the unprecedented expansion and strengthening of American industry and corporate power, frequently at the expense of the environment.[234] Third, law and government undoubtedly had served to promote American empire internationally and resulted in global environmental impacts.[235] And at least as importantly, law had helped facilitate the idea of the American Dream as achieving material wealth, upward mobility, and consumerism.[236]

Nonetheless, the American citizenry and its laws in the Modernization Era were not entirely focused on maximizing private wealth. Other areas of focus included the creation of a robust public bureaucracy, a sophisticated administrative procedural infrastructure, and certain substantive environmental protections. Beyond federal land and wildlife preservation, some cities were well ahead of the curve on pollution regulation. St. Louis and Los Angeles, for example, had already begun to address air quality issues, particularly those related to industry and burning garbage as a form of disposal.[237] However, these experiments while notable were the exception rather than the rule. As the next era dawned, the effects of the law's complicity in environmental degradation were slowly—perhaps far too slowly—being understood as nothing short of devastating.

4

THE ENVIRONMENTAL ERA

FROM PROTEST TO PROTECTION (1960–1980)

INTRODUCTION

From 1960 to 1980, the United States established a staggering legal infrastructure to address environmental harms that had simmered for almost two centuries, steadily building as the consequences of the Modernization Era added up. The first decade of the Environmental Era saw a slow accretion of new public lands laws and courts granting novel relief to environmental litigants, sometimes interpreting well-settled laws in new ways to further environmental protection. The 1970s, however, experienced an avalanche of far-reaching laws aimed at protecting human health and the nation's air, water, land, and wildlife. This environmental progress required significant legal innovation: mandated disclosure and impact assessment; authorizing citizens to sue polluters to enforce public standards; overlapping and coordinated federal and state authority to advance environmental protection. This legal transformation unquestionably positioned the United States as the global leader in environmental protection.

Perhaps more than anyone else, Rachel Carson's personal evolution mirrored the changing focus on the environment at the time. During the Modernization Era, Carson was a noted government scientist and naturalist; though bookish and reserved, she became an unlikely champion for environmental concerns caused by society's swelling excesses. She warned, for example, about the dangers of nuclear fallout alongside other more prominent and confrontational figures, such as Albert Schweitzer, Norman Cousins, and Barry Commoner.[1] As the Modernization Era ended, however, it was her growing advocacy and beautiful prose about the importance of saving oceans and beaches that set her apart.[2]

As the Environmental Era came into being, in due course Carson transitioned into a standard bearer. First, she found herself on the winning side advocating for two important issues central to President John F. Kennedy's agenda: limiting nuclear testing and protecting important ocean shorelines. Only a couple of years later, however, Carson's standing catapulted into the stratosphere, as *Silent Spring* made it to press.[3] Her seminal book highlighted risks related to the pollution legacy of the Modernization Era, particularly those related to toxic chemicals, and challenged the country to think about the environmental and public health consequences of its legacy of pollution. By the 1970s, *Silent Spring* was a touchstone of the emerging environmental movement and played a significant role in focusing the public on the dangers of pollution—a concern that would come to dominate the 1970s' policy agenda. She not only brought concern about pollution into the zeitgeist but also catalyzed the momentum for legal reform, indelibly shaping how the law would attempt to protect the public and environment against these risks.

The many environmental reforms of the era happened amid considerable political tumult. Though ecosystems and public health were already reeling from unrelenting market forces and government policies, environmental protection was not a political priority at the era's outset. Looming anxiety created by the Cold War initially took primacy—highlighted by the Space Race from 1957 to 1975[4] and the Cuban Missile Crisis from 1960 to 1962.[5] Progress was dressed as minimally regulated capitalism and defeating totalitarian communism.[6] The 1960s also saw political protest take center stage: 250,000 people gathering to hear Martin Luther King, Jr.'s 1963 "I Have a Dream" speech on the National Mall; peaceful protestors facing police violence for civil rights demonstrations; and a nation shut down for weeks after King's assassination in 1968.[7] Protests against the Vietnam War in the late 1960s and early 1970s frequently took over universities and public spaces and sometimes ended in violence.[8]

Nonetheless, public consciousness and legal action about wanton and neglected externalities of modernization pivoted away from demanding incremental change to instead focusing on a society-changing agenda to craft legal frameworks that advanced environmental protection. The most meaningful early reforms took shape as President Kennedy championed legislation setting aside prominent beach fronts as the first nationally-designated seashores, which when signed into law led to seashore designations for Point Reyes (California), Padre Island (Texas), and Cape Cod (Massachusetts).[9] The most prominent reform in the Environmental Era's first decade, however, was the Wilderness Act of 1964, which instantiated the natural preservation invoked by John Muir for the safeguarding of major swaths of American public lands in their primeval state. At the same time, often spurred by federal funding, many environmental scholars and scientists began exposing harms from mass industrialization, corporatization, nuclearization, chemicalization, and suburbanization.[10]

In this setting, legal imagination and experimentation helped the country make important strides. The 1960s witnessed a drumbeat of state and federal pollution control legislation—policy experimentation that was persistent but ultimately deficient, with federal law focusing on funding research and incentivizing unwilling states to fill a regulatory void. Yet some citizen-led efforts found new pathways for pollution prevention by scavenging existing law and bringing novel lawsuits.[11] And some states and municipalities made important inroads through legal experiments to tackle environmental harms at more local scales.[12]

In 1970, midway into the Environmental Era, public demand for environmental progress hit a crescendo, stirred by at least three events. First, astronaut Bill Anders snapped "Earthrise" in December 1968 during the first mission to the moon, a photograph of Earth rising over the barren moon that quickly became an iconic symbol of Earth's fragility.[13] Second, public outrage over environmental devastation skyrocketed in early 1969 when a Santa Barbara oil spill resulted in 235,000 gallons of oil fouling the ocean just miles off the California coast.[14] Citizens and the media made their way to witness the destruction, and local residents organized to publicize government inaction and to stop the drilling.[15] The vividness of oil-coated animal corpses dominated news coverage for months.[16] Third, community organizers tapped into Peace and Civil Rights movements to organize the first Earth Day in 1970—an extraordinary public demonstration including about one in ten Americans calling for increased environmental protection.[17]

Action, however, required movement from Congress and the President. A perfect political storm appeared to create a torrent of creative legislative and administrative regulation: an ambitious Senator Ed Muskie, and a President Nixon trained on thwarting Muskie from hogging the limelight. An unlikely two-year political dance resulted in the most concentrated span of consequential environmental lawmaking, including creation of the Environmental Protection Agency (EPA) and passage of the National Environmental Policy Act, Clean Air Act, and Clean Water Act (which Congress passed over Nixon's veto despite Nixon's initially chiding for *not* passing it).

Even as demand for environmental protection subsided, the rest of the decade saw other policymakers working to meet the remaining public demand for environmental action. Congress enacted new laws ranging from species conservation to waste disposal. Agencies and courts wrestled with a new, complex legal infrastructure, struggling to implement these statutes and their ambitious goals. Congress revisited some statutes, whether to tinker with initial assumptions or to revisit the hardest edges. As the decade ended, those closely watching would note key omissions in this procession of environmental legislation and the start of a pendulum swing in the other direction. The vehicle for this oscillation was industry pushback against the avulsion of unprecedented legal change that in significant ways remade the relationship between people and the environment in the United States.

CARRYING FORWARD MUIR'S AND PINCHOT'S LEGACIES IN FEDERAL LAND MANAGEMENT

Congress enacted several new laws promoting the use and protection of the nation's natural resources. These statutes echoed the Progressive Era legacies of, and conflicts between, preservationist John Muir and conservationist Gifford Pinchot. Policymakers, however, advanced a broader set of conservation goals than those that animated the Progressive Era—including natural preservation, historical preservation, and maximizing resource yield—by implementing previous public land laws, designating additional lands within such regimes, and passing new enactments providing for entirely new land protections.

PRESERVATION MEETS THE ENVIRONMENTAL ERA

New preservation efforts in the 1960s came from pressure from environmental, hunting, fishing, and recreation groups.[18] The pathway for preservation frequently ran through Secretary of the Interior Stewart Udall, who served in the U.S. House of Representatives before heading up the Department of the Interior for both Presidents John Kennedy and Lyndon Johnson. Like Harold Ickes before him, when Udall became Secretary of the Interior, he set out to change the role from appeasing resources users and extractive industries; yet more than Ickes, he also set out to serve as a leading public champion for conservation.[19] While Udall struggled to transform Interior's bureaucracy, his connections in Congress provided conservationists unprecedented opportunities.[20]

In 1956, Howard Zahniser, a conservation advocate and nature writer, first proposed the Wilderness Act.[21] The Act, which served as the principal manifestation of John Muir's preservationist vision,[22] provided a process for federal land managers to identify pristine lands (labeled Wilderness Study Areas) and halt commercial development and roadbuilding in these areas until Congress had the chance to consider their fate.[23] True to its natural preservation roots and more poetic that the typical legalese, it required federal land managers to ensure all designated wilderness areas remain "untrammeled by man."[24]

Yet the Wilderness Act, like so many other groundbreaking environmental statutes, faced pushback. Detractors included extractive industries like mining and government agencies too. The Forest Service opposed the bill, claiming it "would strike at the heart of the multiple use policy of national forest administration,"[25] while the Alaskan Commissioner of Mines asked the Senate panel, "[w]hat good are these resources if they must remain in their natural state?"[26] Some companies were "unalterably opposed to the locking up of natural resources of any kind from development for the public good"[27] because this would, they argued, hurt the economy, the tax coffers, access to important consumer goods, and even our national defense by reducing access to mined metals.[28]

As a conciliation to those opposing the Wilderness Act, the negotiated bill included a twenty-five-year exemption for mining in designated wilderness.[29] Nevertheless, in 1964, after a difficult nine-year process and many failed attempts at passage, President Johnson signed the Wilderness Act into law.[30] The enactment still serves as the high watermark of the natural preservation movement.

In the following decades, Congress periodically added the Wilderness Act's protections to more public lands. For instance, in 1978, Congress adopted the Endangered American Wilderness Act, which established ten new designated Wilderness Areas in western national forests.[31] The Wilderness Act ultimately helped preserve and protect over 110 million acres of public lands.[32] The Wilderness Act endured as one of the most important pieces of U.S. natural preservation legislation, serving as a model for wilderness protection for countries around the world.[33]

Other enactments also pushed the nation's land managers toward natural preservation. The Wild and Scenic Rivers Act of 1968,[34] somewhat of an appendage to the Wilderness Act, provided a way to extend natural preservation measures to even private property that sat adjacent to the nation's rivers.[35] The push for dedicating federal lands to natural preservation continued into the next decade. In 1980, Congress enacted the Alaska National Interest Lands Conservation Act,[36] which created most of the National parklands in Alaska and provided nearly eighty million acres of refuge land in Alaska, much of which Congress designated as wilderness.[37]

Meanwhile, other federal laws focused on promoting historical preservation goals—preserving locations that were important historical sites or otherwise tied to history. Most prominently, Congress passed the National Historic Preservation Act of 1966.[38] This statute established a National Register of Historic Places and a process involving the Advisory Council on Historic Preservation to designate and preserve properties of important cultural or historical significance, including sites of historical and cultural significance to Native Americans.[39]

CONSERVATION AND THE ENVIRONMENTAL ERA

Other legislation emphasized a Pinchot-like approach to federal lands, focusing on sustainable yields and wise use of resource exploitation.

Just as Pinchot's approach in the Progressive Era stood in opposition to Muir's preservation, so too did these policies provide a contrast in the Environmental Era and, in many ways, built on the preceding eras' gains by resource users. Still, these new laws provided restrictions designed to protect human health and reduce ecological harm.

This line of legal reforms started with the 1969 Federal Coal Mine Health and Safety Act, which adopted health standards and strengthened safety standards for coal mines, required periodic inspections, and authorized fines and criminal penalties for violators.[40] Then in 1977, Congress enacted the Surface Mining Control and Reclamation Act,[41] which set minimum requirements for all coal surface mining on federal and state lands, including minimizing harm to fish and wildlife.[42]

Other laws emphasized sustained yield in resource exploitation. The Multiple Use and Sustained Yield Act of 1960[43] further solidified Pinchot's vision of the Forest Service—an agency that appeased a wide range of resource users in the management of federal forests.[44] Multiple use became more embedded in national forests in the National Forest Management Act of 1976,[45] even as the enactment also provided for additional opportunities for citizens to participate in government decisions impacting national forests.[46] Similarly, the same year, the Federal Land Policy and Management Act[47] reaffirmed multiple use for federal lands not otherwise set aside for a specific use.[48] As these enactments preserved grazing permits and the use of established roads, they also made official something that had been federal land policy for some time—an implied recognition that federal land would remain public and not be disposed of by the federal government.[49]

HYBRID APPROACHES TO FEDERAL LANDS

Other new laws relied on a hybrid of preservation and sustained yield objectives for wildlife sanctuaries. Specifically, the Refuge Recreation Act of 1962[50] authorized the Secretary of the Interior to administer refuges and other conservation areas for recreational use. The National Wildlife Refuge Administration Act of 1966[51] provided an "organic act" for the National Wildlife Refuge System, \ empowering the Department of the Interior to manage lands for "the protection and conservation of fish and wildlife that are threatened with extinction, wildlife ranges, game ranges, wildlife management areas, or waterfowl production areas."[52] This management of wildlife sought to sustain the "yield" of wildlife populations but also to preserve these areas at least somewhat in their historical condition.

Congress also passed laws that provided funding for conservation projects. The Land and Water Conservation Fund Act of 1965,[53] for instance, bankrolled a steady stream of conservation projects on federal land. The act provided matching grants to federal, state, and local agencies to acquire land and water for public outdoor recreation in the forms of parks, protected forest, and wildlife areas.[54] This fund provided the principal source for land acquisition for outdoor recreation lands by the Forest Service, National Park Service, Fish and Wildlife Service, and Bureau of Land Management.[55]

Finally, the federal government asserted control over ocean resources and Antarctica. First, attempting to provide some restrictions to waters off the U.S. coastline, the Coastal Zone Management Act of 1972 (CZMA)[56] and Magnuson–Stevens Fishery Conservation and Management Act of 1976[57] brought the policy of multiple use to the ocean waters.[58] The CZMA provided a process for coastal states to develop resource use-based zoning plans for offshore waters and submerged lands.[59] Through the CZMA, the federal government, attempted to harmonize federal programs to the extent possible with these local programs and also to provide federal funding for uses that have "more than local significance."[60] While the CZMA baked in a local bias for offshore resource use, it also provided limited safeguards when a state's plan runs countering to important federal and regional interests.[61] Magnuson–Stevens, likewise, provided a mechanism to divide the haul from ocean fisheries among coastal states and different interests (commercial and recreational fishers). In 1978, Congress passed the Antarctic Conservation Act,[62] which adopted major restrictions and responsibilities on U.S. visitors to and U.S. uses of Antarctica—operationalizing obligations that the United States took on through an international treaty in the early 1960s.[63]

CITIZEN LITIGATION AND THE RISE OF THE NATIONAL ENVIRONMENTAL POLICY ACT

Even before the public clamor began as oil washed up on the white beaches of Santa Barbara in 1970, we find early examples of what would become a burgeoning environmental movement focused on federal law reforms—a movement that eventually embraced both statutory change and lawsuits as mechanisms to pursue change.

In 1965, a citizen's group called the Scenic Hudson Preservation Conference sued the Federal Power Commission with the goal of killing a power plant that the Commission had approved for construction on New York's Storm King Mountain by Consolidated Edison.[64] By many accounts, this was the first lawsuit brought against an administrative agency for environmental purposes—in many ways, the birth of modern environmental litigation.[65]

The first hurdle for the environmental group to overcome in court was objections by the government that citizens were not authorized under the U.S. Constitution to bring such a suit. The basis of the objection was rooted in what is commonly referred to as *standing*, a legal requirement found in the U.S. Constitution requiring that parties who bring lawsuits have a legitimate interest in doing so.[66] For the first time ever, in the case of *Scenic Hudson Preservation Conference v. Federal Power Commission*, a federal court of appeals held that members of the group had constitutional standing due to the citizens' "interest in aesthetic, conservational, and recreational aspects" related to the Commission's decision to permit the new plant.[67] Once the environmentalists were allowed to sue, did they ever.[68] Eventually, the project—mired in litigation seeking to prevent the proposed plant's environmental effects—was abandoned.[69]

Environmental litigation would soon become part of almost every controversial federal decision made by administrative agencies related to the environment. As the importance of litigation grew in trying to secure environmental protection, older environmental groups like the Sierra Club became increasingly litigious and new groups, like the National Resources Defense Council (NRDC) and Earth Justice, came into being and relied on litigation as a primary conservation strategy.[70]

A great deal of federal environmental litigation would arise out of a statute called the National Environmental Policy Act (NEPA).[71] When it was debated in Congress, NEPA's future would have been hard to imagine. The most debated provision of NEPA—and this was not that hot of a topic—focused on the creation of a new office within the White House focused on the environment called the Council of Environmental Quality.[72] The most provocative argument made during this debate was bland at best—that the new office would be redundant to other White House operations.[73]

What would become the most important provision of NEPA was substituted in place of a weaker provision after almost all debate on the bill had occurred—at a joint committee of Senate and House members assigned by congressional leadership to reconcile differences between bills passed in both chambers. It was during these final negotiations that provisions were added to the bill that would become the grounds for requiring the federal government to complete environmental impact statements for "major federal actions significantly affecting the quality of the human environment."[74] This requirement provided environmental activists a platform to participate in federal decisions, ranging from decisions to clear cut federal forests to building highways in American cities. As Congress hammered out NEPA's final details, the press failed to grasp its import, and coverage of the passage was scant at best.[75]

The Nixon administration, thick in the throes of shaping its own environmental agenda, also seemed to misapprehend the significance of the bill. When Nixon signed the bill on January 1, 1970, he did not include a photo-op, but rather the administration released a press statement that overlooked the substance of NEPA while focusing on Nixon's confidence that the 1970s would become the decade of the environment.[76]

While unappreciated at its passage, NEPA eventually became regularly known as the *Magna Carta* of modern environmental law.[77] Through decisions such as *Calvert Cliffs' Coordinating Committee v. Atomic Energy Commission*,[78] federal courts parsed out the meaning in the statute's few paragraphs and eventually found that NEPA required detailed impact statements examining not only proposals but also proposals' alternatives for most decisions made by the federal bureaucracy that affected the environment. These same courts also found that NEPA gives citizens procedural protections that force agencies to circulate environmental impact statements to the public and, if needed, an avenue to sue federal agencies that fail to consider the environmental consequences of their actions. NEPA also required virtually every federal agency to address—either by changing their action or articulating why they would not—any comments aimed at criticizing that agency's findings, even including comments from average citizens.[79]

The U.S. Supreme Court has clearly ruled that NEPA's mandates are procedural in nature.[80] Some commentators have argued that NEPA ought to go further than simply *consider* harms and alternatives. Rather, they argue it ought to be interpreted or changed to *require* substantive changes to a proposed action in response to anticipated harms, as some state analogs have required.[81]

Nonetheless, NEPA has served as an invaluable catalyst for environmental protection and democratic participation. The requirement that environmental harms be considered has grown to inform virtually every aspect of federal discretionary regulatory decision making. Underscoring its influence on environmental law, about half the states and over one hundred other nations replicated NEPA.[82] At least as significantly, through its procedural and structural (i.e., interagency consultation) innovations, NEPA promoted a more coordinated administrative state and a more informed and empowered citizenry. The various federal natural resources laws, for instance, only could be successfully implemented through compliance with NEPA's mandates for public participation, interagency consultation, and careful judicial review of such decisions.[83]

AGGRESSIVE FEDERAL POLLUTION CONTROL

For the first time in United States history, pollution control was prominently on the federal policy agenda. The first pollution control law with bite arose in direct response to the Santa Barbara Oil Spill. The spill began just a couple of weeks into Nixon's term and came from a crack in the ocean floor near one of the wells operated by Union Oil. The spill resulted in 235,000 gallons of oil fouling the ocean just miles off the coast of Santa Barbara.[84] When the black tide came to shore, the oil-saturated water changed the physics of the waves—they no longer broke on Santa Barbara's beaches. Instead, in eerie silence, waves washed up oil-soaked birds, fish, and sea mammals. Crowds of Californians made their way up the coast to witness the destruction, and the media coverage was intense.

The vividness of the oil coated corpses of animals became front page news, dominated television news media for months, and resulted in a groundswell of public outrage and support for change.[85]

Because Union Oil's wells were on the federally-owned and -managed sea floor, the federal government faced enormous pressure to act. Congress passed the Oil Pollution Prevention Act,[86] which provided the federal government extensive authority to direct cleanup, recover costs, and impose substantial fines from those who caused oil spills.[87] This enactment, however, was only the beginning of federal environmental protections ushered in during the era.

Modern federal pollution control law was born with the passage of the Clean Air Act of 1970, followed by the 1972 Clean Water Act. Yet this fundamental legal transformation only occurred after earlier iterations of federal law that sought incremental progress by promoting scientific research, funding state regulation, then mandating (but with no consequence for noncompliance) state regulation of pollution. Only after state recalcitrance—and even outright defiance—did Congress eventually mandate significant federal roles in pollution control.

Modern pollution control laws gave rise to an important legal innovation: the "cooperative federalism" structural framework that is copied in many other substantive fields today.[88] Congress encouraged a federal-state partnership by allocating a spectrum of overlapping federal and state authorities and mandates over most governmental functions, with federal primacy over certain government functions (like funding, ambient monitoring, or standard setting) and state primacy over others (such as implementation and enforcement).[89] These laws also involved prescriptive regulation, characterized by strict, ambitious timelines for the federal government to accomplish stated goals, robust monitoring of private entities, strict control standards, and heavy fines for polluters and even jail time for some violations. They also pioneered another significant regulatory innovation: citizen suit enforcement, which allowed citizens to sue not only administrative agencies but also regulated entities for violating environmental laws—and possibly even get reimbursed for their litigation costs in doing so.[90]

Despite these and other triumphal victories, this period was also marked by a succession of impediments in the fight against pollution. In 1977, Congress amended the Clean Air Act[91] and the Clean Water Act[92] to not only establish additional programs but also to extend deadlines and relax certain standards. Some framed these amendments as pragmatic adjustments following Congress's initial inexperience with, and overestimation of the federal government's ability to quickly solve, pollution problems.[93] Others saw the changes, particularly to the Clean Air Act, as effective industry efforts to relax and stall regulations by fueling consumer concerns about restrictions on their freedom and fossil fuel shortages.[94] In many ways, however, these revisions leave much of the original enactments untouched.

CREATING OF THE EPA AND PASSING THE CLEAN AIR ACT

An important wrinkle to the story of how transformational change came to redefine the relationship between people and the environment in this era is the critical role that individuals—even leaders who expressed limited concern for environmental protection—can have on whether legal change occurs, as well as the shape such laws can take. Even before the public began demanding strong federal environmental laws, Senator Ed Muskie—a Democrat from Maine—had worked to advance environmental legislation through Congress in his role of Chair of the Senate's Public Works Committee.[95] While none of these bills in the 1960s shifted the status quo much, they did support the development of significant scientific data about environmental harms and to a certain degree cultivated regulatory experimentation on how to address such harms.

Though they became incrementally more demanding, these early pollution prevention laws initially simply asked or told states and localities to regulate. Sometimes they provided grant opportunities as carrots, but typically they included little by way of sticks for noncompliance. The Clean Air Act Amendments of 1963, for instance, instructed federal officials to assist states by articulating appropriate air quality standards, providing grant money to research and regulate air pollution, and mediating interstate air pollution disputes.[96] The 1965 Water Quality Act directed states to issue water quality standards for interstate waters and authorizing the federal government to do so if states refused.[97] The 1965 Solid Waste Disposal Act, the first federal law focused on helping nonfederal actors improve waste disposal technology,[98] established a framework for states to regulate solid waste disposal as well as landfills. The 1967 Air Quality Act went incrementally further, setting national air pollution standards for some industries, but its primary focus was on providing planning grants to states to meet federal standards.[99] In the 1960s, the only direct regulation by Congress came via the Motor Vehicle Air Pollution Control Act of 1965, which provided direct federal pollution standards for cars; yet even this enactment was spurred on in part by the automobile industry's desire to avoid the potential for more stringent state standards.[100]

As a national consensus for major federal legislation materialized with the 1972 presidential election looming on the horizon, Muskie began to make clear that he had presidential aspirations. Strategically seeing environmental action as a smart way to ward off any challenge from Muskie, President Nixon agreed with his advisers to prioritize environmental legislation.[101] The first public signal of Nixon's intentions to take up environment protection came when he signed NEPA and declared that the 1970s would become the "decade of the environment".[102] Few understood all the plans Nixon had in the works.

In a nation bogged down in an unpopular war in Vietnam and facing political unrest, Nixon caught his rivals and the nation very much by surprise; he made environmental protection the central focal point of his 1970 State of the Union address. Spending approximately half of that address on the environment, he proclaimed, "[c]lean air, clean water, open spaces—these should once again be the birthright of every American. If we act now, they can be."[103] While Nixon received some criticism—particularly from Senator Muskie—that his proposals lacked specifics, Nixon delivered a thirty-seven-point plan calling for aggressive, specific environmental legislation the following month.[104] This Message to Congress on the Environment pointedly called out proposals before Congress (many of them championed by Muskie) as too weak.

To make matters worse for Muskie, the prominent consumer advocate Ralph Nader also began to push a narrative of Muskie's weakness—that the earlier federal environmental legislation lacked teeth because of Muskie's desire to protect Maine's paper industry.[105] Muskie's lead staffer on environmental issues, Leon Billings, reported that Muskie was furious and had instructed Billings of his new marching orders—taking the Clean Air Act and "shoving it up Nader's ass."[106] Muskie and his

Figure 4.1 Richard Nixon (center) and Ed Muskie (right) with Hubert Humphrey (left), the day after Nixon's election in 1968.

subcommittee once again picked up the task of passing air pollution legislation, but this time legislation with much more punch than anything that had come before it.

Some of the most pointed criticisms of past weakness, however, focused on Nixon and not Muskie and Congress. Specifically, the Johnson administration's Department of Justice brought a suit against automakers for what became known as the "smog conspiracy"—industry purposefully stifling the development of pollution-control devices—which was controversially settled by the Nixon administration in 1969.[107] "The consent decree barred the companies from conspiring to delay the use of antipollution devices,"[108] and bound the companies to "follow new and more competitive ground rules in their development activity."[109] Numerous Congressmen, states, Nader, and others decried the settlement for concealing collusive activities, with some seeking new antitrust cases that several years later were ultimately dismissed.[110] Nonetheless, these actions also helped catalyze many in Congress (as well as in state leadership) to act.

While federal legislation and executive actions in the 1960s were not calibrated to advance effective action by many states, consistent with the dual sovereign, overlapping authority embedded in United States federalism, some states did act. The strongest regulations implemented in the 1960s were passed not in Washington, D.C., but in California, which set substantial vehicle emissions standards at the state level.[111] Still, many states had ignored if not explicitly defied federal mandates.[112]

So, as Muskie's subcommittee got to work in the 1970s, it was as much against a backdrop of industrial and state government defiance as it was a strategy to fend off both Nixon and Nader. Other less partisan motivations also seemed to have catalyzed federal action. A key staff member involved on the committee, Tom Jorling, credited the desire of many on the subcommittee to prove to the many protesters who had descended on Washington, D.C., in opposition to the Vietnam War that the federal government could do meaningful things.[113] As the subcommittee and its staff sat behind closed doors drafting the Clean Air Act, all but one of them smoked tobacco, and as the subcommittee left its work and went out into the halls, the smell of tobacco mixed with that of marijuana smoke from the joints of Vietnam War protesters who had occupied the Senate Office Building.[114]

In a similar vein, as Muskie's subcommittee worked, excitement for environmental progress grew and resulted in a public outpouring of support on the first Earth Day.[115] All told, about twenty million people

Figure 4.2 One of many Earth Day events, this one on the University of Michigan's campus, 1970.

(roughly one in ten Americans) participated in Earth Day events, at an estimated ten thousand events—most of which took place at schools and universities across the country.[116] Polling from the time suggests this pivot to focus on the environment pleased most demographic groups.[117]

In the end, it is hard to say if, metaphorically, Muskie's staffer Billings got the bill anywhere near Nader's hindquarters, but the Clean Air Act that made it through Congress went well beyond what Nixon had pushed for and even beyond the policy space where Nixon felt comfortable. The Nixon administration tried to use a cabinet member to lobby Republicans in Congress to walk back some of the most aggressive aspects of the bill to protect industry, but there was no appetite for retreat. The bill received almost unanimous support in both houses of Congress. When Nixon signed the bill, he sought maximum credit for the environmental progress being made by featuring his new EPA Administrator, inviting some Republican leaders in Congress, and refusing to invite Muskie or any other Democrat.[118]

The 1970 Clean Air Act was an enormous step forward in legal imagination. In addition to innovations like citizen suits and cooperative federalism detailed already, the enactment had a host of regulations that made it worthy of claiming title to the most aggressive environmental legislation ever passed by any nation.[119] Perhaps its most ambitious mandate was requiring auto manufacturers selling cars in the United States to cut emissions in their fleets by 90 percent within just five years.[120] It also allowed federal and state governments to closely regulate larger air pollution emitters, like power plants and factories, and gave the federal government a pathway to regulate virtually every product that burned fossil fuels, including planes, trains, and off-road vehicles.[121] It set out a process for the federal government to set national ambient air quality standards (NAAQS), which states were charged with enforcing. While it entrusted the states with ensuring compliance with these standards within their respective jurisdictions, it also provided ways for the federal government to push recalcitrant states, including stepping in and regulating a state directly.[122] It also set aggressive fines for those who violated the enactment—up to $25,000 a day per violation—and even provided criminal liability for those who willingly violated the statute.[123]

As Nixon fought Muskie from pushing the Clean Air Act too far, Nixon made another play to capture the environmental issue by creating a new governmental agency—the EPA.[124] The new agency would oversee fifteen federal programs that were previously scattered across the federal bureaucracy and would also take on the role of administering new environmental laws passed by Congress. By early December 1970, the EPA was formed, and William Ruckelshaus was asked to be its first administrator. His work in establishing the new agency would gain nearly universal praise as bringing credibility to environmental enforcement.[125]

ASSEMBLING THE MODERN CLEAR WATER ACT

President Nixon was very much of two minds about federal environmental policy after having signed the Clean Air Act. On one hand, he looked to take credit for pushing ahead on the environment on the campaign trail. In talking to reelection advisors, discussions about the environment were connected to beating Muskie.[126] In these conversations, Nixon wanted to claim the issue: "I don't mind being a clean air, clean water, open space man."[127] Within the same week, in speaking to policy advisors about future policy strategies, Nixon took a very different tack. "I don't want any of this environment shit," he ranted, "I'm not going to do it. There's nothing in it for us. Not a goddamn thing."[128]

Unlike the Clean Air Act, which was a rough draft before Nixon began to take potshots at it, the Clean Water Act had much further to go both in drafting and in vetting. At the Congressional level, the Federal Water Pollution Control Act of 1948[129] and Federal Water Pollution Control Amendments of 1956[130] had only provided federal funding for research and implementing state programs, which did little to ease the nation's growing water pollution problem. Congress passed the 1965 Amendments requiring states to adopt harm-based water quality standards and implementation plans, with the federal role limited to resolving interstate conflicts.[131] But by 1972, only half the states had even set the required standards, and none had translated the standards into requirements for individual sources.[132]

Meanwhile, as Congress took up the topic, environmental groups sought creative redress for water pollution problems through the courts based on longstanding but long-forgotten federal law. In the early 1960s, environmental litigants rediscovered the Refuse Act, which since 1899 had prohibited the "dumping of refuse" into navigable waters without a permit.[133] Because that law had been largely unheeded for seventy years, no one had a permit, and environmental organizations successfully sued the Army Corps of Engineers (ACE), forcing it to require permits.[134] In response, ACE tried to issue general permits for entire industries, but a court enjoined this strategy, stating that it both was a ploy to undermine the Refuse Act and failed to comply with the newly established NEPA.[135]

Fueled by state incapacity and recalcitrance, judicial directives, and the growing public interest in addressing pollution, Muskie's subcommittee got to work. Over the next year and a half, the subcommittee would put together a very substantial bill, largely keyed to two regulatory programs. The first regulated most of the nation's biggest water polluters, something the enactment referred to as point sources, though for political reasons agricultural runoff was exempted from the bill.[136] Oceans, lakes, and rivers had for centuries been dumping grounds, not

Figure 4.3 Photographs of the Cuyahoga River burning made the river the poster child for water pollution and were published extensively in the late-1960s and early 1970s. However, this iconic photograph was actually not taken during the fire that made headlines (in 1968) but rather during another fire on the same river photographed in 1952. A photo of the 1968 fire apparently does not exist.

only for industry but also for human sewage. One of the rallying cries for those pushing the legislation was that in 1969, the Cuyahoga River in Cleveland had caught on fire.[137] While this became the poster child for the need for legislation, when the river started on fire (or to be more precise the pollutants within it), it was not even front-page news in the Ohio newspapers where the river flows—though later it was picked up by the national press.[138] That river, like many other aquatic resources, had become so polluted that even something as unworldly as water burning was not enough to capture attention of those most immediately affected.

The second program protected waters—and particularly wetlands—from threats related to dredging (removing soils) and filling (adding soils).[139] After hundreds of years of filling wetlands to make real estate for cities and farms, meaningful federal protection of wetlands was finally in place. Neither regulatory program banned regulated activities, but each put certain safeguards in place that would thwart many harmful activities to aquatic systems and reduce the environmental harm of development going forward.

As with the Clean Air Act, there was little opposition to the Clean Water Act in Congress. The main elected official to oppose the bill turned out to be the same Richard Nixon who challenged Congress to pass the bill in his State of the Union Address about two years before. Like with the Clean Air Act, Nixon had grown frustrated that Congress had pushed the Clean Water Act much further than he wanted. There certainly was a countercurrent of resistance, most vocally by the U.S. Chamber of Commerce, which raised dire but unfounded omens of the failure of whole industries because of antipollution laws.[140] Yet Nixon's expressed concerns were not about the market effects but rather with the bill's price tag, largely for much-needed sewer system enhancements around the country.[141] Until this point, cities around the country could shamelessly discharge raw sewage directly to nearby rivers, lakes, and the ocean. Nixon told his staffers: "I don't want to veto the bill and get rolled. Why get the worst of both worlds?"[142]

On October 10, 1972, just weeks before the election, the Senate by a vote of 74–0 and the House by 366–11 passed the Clean Water Act and sent it to Nixon for his signature or veto.[143] At that time, Muskie had failed to receive the Democratic Party's nomination, and Nixon was running strong against the Democratic challenger, George McGovern.

Ultimately, eight days later, despite the looming election, Nixon vetoed the enactment, pointing to the bill's "unconscionable $24 billion price tag."[144] Congress was also aware of the timing of the election, and within hours, Congress overrode the veto by large margins and went home for the elections.[145] Significantly, building off of many of the same features found in the Clean Air Act—ranging from citizen suits and cooperative federalism to a permitting system for larger polluters and aggressive fines for violators—the Clean Water Act had brought, for the first time, consequential federal regulation over surface water pollution.

AN ENDANGERED PRESIDENT AND ENDANGERED SPECIES

While Nixon intended to reshape the nation's environmental policy to be more friendly to industry after his reelection, he infamously hit a wall in his second term—the fallout from the Watergate Scandal. During the 1972 election, five men were arrested for breaking into the Democratic National Committee headquarters located on the sixth floor of the Watergate Office Building in Washington, D.C.[146] The scandal would consume Nixon's administration and every step along the way seemed to get closer to implicating Nixon himself, as it became clear that it was a part of a series of illegal activities and cover-ups designed to undermine Nixon's political opponents.[147] It would result in the firing of central political operatives, prison time for those implicated, and eventually cause Nixon to resign from the presidency altogether.[148] As Nixon's team became increasingly distracted, the environment fell off Nixon's agenda.

Even without the dynamic of one-upmanship between Nixon and Muskie at play, important environmental programs still progressed. Notably, for about a decade, the United States had participated in international negotiations surrounding endangered species. These efforts bore fruit in 1973 with the Convention on International Trade in Endangered Species (CITES), when eighty nations signed an international treaty seeking to prevent species from becoming endangered or extinct because of international trade.[149] (Today, 183 countries and the European Union implement CITES.)[150]

As Congress considered different legislative options to implement CITES and how to protection endangered species more broadly, Nixon was hardly a factor in the negotiations. To be fair, few powerbrokers in Congress paid much attention to the bill either. In fact, as Congress acted, it is hard to imagine that all its members fully grasped the breadth of species that faced the brink of extinction, nor particularly how the enactment would interact with this reality. Most of the debates about what was called the Endangered Species Act (ESA) focused on species that were well recognized, if not celebrated or loved, by Americans—whooping cranes,[151] grizzly bears,[152] or bison.[153] Though the ESA has consistently been one of the most popular environmental laws in the United States,[154] it might have been a different piece of legislation if Congressional deliberations focused on more controversial species that were later to be listed—like a little fish in Tennessee called the snail darter[155] or Southern California's Delhi Sands flower-loving fly.[156] The ESA was passed without much ceremony but with overwhelming support: unanimously by consensus in the Senate and 355 to 4 in the House.[157] While the Nixon White House played virtually no role in passing the legislation, Nixon had a signing ceremony, probably a welcome reprieve from the media's resolute attention on the scandal engulfing his presidency.[158]

The law prohibited the "take" of endangered or threatened species listed by the Fish and Wildlife Service (or the National Marine Fisheries Service in the case of marine species).[159] This prohibition includes not only overt acts ("hunting," "collecting," or "harassing") but also more indirect acts ("hurt," "harm" or even "attempt" to harm).[160] The inclusion of protections triggered by more indirect actions would come to embroil conservationists and property rights advocates in decades to come, but were not a central part of the legislative debate. The statute also regulated the actions of the federal government. Federal agencies were required to ensure that any action "is not likely to jeopardize the continued existence of any endangered species or threatened species or result in the destruction or adverse modification of critical habitat of such species."[161] This aspect of the enactment would severely complicate actions of federal agencies as diverse as military training exercises, energy projects, and new highways.

While the ESA allowed for citizen suits and major fines for "takes," the Supreme Court clarified the real punch of the statute a few years later in *Tennessee Valley Authority v. Hill*.[162] In 1975, recognizing the untapped power of the legal innovation, Zygmunt Plater (a law professor) and Hiram Hill (one of Plater's students) filed the first petition to list a species as endangered under the ESA—the snail darter, a small fish inhabiting the Little Tennessee River below the Tellico dam site near Hill's childhood home.[163] Once listed, they also sued, with Hill serving as the lead plaintiff, seeking to stop construction of a near finished federal dam because it would jeopardize the fish. In 1976, a district court judge ruled it was too late to stop the project, as the government had already spent $80 million and the dam was almost finished.[164] In 1977, the Supreme Court ruled to suspend construction. "It is clear that Congress intended to halt and reverse the trend toward species extinction—whatever the cost," wrote Chief Justice Warren Burger in his opinion.[165] In the decades that followed, the Endangered Species Act would become both a perennial target for those who bemoaned robust federal environmental regulation and the subject of legislative and regulatory compromise to manage the repeated contest between ecological conservation and development.

The Endangered Species Act was the most consequential species law passed during the Environmental Era, but by no means the only one. The year before the Endangered Species Act passed, Congress enacted the Marine Mammal Protection Act, a predecessor of the ESA that made it illegal for anyone in the United States to kill, hunt, injure, or harass all species of marine mammals.[166] Congress also passed the Wild and Free Roaming Horses and Burros Act, making it a federal crime to harass or kill wild horses or burros on federal land[167] and allowing federal land to be set aside for herd management through plans that "maintain a thriving natural ecological balance."[168]

While most of the Environmental Era's wildlife laws focused on preserving and restoring increasingly rare native plants and wildlife where they historically existed, it is worth noting that much of the attention and resources by states and federal land agencies remained focused on sustained yield—that is, maintaining sufficient wildlife for hunting and fishing activities. To partially address this, in 1980, Congress passed the Fish and Wildlife Conservation Act, which provided federal financial and technical assistance to states for developing nongame fish and wildlife conservation plans.[169] Though the contribution of game enthusiasts was unquestionably vital to the passage of virtually all of federal species conservation law, the tension of competing values between species preservation and maximizing yield objectives remained an enduring subplot in the development of federal natural resources law.

CURBING THE HARMS OF MODERN PRODUCTS AND INDUSTRIAL PRODUCTION

The Environmental Era also experienced a legislative revolution that attempted to deal with a wide breadth of harms starting to accumulate from the significant acceleration of industrial and manufacturing activities in post–World War II America. A renowned catalyst for this renaissance was meticulous work by Rachel Carson, a former federal marine biologist who as early as 1945 had (along with a few others) sought to raise concerns about the hazards of the pesticide DDT that fell on deaf ears.[170] But on June 22, 1962, *The New Yorker* began to publish a serialized version of Rachel Carson's book *Silent Spring*,[171] which detailed the horrors of DDT and raised broader fundamental questions about the substantial health risks from modern industrial products unaccounted for in the market or the law. The book also triggered a nationwide outcry, most directly leading to a ban in 1970 of DDT in the United States for agricultural use.[172] The nation's attention in turn sparked a countercurrent of resistance by the chemical industry and agribusiness interests. Some critics questioned whether this burgeoning public health movement was hell-bent on starving Americans,[173] and Monsanto published a brochure—*The Desolate Year*—parodying *Silent Spring* by painting a picture of a pesticide-free world where famine, disease, and insects run rampant.[174] Indeed, despite the substantial evidence of devastating harm to humans and ecosystems, the eventual ban on DDT only occurred over the resistance of countervailing political pressures (including from President Nixon).[175]

Just as had occurred in the Progressive Era, an increasing awareness of the mass occupational, public health, and environmental risks from the rapid proliferation of manufacturing processes and products led to collaboration and even amalgamation of public health and conservation movements. This powerful coalition helped push through a range of laws directed at protecting employee safety, consumer health, and ecological conditions from industrial production and products.

Unsurprisingly, the initial congressional change focused on consumer protection, mostly relying on the disclosure of information to consumers about product content. The 1966 Fair Packaging and Labeling Act directed the Federal Trade Commission to issue regulations requiring all consumer commodities (other than already regulated food, drugs, therapeutic devices, and cosmetics) to be labeled to disclose their contents, the commodity's identity, and the product's manufacturer, packer, or distributor.[176] The statute also authorized regulations to prevent consumer deception (or to facilitate value comparisons).[177]

Drawing on legal innovations that blossomed in the Progressive Era, Congress's attention was directed toward worker safety and health. A 1966 report by the Public Health Service substantiated significant worker safety and health concerns under addressed by Progressive Era laws that had not foreseen new workplace challenges raised by increased technological complexity.[178] In 1970, Congress established the Occupational Safety and Health Administration (OSHA) in the Department of Labor.[179] OSHA was delegated the authority to set and enforce worker safety and health standards for most workplaces.[180]

Chemical safety in structures was next. In 1971, Congress passed the Lead-Based Paint Poisoning Prevention Act, which provided federal financial assistance to help localities develop and implement programs to eliminate the causes, and detect and treat incidents, of lead-based paint poisoning. It also established a federal program to study the extent of the lead-based paint poisoning problem and the methods available for lead-based paint removal, and it prohibited future use of lead-based paint in federal or federally assisted construction.[181]

These laws were prologue for the two primary environmental statutes regulating dangerous products. With the Federal Insecticide, Fungicide, and Rodenticide Act of 1972 (FIFRA) and Toxic Substances Control Act of 1976 (TSCA), Congress asserted control over other particularly toxic products that pose deleterious effects to human health and the environment and transferred responsibility for federal pesticide regulation to the EPA.[182] Before allowing pesticides to be sold or produced in the United States, FIFRA required companies to demonstrate their pesticide had no unreasonable adverse effects on public health or the environment.[183] The idea was to give industry an incentive to develop information about product risks and reduce such risks. Most ambitiously, the statute mandated that fifty thousand pesticides manufactured before the bill passed (in 1972) had to be reviewed for safety by 1976,[184] though Congress repeatedly pushed back these deadlines, with most such reviews incomplete decades later.[185]

Like FIFRA, TSCA[186] was a market-access statute, authorizing the regulation of toxic substances once a product was proposed for the U.S. marketplace economy. TSCA sought to balance promoting a competitive, diverse marketplace of socially desirable products with protecting public safety from dangerous substances.[187] But unlike FIFRA or the Food, Drug, and Cosmetics Act, the burden of proving that regulation was necessary under TSCA was placed on the EPA.[188] As such, the default was that a new product or use was unregulated under TSCA unless the EPA affirmatively found there to be an unreasonable risk from the product.

GARBAGE, HAZARDOUS WASTE, AND SUPERFUND

An unforeseen aspect of the Environmental Era's statutory focus on addressing each pollution medium separately—first air pollution, then water pollution, then products—was the creation of an uneven regulatory scheme. Would-be polluters had an incentive to exploit regulatory gaps and pollute in ways that avoided new federal pollution regulations.[189] In particular, a polluter could opt not to dispose sludge into a river (regulated by the Clean Water Act) and instead transport the sludge for disposal into a much more lightly regulated landfill.

By the mid-1970s, it was clear that the 1965 Solid Waste Disposal Act was far from sufficient to address solid waste pollution, and in particular the most hazardous by-products of "modern" industrial and manufacturing activity. In 1975, Congress passed the Hazardous Materials Transportation Act, which imposed transportation regulations for shipments of hazardous materials along with labeling and packaging requirements for hazardous materials.[190] However, these regulations lacked the bite of the newly passed Clean Air Act and Clean Water Act.

In 1976, Congress added the Resource Conservation and Recovery Act (RCRA), which provided comprehensive regulation of the disposal of conventional garbage and an even more stringent regulatory infrastructure for particularly hazardous wastes.[191] RCRA established a baseline set of rules and a framework for states to take the lead on regulating nonhazardous solid wastes, which brought regulation to ordinary landfills.[192] But RCRA saved its most vigorous restrictions for hazardous wastes, instituting a "cradle to grave" waste-tracking system and robust and detailed regulations focused on generation, transportation, treatment, storage, and disposal.[193]

As comprehensive as RCRA proved in regulating the entire life cycle of newly generated wastes with the goal of preventing new waste sites, the enactment did nothing to address the legacy of innumerable sites throughout the nation that had already been contaminated by decades of careless disposal of hazardous materials. Near the end of the 1970s, however, various high-profile episodes of unremediated hazardous waste captured public and Congressional interest in cleaning up past contamination. The most notorious of these was at Love Canal near Niagara Falls, New York, where in the late-1800s ambitious real estate developer William T. Love initiated excavation of a large canal for ships to bypass Niagara Falls on the Niagara River.[194] Depleting financial support exacerbated by Nikola Tesla's technological innovations in power transmission conspired to hinder and eventually disintegrate the project, leaving only a partially excavated section of the canal by 1910.[195]

In the 1940s, Hooker Chemical purchased the canal and adjacent land.[196] Over the next decade, the chemical company would bury more than twenty thousand tons of toxic waste in the canal. Much of this land was later sold to a real estate developer and became the site of a fifteen-acre suburban neighborhood along with two public schools.

In 1976, the neighborhood became national news, after a torrential rain washed away soil and pushed previously buried toxic waste containers to the surface.[197] This controversy was stoked for more than a year by a constant drumbeat of news coverage that frequently featured Lois Gibbs, the unflinching voice of the neighbors. Eventually President Jimmy Carter used presidential authority to declare Love Canal a federal emergency after a startling increase in skin rashes, miscarriages, and birth defects in the area,[198] leading to the relocation of more than eight hundred households, the destruction of the suburban neighborhood and schools, and eventually the cleanup of Love Canal.[199]

But Love Canal was far from an isolated incident.[200] In 1979, in conjunction with extensive legislative hearings, Congressmen John J. La-Falce and Daniel Patrick Moynihan proposed legislation for paying for and cleaning up toxic waste sites that they called the "Superfund."[201] In

1980, Congress enacted the Comprehensive Environmental Response, Compensation, and Liability Act (CERCLA).[202]

In contrast with the other federal environmental laws enacted up to that point that focused on prospective public agency regulation, CERCLA relied on an extraordinarily creative enforcement regime that profoundly altered the common law court rules regarding tort liability surrounding hazardous waste. It gave the EPA the authority to clean up hazardous waste contamination and then seek reimbursement afterward from "potentially responsible parties" (PRPs).[203] PRPs broadly included any individual or company who currently or in the past owned or operated a site polluted by hazardous waste, arranged for the disposal of hazardous waste at that site, or even transported any hazardous waste to that site.[204] CERCLA also gave EPA broad authority to order private or public entities to cleanup sites themselves and only afterward seek reimbursement in court for those response costs from PRPs (or if they are an innocent party, from the federal Superfund).[205] Perhaps most radically, CERCLA makes virtually any PRP connected to the release or threatened release of any hazardous substance strictly, retroactively, and jointly and severally liable for the full cost of the site's hazardous waste remediation.[206] With substantial public support, Congress made the call that ensuring quick, effective cleanup of incredibly toxic wastes and minimizing administrative costs outweighed any concerns regarding fairness in the allocation of liability among PRPs. In this sense, CERCLA "represents one of the most significant innovations in U.S. law."[207]

THE ENVIRONMENTAL ERA'S UNFINISHED BUSINESS

Even as the country saw major reductions in air pollution (including the virtual elimination of lead air emissions) through implementation of the Clean Air Act, other sorts and sources of pollution went unchecked. Sometimes these regulatory gaps occurred purposefully, as politically engineered loopholes in legislation, like the Clean Water Act's carve out for agricultural pollution to mollify political resistance.[208] Most importantly, while the country began to get many air pollutants under control during the Environmental Era, the greenhouse gases that cause global climate change went unchecked during this period,[209] despite emerging scientific evidence of the potential global threat.[210]

New federal conservation laws raised other limitations. For example, though the Endangered Species Act provided wildlife protections that were unparalleled at the time, a few key drivers of species decline were left unaddressed by the initial enactment: habitat fragmentation, invasive species, and industrialization.[211] The first gap occurred due to centuries of expansion and refining of agriculture and decades of investment in transportation projects, dam building, and other infrastructure that facilitated both urban and suburban growth. Habitat fragmentation, even when not leading to a particular species' demise, resulted in disruptions in species finding food, shelter, and mates. Second, as society became increasingly mobile and commerce increasingly global, native ecosystems became more vulnerable to invasive species, meaning nonnative species disrupted the ecological balance or introduced new competitors and new predators for native species.[212] Third, industrial innovations along with a growing human population meant more pressure on ecosystems from traditional challenges. For example, new technologies in hunting and fishing increased yield. At the same time, new pesticides and chemicals used in agriculture and landscaping posed new threats to species lower on the food chain, particularly beneficial insects, and resulted in the bioaccumulation of such chemicals in species higher on the food chain.[213]

More broadly, federal wildlife management and funding was very narrow. The ESA only focused on species that were on the brink of extinction. Meanwhile, as EPA Administrator Russell Train had previously complained, "97 percent of federal money for wildlife management 'goes to less than three percent of the species—the ones used for hunting, fishing and trapping.'"[214] The 1980 Fish and Wildlife Conservation Act was designed as a way to plan for the protection of biota that were diminishing due to habitat loss before they became imperiled and merited ESA protection.[215] Through the Federal Wildlife Conservation Act, Congress authorized federal financial and technical assistance to the states for inventorying their ecological resources and for the development, revision, and implementation of state nongame fish and wildlife conservation plans and programs.[216] However, unlike the steady revenue available for game species through excise taxes on hunting and fishing, a reliance on general federal revenues for decades was largely inadequate for effective conservation.[217]

Both before initial enactments and during implementation, the countercurrent of political resistance to federal environmental legislation was undoubtedly strong, even if it was repeatedly overcome by waves of legal actors promoting environmental protection. Like the Wilderness Act, there was significant pushback to the passage of the Clean Air Act, with prominent industrial leaders falsely prophesizing the end of their industries and epic national economic crises.[218] Resistance also took the form of President Nixon's characterizations of the Clean Water Act as involving "extreme and needless overspending" in his unsuccessful attempts to veto the bill.[219] Yet often during the Environmental Era, these forces seeking to thwart federal environmental protection were overcome by significant public pressure. For example, President Nixon indicated in private that he would have been "crucified" if he backed off air pollution legislation.[220]

Yet the tidal wave of federal environmental protection was not successful in overcoming political resistance in all realms. For one, many of the land use problems that proliferated in the Modernization Era remained unchecked in the Environmental Era. While some federal enactments required permitting for large polluters and encouraged local planning to address environmental problems, land use remained largely unregulated at the federal level. In 1973, the Nixon administration called for a form of federalization of land use policy, but that effort died on the vine.[221] Suburbanization and sprawl continued to thrive due to the confluence of generally weak local and state land use regulation, federal housing subsidies, and interlocal competition for development, even as the country's population grew substantially. Growth not only resulted in the loss of greenspace and farms on the exurban edge but also in decay of urban cores and air pollution from a car-oriented society. While urban revitalization programs were adopted, such as Lyndon B. Johnson's Great Society programs, these programs had a challenging time keeping up with the structural incentives that pushed the country further toward urban sprawl.[222]

Furthermore, the progress made on environmental issues did not even meaningfully attempt to reach all populations equally. The Civil Rights

Act of 1964 ultimately proved ineffective in addressing environmental justice issues, despite hopes (and litigation efforts) to the contrary.[223] The Civil Rights Act prohibited discrimination based on race, color, religion, sex, or national origin. The enactment would (and still does) prohibit under Title VI recipients of federal financial assistance (e.g., states or private grantees) from discriminating based on race, color, or national origin in any program or activity, which would include programs focused on human health or the environment.[224] This meant, for example, that the federal government, or even state agencies that received funds from the EPA to run a clean air program, were legally prohibited from discriminating because of race, color or national origin when engaging in clean air enforcement activities.

Despite barring such blatant types of discrimination, the Civil Rights Act did not really provide much reach in addressing the increasingly clear disproportionate effects of pollution on lower-income communities and communities of color. In 1971, a Council on Environmental Quality annual report acknowledged that communities of color and the urban poor experienced disproportionate environmental harm.[225]

In 1978, Robert Bullard began an investigation in the Triana, Alabama region where DDT had contaminated a stream. From this study, he wrote his "Cancer Alley" report that in many ways would mark the emergence of the environmental justice movement.[226]

Around the same time, illegal spraying of PCBs on roads in North Carolina led to a plan for dumping the PCB-laden soil in Warren County, a predominantly African American community. A direct-action nonviolent campaign stopped the landfill and raised awareness of environmental racism and the need for environmental justice.[227] Frequently, however, community organizing efforts failed to produce such results. For example, in 1979, a lawsuit was filed on behalf of Houston's Northeast Community Action Group, the first civil rights suit challenging the siting of a waste facility. Southwestern Waste Management won the lawsuit and built a landfill that devastated a middle-class Black neighborhood.[228]

Despite adopting some incremental changes, Congress failed to develop a comprehensive federal energy policy. Much of what constituted federal energy legislation and policy was adopted in response to the energy crisis during the mid-1970s, caused by the Organization of

Petroleum Exporting Countries oil embargo in 1973.[229] Such laws were largely driven by domestic concerns about energy reliability and prices combined with international concerns about U.S. economic and national security. This pressure also led to calls to roll back Clean Air Act provisions to accommodate gas and oil production.[230]

Other energy legislation was piecemeal, with more comprehensive federal policy elusive. In 1975, Congress passed the Energy Policy and Conservation Act (EPCA).[231] EPCA initiated a few disparate programs: a Strategic Petroleum Reserve national stockpile for emergency oil storage (a sort of self-insurance plan for U.S. oil markets);[232] authority for the National Highway Traffic Safety Administration to regulate Corporate Average Fuel Economy standards for automobiles and light trucks,[233] an Energy Conservation Program for Consumer Products to set minimum energy conservation standards for appliances and equipment;[234] a loan guarantee program to promote domestic coal production; and regulatory mechanisms for minimizing disruptions to fuel availability during shortages.[235] Congress also approved an Alaska Oil pipeline in 1973[236] and passed the National Energy Conservation Policy Act (as part of a National Energy Act)[237] to promote conservation in buildings, industry, and transportation largely by requiring states to develop "residential energy conservation plans" and offering limited grants for implementation.[238]

The most significant change to energy law came in the Public Utility Regulatory Policies Act (PURPA) of 1978.[239] The Act's major feature required electric utilities to purchase renewable energy in markets where it is available and pay the cost that the utilities would have paid had they purchased fossil fuel-based energy instead.[240] While the importance of these provisions were largely not experienced in the Environmental Era, they (and the ways that states and utilities implemented them) allowed renewable energy to blossom in decades to come, particularly as the price of producing renewable energy dropped.[241] Beyond providing a pathway for renewable energy growth, it created a conduit for such growth to take place via private investment as pricing for renewables became more affordable. This stood in contrast to the extensive investments in power production generally and hydropower specifically that had occurred as part of public investment in regulated utilities—a legacy of the Progressive Era.

GROWING PAINS, GAPS, AND RESISTANCE DESPITE UNPRECEDENTED PROGRESS

Even as the United States established itself as an international leader in pushing ahead aggressive and innovative domestic legal reforms in service of environmental protection, this new legal infrastructure struggled under the weight of many factors. The challenges of managing an unprecedented eruption in environmental legislation, tensions between idealism and pragmatism, limits in knowledge, and political resistance (particularly from regulated industry) left some environmental challenges inadequately addressed.

First, growing pains in governance complicated the story of the Environmental Era. The proliferation of dozens of new far-reaching statutes, some with incredibly ambitious standards, certainly affected the performance of environmental regulators. This of course was exacerbated by far-from-sufficient funding for the many federal and state agencies now tasked with effectuating Congress's voluminous mandates.[242] Second, scientific and administrative expertise in a range of burgeoning environmental fields was rapidly growing but nonetheless still limited.[243] Third, tensions arose between the idealism that led to aggressive but often unsubstantiated standards and the pragmatism that sought to better tailor standards after it became apparent that those ambitious standards would not be met. These factors hindered the smooth implementation and achievements of federal environmental legislation.

As new regimes were implemented and information was gathered about the capacity of the government to meet statutory goals, subsequent federal legislation reflected the sometimes-competing goals of managing these growing pains, filling in regulatory gaps, and moderating certain stricter elements of the initial enactments. The Clean Air Act Amendments of 1977, for instance, saw some moderations in the extremely ambitious initial law—most notably, extending the deadlines to meet the NAAQS.[244] However, it also created substantial new regulatory standards and programs, such as providing a pathway for places with dirty air to avoid some of the bite of the Clean Air Act if they could demonstrate they were making "reasonable further progress" toward attaining the NAAQS and creating a new program to regulate sources in areas that had clean air in order to ensure that the NAAQS would continue to be met.[245]

Federal water pollution control experienced a parallel story. In 1974, Congress supplemented the Clean Water Act by passing the Safe Drinking Water Act (SDWA).[246] The SDWA sought to protect water quality in public water systems designed for drinking use.[247] It authorized the EPA to establish national minimum standards for drinking water and to oversee state implementation and enforcement of these standards, as well as requiring all owners or operators of privately- and publicly-owned "public water systems" to comply with these EPA standards.[248] States were provided primary responsibility to implement and enforce the drinking water program.[249] In 1977, Congress adopted the Clean Water Act to adjust and enhance the Clean Water Act of 1972. The Clean Water Act of 1977 reflected "a broad congressional consensus that the 1972 legislation was essentially sound, and that with appropriate fine tuning it should be continued without interruption."[250] After passage of the 1972 bill, the EPA had initially concentrated its resources and efforts on regulating conventional pollutants to the detriment of regulation of more toxic pollutants. Through a consent decree—the Flannery Decree, the EPA and environmental groups settled on a plan and schedule to promulgate best available technology standards for toxic pollutants.[251] This plan was largely codified into the 1977 legislation.[252] In addition, the law elaborated on the part of the Clean Water Act passed a few years before that regulated the dredging and filling of wetlands, including procedures for state assumption of such regulatory programs[253] and (to the continued chagrin of environmental organizations) exemptions for farming, silviculture, and ranching from the dredge and fill prohibition.[254]

* * *

While environmentalism became firmly rooted in American culture through legislation during the Environmental Era, resistance came in other forms. It continued during implementation, with the "Sagebrush Rebellion" the most prominent example. This protest movement first started when Westerners opposed designating lands as wilderness under the Wilderness Act on the basis that its protections would interfere with rural livelihoods and opportunities.[255] As the Environmental Era concluded and the Contested Era dawned, this movement expanded to include not only a wide range of legal challenges but also outright defiance of federal land management and federal authority more generally.[256]

Push back, to some extent, also came from more fervent factions of the environmental movement. Though to some a time of unprecedented environmental progress, to others the Environmental Era reflected lost opportunities and unnecessary compromise. Some of this criticism came from those working within the system, including activist Ralph Nader and Senator Gaylord Nelson, founder of Earth Day. This was motivated at least in part to push colleagues reluctant to enact environmental protections.[257]

Some went further than that, advocating for reliance on extra-legal tactics to protect the environment. The rallying call of this arm of the environmental movement went much further than the civil disobedience encouraged by Henry David Thoreau[258] or Martin Luther King, Jr.[259] Instead, they were inspired by works like Edward Abbey's *The Monkey Wrench Gang*, a novel that follows the exploits of a motley foursome of activists, determined to protect the American wilderness from corporate and industrial destruction through acts of sabotage, who openly fantasize about blowing up Arizona's Glen Canyon Dam.[260] The era also saw the advent of Greenpeace, which sought to foil environmental destruction by strategically sailing into nuclear testing zones to disrupt planned explosions and positioning protesters in the pathway of whaling ships, seal harvesters, and forest clear-cutters.[261]

Despite the astonishing environmental progress in law and on the ground during the Environmental Era, as it ended, it is nonetheless also true that in some arenas unprecedented environmental risks were left largely un- or under-addressed. While environmental outrage resulted in a significant environmental movement and a considerable environmental legal infrastructure, other environmental disasters caused significant concern without concomitant structural legal change (though occasionally there were more incremental, case-specific conservation gains). For example, in 1979, the Three Mile Island nuclear power plant partially melted down, which resulted in elevated skepticism about risks from nuclear power and radioactive waste disposal.[262]

Erosion and accretion, borne from the turbulence and the ebb and flow of many disputing forces over a maturing legal infrastructure, became the name of the game in the next era—the Contested Era.

5

THE CONTESTED ERA

BACKLASH, PRAGMATISM, AND GRIDLOCK (1980–PRESENT)

INTRODUCTION

The Contested Era began quite conspicuously with President Reagan's inauguration. Though light on environmental legislation, the contestation throughout the eight years of the Reagan revolution had a lasting effect on the development of U.S. environmental law.[1] It began with the first of many attempts during the era to claw back environmental protections won during the Environmental Era, followed by counteroffensives to restore and build upon what was clawed back. Reagan's antienvironmental efforts took the forms of deregulation, cutting funding, and obstructing implementation of environmental statutes established in the Environmental Era.[2] These efforts were premised on a devotion to the unproven efficacy of "trickle-down" economic policies and a desire to reduce the influence of the government.[3]

Reagan's antienvironmental, antiregulation streak was best illustrated by his appointment of Anne Gorsuch and James G. Watt to head the Environmental Protection Agency and Department of the Interior, respectively.[4] Showy and rough, Gorsuch "wore fur coats and smoked two packs of Marlboros a day."[5] It was said of her that "[s]he could kick a bear to death with her bare feet."[6] After taking the helm at the EPA, Gorsuch was far from an advocate for the agency; instead, she was committed to reducing regulatory "overburden" on businesses and state governments, cutting the EPA's budget, and weakening existing environmental laws.[7] She appointed people in business to provide friendly oversight of their industry's regulations, cut enforcement staff, and even withheld records from Congress about suspected mishandling of money in the newly established Superfund for remediating hazardous waste sites.[8] During the process, she ended up alienating herself from the EPA's key supporters.[9] Bill Ruckelshaus, another Republican-appointed EPA head, said of her, "[s]he treated a lot of people in the agency as the enemy, and they weren't. But within a week, they were."[10] The political heat she created led to bipartisan calls for her removal, then to President Reagan pressuring her to step down, and, ultimately, her resignation.[11] Her legacy remained prominent even after her death in the early 2000s, as her son, Neil, became a Justice on the U.S. Supreme Court in 2017.

In a similar dynamic, Reagan's Secretary of the Interior Watt—a former extractive industry lobbyist and longstanding opponent to federal land regulation—stirred up numerous controversies by adopting anti-environmental positions during the early days of Reagan's first term.[12] While he looked like an unassuming bald man with thick glasses, below the surface he was as much an antienvironmentalist as Stewart Udall or Harold Ickes had been the darlings of conservationists in the same role in prior eras.[13] Watt subscribed to a view that longed to push public lands policy back toward consumptive and extractive uses. He saw conservation and development as in conflict, "preservation vs. people."[14] Watt's main objectives included broad transfers of public lands to private companies, opening wilderness available for mining and drilling, and greatly expanding leasing of public lands and coastal waters for oil drilling.[15] Like Gorsuch, Watt was pushed to resign after a Senate committee voted to cite him for contempt of Congress for failing to provide subpoenaed documents[16] and the broader Senate threatened to pass a resolution calling for his removal.[17]

Beyond what the Gorsuch and Watt appointments tell us about Reagan's approach to the environment, their stories help illustrate the distinctiveness of the Contested Era. In each of the previous eras, the ebb and flow of laws protecting the environment remained directionally stable for decades, even if there were undercurrents pulling in the opposite direction that achieved the occasional modest success. During the Contested Era, however, bold and swift paths by one legal actor in one direction were immediately challenged in another legal venue, held in limbo, or reversed when a political opponent took over. If other eras were ebbs and flows of policy tides, the ebb and flow crashed together during the Contested Era to create something akin to policy turbulence—causing legal whiplash and paralysis in equal measure.

So, even though a countermovement to the environmentalism of the Environmental Era certainly gained momentum early in the 1980s, its dominance was short-lived. Reagan took office in January of 1980, and on March 9, 1983, and October 9, 1983, respectively, Gorsuch[18] and Watt[19] resigned in ignominy.[20] It was the first episode of many in the Contested Era that came to characterize the incremental back and forth that resulted in whiplash in both environmental law and administration.

To be sure, the era could be understood as the period in which the federal environmental statutory infrastructure substantially matured and evolved. Federal and state regulators and managers had promulgated countless regulations, programs, plans, and adjudications. Through slowly developing expertise, these administrative agencies, with occasional judicial and legislative oversight, incrementally filled the scaffolding of modern U.S. environmental law.

The Contested Era, however, became primarily characterized by shifts in political dominance, increased presence of interest groups on all sides on environmental issues, and political polarization.[21] It experienced substantial conflict between the legislative, executive, and judicial branches of government, as well as between levels of government. Fueled by intentional disinformation campaigns,[22] the Contested Era saw the rise of acrimonious political polarization, the worst since the Civil War,[23] even leading to violent insurrection.[24]

Occasionally, Congress managed to pass new legislation during the era, though frequently only trimming at the edges (with key exceptions addressed below). For example, after decades of criticism of the National Environmental Policy Act, in 2023 Congress passed a statute imposing page limits on environmental impact statements but not limiting related reports or appendices.[25] More frequently and meaningfully, Congress tried to control the direction of environmental law through appropriations and regulatory oversight, often undercutting opposing presidential administrations and exerting pressure on existing statutes.[26]

Similarly, courts from different jurisdictions and circuits pushed the law in multiple and conflicting directions.[27] Indicative of the steady increase in polarization, "red" states increasingly sued the federal government during "blue" administrations. Meanwhile, "blue" states resorted to lawsuits against the federal government in "red" ones.[28]

Presidential administrations increasingly relied on executive authority initially through regulations but progressively via executive orders to advance their environmental agendas, allowing them to bypass Congress.[29] Administrations attacked the work done by other administrations, continuingly reinventing or reinstituting administrative rules and even agencies.[30] For example, based on his objection to national monuments designated by Presidents Clinton and Obama, President Trump shrunk the boundaries of two national monuments in Utah.[31] President Biden restored these monuments to their original designated sizes.[32] In 2025, President Trump issued executives orders rescinding over eighty of President Biden's executive orders, including those related to clean energy, environmental justice, climate-related public health protections, fossil fuel development, permitting, mining, and environmental enforcement.[33] Among the most regressive of these efforts was a twofold frontal assault on NEPA seeking to (1) rescind the regulations promulgated over decades that provided a coordinated federal framework for implementing the statute, and (2) direct each federal agency to weaken their NEPA regulations.[34]

Particularly given frequent gridlock in Congress and a closely divided judiciary, most legal turbulence occurred upon changes in presidential administrations. After the Reagan administration, the H. W. Bush and Clinton administrations rode out the remainder of the millennium relying on pragmatism necessitated by threats to the hard-won regimes of environmental protection.[35] Congress frequently faced partisan rancor, most prominently embodied by U.S. Representative Newt Gingrich's response to Clinton's first term—labeled the *Contract with America*,[36] a plan that aimed at reducing regulations, including repealing the Endangered Species Act (ESA), and subjecting federal management agencies to lengthy cost-benefit analyses and comparative risk assessments.[37] Gingrich rode this vision to win a Republican majority in the House along with the Speaker's chair for himself.

While many legal consequences followed, the Contract with America's most obvious environmental legacy was the Clinton administration's response to the pressure facing the ESA: to moderate environmental protection to undercut efforts to gut the law.[38] Clinton's Secretary of the Interior, Bruce Babbitt, ramped up the use of habitat conservation plans as a way to provide more flexibility under the ESA specifically to stymie calls to abolish or substantially pull back the ESA.[39] Other moderate legislators, jurists, and administrators had similar success in building bridges and advancing environmental goals, even if they were subject to critiques of incrementalism by more idealistic forces. Among the most disruptive critics came through the formation of more radical environmental advocacy organizations like Earth First!, which pushed for more aggressive changes and perceived not only pragmatist politicians but even more moderate environmental groups as complicit in environmental destruction.[40]

The new millennium initially saw the ascendancy of more immoderate influences in both parties and particularly in the Republican Party. For the first dozen years, growing ideological rift between parties led to significant battles in the courts and legislatures, but nonetheless resulted in some incremental policy advances.[41] However, mounting partisanship and distrust, fueled by changes in Supreme Court interpretations over campaign financing of elections, pushed polarization to a new level by the start of Trump's first administration.[42]

Fueled by a regressive populism, Trump's administration worked with congressional Republicans to advance a protectionist, antiregulation, and antiscience agenda.[43] Following a successful strategy used during the George W. Bush Administration, an onslaught of lawsuits by environmental organizations resisted efforts by the Trump administration to roll back environmental protection in a wide range of subfields,[44] illustrating the power of environmental law to prevent environmental slippage. Yet reflexive partisanship has ensured that fundamental environmental challenges remain inadequately addressed.

While environmental law under President Biden's administration largely mirrored that of earlier presidencies that pushed for environmental progress, Congress and the Biden Administration, to the surprise of many, ended up taking the single largest governmental step toward addressing climate change in U.S. history. The successful passage of the historic Inflation Reduction Act in 2022 authorized hundreds of billions of dollars for green technologies across the economy along with some infrastructure investments (ranging from car charging stations to new power line corridors) aimed at reducing carbon emissions by roughly 40 percent by 2030.[45] The fact that the bill was packaged to fight inflation rather than climate change, however, was characteristic of the foraging for environmental progress seen frequently during the era. Amid the increasingly strident fighting between those championing bolder environmental restrictions and those calling for rollbacks, this undercurrent of pragmatism continued—focused on getting what was understood to be the best possible deal at the time—either to maximize gains or minimize losses. Nonetheless, the global environmental threats of massive resource exploitation and development, climate change, plastics pollution, and biodiversity loss persisted with weak legal response.

Trump's reelection illustrated that the United States still was as contested as ever, if not more so. Much more targeted and unabashed than his first go round, his administration quickly went to work attempting to defund or dismantle virtually every environmental health and safety action taken under the Biden Administration.[46] Meanwhile, states, municipalities, nonprofit organizations, Congressional Democrats, and even other nations mobilized to rigorously challenge these efforts in the media, the halls of Congress, through state government initiatives, international diplomacy, and the courts.[47] Yet, the actions in his second administration went beyond what had become standard contestation in this era. In just the first year, the Trump administration had begun to weaponize the executive branch to consolidate its authority, promote deregulation, and weaken legal, academic, and scientific institutions to an extent never before witnessed in the United States. Congressional submission to Trump incursions on legislative authority—whether the levying of tariffs, appropriation of funds (e.g., to environmental agencies, programs, and research), or oversight of agency actions[48]—and Supreme Court acquiescence (often through largely deferential emergency "shadow docket" rulings)[49] facilitated unprecedented consolidation of executive power.

UNBRIDLED TECHNOLOGY, CONTESTED FACTS

During the Contested Era, technological change transformed commerce, particularly commerce related to disseminating information. From a legal perspective, the removal of content regulation from existing media and the absence of content regulation on new platforms precipitated misinformation and aggravated political polarization.[50] Misinformation had important implications on a wide range of policy arenas, including the relationship between people and the environment, as well as on the credibility of government and other vital institutions more generally.

While three television networks dominated news dissemination at the beginning of the Contested Era,[51] network viewership plummeted with the advent of cable television.[52] The world's first continuous cable news channel launched in 1980[53] gained traction in 1991 with live on-the-scene broadcasting of the Persian Gulf War.[54] What became a twenty-four-hour news cycle brought an explosion of low-quality sensationalist reporting and relaxed ethical standards, eroding the reliability and integrity of journalism and diminishing public trust.[55]

The gradual repeal of the Fairness Doctrine and its progeny helped foster and reinforce these changes. Goaded by cable and satellite television networks challenging its applicability to their industries,[56] the Federal Communications Commission (FCC) repealed most of the Fairness Doctrine in 1987,[57] the rest of it in 2000,[58] and over eighty other regulations implementing the doctrine in 2011.[59] Emerging cable news outlets increasingly offered opinionated and partisan coverage;[60] cable audiences grew exponentially through the turn of the century.[61]

Around the time we entered in the new millennium, however, the internet revolutionized mass communication,[62] providing unprecedented exchanges of information and opinion globally.[63] However, it also quickly exacerbated disinformation[64] and became a new form of large-scale misinformation, offensive speech, and fraudulent activity.[65] Online deception—later coined "fake news"—permeated the web,[66] but online access soon became the preferred method of news consumption.[67] Higher-quality media outlets increasingly relied on paywalls for revenue instead of advertising,[68] further contributing to audience fragmentation and disinformation.

Meanwhile, smartphones became ubiquitous personal devices for consuming and sharing information,[69] outstripping desktop or laptop computer ownership.[70] Social media further accelerated the news cycle by allowing widespread news transmission in mere seconds with little, if any, verification.[71] Even though transmitted information might be misleading and extreme, large swaths of the population increasingly rely on it as a primary news source.[72] Constitutional limitations on the regulation of even false speech and deficient private regulation by media platforms[73] allowed disinformation to even outperform authentic news stories in user engagement and opportunities for virality.[74] Truths like anthropogenic climate change remained subject to public skepticism despite incontrovertible scientific evidence.[75] Newer technologies such as deep fakes, robotic speech bots,[76] and political imagery generated by artificial intelligence further ensured that the Contested Era remained as contentious as ever.

Even as several environmental problems increasingly became crises during the Contested Era, particularly the problems of climate change and biodiversity loss, the ability (and even the incentives) of the public to receive vital, accurate information rapidly declined.[77] Instead, climate change discussions increasingly became less focused on evaluating the scientific evidence of what was happening to the planet and instead turned into divisive political arguments regarding beliefs and opinion in which shared facts became increasing rare.[78] Some interests invested in the economic status quo particularly used this wedge as a way to obscure the work of scientists, draw doubt about the problem more generally, and obstruct and thwart legal action to address environmental harms.[79]

The second Trump administration took steps that exacerbated this situation a step further. Early in his term, Trump sought to dismantle longstanding sources of information, such as the National Public Radio and the Public Broadcasting Service.[80] His administration further sought to cut allocations for governmental agencies established by Congress to fund critical health and scientific research (including the National Science Foundation and National Institutes of Health), particularly targeting (among other things) climate research.[81] And it threatened to withhold or actually withheld funding for universities that it claimed were not complying with its aggressive interpretations of law.[82] In each of these cases, opponents challenged these actions through lawsuits.

NEGOTIATING WILDLIFE AND SPECIES

Throughout the era, endangered species regulation served as a flashpoint between conservationist and various development industries. For example, the ESA animated resistance by logging and farming interests over protection of endangered spotted owls and their diminishing ecosystems;[83] ranchers opposed to reintroduction of endangered gray wolves;[84] and energy producers and water users frustrated by endangered salmon conservation.[85] Although the ESA consistently maintained overwhelming public support during the Contested Era, it nonetheless is surprising that the statutory language itself remained largely unscathed given the political interests determined to weaken it.

To manage such contestation, policymakers and interested parties regularly found opportunities for collaboration and compromise. In 1982, for example, Congress enacted an amendment to the ESA that allowed for some projects that harmed endangered species in exchange for a permitting system ("incidental take permits") that gave the government power to set out conditions for such projects to proceed. As part of this new permitting system, the amendments included a seemingly innocuous provision that authorized habitat conservation plans (HCPs).[86] The HCP amendment was spurred by a pioneering collaborative planning effort in San Bruno, California, involving local governments, industry, and conservation groups all working to find ways to accommodate both species habitat and development.[87] Despite this amendment and the importance it played in resolving disputes in San Bruno, the government only approved a dozen HCPs over the next decade.

A decade later under the Clinton administration, HCPs flourished.[88] Sensing the potential for repeal of the law in the wake of the Contract with America wave in the mid-1990s, Clinton's Secretary of the Interior Babbitt leaned heavily on HCPs to refashion the ESA. He found HCPs could reduce political opposition to the ESA by providing those seeking permits more certainty[89] and flexibility,[90] while at the same time encouraging (but not requiring) a more collaborative regulator approach, sometimes involving multiple species, landowners, and local governments.[91] The W. Bush and Obama administrations followed suit and transformed the ESA from a strict roadblock[92] to a more pragmatic law able to find compromises balancing economic and conservation concerns. Environmental idealists, however, found Babbitt's attempt to find a middle ground to be nothing less than capitulation to those self-motivated to destroy valuable habitat for endangered species for private benefit.[93]

For the next several decades, the ESA remained very popular and proved successful at preventing extinctions. However, those administering the law still found themselves in the crosshairs of the Contested Era, facing legal challenges from conservationists (e.g., petitions forcing the government to list species)[94] and counterpressure from industry (e.g., convincing Congress to attach exemptions for projects as riders to general appropriation bills).[95] Indeed, using administrative regulations, the first Trump administration found ways to slash several key ESA provisions, including reducing threatened species protections, restricting the ability of agencies to consider climate change effects, making it easier to avoid or limit critical habitat designations, and requiring analysis of economic costs in listing decisions despite statutory prohibitions to consider such costs.[96] The Biden administration restored many of the ESA protections,[97] though it received criticism from more idealistic environmentalists for leaving some rollbacks intact.[98] The second Trump administration almost immediately drove clashes over the ESA into unchartered territory proposing to severely narrow down what constituted prohibited "harm" to a species listed under the ESA. For over thirty years, "harm" had been defined to include significant habitat modification, an interpretation upheld by the Supreme Court in part because of the ESA's goal of protecting ecosystems.[99] In 2025, however, the Trump administration proposed substantially narrowing "harm" to only direct acts injuring a listed animal,[100] a change which would massively reduce the ESA's biodiversity protections. Sixteen states' attorneys general immediately argued that the proposed rule plainly violates the ESA and Supreme Court precedent,[101] setting up an inevitable legal challenge.

ESA implementation thus exemplified the seesaw nature of the Contested Era while also serving as a conduit for compromise, preventing extinction and reducing direct effects on the most vulnerable species and their habitats. Nonetheless, the country faced an ever-growing biodiversity crisis, stoked by indirect effects like invasive species, habitat loss, and the accelerating effects of global climate change. As with many of the Environmental Era's statutes, these more indirect and profound threats raise substantial questions about the law's enduring efficacy and how to adapt or supplement it to address these more complex risks.[102]

SUCCESSES AND FAILURES IN AIR POLLUTION REGULATION

STRENGTHENING AND MODERATING THE CLEAN AIR ACT

The 1990 Clean Air Act Amendments in some ways came out of necessity, as additional problems related to air pollution came into focus. To address a growing hole in the ozone layer (which heightened skin cancer risks), the federal government had negotiated and joined an unprecedented global treaty requiring pollution reductions. The treaty's implementation in the United States required federal legislation.

It also required deft coalition building and statesmanship. Representative Henry Waxman (D-California), who represented a district especially concerned with air pollution problems, spearheaded a broad coalition of Congressmembers powerful enough to strengthen air pollution laws. Almost a decade earlier, President Reagan had worked with Representative John Dingell (D-Michigan), who represented a district concerned more with automobile manufacturing, to potentially gut the Clean Air Act. Not only did Waxman hold off Reagan and Dingell while Reagan occupied the White House, but also, once Reagan left office, Waxman built a strong enough coalition to entice Dingell to support the amendments Waxman crafted.[103] Senator Alan Simpson described Waxman in these efforts as "tougher than a boiled owl."[104]

With a much more environmentally interested President George H. W. Bush, Congress substantially strengthened air quality regulation in some ways and adjusted it in others in pragmatic response to concerns with prior implementation. Its automobile pollution regulation particularly targeted and enhanced the formulation of automobile gasoline. The amendments also created more detailed subclassifications for regions still struggling to meet national ambient air quality standards (tailoring compliance deadlines and stationary source restrictions to each subarea's status), and overhauled the hazardous air pollutant program to replace the ambitious and challenging-to-implement health-based standards with more pragmatic but less stringent technology-based standards.[105] Accordingly, the law was a combination of environmental idealism and pragmatism.

Despite the difficulty in passing meaningful environmental legislation in the Contested Era, the 1990 amendments also created two new programs to address novel air pollution problems. One of these focused on managing atmospheric ozone depletion and the second dealing with acid rain.[106] Each serves as a particularly useful illustration of the potential of using legal creativity and imagination to address important environmental problems, even during times of political gridlock.

Meaningfully Addressing Atmospheric Ozone

The atmospheric ozone reforms passed into law implemented internationally agreed upon controls to phase out ozone-depleting substances like chlorofluorocarbons (CFCs)—many of which originated from U.S. industry—which weakened the global ozone layer that protects the Earth from harmful solar radiation from the sun.[107] In 1987, the international community adopted the Montreal Protocol on Substances that Deplete the Ozone Layer that went into effect in 1989.[108] The Montreal Protocol was designed to protect the ozone layer by phasing out the production of substances that are responsible for ozone depletion. In brokering and signing the Montreal Protocol, the United States found itself a champion of the environment on the international stage.[109]

The accolades were warranted. The Montreal Protocol and the Clean Air Act revisions implementing it in the United States served as a remarkable achievement, addressing a critical problem through international technology-*forcing* regulation—deadlines for ozone-depleting chemicals to be phased out despite the absence of existing technological alternatives.[110] The Montreal Protocol was flexible though, providing a process for applications to delay compliance as well as adjustments that would allow signatories to vote to accelerate deadlines.[111] In addition, the agreement included an excise tax on ozone-depleting chemicals and a fund to assist developing countries.[112]

In the following decades, progress toward phase out was remarkably strong, with developed countries phasing out CFCs, the worst ozone-depleting chemicals, and developing countries close behind, with hydrochlorofluorocarbons (HCFCs) seen as medium-term alternatives and more-advanced hydrofluorocarbons (HFCs) (with no atmospheric ozone-depleting characteristics) the ultimate substitute. However, when scientists learned that HFCs were incredibly potent greenhouse gases that would contribute significantly to global warming, this potential harm was addressed in 2016 through the Kigali Amendment, which was eventually ratified by Congress in 2022.[113] As a result of its global ratification,[114] its success in phasing out ozone-depleting substances, and measurable reductions in the ozone hole,[115] many have called the Montreal Protocol the most successful international agreement in history.[116]

Meaningful Acid Rain Regulation

In addition to the Atmospheric Ozone program, in the 1990 Amendments to the Clean Air Act, Congress and President George H. W. Bush also found enough joint political will to create an innovative market mechanism (a cap-and-trade regulation) to curb a serious environmental problem at the time: acid rain.[117] Acid rain forms when sulfur dioxide and nitrogen oxides are released into the atmosphere, generally by coal-fired power plants, damaging aquatic life and sensitive forest areas.[118] The 1990 amendments first created a cap—an allocation of the total amount of potential emissions coming from power plants. The program initially focused on the 263 biggest power plants, and a few years later it expanded to include another 3,200 plants, though these smaller plants could opt-in earlier if they desired.[119] Once the cap for emissions was allocated to the electric utilities, they were "to trade allowances within the systems and/or buy or sell allowances to and from other affected sources."[120] Trading gave utilities the incentive to find the least expensive reductions possible and, since any additional reductions could be traded away, even rewarded them for doing more than was required. The acid deposition program was largely considered successful in addressing acid rain by reducing sulfur dioxide emissions from power plants across the country,[121] though some critics have argued that a more prescriptive approach would have been even more effective.[122] The program was effectively scrapped by 2012 and replaced with more traditional prescriptive regulation—not due to problems with the trading market but complexities introduced by a court case that severely hampered trading due to concerns of creating localized "hotspot" air quality problems, even as the regional air quality challenges improved.[123]

One major challenge of administering environmental statutes typified by the Clean Air Act was managing the complicated and increasingly technical nature of the march toward environmental progress. Sometimes this manifested in the difficulty to connect the public's environmental concerns with technical and scientific evaluation.[124] The public had a tough time deciphering complex risk analysis, while regulators struggled with how to integrate controversy and outrage into technocratic assessments. A second issue related to the difficulty and unintended consequences that resulted from the way the government measured compliance.

In a glaring example of this, in 2015, the EPA announced that Volkswagen deliberately programmed cars to run differently during EPA tests (performed on car-sized treadmills) than on the road to circumvent Clean Air Act emission standards.[125] The EPA and Volkswagen eventually resolved enforcement cases through three partial settlements,[126] which led to Volkswagen spending $25 billion on vehicle buybacks, repairs, extended warranties, and a large mitigation project.[127] Nonetheless, calculations of the human health impacts of the "defeat" devices predicted the excess emissions likely still caused fifty-nine premature deaths and $450 million in social costs over the sales period from 2008–2015.[128]

SEESAWING REGULATION TO CURTAIL AND ADDRESS THE EFFECTS OF CLIMATE CHANGE

Despite the fact that the Clean Air Act had successfully improved air quality by the measure of many regulated pollutants, we cannot overlook the fact that the United States (along with the rest of the world) failed during this era to adequately tackle the most weighty air pollution problem—climate change.[129] Anthropogenic climate change is largely a result of the global carbon economy, and the United States' culpability in spurring and fostering this economy. This is largely due to great political pressure resulting from its infrastructural lock-in on carbon-intensive industries and technologies. It represents one of the greatest hurdles for effecting change.[130] Still, some progress has been made—even if it only represents (at best) a start to what needs to be done. For the United States, however, every step it has taken during the Contested Era was frequently followed by at least some back tracking.

The United States' Role in International Climate Law

The first meaningful step for the world came in 1988, when the United Nations created the Intergovernmental Panel on Climate Change (IPCC) to provide objective, scientific data on the global trend.[131] The initial work done by the IPCC was the basis for the 1992 United Nations Framework Convention on Climate Change (UNFCCC), which committed countries to reduce their greenhouse gas emissions in recognition of the fact that these human-generated emissions have substantially caused global climate disruption.[132] The UNFCCC also provided an international mechanism to revisit climate change and make subsequent climate agreements.

The Kyoto Protocol was the first meaningful agreement from this framework.[133] It called for an international cap-and-trade program, mainly aimed at countries with more developed economies.[134] Though initially adopted in 1997, it did not come into force until 2005, when the required number of countries to sign on had done so.[135]

Yet the Kyoto Protocol never became law in the United States. The United States delegation led by Vice President Al Gore played a key role in negotiations, and Gore signed it at the end of the meetings. But in the months leading up to the Kyoto meetings, the U.S. Senate passed a resolution unanimously directing climate negotiators that the United States would not participate in any treaty unless developing countries like China and India were bound to reduce greenhouse gas emissions.[136] Because the agreement conflicted with the Senate's resolution, President Bill Clinton opted not to even send the Kyoto Protocol to the Senate for ratification.[137] President George W. Bush went further, withdrawing the United States from Gore's signing of the Accord.[138] Despite public support for participation (catalyzed by ongoing efforts by former Vice President Gore[139] and other activists like Greta Thunberg[140]), the U.S. government remained stagnant on climate change—even if a number of states took steps to address it.[141]

The tides shifted in 2016, as the United States joined 194 other nations (including India and China) to sign the Paris Climate Accords, an agreement to mitigate greenhouse gas emissions, and help (especially developing nations) adapt to climate effects.[142] The agreement was carefully designed by the Obama administration to avoid new commitments that would necessitate Senate ratification.[143] Each signatory was to make voluntary cuts to emissions based on their own reduction goals rather than reciprocal commitments. While it has no enforcement mechanism other than disclosure of noncompliance, many countries (including the United States) made progress toward meeting their commitments, even if global efforts continue to fall short.[144] The Obama administration sought to meet its commitments through adoption of a Clean Power Plan, regulation of auto emissions through the Clean Air Act, state and local government actions, and voluntary reductions by industry.[145]

However, the voluntary nature of the Paris Accord made it particularly vulnerable to backsliding. After President Trump was elected, he ordered the federal government to cease all efforts to implement the Paris Climate Accord.[146] Yet this backtracking was also temporary, as President Biden accepted the Paris Climate Accord and restored the nation's active role in addressing climate change on his first day in office.[147] Even as President Biden pledged to move the climate agenda forward, he did not lean as heavily on the Clean Air Act to get the job done. President Trump, during his second term, again walked away from the Paris Accord, and any other commitment to address climate change through international law (or otherwise).[148]

Domestic Climate Change Law

More durable but slow climate progress for the United States occurred at the domestic level. Similarly, domestic climate change public regulation in the United States took decades to begin, and even then, was still subject to the vagaries of political change. In the face of federal inaction, some states, most notably California as well as a consortium of northeastern states, adopted major climate change regulation seeking to both mitigate greenhouse gases and develop adaptation planning.[149] All this happened as federal action under the Reagan, Bush, Clinton, and the W. Bush administrations had remained minimal, even if tangential and marginal policies (such as the passage of a renewable energy tax credit)[150] sporadically made it across the line.

In a story arc that fits well within the Contested Era, federal inaction also resulted in extensive litigation. A significant effort had been made to appeal to state and federal courts to push for government regulation or seek recovery from energy industries for harms caused from their contributions to climate change or complicity in governmental inaction.[151] Plaintiffs used a creative range of common law and statutory doctrines, including those around since the nation's founding.[152] Some cases, such as *American Electric Power v. Connecticut*,[153] reinforced significant hurdles of bringing these cases, particularly in federal court.[154] Yet a number of these cases, especially at the state level, seemingly broke through some old barriers by obtaining key victories on preliminary issues on the validity of their claims.[155]

Perhaps the most important judicial decision was the landmark ruling by the Supreme Court, *Massachusetts v. EPA*,[156] interpreting the extent to which the Clean Air Act could be used to combat climate change. By deciding that greenhouse gas emissions qualified as "air pollutants" under the Clean Air Act, the Court determined that the EPA had to decide whether and how to regulate them.[157]

What followed for the next fifteen years was a sharp ebb and flow in federal climate policy tied to presidential administrations. Congress undoubtedly relinquished the United States' longstanding position as global environmental leader by failing to act as boldly as other nations.[158] The W. Bush administration dragged its feet to comply with the Supreme Court's ruling in *Massachusetts v. EPA*. While failing to push new legislation through Congress, President Obama's EPA sought to address climate change by leveraging the Clean Air Act to regulate greenhouse gases from cars,[159] trucks and buses,[160] new power plants,[161] and, through the Clean Power Plan, existing power plants, the single largest source of carbon pollution in the United States.[162] President Trump reversed many of these regulatory changes, repealing the Clean Power Plan[163] and limiting the power of states to adopt more stringent auto tailpipe emissions standards.[164]

In his first week in office, however, President Biden adopted Executive Order 14008, which put "the climate crisis at the center of United States foreign policy and national security."[165] The administration pushed the federal government itself to reduce its carbon footprint, be more climate resilient, and be better prepared for climate change.[166] In 2022, the EPA reinstated the power of states to adopt more stringent auto standards under the Clean Air Act.[167] At the same time, the Supreme Court ruled in *West Virginia v. EPA* that the Clean Air Act did not provide the EPA authority to implement the Clean Power Plan.[168] In doing so, the Court determined that had Congress even arguably intended such a dramatic use of the Clean Air Act, it would have expressly addressed such a major question in the statute. Although greenhouse gas regulation continued through other provisions of the Clean Air Act, *West Virginia* certainly raised doubts on the legal viability of aggressive interpretations of the statute to combat climate change.

The Biden administration began to pursue other avenues. Most significantly, for the first time for any president, the Biden administration found Congress a willing partner in furthering a climate-focused agenda. The Infrastructure Investment and Jobs Act (IIJA), Biden's signature infrastructure bill, provided funding for transportation to reduce auto emissions (including alternative fuels like hydrogen and battery production) and upgrading infrastructure to be more resilient against climate change.[169] Building on this, Congress passed the Inflation Reduction Act of 2022 (IRA),[170] perhaps "the most significant climate legislation in U.S. history," including unprecedented levels of funds and incentives to advance a clean energy economy.[171] While also providing resources to the EPA to combat climate change, the IRA primarily used tax policy to encourage renewable energy development, energy efficiency, sale of zero emission vehicles, continued use of nuclear power plants, domestic clean energy manufacturing, along with emerging technologies including green hydrogen and carbon capture at industrial sources.[172]

Upon President Trump's return to office, the administration froze funds that the Biden administration had yet to fully deliver to intended beneficiaries of the IIJA and IRA.[173] This resulted in a barrage of lawsuits that were somewhat successful in shaking loose this funding.[174]

The Trump administration also worked to claw back virtually all funding on climate research, mitigation, or adaptation, or seeking to promote renewable energy, including grants awarded under programs sponsored by the National Science Foundation and the Department of Energy.[175] Some of these efforts received legislative ratification via one of the only bills to make it through Congress in 2025.[176] Yet undoubtedly the Trump administration's most audacious and dangerous initiative to rollback climate action was to initiate regulatory actions seeking to reverse EPA's core finding back in 2009 that greenhouse gases endanger public health and welfare.[177] If finalized and upheld, such an action would effectively eliminate EPA's ability to regulate greenhouse gases under the Clean Air Act.[178]

Each of these attempts to dismantle previous legal efforts to address climate change met stiff political and legal resistance. Some were business interests concerned about economic or legal instability or otherwise invested in climate solutions.[179] Others were youth environmental movements increasingly distraught or incensed by willful inaction despite increasingly conclusive scientific evidence.[180] Some of the more radical protest strategies were countered by government violence and criminalization initiatives goaded if not spearheaded by the fossil fuel industry.[181]

FOSSIL FUEL PRODUCTION AND SPILLS, LEGISLATIVE REPAIRS, AND PROTESTS

America's addiction to oil—a primary driver of the country's contribution to global greenhouse gases—played out in two related narratives during the Contested Era. The first involved continued attempts, especially but not exclusively by proindustry administrations, to use law and governmental policy to accelerate fossil fuel development. The Reagan administration, for example, reversed much of the Carter administration's energy policy measures, including by deregulating the domestic oil and gas market in an effort to increase fossil fuel production.[182] The George W. Bush administration expanded the supply of natural gas, making the nation even more dependent on natural gas than it had been on oil.[183] Under both the first and second Trump administrations' "energy dominance" policy, the United States ramped up its oil production and sought to reduce regulation.[184] Trump started his second term, in fact, attempting to declare an "energy emergency" seeking to expedite any energy projects that were not focused on renewable energy.[185] Though perhaps more measured, Democratic administrations were far from immune from efforts to promote fossil fuel development.[186] Obviously, neither of the parties were monoliths on this or other issues—Republican Senator Richard Lugar of Indiana, for example, warned his colleagues about the risks of associated with the nation's addiction to oil.[187]

These persistent efforts to develop fossil fuels have met intermittent resistance, with mixed results. For instance, the proposed development of a cascade of transcontinental pipelines for transporting fossil fuels have galvanized large-scale protests, most notably involving the Dakota Access Oil Pipeline and the Keystone XL Pipeline,[188] which not only rallied environmentalists from around the country but provided Native American environmental leaders a national platform to articulate the incongruity of U.S. natural resources law with Indigenous epistemologies that offer a different conception of the relationship between humans and the non-human world.[189] Some pipelines like the Dakota Access were completed despite massive demonstrations for months on Lakota lands on and near the Standing Rock Sioux Indian Reservation in North Dakota.[190] Others like Keystone XL were canceled after substantial protest.[191] Yet oil production, at times, has ramped up even when facing longstanding opposition. In 2017, the Senate attached a provision to a vital budget bill that authorized oil production in the Arctic National Wildlife Reserve (ANWR),[192] a controversial proposal first raised in the 1980s[193] and a mainstay in energy policy debates.[194]

The second, unfortunately predictable, narrative has been the pollution and oil-soaked waves caused by unrelenting industrial production; the consequent oil spill disasters; and the limited legal responses to compensate, remediate, and prevent future such pollution. On March 24, 1989, the *Exxon Valdez* spilled eleven million gallons of crude oil into

Figure 5.1 Protestors rally against the Dakota Access Pipeline in Washington, D.C., on March 10, 2017.

Alaska's Prince William Sound.[195] Exxon was eventually fined around $1 billion.[196] The spill spurred the adoption of the Oil Pollution Act (OPA).[197] The OPA sought to streamline and strengthen the EPA's ability to prevent and respond to catastrophic oil spills.[198] It created a trust fund financed by a tax on oil to help pay for the cleanup of spills when responsible parties are not willing or able to do so.[199] OPA began requiring oil storage facilities and vessels to submit to the federal government plans detailing how they will respond to large discharges.[200]

Congress designed the OPA to streamline and strengthen the EPA's ability to prevent and respond to catastrophic oil spills. However, corporate and regulatory laxity[201] ensured that a later spill in the Gulf of Mexico eclipsed all other environmental disasters in the country.[202] British Petroleum and its partners, as well as the federal government, all proved completely ineffective to stop the Deepwater Horizon spill for weeks. Still, based in significant part on OPA's force, litigation followed, a compensation fund was established, and the federal government declared a moratorium on ocean oil production while

Figure 5.2 BP Deepwater Horizon oil spill, 2010.

it reassessed the risks of such development.[203] These actions spurred vocal protests from oil workers and local government leaders off the coast of Louisiana who voiced concerns about economic hardship caused first by the spill and then compounded by the moratorium.[204]

COAL, FRACKING, AND RENEWABLES: SHIFTING ENERGY MARKETS AND POLICY

While coal-fired energy dominated energy production for almost a century, natural gas's importance skyrocketed during the Contested Era.[205] Technological advances in fracking during the 2000s made natural gas production substantially more competitive.[206] The fracking boom made natural gas much more affordable while resulting in a wide range of environmental harms.[207] In the absence of federal and state public laws sufficient to prevent or mitigate harms, landowners across the nation resorted to the time-honored strategy of pursuing state common law tort litigation.[208] These fracking cases sought redress for an array of harms, including water contamination and subsurface trespass, air contamination and pollution, and property damage tied to waste injection.[209] In response to the limitations of common law strategies—including their focus on largely private disputes, remedying rather than preventing harm, limited judicial technical expertise, and unpredictability—public regulations across the nation began to emerge. States adopted and expanded regulations through legislation.[210] Such state regulations varied greatly in how they addressed critical questions, ranging from choices about regulatory bodies for oversight to regulations related to fracking fluids.[211] At the federal level, in response to a lawsuit alleging failure to address fracking harms, the EPA adopted regulations in 2012 to decrease smog-forming volatile organic compounds created from fracking,[212] with more extensive state[213] and federal regulations adopted later.[214] Much of the politics surrounding energy production across the spectrum included an "all of the above" mentality, embracing all sorts of energy production even if particular decision makers would put a finger on the scale for certain types of energy from time to time.

Meanwhile, outdated and largely dirtier coal-fired plants became increasingly less competitive, and newer coal plants became unviable for new energy development.[215] During this time, the coal industry limped along, but many coal-fired plants still shuttered,[216] even as both the Trump administrations used executive authority to try to prop up coal (such as attempting to rollback Obama's Clean Power Plan and coal mining moratorium on public lands).[217] Nevertheless, the gas boom propelled the United States to be a net energy exporter.

While Congress and a number of states boosted renewable energy by adopting tax subsidies, energy portfolio standards, and marketing green energy to end users, a real breakthrough occurred as technological changes began making renewable energy cheaper.[218] Even into the 2020s, renewable energy did not occupy a large percentage of energy produced.[219] However, renewables came to represent a significant growth area in the energy market,[220] and—in no small part due to the increased affordability of green energy—policymakers increasingly added mandates to the substantial incentives for the development of renewable energy infrastructure. As the prices of renewables decreased, renewable energy not only boomed in places like California, which had plenty of sun for solar energy along with supportive policies, but also places without regulations and policy supports, allowing the comparatively unregulated State of Texas to become the leading state for renewable energy.

Meanwhile, Congress had adopted piecemeal energy legislation over the decades, but the United States continued to lack a comprehensive energy policy. In 1992, the EPA and the Department of Energy launched the Energy Star program to promote energy-efficient products and practices.[221] Energy Star was subsequently adopted by international partner countries of Canada, Japan, Switzerland, and Taiwan.[222] In 1992, the Energy Policy Act created a framework for a competitive wholesale electricity generation market.[223] It also made it easier for nonutility producers to enter the wholesale electricity market and revised energy reduction goals and performance requirements for federal buildings, including a timetable for reduced energy consumption. Finally, the Energy Policy Act of 2005 provided incentives to produce greener energy by "provid[ing] loan guarantees for entities that develop or use innovative technologies that avoid the by-production of greenhouse gases" and "increas[ing] the amount of biofuel that must be mixed with gasoline sold in the United States."[224]

INDUSTRIAL CONTROLS, NONPOINT POLLUTION, AND "WATERS OF THE UNITED STATES"

Despite the push and pull, in the Contested Era, the Clean Water Act (CWA) proved to be very effective in getting a handle on the most harmful water pollutants from industry.[225] In a talk commemorating the fortieth anniversary of the CWA and its achievements, Bill Ruckelshaus, who was appointed by President Nixon as the first Administrator of the EPA, where he oversaw the initial implementation of the CWA, quipped that while the nation's waters were not all "fishable" or "swimmable," as required by the CWA, at least they were no longer "flammable."[226]

The era also saw bipartisan actions involving public drinking water. In 1986, President Reagan signed the Safe Drinking Water Act (SDWA) Amendments.[227] By 1991, just five years after passage, the SDWA audaciously required the EPA to regulate more than one hundred pollutants and expanded EPA enforcement power.[228] The legislation also banned the use of lead materials in water systems and called for tighter regulation of drinking water wells. A decade later, President Clinton signed additional SDWA Amendments and increased water quality protections for public drinking water systems.[229] The law made funding available to upgrade water treatment plants and requires public drinking water suppliers to inform customers about chemicals and microbes in their water.[230]

Despite the meaningful improvements in many water systems, the goal of adequate drinking water in every municipal system was certainly far from realized. The harshest example of this arrived in 2014 in Flint, Michigan, when, in an act of gross negligence, the city switched its drinking water source to the Flint River. Due to its elevated levels of chloride, this resulted in dangerous corrosion of the city's lead pipes, a public health emergency, and criminal action against the responsible public officials.[231]

As Flint reminds us, even after making significant progress in cleaning up the aquatic environment, much was left to be done.[232] Addressing this pollution challenge presented a complex range of sources of pollution, some outside of regulatory reach.[233] While this is true of drinking water infrastructure and safety, this is even more pressing for what became known as "nonpoint pollution"—initially exempted from the Clean Water Act's "point source" regulations—like farm and urban runoff.[234] The Water Quality Act of 1987 amended the CWA for the first time to authorize measures to address such pollution by directing states to develop and implement nonpoint pollution management programs.[235] Still, through financial incentives, stormwater pollution reduction programs, and increased regulatory and citizen-suit attention to particularly impaired water bodies (the Total Maximum Daily Load program), the EPA and the states began to make inroads in managing nonpoint source pollution.[236] Yet nonpoint source pollution remains a substantial problem.

Perhaps no better illustration of the ebb and flow of environmental law during the Contested Era can be found than the decades-long drama surrounding the interpretation of the phrase "waters of the United States," an important term in establishing the regulatory reach of Clean Water Act programs.[237] For decades, administrations pushed in different directions, undoing and redoing what had gone before them.[238] The Supreme Court, meanwhile, stepped in periodically and increased uncertainty.

The latest versions of this involved back and forth between the Obama, Trump, and Biden administrations, followed by another intervention by the Supreme Court. In 2015, the Obama EPA adopted the Clean Water Rule to protect critical streams and wetlands by ensuring that waters protected under the Clean Water Act were more precisely defined and predictably determined.[239] But in 2017, Trump's EPA and Army Corps of Engineers proposed rules to rescind the Obama-era rule and redefine the phrase "waters of the United States."[240] In 2019, the Trump EPA finalized this repeal,[241] and in 2020 narrowed the definition with the Navigable Waters Protection Rule.[242] When the Biden administration took over, it repealed the Trump administration's effort[243] and in 2021 proposed a new definition.[244] States and interest groups brought litigation, while others took different sides and pressed different actions taken by different administrations.[245] In 2023, the Supreme Court unanimously overturned the Biden administration's determination that wetlands on a couple's property were "waters of the United States."[246] The Court sharply reduced federal authority over wetlands to only protect those that have "a continuous surface connection" with "a relatively permanent body of water connected to traditional interstate navigable waters."[247] The EPA promulgated regulations to conform its interpretation to the Court's decision,[248] but industry advocates challenged these regulations as well.[249] The constraints the Court put on the reach of "waters of the United States" has left large swathes of wetlands traditionally protected by the Clean Water Act seemingly outside of the reach of the statute.[250] With an ossified Congress for decades failing to clarify the statute's language, the second Trump administration's EPA and environmental organizations continued the fight in court to clarify the full scope of waters subject to federal authority.

THE ENVIRONMENTAL JUSTICE MOVEMENT

After centuries of environmental inequalities, the Contested Era saw the full blossoming of a movement focused on the disproportionate effects of pollution on disadvantaged populations and communities of color.[251] In the 1980s, communities of color began fighting siting decisions of particularly undesirable land uses, such as hazardous waste treatment facilities.[252] Government[253] and private[254] studies showed a strong correlation between the location of toxic waste dump sites and the location of minority communities.

The environmental justice movement grew out of the activism of individuals, communities, and community organizations (particularly churches).[255] In 1982, a predominantly poor, African American community developed a grassroots campaign in Warren County, North Carolina to protest a polychlorinated biphenyl landfill, seeking fair treatment and meaningful involvement in public environmental regulatory decisions.[256] Civil rights protesters stood side-by-side with environmental activists to decry both the effect such decisions have on minority communities and the racial bias that cause minority communities to be targeted for these unpopular facilities.[257]

Despite government recognition of the problem during the Clinton administration, progress through the legal system was limited. For example, in 1992, an EPA report revealed that those populations were exposed more than others to air pollution and other environmental hazards.[258] In 1994, President Clinton issued an executive order that all federal agencies prioritize environmental justice for minorities and low-income populations to the greatest extent practicable and permitted by law.[259] However, after a number of lawsuits rooted primarily in civil rights law were unsuccessful, it became clear to many that the most effective tools of the movement were those related to political organizing,[260] bolstered by the processes, disclosure, and public scrutiny called for by procedural statues like the National Environmental Policy Act.[261] For the next three decades, however, these various tools only provided at best limited success.

While litigants struggled to find a foothold in securing legal tools that advanced environmental justice by relying on existing legal frameworks, in 2021, the Biden administration made environmental justice a key focus of its administration.[262] Within days of taking office, Executive Order 14008 proposed a "Justice40 Initiative," with the ambitious goal for the federal government of ensuring that "40 percent of the overall benefits of certain Federal investments flow to disadvantaged communities that are marginalized, underserved, and overburdened by pollution."[263] The President also established the White House Environmental Justice Advisory Council,[264] an Office of Environmental Justice, and a comprehensive environmental justice enforcement strategy by the Justice Department.[265] The Department of Energy also adopted programs designed to help disadvantaged communities.[266] In 2023, Executive Order 14096 expanded the definition of "environmental justice" to encompass more affected communities including those with tribal affiliations and disabilities.[267] Most importantly, primarily relying on funds from the IRA and IIJA, the Biden administration made the largest single investment in environmental justice that the country has had thus far.[268]

The Trump administration, in turn, quickly went to work to undo as many efforts as possible focused on environmental justice. During his first week back in office during his second term, President Trump issued an executive order targeting a wide range of civil rights and other diversity, equity, and inclusion programs, including those related to environmental justice.[269] Perhaps the executive order's most draconian provision involved something even Trump did not consider proper during his first term: rescission of the foundational 1994 Clinton executive order that for decades had integrated environmental justice into federal agency decision making. The administration then moved ahead with efforts to fire employees working on environmental justice and close programs and offices focused on them.[270]

CELEBRATION AND PUSHBACK OVER NATURAL RESOURCES LAW

Turbulence was also the dominant theme in public lands management. Highlighting the durability of legal institutions, an 1870s mining law[271] and a 1930s grazing law[272] continued to serve as the primary mechanisms for controlling resource allocation decisions on federal lands, even as the U.S. population became less rooted economically in mining and agriculture and increasingly valued recreational uses. While many rural areas outside of tourist hubs faced substantial economic and population decline, gateway communities surrounding public lands (like Jackson Hole, Wyoming; Gatlinburg, Tennessee; Moab, Utah; and Bar Harbor, Maine) steadily grew due to increasing demand for tourism and recreation. Burgeoning telecommuting allowed some to leverage perceived quality of life linked to proximity to public lands. These factors created a new local constituency dedicated to pressing federal managers for increased recreational access and protections from extractive industries.[273] Recreational and environmental interests expressed frustration that public lands law was stuck in the nineteenth century and failed to address these modern needs and realities.[274] The steady increase to over 111 million acres of designated federal wilderness lands represented the biggest shift of federal lands management toward natural preservation, but most of these lands were not readily accessible to resource extractors prior to their designation anyway.[275]

Even as environmental interests complained of slow progress, longstanding resource users, given voice by those like James Watt, felt under siege by modest inroads made by environmental interests.[276] This set off enormous pushback in many areas with a history of relying on public lands for resource extraction. This conflict boiled over as Cliven Bundy and other "Sagebrush Rebels" staged a demonstration of wills and armed resistance, first in Nevada and later in Oregon, and openly flaunted the federal government's authority to manage public lands.[277]

Probably the biggest changes to land management that seemed to interfere with prospective resource extraction came in the form of national monument designations by presidents invoking the Antiquities Act.[278] Most notably, this includes the designation of two monuments in Utah—Grand Staircase–Escalante Monument by President Clinton[279] and Bears Ears Monument by President Obama.[280] Responding to those who opposed changing public lands management to further environmental and recreational values, President Trump dramatically shrank both monuments.[281] President Biden later restored both Utah monuments to their original sizes[282] and designated the nearby Baaj Nwaavjo I'tah Kukveni–Ancestral Footprints of the Grand Canyon National Monument,[283] advancing his administration's goal to conserve 30 percent of United States lands and waters by 2030.[284] The second Trump administration continued to target national monuments and these three particularly. More radically, Trump's Department of Justice purported to overrule a legal interpretation in place since 1938, asserting that it is within presidential authority to revoke or reduce previous monument designations.[285]

LAND POLLUTION LEGAL DEVELOPMENTS

Although hazardous waste cleanup and prevention on land during this Era at times was also the subject of contest and turbulence, it is notable that Congress and Presidents from both political parties were more willing to support and adjust these laws to reduce risks and promote cleanup of hazardous substances. At the dawn of the Contested Era, the EPA would need to immediately begin to implement the Comprehensive Environmental Response, Compensation, and Liability Act (CERCLA) enacted by Congress in 1980. This was the "Superfund" law, which aimed at cleaning up the many existing sites polluted by toxic waste. While implementation had a rocky start, CERCLA (along with several supporting pieces of legislation passed during the era) resulted in vital, though sometimes controversial, cleanup of some of the worst toxic waste sites in the United States.

The first few years of CERCLA necessarily focused by Congressional design on identifying potential contaminated sites, assessing risks associated with the sites, and then creating the National Priority List of sites to prioritize federal remediation action.[286] EPA Administrator Anne Gorsuch complicated that work by cutting the EPA's budget, allowing misappropriation of CERCLA funding, and undermining CERCLA enforcement.[287] After a few turbulent years, however, the EPA turned to accomplishing the work envisioned by CERCLA, even if those facing litigation or orders to clean up or pay for Superfund sites attempted to stall and resist any responsibility.

In 1986, following a growing realization in Congress that the hazardous waste problem was far more substantial than initially believed, Congress passed and President Reagan signed the Superfund Amendments and Reauthorization Act (SARA).[288] SARA increased funding for cleanups by more than five times what was provided originally under CERCLA,[289] prioritized permanent remedies for cleanup,[290] and increased the ability of states and interested citizens to participate in and monitor cleanup decisions made under CERCLA.[291]

Through the 2000s, the EPA made progress in securing site cleanups, even if the work in reaching the finish line was by its nature slow going, and political resistance of those facing cleanup costs was ever present. Under the Clinton administration in the 1990s, the EPA started its Brownfields Program, which provided investment and focus on cleaning up abandoned, contaminated sites and returning them to productive community use.[292] This resulted in almost three thousand cleanups of contaminated sites since the program began.[293] However, facing resistance from manufacturers of toxic products and others forced to pay the Superfund tax, Congress allowed Superfund taxes to expire.[294] Direct appropriations from Congress also diminished, leaving the only continued source of funding those monies paid by parties found liable under CERCLA. This reduction in funding led to years of delays in CERCLA remediation.[295] Nonetheless, the EPA continued to prioritize cleanups of sites on the National Priority List, and almost five hundred of these sites have been cleaned up.[296]

Decades after their expiration, Congress and the Biden administration reinstated two Superfund taxes—a chemical excise tax through the IIJA[297] and an oil and petroleum product tax through the IRA.[298] Consistent with the administration's efforts in other environmental law subfields, this period saw a heightened focus by the EPA on environmental justice and community engagement in CERCLA cleanup efforts.[299] Beyond actions of the federal government, increasingly CERCLA suits brought by private parties (whether voluntary or required by EPA order) have addressed many more sites not on the list.[300]

Congressional enactments also strengthened toxic waste management. For example, in 1982, President Ronald Reagan signed the Nuclear Waste Policy Act, which focused on safe storage and disposal of nuclear waste.[301] It established procedures to develop, evaluate, and select sites for the disposal of high-level radioactive waste and spent nuclear fuel.[302] The statute also established a program of research, development, and demonstration regarding the disposal of high-level radioactive waste and spent nuclear fuel.[303]

The inability of the federal government to secure a safe site for long-term storage of nuclear waste during the era represented a major failure of hazardous waste management. Though Congress approved the Yucca Mountain Nuclear Waste Repository in Nevada in 2002, Congress ended federal funding for it in 2011[304] due to substantial resistance from Nevadan policymakers and communities.[305]

In 1984, amendments to the Resource Conservation and Recovery Act (RCRA) established requirements governing generators, transporters, and disposers of small quantities of hazardous wastes who had generally not been subject to full regulation under RCRA.[306] It also mandated that land disposal of hazardous waste must be banned unless the EPA determines that the prohibition of such disposal is not necessary to protect human health and the environment.[307] In many ways, RCRA and these amendments in particular helped reduce the prospect of additional toxic waste sites needing remediation under CERCLA going forward.

In 1986, Congress declared the public has a right to know when toxic chemicals that are released into the air, land, and water through Emergency Planning and Community Right-to-Know Act (EPCRA).[308] Its purpose was to encourage and support emergency planning efforts at the state and local levels and to provide the public and local governments with information concerning potential chemical hazards present in their communities.[309] In 1990, the EPA inaugurated the Toxic Release Inventory, which was created to tell the public which pollutants are being released from specific facilities in their communities.[310]

PRODUCT REGULATION DEVELOPMENTS

The Contested Era experienced substantial globalization and thus the expansion of worldwide markets, with the accompanying exportation and compounding of environmental problems around the world. Several statutes were enacted that sought to address some of the effects on products domestically.

As was often the case, California took the lead in innovative approaches to product regulation. The Safe Drinking Water and Toxic Enforcement Act of 1986, commonly referred to as "Prop. 65," passed in California by direct voter ballot proposition initiative in 1986.[311] Prop. 65's most noteworthy regulatory innovation required any business that exposes others to a carcinogenic or a reproductive toxicant to provide a "clear and reasonable warning."[312] By targeting products rather than proposed agency actions, Prop. 65 was fundamentally different than the National Environmental Policy Act. Yet its fundamental strategy was quite similar: Both relied on the disclosure of information, rather than prescriptive rules, to educate regulated entities, regulators, and the public (in this case, consumers) about the potential risks to health and the environment. While popular among environmentalists and industry alike, assessments of the effectiveness of disclosure regulation in the succeeding decades vary.[313]

In 1996, Congress unanimously passed, and President Bill Clinton signed the Food Quality Protection Act, amending the Federal Insecticide, Fungicide, and Rodenticide Act (FIFRA) and the Federal Food Drug and Cosmetic Act (FFDCA).[314] The law tightened standards for pesticides used to grow food, with particular attention to ensuring that foods were safe for children to eat.[315] Twenty years later, Congress passed the Global Food Security Act, which requires the President to develop and implement a Global Food Security Strategy to promote global food security, resilience, and nutrition.[316]

In an increasingly rare bipartisan effort, in 2016, President Obama signed the Lautenberg Chemical Safety for the 21st Century Act.[317] The law amended the Toxic Substances Control Act (TSCA), the nation's primary chemicals management law, and required the EPA to evaluate existing chemicals with clear and enforceable deadlines.[318] TSCA continued to require premanufacture notifications for "new chemical substances," testing of chemicals when risks or exposures of concern are determined, and compliance with certification reporting for importing and exporting chemicals listed in the TSCA Inventory.[319] Despite the fanfare, however, the years that followed indicate the amendments insufficiently addressed the many problems with TSCA. The Act continued to place the burden of obtaining the necessary data to evaluate chemicals on the EPA rather than manufacturers.[320] This burden, combined with allocating authority to the EPA over many critical implementation decisions (and preempting certain state actions), as well as very limited resources dedicated to address the massive backlog of assessments, ensured toxic product regulation remains very slow.[321]

* * *

While the foundations of environmental law were largely established earlier, the Contested Era witnessed the indelible role that law can play in repairing and preventing harm to the environment and public health—as well as its limitations so far. Modern environmental law immediately and resolutely tackled many of the lowest hanging fruits of environmental harms, maturing as it was implemented and tested by private litigants as well as federal and state administrations. While the era saw considerable growth in population and wealth, environmental law—particularly the laws passed during the Environmental Era—resulted in considerable improvements in environment and public health by many measures. Nonetheless, many challenges remained inadequately addressed. Typically, these are the issues that are practically, legally, and politically the most complex and critical to address—such as environmental justice, indirect pollution, biodiversity loss, and climate change. However, as illustrated by the substantial gains in air quality during this Era, government has the capacity to overcome complexity when sufficient political will materialized.

Decades into the era, the complexity of environmental problems has combined with increasingly specialized knowledge to change the landscape of environmental governance. Addressing environmental problems requires scientific data, and such knowledge is increasingly sophisticated and robust. However, this often had the unintended consequence of creating a scientific paywall in front of conversations about values and ethics. While public participation became fundamental, technocracy also provided an inside track to sophisticated actors like industry and conservation organizations. Not only has this left ordinary people with limited opportunity to engage in meaningful ways; it also too often tempered passion that used to fundamentally animate the protection of environmental and human health. Relatedly, intensifying partisanship precipitated increased gridlock and incrementalism.

The second Trump administration threw the Contested Era's disputation to a level never witnessed before. Taking a more aggressive interpretation of executive power than any U.S. president had ever offered, it issued a deluge of executive orders purporting to dismantle statutory programs. It delegated authority to slash administrative funding and personnel to private individuals outside the conventionally understood separation of constitutional powers. It advanced regulations that, if upheld by the courts, would require less public participation in agency decision making and weaken environmental statutes that served as the bedrock of environmental law for half of a century. It waged attacks on private law firms and nongovernmental legal institutions. And, as described earlier, it slashed funding of both agencies and universities dedicated to engaging in scientific research, particularly targeting public health and environmental research.

Yet that, of course, is not immutable. It remains unclear for now how long the Contested Era will last (or even if we have entered a new era. What seems evident is that the closing and beginning of eras in environmental law have been shaped by political, social, and economic movements; technological change; and, perhaps most importantly, the dawning of a new legal consciousness and imagination. Scholars, activists, students, and policymakers interested in addressing environmental problems must be ready if or when incremental or transformational opportunities develop for addressing the environmental problems that have become increasing fraught and tangled during the Contested Era. The question is, of course, how? The Conclusion, which follows, tries to provide some answers, based in part on the lessons from the past.

CONCLUSION

LOOKING BACK AND MOVING FORWARD

The story of U.S. law and the environment weaves together numerous contrasts, competitions, overlaps, movements, and tensions. It is one of exploitation and temperance. Of excess and forbearance. Of destruction and restoration. Of resistance and adaptation. Taken together, the many intersecting narratives provide vital lessons for a nation, and even a world, navigating today's pressing environmental challenges.

THE CENTRALITY OF LAW TO ENVIRONMENTAL HISTORY

Even before the Founders established the United States of America, the law often directed humanity's relationship and served as the core engine of environmental protection and degradation. To be sure, law was not singular in its influence—social, economic, political, philosophical, and scientific developments have each shaped our environmental history. Still, it is the law that most directly promoted development and exploitation, rearranged people's relationship with the environment in the eras of major environmental lawmaking, and mediated different objectives in more dormant times of implementation and contestation.

Legal infrastructure has served and likely will serve as *the* fundamental building block in the societal reckoning in relation to environmental harm. At times, the law enabled the exploitation of peoples and resources. In others, laws directly facilitated prevention, abatement, mitigation, or even repair of such harm—sometimes even emerging when legal development may have seemed unlikely.

Despite differences between the past and the present, we can learn from our past—both in its times of progress and in times of unheeded warnings. Looking back, we can see the law's potential and limitations. Indeed, despite an imperfect fit with today's context, the stakes of current environmental challenges compel a careful review.

THE BREADTH OF LAW AFFECTING THE ENVIRONMENT

First, descriptively, history shows that the law's impact on the environment extends well beyond the boundaries typically assumed and discussed. Environmental law is commonly understood to focus on public pollution control law and natural resources law. However, the reach of law affecting the environment is much broader. A core motivation for the book was our surprise that no prior book on the history of environmental law had taken this broader view, with most focusing on environmental protections that have grown out of the Environmental Era through the Contested Era. This leaves a lot out.

U.S. law incentivized the consumption, use, and impairment of environmental resources for centuries before Theodore Roosevelt schemed with Pinchot or Muir, let alone before the first Earth Day. Sweeping legislative actions and judicial interpretations of property law and other historical doctrines dating back to at least the sixteenth century sanctioned, even instigated, massive actions of environmental and human exploitation in what is now the United States.[1] In rare cases, early conservation efforts arose, but these efforts became increasingly common and impactful as time marched on.

A core message from this broader examination of the history of environmental law, then, is that major environmental problems often have been caused, influenced, mitigated, or undone by broader legal developments than those generally considered within the conventional environmental law canon. The causes of environmental harms—and the role that the law has played and presumably will play in those problems—very frequently require both observers and change agents to increase their aperture. Indeed, addressing consumption, use, and degradation often begins with changes in legal fields not traditionally considered to be environmental law. This list includes civil rights, property, constitutional, administrative, corporate, local government, consumer protection, employment, or communications law.

Contemporary weighty problems like anthropogenic climate change and emerging artificial intelligence (AI) and biotechnologies are likely to require this wider aperture. Understanding the broader legal picture will likely prove necessary to not only understand how important environmental challenges unfolded but also to assess roadblocks, see pathways forward, and ultimately solve these problems.

THE OSCILLATIONS OF ENVIRONMENTAL LAW

As a descriptive matter, legal change related to the environment has been characterized by eras of ebbs and flows, with dominant currents in each era accompanied by subordinate countercurrents. The last and current era, spanning over five decades—the Contested Era—is unique in that it has relied on incrementalism both in the ebbs and flows, a turbulence of sorts. The ushering in of each new era frequently involved a course correction in which prior undercurrents gained ascendancy, building enough momentum in response to unaddressed harms or prior legal change that the reaction ultimately overwhelms the previously dominant current. While some marginal countercurrents never fully ascend, the U.S. history of environmental law is largely a history of marginal countercurrents that later—sometimes suddenly—crest into waves. Sometimes even tidal waves. Indeed, massive changes to environmental law regularly grew out of earlier failures and failed attempts. New incentives and events—too often disasters—recreated the social, political, and (eventually) legal state of play that ushered in legal change. Taking a closer look at those changes and their context seems particularly important.

SOME ENVIRONMENTAL LAW SUCCESSES

While law enabled the environmental challenges faced today, U.S. law has also made remarkable gains in protecting the environment:

- *Public and Preserved Lands.* In addition to millions of acres of state, local, and private lands, environmental law has conserved as federal more than a quarter of the lands in the United States, including some of the most beautiful and ecologically important places in the planet.[2]

- *Endangered Species*. The Endangered Species Act protects over 1,600 species just in the United States,[3] saving 99% of imperiled species from extinction.[4] At least 227 likely would have gone extinct if not for the law,[5] and over 60 have been recovered.[6] Nearly half have stabilized or improved their populations under ESA protection,[7] despite chronic underfunding.[8] Meanwhile, the ESA provides over $1 trillion in ecological, economic, and other benefits every year that vastly outweigh its costs,[9] with other natural resources laws adding trillions more.
- *Air Pollution*. By most measures, air quality has improved since passage of the Clean Air Act, with dramatic reductions in exposure to ground-level ozone and particulates;[10] lead pollution from cars virtually eliminated; other pollutants at just a fraction of pre--Clean Air Act levels;[11] great strides in acid rain elimination; and virtual elimination of the primary pollutants that created the ozone hole.[12] In contrast with industry assertions before and after passage, studies show the Clean Air Act has led to trillions in net economic benefits annually.[13]
- *Water Pollution*. The Clean Water Act has produced dramatic improvements in water quality, keeping billions of pounds of pollution particularly from industrial "point" sources out of the nation's waters.[14] Dumping of raw sewage into rivers, lakes, and oceans—commonplace just decades ago—is now almost unthinkable.
- *Hazardous Waste and Toxic Products*. Many toxic waste sites have been remediated, and meaningful federal restrictions on hazardous waste disposal have radically limited the risks of creating future sites. And while research continues to identify toxic products, many of the most problematic, including lead, DDT, and asbestos, have been banned or controlled.[15]
- *Better Government and Decision Making*. NEPA helped improve American democracy and numerous government decisions by providing a government-wide architecture for integration of environmental concerns and public involvement in federal decisions, interagency coordination, and government accountability.[16] Many state and national governments have followed suit and created similar protections,[17] so much so that international law has begun to treat environmental impact assessment as an enforceable international legal norm.[18]

Figure C.1 Photographs of Bubbly Creek, taken in the early 1900s, about when Upton Sinclair described the river as a polluted waste dump, compared to the river today is one of many success stories of environmental law.

- *Renewable Energy.* Countries around the globe, notably including the United States, are making substantial progress toward a renewable energy transformation, supported by government investment. Battery storage has grown substantially, with each of the past several years setting a renewable energy generation record.[19] Even without direct government investment, this trend is expected to continue as wind, solar, and storage become increasingly less expensive (substantially less so than fossil fuels).[20] Governments at various scales continue to push industry to continue this transition.[21] This progress would not have been possible without 1970s-era federal energy laws that helped create the conditions that eventually ignited the explosion of new renewable projects.[22] The Inflation Reduction Act of 2022, which provided financial incentives to move the energy transition ahead, helped spur a major spike in growth in the United States.[23]

THE CHALLENGES AHEAD

Despite many successes, persistent resource development and exploitation has perpetuated fossil fuels dependency, resource overuse and scarcity, and habitat and biodiversity loss. As in prior eras, our era's most pressing environmental problems are insufficiently addressed by the law. In attempting to dismantle the ability of the federal government to address environmental and other social problems, the second Trump Administration has introduced a new set of challenges.

- *Climate.* Global anthropogenic climate change has exacerbated, broadened, and transformed the ecological effects of each of the persistent issues of prior eras. It poses the most complex, profound, and potentially catastrophic set of environmental challenges faced in modern human \ history.[24] Climate change already has caused harm to human and natural systems, harm which is only expected to increase over the coming decades.[25] While there have been some pockets of progress in limiting greenhouse gas emissions, aggressive national and global legal changes are needed to have any hope to keep climate change in check.
- *Emerging Technologies.* As in every other era, new technologies are both a source of environmental risk and a potential strategy for reducing such risks. Technologies like geoengineering, synthetic biology, and AI raise

ethical, political, and legal questions that will shape the future of life on the planet, including the environment. Geoengineering (i.e., the use of deliberate and large-scale intervention strategies for manipulating the global climate system)[26] raises catastrophic global risks from potentially unilateral actions to manipulate and alter global climatic processes.[27] Synthetic biotechnologies suggest a range of new but untested ways to promote human and ecological health through human intervention.[28] While a few laws governing biotechnologies consider the wider trade-offs of their deployment, most narrowly focus only on keeping technologies and "natural" systems apart.[29] And increased use of AI will lead to considerable pressures on energy[30] and freshwater resources,[31] not to mention unprecedented risks to ecosystems and human health.[32]

- *Environmental Injustice.* Environmental law's inability to address meaningfully the economic and racial injustice of unequal distribution of environmental harms remains a critical limitation.[33] Added to this shortcoming of prior eras are new important questions of intergenerational justice and the state of the planet that will be passed to future generations.
- *Attacks on the Environmental Administrative State and the Rule of Law.* While politicians have long criticized the administrative state, the first and second Trump administrations took it much further. Leaning on the guise of government efficiency, Trump has sought to starve and

Figure C.2 **Climate change will increase the incidence of and severity of fires like the Dixie Fire in California, along with other disasters like hurricanes and heat waves.**

> hollow out environmental agencies, particularly those focused on climate change, environmental justice, and renewable energy. Forces, particularly outside the government, resisted by bringing lawsuits and rallying allies in Congress and within other levels of government. Even when successful, this resistance had difficulty in stemming the barrage of destabilizing actions. At a broader level of governance, the Trump administrations not only attacked political opponents but also the courts, and they harnessed the power of the administrative state not only as a partner in pursuing a policy agenda but also an accomplice in settling Trump's personal and political vendettas. Such attempts to turn the legal system into something less democratic and more autocratic have found some success.[34]

These developments bring into sharp relief the limitations of law created and shaped in prior eras for managing emerging environmental problems. The political and legal ebb and flow of environmental protection undoubtedly continues, but will the incremental contestation of the current era be enough in an age of rising tides and AI? That seems doubtful. The conflict and stagnancy that characterizes the Contested Era has hindered meaningful legal solutions at a time when incremental progress is unlikely to be enough. It also amplified fissures between environmental pragmatists who stress averting deregulation or scavenging for incremental gains and idealists focused on ambitious political and even extra-legal campaigns for fundamental (though still elusive) transformations in governance.[35]

The second Trump administration's approach to governance and unwillingness to accept the core problems facing the planet—not just environmental harms, but also unprecedented wealth disparities and basic facts—raise particularly concerning risks to long-term governance. These hazards extend further than failing to reassemble lost expertise, or even the dire and irreparable consequences at risk when ignoring acute and unprecedented environmental problems. Rather, they raise the specter that the next era of governance might prove to be an era dominated by autocratic rule, development, and exploitation of diminishing natural resources.

On the other hand, the second Trump administration's extreme tactics also set up a real possibility of outrage and backlash that leads to a pendulum swing into a new era that is quite amenable to environmental protection and justice, renewable energy, and significant changes in governance. Looking back at history, there is evidence that such changes are possible even when they seem improbable. Either way, overwhelming evidence today suggests that as the Anthropocene dawns, the United States—indeed the world—is due for another substantial course correction related to the environment. If or when a paradigm shift actually occurs may not be clear for some time, and perhaps only in hindsight.

ACCRETIONS, EROSIONS, AND AVULSIONS THROUGH SUBSTANTIVE, PROCEDURAL, AND STRUCTURAL GOVERNANCE

Sometimes the production or dismantling of law affecting the environment has occurred through accretion and erosion, incrementally and gradually accumulating over decades. In some eras, however, solutions came in the form of transformative avulsions, frequently as urgent responses to untenable harms or powerful fears. Particularly when resistance to change was especially strong, incremental progress proved difficult, with legal change occurring only after an extreme circumstance or crisis. Whether incremental or radical changes, environmental law evolved through the successive invention or reinvention of substantive, procedural, and structural law and governance. Changes to protect the environment have involved not only undoing incentives created in the past, but also frequently adopting new goals, strategies, processes, and institutions.

While any positive incremental change is a reason to celebrate, it is hard to imagine that many of the environmental challenges facing the nation and the planet today can be surmounted without some form of transformational change.

ADJUSTING AND TRANSFORMING GOALS AND STRATEGIES

In each era, policymakers have adopted new legal goals and strategies that have shaped our relationship with the environment. Economic development and job creation were almost exclusively the substantive goals for more than a century after the United States was formed—and undoubtedly these remain core goals today. Yet in each era, the country created and expanded the range of goals relied upon to address emerging environmental problems and supplant, or at least rein in, unfettered exploitation. While these goals may seem like obvious precepts of the policy landscape now, it is important to recognize how novel and innovative fundamental goals like promotion of public health, historical preservation, natural preservation, sustained yield, and environmental justice were in previous eras.

Moreover, the law developed a wide range of strategies to advance one or more of these substantive goals. In the earliest era, these strategies were almost exclusively limited to legislative subsidies and development of new (or reinterpretations of old) liability doctrines in the common law. In latter eras, policymakers at every scale invented a constellation of public law strategies for advancing one or more of these substantive goals, including prescriptive standards, planning, information disclosure, bans or use limitations, as well as market-enlisting strategies such as marketable allowances, pollution charges or taxes, or even contracts.

It seems evident that there are great opportunities for transformational legal innovations to both the substantive purposes and tools of environmental law, tailored to meet the distinctive challenges of today. Undoubtedly, past legal goals and tools persist, and some are being partly adapted to try to manage new challenges—such as common law nuisance,[36] the Clean Air Act and the ESA to address climate change;[37] or existing environmental law's ability to regulate biotechnologies.[38]

However, it is equally evident that at least some of the foundational goals and strategies of U.S. environmental law have proven to be outmoded for the challenges we face. Let's take, for example, the reality that existing U.S. environmental laws are at best an awkward fit for effectively mitigating climate change through reducing greenhouse gas emissions. These laws were not designed to ensure that all responsible for climate change fairly share in developing the solutions. And they also were not established to promote effective adaptation to the inevitable effects of climate change. They were not built for the job. Although (as in prior eras) they may be adjusted to accommodate new problems, there is a limit to their legal adaptive capacity absent some major changes.[39]

So, what might such change in substantive goals and strategies look like? Climate change, for example, will require substantial reductions in, if not elimination of, our reliance on fossil fuels in favor of more renewable and/or sustainable sources, as well as a wide range of planning and regulatory strategies to resist, prepare for, and manage its effects. Long-proposed strategies include cap-and-trade regimes, carbon taxes, renewable energy subsidies, and adaptation planning, with each of these adopted to some degree at state, regional, and federal levels.[40] The history of environmental law suggests that adopted strategies over the coming decades likely will include options that scholars, activists, and policymakers have only begun to imagine.

Yet another potential avenue for innovation might focus on the aims of environmental law. Indeed, the fundamental goals of current environmental law focus on maximizing productivity or reducing direct harm to human health. Some of these and other legal regimes, however, treat ecological processes as both relatively static and distinct from human action. Some of the statutes incorporating the assumption of a static environment include some water law regimes and conservation laws seeking to advance strategies rooted in nonintervention and historical preservation.

Climate change raises questions about the fitness—or possible narrowness—of these objectives. Legal change may need to increase prioritization of ecological and human health as their primary objectives. In the past, other conservation goals—like those embedded in the Endangered Species Act—were used as surrogates for ecological health. Given the scale of ecosystem collapse expected unless major changes are made quickly, it may prove necessary to embrace a goal focused more on promoting ecological health and congruent with ecological dynamics—despite the hot debates inevitably to come with defining and effectuating such a goal through law. Changes could take other forms. Policymakers, for example, may need to de-emphasize (but not necessarily eliminate) strategies that emphasize wildness/naturalness, as ecological conditions may increasingly call for unprecedented interventions. Historical preservation—meaning maintaining preexisting conditions—may flatly be out of our reach as the planet changes. Moreover, laws that focus on maximizing economic productivity (whether operationalized as sustained or maximizing yield or economic output) may require a broader ecological outlook.

Failing to address current global environmental threats is likely to raise existential threats not only to ecological health but also to many industries and the fabric of many societies. Because of this, to find a fair solution, law will almost certainly need to be involved actively in developing a fair outcome, one that grapples with racial, ethnic, and economic injustices that to date have largely been neglected.

ADAPTING PROCEDURAL GOVERNANCE

It is not just the substance of law that matters. Procedural innovations have proven enormously important for developing modes of deciding among various potential substantive governance strategies. Adopting federal and state constitutions and amendments, legislative statutes, and judicial procedures were the only three alternative paradigms on the table up to the Progressive Era, with administrative processes ascending in both prominence and incidence up to the present day. Yet these processes were augmented in the Environmental and Contested Eras through a range of procedural innovations including citizen suit provisions, environmental impact assessment, and, to a limited extent, collaborative adaptive management.

One warning gleaned from U.S. environmental legal history, however, is that policymakers have generally neglected to incorporate mechanisms that provide any semblance of systematic and periodic adjustments as they learn more about the challenges being faced.[41] Despite all the procedural innovations that have pushed environmental protection, changes have typically focused on putting out a particular fire but left plenty of embers burning.

The history of environmental law illustrates the procedural rigidity of legal innovations. From the Mining Law of 1872 to the persistence of the Endangered Species Act in withstanding attack, legal innovations were often not only durable, but arguably incredibly rigid. There has been limited investment in procedural innovations that help laws adapt. That is not to say that none of these kinds of innovations exist. For example, many of the environmental laws passed during the Environmental Era require regulators to look at the best available science when decisions are made.[42]

Still, most of environmental law does not have much give. Climate change particularly increases the need for the development of an adaptive and more resilient climate adaptation infrastructure that reduces the level of harm resulting from climate change.[43] Because most laws assume a world that is static, these same laws are likely to prove increasingly ineffective in averting and managing the effects of increasingly dynamic phenomena like climate change and emerging technologies on ecosystems and markets. Frequently these problems arise because environmental law and management focus on front-end planning[44] and not on the need to manage uncertainty or adjust for the almost inevitable missteps.[45] The law frequently even fails to incorporate opportunities to revisit decisions to account for change or new information.[46] Furthermore, monitoring necessary to learn lessons and spot mistakes is typically weak for under-resourced agencies.[47]

As policymakers confront the task of creating a new legal infrastructure, they will have the opportunity to develop measures that integrate increased reliance on more adaptive management and governance processes. Indeed, the uncertainty and volatility of climate-related problems require no less—until the climate stabilizes, change is the new normal. Policymakers need to rely on not only provisional decisions based on existing information, but also incremental policy and decision adjustments at the back end if conditions warrant.[48] Effective adaptive procedures may require not only empiricism and experimentalism in implementing on-the-ground strategies but also more systematic monitoring, assessment, and adjustment of agency policies, programs, and processes.[49] Learning over time is important because in facing such dynamic problems, even if one gets it right, *rightness* is going to change as new information is gathered and circumstances shift.

Similarly, while emerging technologies raise significant risks, many also offer the potential to reduce ecological harms or improve the implementation of environmental law. Geoengineering and AI may facilitate significant ecological benefits.[50] Remote sensing combined with machine learning may revolutionize environmental enforcement.[51] It will be crucial for legal processes to harness and manage technologies like these to support more effective environmental protection.[52] As always, policymakers will also need to adjust and adapt substantive environmental law strategies to avoid new risks, but the history of environmental law suggests (and our current reality confirms) that it is important for legal processes to adapt, respond to, and remediate ecological and human health harms quickly as new information about them becomes available.

RETHINKING THE STRUCTURAL RELATIONSHIP BETWEEN LEGAL INSTITUTIONS

The history of environmental law shows that successful environmental policy requires careful consideration of not only goals, tools, and processes, but also the design of environmental legal institutions. This is true for both strategies addressing environmental harms and assessing the effectiveness of strategies used to advance environmental protection.

The legal institutions that developed for promoting use, management, and eventual protection of the environment evolved across the eras. Since the United States arose, legislative, executive, and judicial branches each played their role, as did federal, state, and local governments, with relationships between these institutions governed by constitutional doctrines including separation of powers and federalism. Though the focus of attention for environmental law over the course of the past fifty years has been at the federal level, throughout history much of public authority over environmental resources has primarily been decentralized to local and state authorities. Even today, local and state governments retain primary control over key environmental authority in the United States, most notably the ownership, development, and regulation of resources such as water and land.[53] As such, many environmental resources remain largely decentralized, with some overlap and only limited coordination over a few governmental functions.[54]

At various key political moments, however, new forms of federal law emerged to authorize limited-purpose, often overlapping, centralized institutions to address evident inadequacies of relying on decentralized, independent institutions to address environmental harms. At times these involved preemptive federal assumption of authority, such as the establishment of federal lands in the Progressive Era or nuclear waste disposal and hazardous waste remediation in the Environmental Era. Under other regimes, federal authority only served as a floor that state regulation could supplement with more stringent regulation but not abrogate.[55] The surfacing of a robust federal and state public administrative state in the Modernization and Environmental Eras thus led to the development of a complex structural legal infrastructure, in certain contexts decentralized and others centralized—with some exclusive but more commonly overlapping authority, as well as some independently exercised jurisdiction but more often subject to various forms of coordination.[56]

One replicated legal innovation that arose during the Environmental Era took the form of "cooperative federalism" regimes that vested federal authority over key regulatory functions—for example, funding, ambient monitoring, and ambient and even source standard setting—while maintaining substantial roles for states, particularly over implementation and enforcement.[57] Again, in some regimes authority was not fully centralized, as federal jurisdiction continued to overlap with state authority through floor preemption.[58] Such regimes often include federal-state coordination in the performance of their overlapping authority.[59]

Similarly, flexible standards built into common law doctrines have proven to be a vital backstop to public law regimes for addressing emerging environmental problems. Even unsuccessful lawsuits have raised awareness and catalyzed action by legislatures and the executive branch. A lengthy list of unsuccessful common law cases preceded *Massachusetts v. EPA*. The persistence of overlap between the common and public law regimes has been invaluable in protecting human health and the environment.

As the Anthropocene emerges, the structural governance of environmental law needs to be reconsidered, even as it is rebuilt to address threats to administrative governance and the rule of law. As in prior eras, the trade-offs of allocations of authority are likely to vary depending on the context and risks at hand. Climate mitigation might require more robust governance at scales that so far have been elusive, as illustrated by decades of global diplomacy seeking to create a robust international legal infrastructure to reduce greenhouse gas emissions.

As for climate change adaptation, particularly given the diversity and uncertainty of most climate effects, policymakers are most likely to succeed if planning and implementation strategies are largely addressed at the local level. Federal interventions, on the other hand, are more likely to prove helpful in circumstances in which cross-jurisdictional harms are of particular concern or when uniform standards or economies of scale are especially advantageous. Of course, intergovernmental coordination will frequently pay dividends, and though overlapping authority may be inefficient, it nonetheless might be worth it for protecting resources that are especially precious or irreplaceable.[60] Regardless, the particular configuration of and legal relationship between these institutions ought to vary by context.

Climate geoengineering activities, in contrast, are likely to be spurred by perceived local benefits and could be deployed unilaterally but raise potentially global catastrophic risks. As such, while research on geoengineering technologies may be suited for independent, decentralized governance, geoengineering risks might appropriately push U.S. environmental governance toward more centralized and overlapping controls on research and deployment to minimize cross-jurisdictional spillovers and access the redundancy benefits of overlapping authority. International coordination may even be necessary to minimize unilateral deployment.[61]

Given the attacks on legal institutions that have become increasingly pronounced, in addition to investing in ideal legal innovations, it seems increasingly prudent to invest in backup plans. Redundancy is the key to reduce disruptions when institutions are under siege.

BUILDING COALITIONS, POLICY EXPERIMENTATION, AND LEGAL IMAGINATION

Finally, the history of U.S. environmental law offers some lessons for how, and in what form, legal innovations in substantive, procedural, and structural governance may arise. Prior to the eras of major environmental protection, it typically was unclear whether the United States had the interest, will, or capacity to engage in the transformative change necessary to mend its environmental wounds. Yet various factors served to catalyze a legal transformation. From President Theodore Roosevelt[62] to Richard Nixon,[63] personal leadership, charisma, and resolute political expediency all played a role in instigating change. Change frequently began from people outside of the government. It also came from disciplines other than law: Sinclair's *The Jungle*;[64] Carson's *Silent Spring*;[65] public health officers tracing urban ills to deficient waste disposal and treatment. Effective narrative and dissemination of ideas and insights could mobilize hearts and minds.

Despite the myriad of factors that are at play in creating change, the history of U.S. environmental law suggests three stimulants of legal change particularly worthwhile for closer exploration: building coalitions, legal imagination, and policy experimentation.

A CONVERGENCE (AND DIVERGENCE) OF INTERESTS

From the American Revolution to modern day, the coalitions that were successful at cultivating meaningful environmental lawmaking were diverse, overlapping, and decentralized. The movements often blended the insights of intellectuals and scientists with policymakers, environmental advocacy groups, student organizations, labor unions, and business interests. The Environmental Era combined forces of organizers of a civil rights advocacy network with a growing environmental advocacy network to demand change.[66] These different types of interests were themselves quite diverse, ranging from the local grassroots to the multinational, and they frequently took aim at various governmental scales and relied upon a range of efforts to bring about legal change.

Importantly, at least some key constituencies from industry and commerce were often vital to accepting, if not promoting, conservation of human health and environmental resources and reduction of environmental harms. Undoubtedly, as environmental harms escalated and public awareness swelled, some business interests led antiregulatory forces that opposed legal change, ranging from Progressive Era trusts[67] to today's fossil-fuel industries.[68] Often business interests found support from ideological or grassroots resistance, whether Progressive Era proponents of laissez-faire economics;[69] 1960s neoliberal economics;[70] or the Contested Era's wise-use movement, antigovernment activists like the "Sagebrush Rebels" and Cliven Bundy,[71] and evangelical antienvironmentalism.[72] Additionally, antienvironmental regulation efforts frequently rejected established scientific evidence and even engaged in disinformation campaigns.[73]

Nonetheless, interest convergence[74] has played a notable role in the development of environmental law. The significant political, ideological, and economic barriers to transformative legal change in U.S. environmental history were, when successful, ultimately surmounted not only by savvy news outlets, charismatic political leaders, intellectuals, and grassroots movements, but at times in tandem with business leaders and interests. Indeed, businesses—whether motivated by relative market advantages, economic certainty, entrepreneurism, or socially consciousness—were consistently a key component in every era in which incremental or transformational environmental legal change occurred. Frequently business interests have aligned to press against environmental change, but critical innovations of environmental protection have also relied on these interests. For example, the Progressive Era relied on organized hunting affinity groups to advocate for conservation; Yellowstone National Park's creation leaned heavily on railroad interests. Similarly, during the Contested Era, regulation of products causing the ozone hole became politically possible with the help of those businesses that profited from these products but could shift to alternatives.[75]

Throughout U.S. history, another consistent thread of environmental social movements has been the tension between two strands of reformers over either the ambition and rigor of conservation goals or the best approach to legal change. From the Transcendentalists to the Sunrise Movement, idealists have sought to fundamentally transform, and even revolutionize, the political, economic, and legal system to advance conservation and public health. On the other side, pragmatists from Gifford Pinchot to President Biden and the Abundance Movement pushed for environmental protection or conservation as important goals, but either identify other social objectives as similarly important or are willing to compromise the ideal for action regarded as more realistic.

In truth, this dichotomy can be a false one, as many individuals likely have both pragmatist and purist impulses, uncertain about whether to shoot for the stars or keep both feet firmly planted on the ground. Many are willing to settle, even if they root for idealism to win the day. Moreover, it is also important to note key insights from the social science on social movements. When courts are unable to achieve systemic change, more strident social movements can complement litigation to move the needle,[76] even if some might find such radical efforts objectionable. Additionally, more rebellious organizations like Greenpeace and Earth First! have generated attention, time, and space for more mainstream legal actions and advocates to deliver meaningful change.[77]

In thinking about possible pathways to address existing and emerging environmental problems, it is also productive to consider how interests might align across different policy forums. While it is debatable whether, for example, proposals that might appeal to labor interests (like the Green New Deal[78]) and even combine business innovators (like the Inflation Reduction Act[79]) will carry the day, it seems certain that a coalition with labor and/or green entrepreneurs is more likely to be effective than a coalition without either. In determining what is possible, the answer is likely to change depending on the coalitions built. History shows that designing policies that seek to harmonize interests is undoubtedly an important aspect of coalition building.

Relatedly, advocates for environmental conservation historically have pointed to the co-benefits of addressing a particular environmental problem. This is a form of coalition building. In some circumstances, climate advocates might want to consider whether policies that do not scream climate action (such as addressing local air pollution or transit mobility) might be more politically viable pathways to address climate change. While existing evidence suggests transformational change is likely necessary to address climate change, AI, and other emerging technologies,[80] it might be that in some fora more might be accomplished to promote environmental protection in the interim if cultural flashpoints like climate change are deliberately not front and center.[81]

Finally, history indicates that there might be ways to make inroads in some venues more quickly than others. For instance, even as the politics around climate action is fraught at the national level, within many states and metropolises, the politics are less fractious. Even if it might seem logical that a larger scale for mobilization is more appropriate for large-scale issues like climate change, in some instances the politics of securing change might point in other directions.

LEGAL IMAGINATION

Another key factor in the successful development of environmental laws has been the initial capacity to cultivate legal imagination. Legal imagination refers to "the collective mental constructs that are deployed by lawyers and legal scholars in thinking about law and how it operates."[82] At certain points in the history of U.S. environmental law, scholars and policymakers imagined new substantive goals, legal processes, and legal structures and institutions to address novel or previously unaddressed harms. As stated by Elizabeth Fisher, "[L]egal imagination is a feature of all law. But, . . . the complexity of environmental problems and the institutions needed to govern them, means that legal imagination is a particularly necessary feature of environmental law."[83]

While there undoubtedly were instances in which the deployment of imaginative legal or policy strategies occurred fairly swiftly, the seeds of responses and solutions to degradation were often planted much earlier than their eventual instantiation in policy. Pinchot studied forestry in Europe many years before implementing scientific forestry management in the United States.[84] Muir developed a conservation agenda well before his ideas were implemented;[85] the Wilderness Act, the closest manifestation of Muir's ideas about natural preservation, was adopted fifty years after his death.[86]

Undoubtedly, today many diverse legal theories have been offered for refashioning legal goals, processes, or institutions in the United States to better address and repair environmental harm, particularly in light of global climate change and emerging technologies. The most prominent recent social movement discourses in the United States that have made legal inroads include (1) the Green New Deal,[87] which promotes clean energy transition and social justice policies to address climate change and income inequality; (2) environmental rights amendments, which seek to instantiate or reaffirm human rights to a healthy environment in state constitutions;[88] and (3) rights of nature jurisprudential theories, which advocate for recognition of legal rights for non-human species and ecosystems.[89] Relatedly, a long-overlooked jurisprudential strand in conventional U.S. environmental law that more recently has seen traction among tribal scholars[90] and social movement leaders[91] are Indigenous epistemologies asserting that U.S. law's focus on anthropocentric value is at fundamental odds with Indigenous understandings of the relationship between humans and the non-human environment. These and other perspectives seek to expand what is possible in environmental law.

It would be folly, however, to offer concrete legal solutions with the expectation that they would effectively and definitively manage the environmental problems of today and tomorrow. A review of the past also highlights a large degree of unpredictability. Given the inherent difficulty of the task, what seems to offer the most promising avenues for legal innovations? Perhaps default rules that take into consideration interests of future generations might prove vital.[92] Or public governance processes might rely more heavily on cautious risk assessments of the trade-offs of strategies—perhaps combined with rebuttable presumptions of the acceptability of preexisting baseline conditions—rather than reflexive protection of natural and historical phenomena (or prohibition on intentional and novel interventions).[93]

Despite uncertainties, however, what the history of U.S. environmental law makes clear is that it is critical to invest in a platform for the development of information and creativity. Legal imagination was certainly prompted by imagination and the development of knowledge in other fields. Developments in economics, politics, philosophy, psychology, chemistry, biology, medicine, sociology, and engineering explored environmental and human health and the causal relationships between humans and the environment. Insights in these fields not only spurred legal change but also increased legal creativity. Public health innovations in the Allocation Era followed public health science, particularly after military encampments implemented standards and saw dramatic gains.[94] The Wilderness Act was championed by prominent writings and writers. And *Silent Spring* and a NASA photograph of the earth focused the Environmental Era.[95] Foraging in the realm of ideas requires an initial planting of seeds, however eccentric or outlandish they may initially seem. Without investment, there is not a potential of dividends.

Accordingly, to increase the adaptive capacity of the law to address new harms in an increasingly complex natural and legal environment, there is a need to invest in scientific, technological, and legal imagination. Legislative investment in the monitoring or scientific study of environmental harms, whether through statutes directed specifically at researching pollution or health harms or more generally in creating and funding entities like the National Science Foundation and the National Institutes of Health, have played an incalculable role in helping develop environmental law. These very institutions were attacked under the second Trump Administration.[96] While the severity of the problems and the context of the time might point to focusing on short-term strategies, to surmount what are long-term environmental challenges necessitates tracing long-term alternatives that might eventually serve as the pathway forward.

REGULATORY EXPERIMENTATION

Beyond the initial planting, ideas need to germinate, sprout, and pollinate. The history of environmental law has illustrated the incredible value of legal experimentation in promoting the study and proliferation of legal innovation. For example, state and local policy often proved important precedent for federal action, with the influence of California's regulation of air pollution on development of the Clean Air Act serving as a key example.[97] Similarly, even as the federal government has experienced the seesaw of environmental policy during the Contested Era, many states and local governments have boldly invested in and made progress toward addressing greenhouse gas emissions.[98] The idea of National Parks, founded on promoting historical preservation as a method of conservation, spurred such nature reserves around the world.[99] Similarly, the National Environmental Policy Act's innovation requiring federal agency planning and analysis for any major federal action significantly affecting the environment not only helped legitimate administrative processes and advance the consideration of environmental harms in decision making; it also led to the proliferation of environmental impact assessment in half the states and over a hundred nations worldwide.[100]

Change can happen through the iterative interplay between multiple levels of governance. For this to happen, a social and legal system must be in place that not only allows for policy experimentation but cultivates it. Historically, this has occurred in the United States through its federalist governance system, with change at one level having the potential to alter the state of play at other levels—such as state common law liability softening up federal regulatory reform, or federal unwillingness to legislate amping up pressure to act at state or local levels.

Despite the examples of experimentation, the United States' current procedural and structural governance remain far from models of regulatory experimentation. There are more systematic and rigorous ways to percolate effective governance than just relying on ideas arising from fragmented, haphazard, and serendipitous regulatory innovations. To maximize the capacity to cultivate legal experimentation, policymakers may need to treat United States governance as a way to coordinate intergovernmental learning to increase information and manage uncertainty about policy experiments—that is, to incorporate *empiricism* (i.e., systematic monitoring, evaluation, of regulatory strategies, processes, and programs) and *experimentalism* (i.e., provisional adoption and periodic adjustment of regulatory strategies, processes, and programs to account for disseminated evidence) into governance itself.[101] Cultivating such a system would help manage the unprecedented challenge of leveraging democratic, market, and regulatory institutions to manage latent, dispersed, unpredictable, and unquantifiable problems—traits that typify the most pressing environmental problems we face today.

* * *

As for every prior generation, the choices of current generations will define the kind of world inherited by those who come next. History highlights the importance of legal and policy choices in not only defining people's relationship with the environment but also in reorienting it when needed. In the face of unprecedented environmental challenges, the law has and will continue to be a primary conduit for change. Given the stakes of the environmental challenges we now face, the directions law pushes us will prove consequential to the planet and to future generations. Our legal system will either promote exploitation, consumption, and pollution; or it will reduce harm, advance conservation, and cultivate effective and fair democratic governance. More than likely, it will do both, but to what extent in either direction is entirely up for grabs.

Whether the public and their policymakers are willing to fundamentally shift governance to address the latest intimidating set of environmental harms remains to be seen. Two ideas made famous by Dr. Martin Luther King, Jr. warrant our attention—that "the line of progress is never straight"[102] and that "the arc of the moral universe is long but it bends toward justice."[103] While there undoubtedly have been rollbacks and complexities, the history of U.S. law and the environment suggests that the arc of law is largely bent toward environmental protection. Whether through a flood of executive actions, judicial relief, or statutes, each period of environmental degradation has been followed by a period of substantial legal restoration and even progression.

Scholars, students, and policymakers must prepare for the moment in which transformational environmental protection is possible. If serious consideration of a legal paradigm shift is in the offing, whether such a transformation occurs will at least partially depend on the available portfolio of potential and practicable legal solutions. Like the drafters of the Wilderness Act, advocates not only need to be ready when the moment arrives but also work tirelessly to create it.[104]

In building this portfolio of change, it is important to keep in mind the lessons of the past. Foraging for explanations and solutions in areas of law not conventionally associated with the environment will likely prove crucial, as will insights from complementary environmental fields. A review of the range of potential strategies, goals, processes, and institutions previously adopted will help cultivate an understanding of what has worked before, what has not, and perhaps what else might be possible. The portfolio should also invest in exploring how the values typically used to protect the environment (such as public health) or emerging values (equity or rights of nature) could be leveraged for change. For some, building the portfolio will mean pragmatic plotting for incremental change; for others, ardent optimistic ambition seeking to rearrange legal relationships in ways never previously tried; for many it will be both. Building a robust portfolio of change will entail identifying places where interests converge, investing in legal imagination, and participating and learning from legal experimentation. For those working and hoping to create a better world, such investments are vital.

Given the stakes, such investments are hardly optional. For the sake of the planet and all those who currently or will call this home, we have to rise to the occasion. While the hurdles to change may feel insurmountable, the same was true in the past. Perhaps the most important lesson to take from history is that there is reason to work together, to imagine, to experiment, and to pursue many pathways forward. While this idea provides hope, to overcome the challenges ahead of us, hope is not enough. What our era requires is our commitment and work.

ACKNOWLEDGMENTS

We thank Clara Platter, our editor at NYU Press, who saw value in our proposal and shepherded it through the approval process. We also thank Brianna Jean and Malathi Balamurugan, who guided us through the manuscript preparation process. Although they remain anonymous, we are grateful for the feedback and suggestions provided by the reviewers of the proposal and draft manuscript recruited by NYU Press.

We benefited enormously from the insights provided to us by our academic and professional colleagues. We received critically helpful feedback from participants in workshops at Loyola University Chicago School of Law; the University of California, Irvine School of Law; University of Minnesota Law School; Texas A&M School of Law; Utah's Premier Environmental Reading Group; and University of Utah S. J. Quinney College of Law. At the risk of omitting some whose observations aided us, we acknowledge Sameer Ashar, Swethaa Ballakrishnen, Rebecca Bratspies, Ann Carlson, Scott Daniels, Victor Fleischer, Lisa Grow, George Handley, Bruce Huber, Don Jarvis, Lance Long, Felix Mormann, Tim Mulvaney, Chip Oscarson, Vanessa Casado Pérez, Justin Pidot, Troy Rule, Kalyani Robbins, Michael Robinson-Dorn, Ari Waldman, Rachel Whipple, and Sonya Ziaja for their wise and perceptive critiques of our ideas and previous drafts.

Special thanks are due to research librarians Ellen Augustiniak, Matthew Flyntz, Annalee Hickman Pierson, Jessica Pierucci, Christina Tsou, as well as Maria Gonzalez De Toro, Rabie Kadri, and Veronica Przybyl for their editorial assistance. We relied heavily on our research assistants, including Rosanna Barrett, Danny Dudley, Willie Duhart, Avery Emery, William Funk, Kemarie Jorgensen, Duncan Justice, Ariana Keshishian, Jennifer Keute, Gabrielle Moore, Victor Moxley, Adriana Perera, London Powers, Allison Rabe, Skylar Reed, Madelyn Sickle, Anastasia Sun, Tran To, and Isadora Weiner.

We also thank the University of California, Irvine School of Law and the University of Utah S. J. Quinney College of Law for providing financial research support for the project.

Finally, we appreciate the support of our families, without whose patience we could not possibly have completed this book. In particular, our spouses Kathleen and Kellie supported us through the process of writing the book—graciously listened to us recount the book's progress and challenges endless times, tolerated our long conversations as we agonized over the thornier trade-offs in the writing and editing processes, and provided us invaluable advice and encouragement without which the book may not have come to fruition.

Alejandro Camacho
Laguna Beach, CA

Brigham Daniels
Salt Lake City, UT

NOTES

INTRODUCTION

1 Boston has a rich environmental history, which is well told in REMAKING BOSTON: AN ENVIRONMENTAL HISTORY OF THE CITY AND ITS SURROUNDINGS (Anthony N. Penna & Conrad Edick Wright eds., 2009).

2 WILLIAM CRONON, CHANGES IN THE LAND: INDIANS, COLONISTS, AND THE ECOLOGY OF NEW ENGLAND (2011); JEAN O'BRIEN, FIRSTING AND LASTING: WRITING INDIANS OUT OF EXISTENCE IN NEW ENGLAND (2010).

3 CRONON, *supra* note 2.

4 RITA KIKI EDOZIE ET AL., CHANGING FACES OF GREATER BOSTON 41 (2019).

5 The Charter of the Colony of the Massachusetts Bay in New England, 1628–9 (Mar. 4, 1629).

6 Dean R. Snow & Kim M. Lanphear, *European Contact and Indian Depopulation in the Northeast: The Timing of the First Epidemics*, 35 ETHNOHISTORY 15 (1988).

7 Michael Rawson, *What Lies Beneath: Science, Nature, and the Making of Boston Harbor*, *in* REMAKING BOSTON: AN ENVIRONMENTAL HISTORY OF THE CITY AND ITS SURROUNDINGS 33, 58 (Anthony N. Penna & Conrad Edick Wright eds., 2009).

8 *Id.*

9 *Id.*

10 HENRY DAVID THOREAU, WALDEN AND CIVIL DISOBEDIENCE 15 (Signet 1960).

11 Paul F. Levy & Michael S. Connor, *The Boston Harbor Cleanup*, 8 NEW ENGLAND J. PUB. POL'Y 91, 92 (1992); *see also* ELIOT C. CLARKE, MAIN DRAINAGE WORKS OF THE CITY OF BOSTON 107 (1885).

12 Steven M. Rudnick, *Remaking Boston Harbor: Cleaning Up After Ourselves*, *in* REMAKING BOSTON: AN ENVIRONMENTAL HISTORY OF THE CITY AND ITS SURROUNDINGS 56, 58 (Anthony N. Penna & Conrad Edick Wright eds., 2009).

13 *Id.* at 66. *See also* Jeff Hecht, *Raising a Stink in Boston*, NEW SCIENTIST, Dec. 5, 1992, at 32.

14 David M. Culver, Tenement House Reform in Boston, 1846–1898 229 (1972) (Ph.D. dissertation, Boston University).

15 James C. O'Connell, *How Metropolitan Parks Shaped Greater Boston, 1893–1945*, *in* REMAKING BOSTON: AN ENVIRONMENTAL HISTORY OF THE CITY AND

ITS SURROUNDINGS 168, 168–81 (Anthony N. Penna & Conrad Edick Wright eds., 2009).

16 J. L. Bowen et al., *Boston Harbor, Boston, Massachusetts, USA: Transformation from 'the Harbor of Shame' to a Vibrant Coastal Resource*, 25 REG'L STUD. MARINE SCI. 1, 4 (2019).

17 Rudnick, *supra* note 12, at 67.

18 *Id.* at 68.

19 Michael J. Brennan, *The Environmental Roots of Urban Renewal in Boston*, 45 J. URB. HIST. 23, 39 (2019).

20 DOUGLAS BRINKLEY, SILENT SPRING REVOLUTION: JOHN F. KENNEDY, RACHEL CARSON, LYNDON JOHNSON, RICHARD NIXON, AND THE GREAT ENVIRONMENTAL AWAKENING 119–21 (2022).

21 Levy & Connor, *supra* note 11, at 92–93.

22 This history of recalcitrance is laid out concisely in MASSACHUSETTS ENVIRONMENTAL LAW § 17.3.1 (Mass. Cont. Legal Educ. 5th ed. & Supp. 2024).

23 BRINKLEY, *supra* note 20, at 70.

24 United States v. Metropolitan Dist. Comm'n, [1985] 23 Env't Rep. (BNA) 1350 (D. Mass. Jan. 31, 1985). For an interesting history of this case (and related cases) and how the state ultimately responded, see Andrew Thomas Savage, *Comment: Boston Harbor: The Anatomy of a Court-Run Cleanup*, 22 B.C. ENV'T AFF. L. REV. 365 (1995).

25 Dalia Munenzon & Yair Titelboim, *Transformative Actions in the Boston Harbor: Lessons Learned from Past Projects Toward a Resilient and Sustainable Urban Future, in* URBAN AND TRANSIT PLANNING 55, 69 (Francesco Alberti et al. eds., 2022).

26 CITY OF BOSTON, IMAGINE BOSTON 2030: A PLAN FOR THE FUTURE OF BOSTON (2017), www.boston.gov/sites/default/files/imce-uploads/2018-06/imagine20boston202030_pages2.pdf.

27 Futu Chen et al., *Disparities in Joint Exposure to Environmental and Social Stressors IN Urban Households in Greater Boston*, 238 ENV'T RSCH. 1, 10 (2023).

28 *Id.*

29 CHARLES DICKENS, A TALE OF TWO CITIES 3 (1859).

30 DAVID HUME, AN ENQUIRY CONCERNING THE HUMAN UNDERSTANDING: AND CONCERNING THE PRINCIPLES OF MORALS 33–34 (1894). ("As to past Experience, it can be allowed to give direct and certain information of those precise objects only, and that precise period of time, which fell under its cognizance: but why this experience should be extended to future times, and to other objects, which for aught we know, may be only in appearance similar; this is the main question on which I would insist."); Amit Tubi et al., *Can We Learn from the Past? Towards Better Analogies and Historical Inference in Society-Environmental Change Research*, 76 GLOB. ENV'T CHANGE 1, 2 (2022). ("[A]lthough we believe that history can provide useful lessons, any attempt to draw parallels between past and present societies must account for the divergences between them in its analysis and consequent derived insights.").

31 *See* Douglas Fox, *Back to the No-Analog Future?*, 316 SCI. 823 (2007); Peter Cox & David Stephenson, *A Changing Climate for Prediction*, 317 SCI. 207 (2007); P. C. D. Milly et al., *Stationarity Is Dead: Whither Water Management?*, 319 SCI. 573 (2008).

32 *See, e.g.*, Alejandro E. Camacho, *Transforming the Means and Ends of Natural Resources Management*, 89 N.C. L. REV. 1405, 1426–27 (2011).

33 Wilderness Act, Pub. L. No. 88–577, 78 Stat. 890 (1964) (codified as amended at 16 U.S.C. §§ 1131–1136).

34 *See, e.g.*, Sebastián Ureta et al., *Baselining Nature: An Introduction*, 3 ENV'T & PLAN. E: NATURE & SPACE 3, 4–7 (2020).

35 Alfred C. Aman, Jr., *Administrative Law in A Global Era: Progress, Deregulatory Change, and the Rise of the Administrative Presidency*, 73 CORNELL L. REV. 1101, 1236 (1987).

36 *See* Barry Boyer & Errol Meidinger, *Privatizing Regulatory Enforcement: A Preliminary Assessment of Citizen Suits Under Federal Environmental Laws*, 34 BUFFALO L. REV. 833 (2025); Nicholas A. Robinson, *International Trends in Environmental Impact Assessment*, 19 B.C. L. REV. 591 (1991); J. B. Ruhl & Robert L. Fischman, *Adaptive Management in the Courts*, 95 MINN. L. REV. 424 (2010); Jody Freeman, *Collaborative Governance in the Administrative State*, 45 UCLA L. REV. 1 (1997).

37 Jon D. Michaels, *An Enduring, Evolving Separation of Powers*, 115 COLUM. L. REV. 515 (2015); MATTHEW E. GLASSMAN, CONG. RSCH. SERV., R44334, SEPARATION OF POWERS: AN OVERVIEW (2016).

38 Jody Freeman & Jim Rossi, *Agency Coordination in Shared Regulatory Space*, 125 HARV. L. REV. 1131 (2012); ALEJANDRO E. CAMACHO & ROBERT L. GLICKSMAN, REORGANIZING GOVERNMENT: A FUNCTIONAL AND DIMENSIONAL FRAMEWORK (2019).

39 CHAR MILLER, GIFFORD PINCHOT AND THE MAKING OF MODERN ENVIRONMENTALISM (2013).

40 C. Michael Hall, *John Muir: Pioneer of Nature Preservation*, *in* GIANTS OF TOURISM 229 (Richard W. Butler & Roslyn Russell eds., 2010).

41 Brigham Daniels, *Emerging Commons and Tragic Institutions*, 37 ENV'T L. 515 (2007).

42 ALFRED RUNTE, NATIONAL PARKS: THE AMERICAN EXPERIENCE 48–64 (4th ed. 2010).

43 Rivers and Harbors Appropriation Act of 1899, ch. 425, 30 Stat. 1121 (codified as amended at 33 U.S.C. §§ 401–418).

44 Federal Meat Inspection Act, Pub. L. No. 59–242, 34 Stat. 1256 (1907) (codified as amended at 21 U.S.C. §§ 601–695).

45 Migratory Bird Treaty Act of 1918, ch. 128, 40 Stat. 755 (codified as amended at 16 U.S.C. §§ 703–712).

46 *See* Rachel Carson, Silent Spring (1962).

47 *See, e.g.*, Christine Mai-Duc, *The 1969 Santa Barbara Oil Spill that Changed Oil and Gas Exploration Forever*, L.A. Times (May 20, 2015), www.latimes.com/local/lanow/la-me-ln-santa-barbara-oil-spill-1969-20150520-htmlstory.html.

48 George Santayana, The Life of Reason (1905).

CHAPTER 1. EXPLOITING A NEW COUNTRY

1 For a probing explanation of Clay's life and the important role he played in early American history, see David S. Heidler & Jeanne T. Heidler, Henry Clay: The Essential American (2010).

2 Robert C. Byrd, The Senate, 1789–1989: Classic Speeches, 1830–1993 84 (1994) (quoting Henry Clay's Defense of the American System speech from Feb. 2, 3, and 6, 1832).

3 *Id.*

4 While many writers and thinkers could be cited, see particularly Ralph Waldo Emerson, *Nature*, *in* Ralph Waldo Emerson: The Major Prose 61 (Ronald A. Bosco & Joel Myerson eds., 2015); Henry David Thoreau, Walden: a fully Annotated Edition (Jeffrey S. Cramer ed., 2004). *See also* Jedediah Purdy, *The Politics of Nature: Climate Change, Environmental Law, and Democracy*, 119 Yale L.J. 1122 (2010).

5 David Reich et al., *Reconstructing Native American Population History*, 488 Nature 370, 370–74 (2012).

6 William M. Denevan, The Native Population of the Americas in 1492 (2d rev. ed. 1992).

7 Raymond Hames, *The Ecologically Noble Savage Debate*, 36 Ann. Rev. Anthropol. 177 (2007); Shepard Krech III, The Ecological Indian: Myth and History (1999).

8 Charles C. Mann, 1493: Uncovering the New World Columbus Created 37–42 (2011).

9 William Cronon, Changes in the Land: Indians, Colonists, and the Ecology of New England 48–50 (1983). Even late into the nineteenth century, the ways in which fire was used by Native Americans was still largely misunderstood. For example, the explorer John Wesley Powell—who in many ways had a prophetic eye in understanding the challenges western landscapes would challenge the desires of the settlers in the West—saw it as destructive and wasteful. John Wesley Powell, Report on the Lands of the Arid Region of the United States, H.R. Exec. Doc. No. 73 (1878), reprinted in John Wesley Powell, Lands of the Arid Region of the United States 15–17 (1983).

10 *See, e.g.*, Biloine Whiting Young & Melvin L. Fowler, Cahokia, the Great Native American Metropolis (2000).

11 Barbara E. Mundy, The Death of Aztec Tenochtitlan, the Life of Mexico City 1–3 (2015).

12 M. Kat Anderson & Michael J. Moratto, *Native American Land-Use Practices and Ecological Impacts*, *in* SIERRA NEVADA ECOSYSTEM PROJECT FINAL REPORT TO CONGRESS, VOL. 2: ASSESSMENTS AND SCIENTIFIC BASIS FOR MANAGEMENT OPTIONS 187 (University of California Centers for Water and Wildlife Resources, 1996).

13 CRONON, *supra* note 9.

14 *See, e.g.*, DONALD I. DICKMANN & DAVID T. CLELAND, FIRE RETURN INTERVALS AND FIRE CYCLES FOR HISTORIC FIRE REGIMES IN THE GREAT LAKES REGION: A SYNTHESIS OF THE LITERATURE (2002); Richard P. Guyette et al., *350 Years of Fire-Climate-Human Interactions in a Great Lakes Sandy Outwash Plain*, 7 FORESTS 189, 199–200 (2016).

15 *See* Ron Rosenbaum, *The Shocking Savagery of America's Early History*, SMITHSONIAN MAG. (Mar. 2013), www.smithsonianmag.com/history/the-shocking-savagery-of-americas-early-history-22739301/; BERNARD BAILYN, THE BARBAROUS YEARS: THE PEOPLING OF BRITISH NORTH AMERICA: THE CONFLICT OF CIVILIZATIONS, 1600–1675 (2012).

16 JARED M. DIAMOND, GUNS, GERMS, AND STEEL 80–90 (1997).

17 MANN, *supra* note 8, at 38–41; DIAMOND, *supra* note 16, at 80; FREDERICK JENNINGS, THE INVASION OF AMERICA 22 (1975).

18 Cynthia Fowler & Evelyn Konopik, *The History of Fire in the Southern United States*, 14 HUM. ECOLOGY REV. 165, 169–70 (2007).

19 William Ruddiman, *The Anthropogenic Era Began Thousands of Years Ago*, 61 CLIMATIC CHANGE 261 (2003). *See also* MANN, *supra* note 8.

20 Tsim D. Schneider & Lee M. Panich, *Native Agency at the Margins of Empire: Indigenous Landscapes, Spanish Missions, and Contested Histories*, *in* INDIGENOUS LANDSCAPES AND SPANISH MISSIONS: NEW PERSPECTIVES FROM ARCHAEOLOGY AND ETHNOHISTORY 5, 5–22 (Lee M. Panich & Tsim D. Schneider eds., 2014).

21 Laurent Dubois, *The French Atlantic*, *in* ATLANTIC HISTORY: A CRITICAL APPRAISAL 137,137–62 (Jack P. Greene & Philip D. Morgan eds., 2009).

22 *Id.*

23 LAWRENCE M. FRIEDMAN, A HISTORY OF AMERICAN LAW 33–48 (2d ed. 1985).

24 O.W. HOLMES, JR., THE COMMON LAW (1881). *See also*, Daniel M. Klerman et al., *Legal Origin or Colonial History?*, 3 J. LEGAL ANALYSIS 379, 379–409 (2011).

25 *See, e.g.*, Allan Greer, *Commons and Enclosure in the Colonization of North America*, 117 AM. HIST. REV. 365, 365–86 (2012); Dale D. Goble, *Three Cases/Four Tales: Commons, Capture, the Public Trust, and Property in Land*, 35 ENV'T L. 807, 822 (2005); Joseph W. Dellapenna, *The Evolution of Riparianism in the United States*, 95 MARQ. L. REV. 53, 55 (2011); Thomas A. Lund, *Early American Wildlife Law*, 51 N.Y.U. L. REV. 703, 706–07 (1976).

26 *See, e.g.*, Sally K. Fairfax et. al., *Historical Evolution and Future of Natural Resources Law and Policy, in* THE EVOLUTION OF NATURAL RESOURCES LAW AND POLICY 3, 3–4 (Lawrence J. MacDonnell & Sarah F. Bates eds., 2010).

27 *See, e.g.*, Christine Meisner Rosen, *'Knowing' Industrial Pollution: Nuisance Law and the Power of Tradition in a Time of Rapid Economic Change, 1840–1846*, 8 ENV'T HIST. 565, 566 (2003); Goble, *supra* note 25, at 845; Jouni Paavola, *Water Quality as Property: Industrial Water Pollution and Common Law in the Nineteenth Century United States*, 3 ENV'T & HIST. 295, 298 (2002).

28 Pierson v. Post, 3 Cai. 175 (N.Y. 1805).

29 Dean Lueck, *Property Rights and the Economic Logic of Wildlife Institutions*, 35 NAT. RES. J. 625, 631 (1995).

30 Michael C. Blumm & Lucus Ritchie, *The Pioneer Spirit and the Public Trust: The American Rule of Capture and State Ownership of Wildlife*, 35 ENV'T L. 673, 675–77 (2005).

31 *See, e.g.*, Fairfax et al., *supra* note 26.

32 Paul Frymer, *"A Rush and a Push and the Land Is Ours": Territorial Expansion, Land Policy, and U.S. State Formation*, 12 PERSPS. ON POL. 119, 121 (2014).

33 John P. Bowes, *American Indian Removal Beyond the Removal Act*, 1 NATIVE AM. & INDIGENOUS STUD. 65, 68–69 (2014).

34 Johnson v. M'Intosh, 21 U.S. 543 (1823).

35 *See* Cheryl I. Harris, *Whiteness as Property*, 106 HARV. L. REV. 1707, 1715–24 (1993).

36 *Johnson*, 21 U.S. at 572–90.

37 *See Native American Ownership and Governance of Natural Resources*, U.S. DEP'T INTERIOR, https://revenuedata.doi.gov/how-revenue-works/native-american-ownership-governance/ (last visited Feb. 3, 2022).

38 *See Johnson*, 21 U.S. 543; Eric Kades, *History and Interpretation of the Great Case of* Johnson v. M'Intosh, 19 LAW & HIST. REV. 67 (2001).

39 Kades, *supra* note 38.

40 Louisiana Purchase Treaty, U.S.-Fr., Apr. 30, 1803, T.S. No. 86.

41 MIKE WILSON, BROKEN PROMISES: THE U.S. GOVERNMENT AND NATIVE AMERICANS IN THE NINETEENTH CENTURY (2003).

42 Winters v. United States, 207 U.S. 564, 576 (1908). *See also* DAVID RICH LEWIS, NEITHER WOLF NOR DOG : AMERICAN INDIANS, ENVIRONMENT, AND AGRARIAN CHANGE 2-21 (1994).

43 Angela P. Harris, *[Re]Integrating Spaces: The Color of Farming*, 2 SAVANNAH L. REV. 157, 174 (2015).

44 STEPHANIE A. MERCIER & STEVE A. HALBROOK, AGRICULTURAL POLICY OF THE UNITED STATES: HISTORIC FOUNDATIONS AND 21ST CENTURY ISSUES 7–24 (2020).

45 *See, e.g.*, Andrew Smith, *The First Thanksgiving*, 3 GASTRONOMICA 79 (2003).

46 Thomas R. Wessel, *Agriculture, Indians, and American History*, 50 AGRIC. HIST. 9, 9 (1976).

47 *Id.* at 15.

48 *Id.*

49 Alfred A. Cave, *Abuse of Power: Andrew Jackson and the Indian Removal Act of 1830*, 65 HISTORIAN 1330, 1332 (2003).

50 *See, e.g.*, GRANT FOREMAN, THE FIVE CIVILIZED TRIBES: CHEROKEE, CHICKASAW, CHOCTAW, CREEK, SEMINOLE (1989).

51 Worcester v. Georgia, 31 U.S. 515, 561 (1832).

52 Cave, *supra* note 49, at 1349–50.

53 *Id.* at 1333.

54 AMY H. STURGIS, THE TRAIL OF TEARS AND INDIAN REMOVAL 55–64 (2007).

55 *Id.* at 60.

56 *See* John D. Wilsey, *"Our Country Is Destined to be the Great Nation of Futurity": John L. O'Sullivan's Manifest Destiny and Christian Nationalism, 1837–1846*, 8 RELIGIONS 68 (2017).

57 *See, e.g.*, CHAR MILLER, FLUID ARGUMENTS: FIVE CENTURIES OF WESTERN WATER CONFLICT (2001).

58 *See* ROBERT H. JACKSON & EDWARD CASTILLO, INDIANS, FRANCISCANS, AND SPANISH COLONIZATION: THE IMPACT OF THE MISSION SYSTEM ON CALIFORNIA INDIANS (1996).

59 *See* George B. Eckhart, *Spanish Missions of Texas 1680–1800: An Outline of Spanish Mission History in Texas from 1680 to 1800*, 32 J. SW. ANTHROPOLOGY & HIST. 73 (2016).

60 Schneider & Panich, *supra* note 20.

61 Julius W. Pratt, *The Origin of 'Manifest Destiny,'* 32 AM. HIST. REV. 795 (1927).

62 *Id.*

63 *Id.* at 796.

64 *See* WALLACE EARLE STEGNER, THE GATHERING OF ZION: THE STORY OF THE MORMON TRAIL (3d ed. 1992).

65 *See* Leonard J. Arrington & Dean May, *"A Different Mode of Life": Irrigation and Society in Nineteenth-Century Utah*, 49 AGRIC. HIST. 3 (1975).

66 *See* THOMAS MAXWELL-LONG, DAILY LIFE DURING THE CALIFORNIA GOLD RUSH (2014).

67 *See* HERBERT M. WILSON, U.S. GEOLOGICAL SURVEY PUMPING WATER FOR IRRIGATION 25–26 (1896).

68 Adam Smith, *History of Astronomy*, *in* ADAM SMITH: ESSAYS ON PHILOSOPHICAL SUBJECTS 33 (W. P. D. Wightman & J. C. Bryce eds., Liberty Classic ed. 1982); ADAM SMITH, AN INQUIRY INTO THE NATURE AND CAUSES OF THE WEALTH OF NATIONS, VOL. I, BOOK IV, at 477–78 (Edwin Cannan ed., Chicago 1976) (1776).

69 FRANK BOURGIN, THE GREAT CHALLENGE: THE MYTH OF LAISSEZ-FAIRE IN THE EARLY REPUBLIC (1989).

70 *See, e.g.*, *A History of Central Banking in the United States*, THE FED. RSRV. BANK OF MINNEAPOLIS, https://web.archive.org/web/20100103085054

/http://www.minneapolisfed.org/community_education/student /centralbankhistory/bank.cfm (last visited June 12, 2025).

71 *See* P. J. Federico, *Operation of the Patent Act of 1790*, 18 J. PAT. OFF. SOC'Y 237 (1936).

72 *See* J. L. Allen, *Horizons of the Sublime: The Invention of the Romantic West*, 18 J. HIST. GEOGRAPHY 27 (1992).

73 *See* Federico Bonomi, *The United States Immigration Laws: History of a Nation Set up by Migrants*, 9 VERGENTIS 253 (2019).

74 Naturalization Act of 1790, ch. 3, 1 Stat. 103.

75 Carla L. Reyes, *Naturalization Law, Immigration Flow, and Policy*, *in* PERSPECTIVES ON IMMIGRATION: HISTORY AND ISSUES 145, 145–48 (2013).

76 Frymer, *supra* note 32, at 119–44.

77 *Id.*

78 *See, e.g.*, John T. Ganoe, *The Desert Land Act in Operation, 1877–1891*, 11 AGRIC. HIST. 142, 146–47 (1937); Karl S. Landstrom, *Reclamation Under the Desert-Land Act*, 36 J. FARM ECON. 500 (1954); Robert W. Harrison & Walter M. Kollmorgen, *Land Reclamation in Arkansas Under the Swamp Land Grant of 1850*, 6 ARK. HIST. Q. 369, 370 (1947).

79 *See* Harris, *supra* note 35, at 1715–20.

80 *See, e.g.*, EUGENE D. GENOVESE, THE POLITICAL ECONOMY OF SLAVERY: STUDIES IN THE ECONOMY AND SOCIETY OF THE SLAVE SOUTH (2d ed. 1988).

81 Letter from Thomas Jefferson to George Washington (Aug. 14, 1787).

82 Mark D. McGarvie, *"In Perfect Accordance with His Character": Thomas Jefferson, Slavery, and the Law*, 95 IND. MAG. HIST. 142 (1999).

83 *See* R. Daniels Hank et al., *Mapping Antebellum Rice Fields as a Basis for Understanding Human and Ecological Consequences of the Era of Slavery*, 10 LAND 831 (2021).

84 Douglas W. Allen, *Homesteading and Property Rights; Or "How the West Was Really Won,"* 34 J.L. & ECON. 1, 7–8, 19 (1991).

85 *See, e.g.*, Frymer, *supra* note 32, at 119–44; *About the Homestead Act*, NAT'L PARK SERV. NAT'L HIST. PARK, NEB. (Oct. 12, 2022), www.nps.gov/home/learn /historyculture/abouthomesteadactlaw.htm.

86 *See, e.g.*, Allen, *supra* note 72, at 6–12.

87 *See, e.g.*, Greg Bradsher, *How the West Was Settled: The 150-Year-Old Homestead Act Lured Americans Looking for a New Life and New Opportunities*, 44 PROLOGUE 26, 27 (2012).

88 *See* Allen, *supra* note 72, at 11.

89 U.S. DEP'T OF THE INTERIOR, PRESIDENT KENNEDY'S MESSAGE ON CONSERVATION TO THE CONGRESS OF THE UNITED STATES 11 (1962).

90 *See, e.g.*, HARRY N. SCHEIBER, OHIO CANAL ERA: A CASE STUDY OF GOVERNMENT AND THE ECONOMY, 1820–1861 193–95, 198–200, 238 (2012).

91 Pamela L. Baker, *The Washington National Road Bill and the Struggle to Adopt a Federal System of Internal Improvement*, 22 J. Early Republic 437 (2002).

92 Peter L. Bernstein, Wedding of the Waters: The Erie Canal and the Making of a Great Nation 26 (2005)

93 Ronald E. Shaw, Erie Water West: a history of the Erie Canal, 1792–1854 298 (1990).

94 Bernstein, *supra* note 92, at 256.

95 *See* Camden Burd, *A New, Historic Canal*, 42 J. Soc'y for Indus. Archeology 23, 24 (2016).

96 *See* Shaw, *supra* note 93.

97 John T. Cumbler & Mark R. Stoll, Northeast and Midwest United States: An Environmental History 136 (2005).

98 David Sommerstein, *Ten Threats: The Earliest Invader*, The Env't Rep. (Oct. 17, 2005).

99 *See* Charles W. Ramsdell, *The Confederate Government and the Railroads*, 22 Am. Hist. Rev. 794, 794 (1917).

100 Pacific Railway Act, ch. 120, 12 Stat. 489 (1862).

101 Roger D. Billings, *The Homestead Act, Pacific Railroad Act and Morrill Act*, 39 N. Ky. L. Rev. 699, 705–06 (2012).

102 *See Railroad Maps, 1828 to 1900: Land Grants*, Libr. Congress, www.loc.gov/collections/railroad-maps-1828-to-1900/articles-and-essays/history-of-railroads-and-maps/land-grants/ (last visited June 12, 2025).

103 *See Abraham Lincoln, Fourth Annual Message (Dec. 6, 1864)*, The American Presidency Project, https://www.presidency.ucsb.edu/documents/fourth-annual-message-8 (last visited Sept. 20, 2025).

104 *See, e.g.*, The Chinese and the Iron Road: Building the Transcontinental Railroad (Gordon H. Chang & Shelley Fisher Fishkin eds., 2019).

105 George W. Geib, *The Land Ordinance of 1785: A Bicentennial Review*, 81 Ind. Mag. History 1, 6 (1985).

106 *See, e.g.*, Anthony Scott & Georgina Coustalin, *The Evolution of Water Rights*, 35 Nat. Res. J. 821, 825 (1995).

107 Tyler v. Wilkinson, 24 F. Cas. 472 (C.C.D.R.I. 1827).

108 T. E. Lauer, *The Common Law Background of the Riparian Doctrine*, 28 Mo. L. Rev. 60 (1963).

109 *Tyler*, 24 F. Cas. 472.

110 *Id.* at 474.

111 *Id.*

112 *See The Annexation of Texas, the Mexican-American War, and the Treaty of Guadalupe-Hidalgo, 1845–1848*, Off. of the Historian, Dep't of State, https://history.state.gov/milestones/1830-1860/texas-annexation (last visited Feb. 8, 2022); *Government and Law, in Early California History: An Overview*, Libr. of Congress, www.loc.gov/collections/california-first-person-narratives

/articles-and-essays/early-california-history/government-and-law/ (last visited Feb. 8, 2022).

113 Irwin v. Phillips, 5 Cal. 140 (1855).

114 *Id.* at 146.

115 *Id.*

116 *See* Norman K. Johnson & Charles T. DuMars, *A Survey of the Evolution of Western Water Law in Response to Changing Economic and Public Interest Demands*, 29 NAT. RES. J. 347, 348–51 (1989).

117 *See, e.g.*, ALLAN PRED, URBAN GROWTH AND CITY SYSTEMS IN THE UNITED STATES, 1840–1860 6 (1980).

118 *See* Scott Kirsch, *John Wesley Powell and the Mapping of the Colorado Plateau, 1869–1879: Survey Science, Geographical Solutions, and the Economy of Environmental Values*, 92 ANNALS ASS'N AM. GEOGRAPHERS 548 (2002).

119 *See id.*

120 DONALD WORSTER, A RIVER RUNNING WEST: THE LIFE OF JOHN WESLEY POWELL 166 (2002).

121 *Id.* at 495.

122 Cnty. of Imperial v. Superior Court, 152 Cal. App. 4th 13, 18 (2007) (citing Twain). Note, however, that while this turn of phrase is enough of a clever truism that it might ring of Twain, we cannot find a source to verify that these are Twain's words.

123 *See also* Daina Dravnieks Apple, *Evolution of U. S. Water Policy: Emphasis on the West*, 24 WOMEN IN NAT. RES. 16 (2004).

124 Yasuhide Kawashima & Ruth Tone, *Environmental Policy in Early America: A Survey of Colonial Statutes*, 27 J. FOREST HIST. 168 (1983).

125 *Id.*

126 *See* Thomas R. Dunlap, *Sport Hunting and Conservation, 1880–1920*, 12 ENV'T REV. 51 (1988).

127 ANDREW C. ISENBERG, THE DESTRUCTION OF THE BISON: AN ENVIRONMENTAL HISTORY, 1750–1920, 25–27 (2020).

128 *See* Andrew C. Isenberg, *Toward a Policy of Destruction: Buffaloes, Law, and the Market, 1803–83*, 12 GREAT PLAINS Q. 227 (1992).

129 *See* Clay Duval, *Bison Conservation: Saving an Ecologically and Culturally Keystone Species*, DELIBERATIONS, Fall 2006, 21, https://web.archive.org/web/20120308011257/http://twp.duke.edu/uploads/assets/Duval.pdf.

130 *See, e.g.*, WILLIAM TEMPLE HORNADAY, THE EXTERMINATION OF THE AMERICAN BISON (1889).

131 *See* Isenberg, *supra* note 128, at 227.

132 HORNADAY, *supra* note 130, at 525; ISENBERG, *supra* note 127, at 12.

133 Barry Yeoman, *Why the Passenger Pigeon Went Extinct*, AUDUBON (May/June 2014), www.audubon.org/magazine/may-june-2014/why-passenger-pigeon-went-extinct.

134 *See* Jonathon Rosen, *The Birds*, THE NEW YORKER (Dec. 29, 2013), www.newyorker.com/magazine/2014/01/06/the-birds-4.

135 *See* Taylor Waters, *Passenger Pigeons: The De-Extinction and Reintroduction of a Bird*, 15 J. ANIMAL & NAT. RES. L. 19, 25 (2019).
136 ERROL FULLER, EXTINCT BIRDS 96–97 (rev. ed. 2001).
137 Norwegian University of Science and Technology, *Why Did the Passenger Pigeon Die Out? Turns out that Humans Really Did Cause the Extinction of this Species*, SCIENCE DAILY (Jan. 11, 2018), www.sciencedaily.com/releases/2018/01/180111084953.htm.
138 *See* Steinar Brandslet, *Why the Passenger Pigeon Died Out*, NORWEGIAN SCITECH NEWS (Jan. 11, 2018), https://norwegianscitechnews.com/2018/01/passenger-pigeon-died/.
139 *See* Garrett Power, *More About Oysters than You Wanted to Know*, 30 MD. L. REV. 199, 200 (1970).
140 *Id.*
141 *See* Charles F. Wilkinson & Daniel Keith Conner, *The Law of the Pacific Salmon Fishery: Conservation and Allocation of a Transboundary Common Property Resource*, 32 U. KAN. L. REV. 17, 30–35 (1983).
142 *See* Kendall Beaton, *Dr. Gesner's Kerosene: The Start of American Oil Refining*, 29 BUS. HIST. REV. 28 (1955).
143 J. David Hacker, *Top of Form, Bottom of Form: A Census-Based Count of the Civil War Dead*, 57 CIVIL WAR HIST. 307 (2011).
144 Jack Temple Kirby, *The American Civil War: An Environmental View*, NAT'L HUMANITIES CTR. (2001), http://nationalhumanitiescenter.org/tserve/nattrans/ntuseland/essays/amcwarb.htm (last visited June 12, 2025).
145 *See* Carl E. Bruch, *All's Not Fair in (Civil) War: Criminal Liability for Environmental Damage in Internal Armed Conflict*, 25 VT. L. REV. 695, 695 (2000).
146 TED STEINBERG, DOWN TO EARTH: NATURE'S ROLE IN AMERICAN HISTORY 89 (2002).
147 Ted Widmer, *The Civil War's Environmental Impact*, N.Y. TIMES (Nov. 15, 2014), https://archive.nytimes.com/opinionator.blogs.nytimes.com/2014/11/15/the-civil-wars-environmental-impact/.
148 *See generally* WHY THE NORTH WON THE CIVIL WAR (David Herbert Donald ed., 1960).
149 *See* Leland H. Jenks, *Railroads as an Economic Force in American Development*, 4 J. ECON. HIST. 1, 4–11 (1944).
150 *See* Alfred D. Chandler, Jr., *Anthracite Coal and the Beginnings of the Industrial Revolution in the United States*, 46 BUS. HIST. REV. 141 (1972).
151 *See, e.g.*, MARTIN V. MELOSI, EFFLUENT AMERICA: CITIES, INDUSTRY, ENERGY, AND THE ENVIRONMENT 39 (2001).
152 *See* Rosen, *supra* note 134.
153 *See* MELOSI, *supra* note 151, at 50–52.
154 *See* Chandler, *supra* note 150.
155 CLAYTON J. RUMINSKI, IRON VALLEY: THE TRANSFORMATION OF THE IRON INDUSTRY IN OHIO'S MAHONING VALLEY, 1802–1913 77–111 (2017).

156 David Favre & Vivien Tsang, *The Development of the Anti-Cruelty Laws During the 1800s*, 1993 DET. COLL. L. REV. 1 (1993).

157 ROBERT P. WOLENSKY & JOSEPH M. KEATING, TRAGEDY AT AVONDALE: THE CAUSES, CONSEQUENCES, AND LEGACY OF THE PENNSYLVANIA ANTHRACITE COAL INDUSTRY'S MOST DEADLY MINING DISASTER, SEPTEMBER 6, 1869 (2008).

158 Jeffrey S. Sartin, *Infectious Diseases During the Civil War: The Triumph of the "Third Army,"* 16 CLINICAL INFECTIOUS DISEASES 580 (1993).

159 *See, e.g.*, Thomas Fisher, *Frederick Law Olmsted and the Campaign for Public Health*, PLACES (Nov. 2010), https://placesjournal.org/article/frederick-law-olmsted-and-the-campaign-for-public-health/?cn-reloaded=1.

160 *See* SANDRA HEMPEL, THE STRANGE CASE OF THE BROAD STREET PUMP: JOHN SNOW AND THE MYSTERY OF CHOLERA (2007).

161 *See* Fisher, *supra* note 159.

162 *Id.*

163 *See, e.g.*, JOHN DUFFY, THE SANITARIANS: A HISTORY OF AMERICAN PUBLIC HEALTH 110–25 (1992); H. Toledo-Pereyra Luis & Horacio Toledo Alexander, *American Civil War. Part II*, 17 J. INVESTIGATIVE SURGERY 185, 187 (2009).

164 *See* DUFFY, *supra* note 163.

165 *See* N.Y.C. DEP'T OF HEALTH & MENTAL HYGIENE, PROTECTING PUBLIC HEALTH IN NEW YORK CITY: 200 YEARS OF LEADERSHIP (2005), www1.nyc.gov/assets/doh/downloads/pdf/bicentennial/historical-booklet.pdf.

166 *See* Stanley K. Schultz & Clay McShane, *To Engineer the Metropolis: Sewers, Sanitation, and City Planning in Late-Nineteenth-Century America*, 65 J. AM. HIST. 389 (1978).

167 *See* Lawrence O. Gostin, Note, *Public Health Law in a New Century: Part I: Law as a Tool to Advance the Community's Health*, 283 HEALTH L. & ETHICS 2837 (2000).

168 *See* HAROLD U. FAULKNER, AMERICAN ECONOMIC HISTORY 345 (7th ed. 1954).

169 *See* ROY ROSENZWEIG & ELIZABETH BLACKMAR, THE PARK AND THE PEOPLE: A HISTORY OF CENTRAL PARK 90–91 (1992).

170 LAWRENCE B. CONYERS, GPR SURVEYS, SENECA VILLAGE PROJECT SITES, CENTRAL PARK, NEW YORK, FINAL REPORT (2005).

171 *See* Theodore S. Eisenman, *Frederick Law Olmsted, Green Infrastructure, and the Evolving City*, 12 J. PLAN. HIST. 290 (2013).

172 *See* FREDERICK LAW OLMSTED, LANDSCAPE ARCHITECT, 1822–1903 (Frederick Law Olmsted & Theodora Kimball Hubbard eds., 1970).

173 *Id.*

174 Wallace Stegner, *The Best Idea We Ever Had*, *in* MARKING THE SPARROW'S FALL: THE MAKING OF THE AMERICAN WEST 135, 137 (Page Stegner ed., 1999).

175 *See, e.g.*, W. Turrentine Jackson, *The Creation of Yellowstone National Park*, 29 MISS. VALLEY HIST. REV. 187, 187–88 (1942); *Expeditions Explore Yellowstone*, NAT'L PARK SERV. (Apr. 18, 2025), www.nps.gov/yell/learn/historyculture/expeditions.htm.

176 *See* U.S. GEOLOGICAL SURV., FERDINAND VANDIVEER HAYDEN AND THE FOUNDING OF THE YELLOWSTONE NATIONAL PARK 5 (1973); Jackson, *supra* note 175, at 192; Sam Kalen, Rekindling Yellowstone's Early History: 150 Years Later, 22 WYO. L. REV. 217, 222–224 (2022).

177 MARK DAVID SPENCE, DISPOSSESSING THE WILDERNESS: INDIAN REMOVAL AND THE MAKING OF THE NATIONAL PARKS 57–68 (1999); Robert B. Keiter, *Preserving Nature in the National Parks: Law, Policy, and Science in a Dynamic Environment*, 74 DENV. U.L. REV. 649, 653–654 (1997); Isaac Kantor, *Ethnic Cleansing and America's Creation of National Parks*, 28 PUB. LAND & RES. L. REV. 41 (2007).

178 *See* GARY E. MACHLIS & DONALD FIELD, NATIONAL PARKS AND RURAL DEVELOPMENT: PRACTICE AND POLICY IN THE UNITED STATES 51–55 (2000).

179 *See Today in History—June 30: Yosemite*, LIBR. OF CONGRESS, www.loc.gov/item/today-in-history/june-30 (last visited June 12, 2025).

180 *See* LINDA WEDEL GREENE, YOSEMITE: THE PARK AND ITS RESOURCES: A HISTORY OF THE DISCOVERY, MANAGEMENT, AND PHYSICAL DEVELOPMENT OF YOSEMITE NATIONAL PARK, CALIFORNIA 51–55 (1987).

181 Frederick Law Olmsted & Laura Wood Roper, *The Yosemite Valley and the Mariposa Big Trees: A Preliminary Report (1865)*, 43 LANDSCAPE ARCHITECTURE MAG. 12, 14 (1952).

182 *See, e.g.*, Bruce M. Kramer & Owen L. Anderson, *The Rule of Capture—An Oil and Gas Perspective*, 35 ENV'T L. 899 (2005); Goble, *supra* note 25, at 39; *Pierson*, 3 Cai. 175.

183 *See, e.g.*, Mary C. Suter, *Swamp Land Act of 1850*, ENCYCLOPEDIA OF ARK. (Sept. 1, 2022), https://encyclopediaofarkansas.net/entries/swamp-land-act-of-1850-7402/; *see also* U.S. NAT'L ARCHIVES AND RECS. ADMIN., LAND ACTS (2014), www.archives.gov/files/calendar/genealogy-fair/2014/handouts/session-11-handout-5of5-martinez-land-other-land-acts.pdf.

184 *See* U.S. NAT'L ARCHIVES AND RECS. ADMIN., *supra* note 183.

185 General Mining Act of 1872, ch. 152, 17 Stat. 91 (codified as amended at 30 U.S.C. §§ 21–54 (1982)).

186 Carl J. Mayer, *Historical Origins of the Discovery Rule: The 1872 Mining Law*, 53 U. CHI. L. REV. 624 (1986).

187 *Id.*

188 *See* CHARLES F. WILKINSON, CROSSING THE NEXT MERIDIAN: LAND, WATER, AND THE FUTURE OF THE WEST 49 (2013) (describing "[T]he General Mining Law . . . lack[s] . . . any provision for environmental protection . . . [T]he legacy continues long after mines have been abandoned. Approximately

50 billion tons of mining and processing waste have been left behind at mining sites . . . 12,000 miles of rivers and streams and 180,000 acres of lakes and reservoirs have been adversely affected . . . 1,298 river miles in Colorado alone have been contaminated by mining wastes.").

CHAPTER 2. THE PROGRESSIVE ERA

1 Frederick Jackson Turner, *The Significance of the Frontier in American History*, *in* REPORT OF THE AMERICAN HISTORICAL ASSOCIATION FOR 1893, 199–227 (1894), reprinted in FREDERICK JACKSON TURNER, THE FRONTIER IN AMERICAN HISTORY 1–38 (1st ed. 1920).

2 ROBERT P. PORTER, U.S. CENSUS OFFICE, EXTRA CENSUS BULLETIN 4 (1891).

3 Turner, *supra* note 1.

4 JOHN WHITECLAY CHAMBERS, THE TYRANNY OF CHANGE: AMERICA IN THE PROGRESSIVE ERA, 1890–1920 45 (2d ed. 2000); RANDALL WILSON, AMERICA'S PUBLIC LANDS: FROM YELLOWSTONE TO SMOKEY BEAR AND BEYOND 17 (2d ed. 2020).

5 *See supra* chap. 1 notes 125 to 140 and accompanying text.

6 *Increasing Urbanization: Population Distribution by City Size, 1790 to 1980*, U.S. CENSUS BUREAU (July 19, 2012), www.census.gov/dataviz/visualizations/005/.

7 *See generally* Stewart E. Tolnay, *The African American "Great Migration" and Beyond*, 29 ANN. REV. OF SOCIO. 209 (2003).

8 ROBERT G. SPINNEY, CITY OF BIG SHOULDERS: A HISTORY OF CHICAGO 40 (2020).

9 *See, e.g.*, Sean M. Kammer, *Railroad Land Grants in an Incongruous Legal System: Corporate Subsidies, Bureaucratic Governance, and Legal Conflict in the United States, 1850–1903*, 35 L. & HIST. REV. 391, 401 (2017).

10 ERIK LARSON, DEVIL IN THE WHITE CITY 11 (2003).

11 SPINNEY, *supra* note 9, at 40–61.

12 *See* Ronald H. Carpenter, *Frederick Jackson Turner and the Rhetorical Impact of the Frontier Thesis*, 63 Q.J. SPEECH 117 (1977).

13 Javier Monclús & Carmen Díez Medina, *City Beautiful and 'Architectural Urbanism' (1893–1940)*, *in* URBAN VISIONS 3 (Carmen Díez Medina & Javier Monclús eds., 2018).

14 LARSON, *supra* note 11, at 254.

15 *See, e.g.*, The Rural Electrification Act of 1936, Pub. L. No. 74–605. *See also* Elizabeth Adams, *The Third Wave of Electrification: A Normative Tool Against Climate Change*, 1 NOTRE DAME J. ON EMERGING TECH. 415, 417 (2020).

16 GIFFORD PINCHOT, THE FIGHT FOR CONSERVATION (1910).

17 *See* Grant McConnell, *The Environmental Movement: Ambiguities and Meanings*, 11 NAT. RES. J. 427, 430 (1971).

18 Thomas G. Alexander, *Senator Reed Smoot and Western Land Policy, 1905–1920*, 13 ARIZ. & WEST 245, 246 (1971).

19 Stuart W. Shulman, *The Business of Soil Fertility: A Convergence of Urban-Agrarian Concern in the Early 20th Century*, 12 ORG. & ENV'T 401 (1999).

20 *See, e.g.*, SAMUEL P. HAYS, CONSERVATION AND THE GOSPEL OF EFFICIENCY: THE PROGRESSIVE CONSERVATION MOVEMENT, 1890–1920 83 (1968).

21 John T. Cumbler, *Conflict, Accommodation, and Compromise: Connecticut's Attempt to Control Industrial Wastes in the Progressive Era*, 5 ENV'L HIST. 314, 315 (2000).

22 GERALD D. NASH, UNITED STATES OIL POLICY, 1890–1964; BUSINESS AND GOVERNMENT IN TWENTIETH CENTURY AMERICA (1968); AUGUST W. GIEBELHAUS, BUSINESS AND GOVERNMENT IN THE OIL INDUSTRY: A CASE STUDY OF SUN OIL, 1876–1945 (1980).

23 *See* Jason Scott Johnston, *The Tragedy of Centralization: The Political Economics of American Natural Resource Federalism*, 74 U. COLO. L. REV. 487, 538–39 (2003).

24 *See generally* ROY M. ROBBINS, OUR LANDED HERITAGE: THE PUBLIC DOMAIN, 1776–1970 (2d ed. 1976).

25 ELMO R. RICHARDSON, THE POLITICS OF CONSERVATION: CRUSADES AND CONTROVERSIES, 1897–1913 (1962).

26 Ernest Engelbert, *Richardson, Elmo R., The Politics of Conservation: Crusades and Controversies, 1897–1913*, 5 NAT. RES. J. 193, 194 (2017).

27 RICHARDSON, *supra* note 26.

28 ROBERT H. WIEBE, THE SEARCH FOR ORDER, 1877–1920 166 (1967).

29 J. Leonard Bates, *Fulfilling American Democracy: The Conservation Movement, 1907 to 1921*, 44 MISS. VALLEY HIST. REV. 29, 30 (1957).

30 Grant McConnell, *The Conservation Movement—Past and Present*, 7 W. POL. Q. 463, 466 (1954); Penick James, *The Progressives and the Environment: Three Themes from the First Conservation Movement*, *in* THE PROGRESSIVE ERA IN THE USA: 1890–1921 (Kristofer Allerfeldt ed., 2007).

31 Bryan McDonald, *Considering the Nature of Wilderness: Reflections on Roderick Nash's Wilderness and the American Mind*, 14 ORG. & ENV'T 188, 189, 193–94 (2001).

32 *See, e.g.*, KURKPATRICK DORSEY, THE DAWN OF CONSERVATION DIPLOMACY: U.S.-CANADIAN WILDLIFE PROTECTION TREATIES IN THE PROGRESSIVE ERA (2009).

33 *See generally* THE LETTERS OF THEODORE ROOSEVELT, VOL. III-IV, THE SQUARE DEAL, 1901–1905 (Elting E. Morison ed., 1951).

34 Daniel Rodgers, *In Search of Progressivism*, 10 REVS. AM. HIST. 113, 123 (1982).

35 SHELTON STROMQUIST, REINVENTING "THE PEOPLE": THE PROGRESSIVE MOVEMENT, THE CLASS PROBLEM, AND THE ORIGINS OF MODERN LIBERALISM (2006).

36 Federal income taxes were provided for through ratification of the Sixteenth Amendment of the U.S. Constitution. U.S. CONST. amend. XVI.

37 U.S. CONST. amend XVIII.

38 *See, e.g.*, Oscar Kraines, *Brandeis' Philosophy of Scientific Management*, 13 W. Pol. Q. 191, 191 (1960); Woodrow Wilson, *The Study of Administration*, 2 Pol. Sci. Q. 197 (1887).
39 *See* Mordecai Lee, Bureaus of Efficiency: Reforming Local Government in the Progressive Era (2008).
40 Henry George, Progress and Poverty (1879).
41 *See generally* Louis Filler, The Muckrakers (1968); *see, e.g.*, Ida Tarbell, The History of the Standard Oil Company (1904).
42 Joseph L. Tropea, *Rational Capitalism and Municipal Government: The Progressive Era*, Soc. Sci. Hist. 137 (1989); Martin J. Schiesl, The Politics of Efficiency: Municipal Reform in the Progressive Era 1880–1920 (1972); Kenneth Fox, Better city government: Innovation in American Urban Politics, 1850–1937 (1977).
43 Upton Sinclair, The Jungle (1906).
44 *See generally* Michael P. Cohen, The History of the Sierra Club 1892–1970 (1988).
45 Mildred Chadsey, *Municipal Housekeeping*, 7 J. of Home Econ. 53 (1915).
46 *See, e.g.*, Richard Hofstadter, Social Darwinism in American Thought 167 (1992).
47 *Id.* at 170.
48 Booker T. Washington, Up from Slavery: An Autobiography: Electronic Edition 264–65 (1997).
49 W. E. B. DuBois, *Hopkinsville, Chicago and Idlewild*, 22 The Crisis 158 (1921).
50 *See, e.g.*, Brian McCammack, Landscapes of Hope: Nature and the Great Migration in Chicago (2017).
51 *See* Leslie Vincent Tischuaser, Jim Crow Laws xi-xv (2012).
52 *Id.* at 29–33; *see also* Plessy v. Ferguson, 163 U.S. 537 (1896).
53 New York State Legislature, Testimony Taken by the Assembly Committee on Public Lands and Forestry Concerning the Administration of Laws in Relation to the Forest Preserve by the Forest Commission, Etc., 114 Documents of the Assembly of the State of New York 74–82 (1891) (Statement of Theodore Basselin).
54 *See generally* Natasha N. Jones & Miriam F. Williams, *Technologies of Disenfranchisement: Literacy Tests and Black Voters in the U.S. from 1890 to 1965*, 65 Tech. Commc'n 371 (2018); *see also* Chambers, *supra* note 4, at 8–10.
55 Letter from Captain Jim to Commissioner of Indian Affairs (Sept. 25, 1915), File 115, Havasupai Agency, Central Classified Files, 1907–39, Records of the Bureau of Indian Affairs, RG 75, National Archives.
56 *See generally* Jason Corburn, Toward the Healthy City: People, Places, and the Politics of Urban Planning 25–60 (2009).
57 *See* John Copeland Nagle, *What if the Grand Canyon Had Become the Second National Park?*, 51 Ariz. St. L.J. 675 (2019).
58 *Id.* at 683.

59 *Id.*

60 *See B&C Member Spotlight—Gifford Pinchot*, BOONE AND CROCKETT CLUB, www.boone-crockett.org/bc-member-spotlight-gifford-pinchot (last visited Sept. 25, 2025).

61 Act of March 3, 1891, ch. 561, 26 Stat. 1095. *See generally* DOUGLAS BRINKLEY, THE WILDERNESS WARRIOR: THEODORE ROOSEVELT AND THE CRUSADE FOR AMERICA 237 (2009).

62 BRINKLEY, *supra* note 62, at 237–40.

63 HAROLD K. STEEN, THE U.S. FOREST SERVICE: A HISTORY 27–28 (1976).

64 Lance F. Sorenson, *The Hybrid Nature of the Property Clause: Implications for Judicial Review of National Monument Reductions*, 21 U. PA. J. CONST. L. 761, 799 (2019).

65 Lacey Act of 1894, ch. 72, 28 Stat. 73 (also referred to as the Yellowstone Game Protection Act) (codified as amended at 16 U.S.C. §§ 24–31).

66 BRINKLEY, *supra* note 62, at 270.

67 *Id. at* 274–75, 288–90.

68 *Id. at* 290.

69 *Id.* at 292.

70 Robert Bassman, *The 1897 Organic Act: A Historical Perspective*, 7 NAT. RES. LAW. 503, 509–11 (1974).

71 Gerald W. Williams & Char Miller, *At the Creation: The National Forest Commission of 1896–97*, FOREST HIST. TODAY, Spring/Fall 2005, at 32, 38–39.

72 *Id.* at 39; *see also* GERALD W. WILLIAMS, THE USDA FOREST SERVICE: THE FIRST CENTURY 9–10 (2000).

73 JOHN CLAYTON, NATURAL RIVALS: JOHN MUIR, GIFFORD PINCHOT, AND THE CREATION OF AMERICA'S PUBLIC LANDS 80, 190–91 (2019).

74 Act of June 4, 1897, ch. 2, 30 Stat. 11 (codified as amended at 16 U.S.C. §§ 473–482, 551).

75 Sorenson, *supra* note 65, at 800; Scott W. Hardt, *Federal Land Management in the Twenty-First Century: From Wise Use to Wise Stewardship*, 18 HARV. ENV'T L. REV. 345, 354 (1994).

76 16 U.S.C. § 475; *see also* Bassman, *supra* note 71, at 504–14.

77 16 U.S.C. § 475.

78 *Id.*

79 *Id.*

80 Jedediah Purdy, *American Natures: The Shape of Conflict in Environmental Law*, 36 HARV. ENV'T L. REV. 169, 191–92 (2012).

81 BRINKLEY, *supra* note 62, at 238–39.

82 *Id.* at 342–47.

83 THEODORE ROOSEVELT, THE WILDERNESS HUNTER (1893); THEODORE ROOSEVELT & GEORGE BIRD GRINNELL, AMERICAN BIG GAME HUNTING (1893); THEODORE ROOSEVELT & GEORGE BIRD GRINNELL, HUNTING IN MANY LANDS (1895); THEODORE ROOSEVELT, SOME AMERICAN GAME (1897).

84 *See* CHAR MILLER, GIFFORD PINCHOT AND THE MAKING OF MODERN ENVIRONMENTALISM 10 (2001).

85 *Id.* at 147.

86 CLAYTON, *supra* note 74, at 75–78.); BRINKLEY, *supra* note 62, at 341–42.

87 PINCHOT, *supra* note 17, at 46. For a probing look into the values that sat of the root of Progressive conservation efforts, see Michael C. Blumm and Andkara Teabeau, *Antimonopoly in American Public Land Law agency as Principal*, 48 GEO. ENVTL. L. REV. 155, 186–199 (2016).

88 Hardt, *supra* note 76, at 355–56.

89 *Id.*

90 Brigham Daniels, *Agency as Principal*, 48 GA. L. REV. 335, 396–401 (2014).

91 *Id.*

92 *See* BRINKLEY, *supra note* 62, at 676–77.

93 JOHN MUIR, THE YOSEMITE (1912). *See also* John Copeland Nagle, *The Spiritual Values of Wilderness*, 35 ENV'T L. 955, 976–77 (2005); Fred Bosselman, *Four Land Ethics: Order, Reform, Responsibility, Opportunity*, 24 ENV'T L. 1439, 1478–82 (1994).

94 *See generally* LINNIE MARSH WOLFE, SON OF THE WILDERNESS: THE LIFE OF JOHN MUIR (1930).

95 Purdy, *supra* note 81, at 187–92.

96 Alejandro E. Camacho, *De- and Re-constructing Public Governance for Biodiversity Conservation*, 73 VAND. L. REV. 1585, 1601–05 (2020).

97 *See* CAROLYN MERCHANT, SPARE THE BIRDS! GEORGE BIRD GRINNELL AND THE FIRST AUDUBON SOCIETY 235 (2016).

98 *See* BRINKLEY, *supra* note 62, at 13–14; PAUL RUSSELL CUTRIGHT, THEODORE ROOSEVELT: THE MAKING OF A CONSERVATIONIST 233 (1985); EDMUND MORRIS, THE RISE OF THEODORE ROOSEVELT 17 (1979).

99 Rachel F. Levin, *Leading the Way: Early Pioneers of the Refuge System*, FISH & WILDLIFE NEWS, Mar./Apr. 2000, at 14.

100 *See* Robert L. Fischman, *The Significance of National Wildlife Refuges in the Development of U.S. Conservation Policy*, 21 J. LAND USE & ENV'T L. 1, 5 (2005).

101 Antiquities Act of 1906, Pub. L. No. 59–209, 34 Stat. 225 (codified at 54 U.S.C. §§ 320301–320303).

102 *See* Robert W. Righter, *National Monuments to National Parks: The Use of the Antiquities Act of 1906*, 20 W. HIST. Q. 281 (1989).

103 Mark Squillace, *The Monumental Legacy of the Antiquities Act of 1906*, 37 GA. L. REV. 473, 477 (2003); David H. Getches, *Managing the Public Lands: The Authority of the Executive to Withdraw Lands*, 22 NAT. RES. J. 279, 301–02 (1982); James R. Rasband, *Utah's Grand Staircase: The Right Path to Wilderness Preservation?*, 70 U. COLO. L. REV. 483, 501 (1999).

104 Squillace, *supra* note 105, at 85.

105 16 U.S.C. § 431.

106 *See generally* Francis P. McManamon, *The Antiquities Act and How Theodore Roosevelt Shaped It*, 31 George Wright F. 324 (2014).

107 Brinkley, *supra* note 62, at 631–790.

108 *See* Clayton, *supra* note 74.

109 *Id.*

110 *Id.*

111 Horace M. Albright as told to Robert Cahn, The Birth of the National Park Service, The Founding Years, 1913–33, 6 (1985).

112 National Park System Organic Act of 1916, ch. 408, 39 Stat. 535 (codified at 16 U.S.C. §§ 1–4).

113 16 U.S.C. § 1.

114 John Muir, *The Hetch Hetchy Valley*, 6 Sierra Club Bull. 211 (1908) (republished in 13 Hastings W.-Nw. J. of Env't L. & Pol'y 223 (2007)).

115 Federico Cheever, *The United States Forest Service and National Park Service: Paradoxical Mandates, Powerful Founders, and the Rise and Fall of Agency Discretion*, 74 Denv. U.L. Rev. 625, 637–38 (1997); Denise E. Antolini, *National Park Law in the U.S.: Conservation, Conflict, and Centennial Values*, 33 Wm. & Mary Env't L. & Pol'y Rev. 851, 857 (2009).

116 Muir, *supra* note 115.

117 Brian E. Gray, *The Battle for Hetch Hetchy Goes to Congress*, 6 Hastings W.N.W. J. Env. L. & Pol'y 199, 213 (2000).

118 Clayton, *supra* note 74, at 199–206.

119 *See* Wilson, *supra* note 39; Fredrick W. Taylor, The Principles of Scientific Management (1911). The ties between these theorists and the work of federal land management during the era is well recognized. *See* R. McGreggor Cawley, *We May Help to Make up the General Mind: Reuniting Wilson, Taylor, and Pinchot*, 20 Admin. Theory & Praxis 55 (1988).

120 Johnston, *supra* note 24, at 552–57.

121 *See, e.g.*, Mark Damian et al., The Sportsman's Voice: Hunting and Fishing in America 1–8 (2010); Francis Coats & Karrigan Börk, *California's Constitutional Right to Fish*, 51 Env't L. 1085, 1102–08 (2021). For an in-depth look at these early wildlife conservation efforts, see Karrigan Börk, et al., *The Rebirth of California Fish & Game Code Section 5937*, 45 U.C. Davis L. Rev. 809, 817–826 (2012) (discussing California's early fish protections measures, put in place during the Progressive Era).

122 Geer v. Connecticut, 161 U.S. 519, 528–29 (1896).

123 16 U.S.C. §§ 3371–3378.

124 16 U.S.C. § 3372.

125 16 U.S.C. §§ 703–712.

126 16 U.S.C. § 703.

127 *See, e.g.*, Greg Mitman, The State of Nature: Ecology, Community, and American Social Thought, 1900–1950 (1992); Mark

HERSEY, *"What We Need is a Crop Ecologist": Ecology and Agricultural Science in Progressive-Era America*, 85 AGRIC. HIST. 297 (2011).

128 Robert H. Nelson, *The Federal Land Management Agencies*, *in* A NEW CENTURY FOR NATURAL RESOURCES MANAGEMENT 37, 42–44 (Richard L. Knight & Sarah F. Bates eds., 1995).

129 *Id.* at 44–47.

130 *See* BUREAU OF LAND MGMT., JOHN DAY BASIN PROPOSED RESOURCE MANAGEMENT PLAN AND FINAL ENVIRONMENTAL IMPACT STATEMENT 238 (2012).

131 *See e.g.*, ALDO LEOPOLD, SAND COUNTY ALMANAC 129–133 (1949); RACHEL CARSON, SILENT SPRING 245–261 (1962). Note, however, while little dispute exists about the damage of overgrazing, some dispute exists about whether the Kaibab herd in the 1920s is an historically accurate example of it. *See* Dan Binkley, et al., *Was Aldo Leopold Right about the Kaibab Deer Herd?*, 9 ECOSYSTEMS 227 (2006).

132 David Cherney, *Securing the Free Movement of Wildlife: Lessons from the American West's Longest Land Mammal Migration*, 41 ENV'T L. 599, 603 (2011).

133 Richard W. Wahl, *Redividing the Waters: The Reclamation Act of 1902*, 10 NAT. RES. & ENV'T 31 (1995).

134 THEODORE ROOSEVELT, MESSAGE OF THE PRESIDENT OF THE UNITED STATES COMMUNICATED TO THE TWO HOUSES OF CONGRESS AT THE BEGINNING OF THE SECOND SESSION OF THE FIFTY-SEVENTH CONGRESS (1902).

135 *The Bureau of Reclamation: A Very Brief History*, BUREAU OF RECLAMATION (Aug. 15, 2018), www.usbr.gov/history/borhist.html.

136 WILLIAM STULL HOLT, THE BUREAU OF PUBLIC ROADS: ITS HISTORY, ACTIVITIES, AND ORGANIZATION 1–2 (1923).

137 Act of March 3, 1899, ch. 425, 30 Stat. 1151 (codified as amended at 33 U.S.C. §§ 401–420.

138 United States v. Standard Oil, 384 U.S. 224 (1966). The history of the Refuse Act is concisely laid out in N. William Hines, *History of the 1972 Clean Water Act: The Story Behind How the 1972 Act Became the Capstone on a Decade of Extraordinary Environmental Reform*, 4 GEO. WASH. J. ENERGY & ENV'T L. 80, 83–85, 91 (2013).

139 *See* Bruce R. Huber, *The Fair Market Value of Public Resources*, 103 CALIF. L. REV. 1515, 1535–40 (2015).

140 Sara M. Gregg, *Imagining Opportunity: The 1909 Enlarged Homestead Act and the Promise of the Public Domain*, 50 W. HIST. Q. 258 (2019).

141 *Id.*

142 WILSON, *supra* note 4, at 32. The Placer Act "allow[ed] miners to preempt 160 acres for $2.50 per acre, with no limits on the number of separate 160-acre claims made per individual." *Id.* The General Mining Law, *inter alia*, "allowed mining claims to be 'patented' (i.e., purchased) as private property and put to any use deemed appropriate by the owner, not just mineral development. This created a powerful incentive for land speculators to acquire portions of the public domain under the guise of mining, but with the intention of using it for other purposes once patented." *Id.*

143 Winters v. United States, 207 U.S. 564 (1908).

144 Arizona v. California, 373 U.S. 546, 601 (1963).

145 John E. Thorson et al., *Dividing Western Waters: A Century of Adjudicating Rivers and Streams*, 8 U. DENV. WATER L. REV. 355, 412 (2005).

146 *See, e.g.*, 1881 Idaho Terr. Sess. Laws 267; *see also* Thorson et al., *supra* note 147, at 409–11, 412–14.

147 *See, e.g.*, FRED WELDEN, HISTORY OF WATER LAW IN NEVADA AND THE WESTERN STATES 3 (2003).

148 *See* WATERS AND WATER RIGHTS §§ 11.04(b), 12.02(c)(2) (Amy K. Kelley ed., 3d ed. 2023).

149 Thorson et al., *supra* note 147, at 409–11, 415.

150 RON CHERNOW, TITAN: THE LIFE OF JOHN D. ROCKEFELLER (2004).

151 Barak Orbach & D. Daniel Sokol, *Antitrust Energy*, 85 S. CAL. L. REV. 429, 431 (2012) (quoting WILLIAM HOWARD TAFT, THE ANTI-TRUST ACT AND THE SUPREME COURT 85–86 (1914)).

152 15 U.S.C. §§ 1–7.

153 William Kolasky, *Trust Busters, Theodore Roosevelt and William Howard Taft: Marching Toward Armageddon*, 25 ANTITRUST 97 (2011).

154 Standard Oil Co. v. United States, 221 U.S. 1 (1911).

155 Alexandra B. Klass & Danielle Meinhardt, *Transporting Oil and Gas: U.S. Infrastructure Challenges*, 100 IOWA L. REV. 947, 959 (2015).

156 Jacqueline Lang Weaver, *The Federal Government as a Useful Enemy: Perspectives on the Bush Energy/Environmental Agenda from the Texas Oilfields*, 19 PACE ENV'T L. REV. 1, 9 (2001).

157 *Id.*

158 *Id.*

159 *See* KINGSLEY DENNIS & JOHN URRY, AFTER THE CAR 32–34 (2009).

160 *See* RICHARD W. BOUBEL ET AL., FUNDAMENTALS OF AIR POLLUTION: THIRD EDITION 8–9 (1994).

161 James W. Coleman, *The Third Age of Oil and Gas Law*, 95 IND. L.J. 389, 392–407 (2020).

162 Ohio Oil Co. v. Indiana, 177 U.S. 190, 200 (1900).

163 NASH, *supra* note 23, at 15.

164 *Ohio Oil*, 177 U.S. at 200.

165 *Id.* at 204–05.

166 *See, e.g.*, Illinois Central R. Co. v. Illinois, 146 U.S. 387 (1892).

167 *See* JOSEPH D. KEARNEY & THOMAS W. MERRILL, LAKEFRONT: PUBLIC TRUST AND PRIVATE RIGHTS IN CHICAGO 13–40 (2021).

168 LARSON, *supra* note 11, at 19.

169 *See Illinois Central*, 146 U.S. at 448; *see also* Joseph D. Kearney & Thomas W. Merrill, *The Origins of the American Public Trust Doctrine: What Really Happened in Illinois Central*, 71 U. CHI. L. REV. 799, 860–94 (2004).

170 KEARNEY & MERRILL, *supra* note 169, at 13–29.

171 *Id.* at 40–42.

172 *Id.*

173 *Illinois Central*, 146 U.S. at 458–60.

174 *Id.* at 458.

175 Erin Ryan, *Short History of the Public Trust Doctrine and Its Intersection with Private Water Law*, 38 VA. ENV'T L.J. 135, 140–46 (2020).

176 *See generally* SINCLAIR, *supra* note 44.

177 *Id.* at 167–81.

178 The Supreme Court has original jurisdiction over cases between states. U.S. CONST. art. III, § 2, cl. 2. For a thoughtful review of these and other seminal environmental nuisance cases, see Michael C. Blumm, *A Dozen Landmark Nuisance Cases and Their Environmental Significance*, 62 ARIZ. L. REV. 403 (2020).

179 Missouri v. Illinois, 200 U.S. 496 (1906).

180 Blumm, *supra* note 180, at 416.

181 *Id.*

182 *Missouri*, 200 U.S. at 523.

183 *Id.* at 518.

184 *Id.* at 523.

185 Georgia v. Tennessee Copper Co., 206 U.S. 230 (1907).

186 *Id.*

187 Ducktown v. Barnes Sulphur, Copper & Iron Co., 60 S.W. 593 (Tenn. 1900).

188 Whalen v. Union Bag & Paper Co., 208 N.Y. 1, 101 N.E. 805 (1913).

189 Pennoyer v. Allen, 56 Wis. 502 (1883).

190 New York Continental Jewell Filtration Co. v. Wynkoop, 29 App. D.C. 594 (1907).

191 Interstate Commerce Act, ch. 104, 24 Stat. 445 (1887).

192 State-level reforms included requirements for direct primaries, secret ballots, referenda, initiatives, and recall elections. *See* Jamie L. Carson & Joel Sievert, *Electoral Reform and Changes in Legislative Behavior: Adoption of the Secret Ballot in Congressional Elections*, 4 LEGIS. STUD. Q. 83 (2015).

193 *See* Federal Reserve Act of 1913, ch. 6, 38 Stat. 251.

194 *See* James T. Bennett & Jason E. Taylor, *Labor Unions: Victims of Their Political Success?*, 22 J. LAB. RSCH. 261, 267 (2001).

195 D. Rosner & G. Markowitz, *A Short History of Occupational Safety and Health in the United States*, 110 AM. J. PUB. HEALTH 622, 624 (2020).

196 29 U.S.C. § 551.

197 Rosner & Markowitz, *supra* note 197, at 624.

198 PHILIP J. HILTS, PROTECTING AMERICA'S HEALTH: THE FDA, BUSINESS, AND ONE HUNDRED YEARS OF REGULATION 49 (2003).

199 LAWRENCE M. FRIEDMAN, A HISTORY OF AMERICAN LAW 681 (2d ed. 1985).
200 HILTS, *supra* note 200, at 51.
201 JON A. YODER, UPTON SINCLAIR 40 (1975) (quoting Upton Sinclair, *What Life Means to Me*, COSMOPOLITAN MAG., Oct. 1906, at 591, 594).
202 While the power to constrain monopolists predated Roosevelt, his Department of Justice made ample use of the Sherman Anti-Trust Act (15 U.S.C. §§ 1–7 (1890)) to constrain monopolists. Spencer Weber Waller, *Prosecution by Regulation: The Changing Nature of Antitrust Enforcement*, 77 OR. L. REV. 1383, 1388 (1998).
203 HILTS, *supra* note 200, at 51.
204 Letter from Theodore Roosevelt to William Allen White (July 31, 1906), *in* 5 THE LETTERS OF THEODORE ROOSEVELT, 340 (Elting E. Morison & John M. Blum eds., 1952).
205 JAMES BRONSON REYNOLDS & CHARLES P. NEILL, CONDITIONS IN CHICAGO STOCKYARDS, H.R. DOC. NO. 59–873, at 1 (1906), https://wp-cpr.s3.amazonaws.com/uploads/2019/06/rooseveltletter.pdf (last visited Sept. 20, 2025).
206 *Id.* at 2.
207 *Id.*
208 *Id.* at 7.
209 James Harvey Young, *The Pig that Fell unto the Privy: Upton Sinclair's* The Jungle *and the Meat Inspection Amendment of 1906*, 59 BULL. HIST. MEDICINE 467 (1985).
210 Federal Meat Inspection Act of 1906, Pub. L. No. 59–382, 34 Stat. 669. It also indirectly regulates any intrastate meatpacking through federal funding and technical assistance of state-certified inspection programs.
211 *Id.*
212 LESTER M. SALAMON, THE TOOLS OF GOVERNMENT: A GUIDE TO THE NEW GOVERNANCE 156 (2002).
213 The Pure Food and Drug Act of 1906, Pub. L. No. 59–384, 34 Stat. 768.
214 LOUIS D. BRANDEIS, OTHER PEOPLE'S MONEY AND HOW THE BANKERS USE IT 92 (1914).
215 The Federal Insecticide Act of 1910, Pub. L. No. 80–104, 61 Stat. 163.
216 *Id.*
217 JERRY H. YEN & ROBERT ESWORTHY, CONG. RSCH. SERV., RL31921, PESTICIDE LAW: A SUMMARY OF THE STATUTES (2012).
218 *See generally* IAN TYRELL, WOMAN'S WORLD, WOMAN'S EMPIRE: THE WOMAN'S CHRISTIAN TEMPERANCE UNION IN INTERNATIONAL PERSPECTIVE, 1880–1930 (1991).
219 *See* Molly Ladd-Taylor, *Toward Defining Maternalism in U.S. History*, 5 J. WOMEN'S HIST. 110 (1993).
220 MAUREEN A. FLANAGAN, AMERICA REFORMED: PROGRESSIVES AND PROGRESSIVISMS, 1890–1920S 46 (2007).

221 *Id.* at 45–46.

222 *See* Landon R. Y. Storrs, Civilizing Capitalism: the National Consumers' League, Womens' Activism, and Labor Standards 44–46 (2000).

223 *See* Richard A. Meckel, Save the Babies: American Public Health Reform and the Prevention of Infant Mortality 124 (1990).

224 *See, e.g.*, Brenda D. Frink, *San Francisco's Mother Monument: Maternalism, Racial Order, and the Politics of Memorialization, 1907–1915*, 64 Am. Q. 88 (2012); Ladd-Taylor, *supra* note 221, at 12.

225 *See* Angela Gugliotta, *Class, Gender, and Coal Smoke: Gender Ideology and Environmental Injustice in Pittsburgh, 1868–1914*, 5 Environmental History 165 (2000) ("Early writers described smoke as ubiquitous and pervasive, but smoke burdens were distributed differentially with respect to both gender and class. . . . The poorest men, women, and children were most heavily exposed to environmental pollution."); Julie Sze, Noxious New York 39–40 (2007) ("Based on census data, . . . life expectancy at birth for African Americans in 1900 was ten years shorter than the life expectancy for whites. The black-white gap continued to increase, peaking at twelve years in 1930. . . . The gains being made to reduce immigrant and white infant mortality were not being translated to blacks in the South and the North. . . . The discursive logic of black health activism during the Progressive era emphasized institutional factors and social structures to explain disproportionate rates of black disease in the context of scientific racism and a widespread acceptance of eugenic thought and policy.").

226 Edmund Morris, Theodore Rex 227 (2001).

227 *See, e.g.*, John F. Reiger, *For "Generations Yet Unborn": George Bird Grinnell, Theodore Roosevelt, and the Early Conservation Movement*, *in* Theodore Roosevelt, Naturalist In The Arena 81, 92 (Char Miller & Clay S. Jenkinson eds., 2020).

228 Michael C. Blumm, *Present at the Creation: The 1910 Big Burn and the Formative Days of the U.S. Forest Service*, 37 Ecology L.Q. 1217, 1220 (2010).

229 *Id. See also* Timothy Egan, The Big Burn: Teddy Roosevelt and the Fire That Saved America 94–95 (2009).

230 Blumm, *supra* note 230, at 1219; Michael C. Blumm, *Pinchot, Property Rights, and Western Water (A Reply to Greg Hobbs)*, 24 Env't L. 1203, 1204 (1994).

231 Egan, *supra* note 231, at 135.

232 Timber and Stone Act, 20 Stat. 89 (1878).

233 Stephen E. Ponder, *Executive Publicity and Congressional Resistance, 1905–1913: Congress and the Roosevelt Administration's PR Men*, 13 Cong. & Presidency 177, 181–82 (1986).

234 Blumm, *supra* note 230, at 1219.

235 Egan, *supra* note 231, at 9, 13.

236 Petition for a Writ of Certiorari, *Makah Indian Tribe v. Quileute Indian Tribe*, 586 U.S. 908 (2018) (No. 17–1592).
237 EGAN, *supra* note 231, at 239.
238 *Id.* at 135.
239 *See, e.g.*, Reiger, *supra* note 229, at 94.
240 EGAN, *supra* note 231.
241 Reiger, *supra* note 229, at 92.
242 Blumm, *supra* note 230, at 1222; *see also* EGAN, *supra* note 231, at 67.
243 CLAYTON, *supra* note 74, at 17.

CHAPTER 3. THE MODERNIZATION ERA

1 JAMES TRUSLOW ADAMS, THE EPIC OF AMERICA (1943).
2 Claude S. Fischer & Glenn R. Carroll, *Telephone and Automobile Diffusion in the United States, 1902–1937*, 93 AM. J. SOCIOLOGY 1153 (1988); David J. St. Clair, *The Motorization and Decline of Urban Public Transit, 1935–1950*, 41 J. ECON. HIST. 579 (1981).
3 Muyesaier Tudi et al., *Agriculture Development, Pesticide Application and Its Impact on the Environment*, 18 INT'L J. ENV'T RSCH. & PUB. HEALTH 1112 (2021).
4 U.S. CENSUS BUREAU, STATISTICAL ABSTRACT OF THE UNITED STATES: 1999 885 (1999).
5 Susannah Locke, *How Air Conditioning Changed America Forever*, VOX (Sept. 9, 2014), www.vox.com/2014/9/9/6124321/the-history-of-air-conditioning-is-more-interesting-than-it-sounds-i.
6 Marian Moser Jones & Isidore Daniel Benrubi, *Poison Politics: A Contentious History of Consumer Protection Against Dangerous Household Chemicals in the United States*, 103 AM. J. PUB. HEALTH 801 (2013).
7 Raffaele Porta, *Anthropocene, the Plastic Age, and Future Perspectives*, 11 FEBS OPEN BIO 948 (2021).
8 Lenore Marshall, *The Nuclear Sword of Damocles*, LIVING WILDERNESS, Spring 1971, at 17.
9 Becky Nicolaides & Andrew Wiese, *Suburbanization in the United States After 1945*, OXFORD RSCH. ENCYCLOPEDIA OF AM. HIST. (Apr. 26, 2017), https://oxfordre.com/americanhistory/display/10.1093/acrefore/9780199329175.001.0001/acrefore-9780199329175-e-64.
10 *Id.*
11 John Armour, *Share Capital and Creditor Protection: Efficient Rules for a Modern Company Law*, 60 MOD. L. REV. 355 (2000).
12 Joe Weber, *The Evolving Interstate Highway System and the Changing Geography of the United States*, 25 J. TRANSP. GEOGRAPHY 70 (2012).
13 Memorandum from Lt. Col. Dwight D. Eisenhower to Chief Motor Transport Corps, Report on Trans-Continental Trip (Nov. 3, 1919), www.eisenhowerlibrary.gov/sites/default/files/research/online-documents/1919-convoy/1919-11-03-dde-to-chief.pdf.

14 *Id.*

15 *See infra* notes 28 to 38 and accompanying text.

16 Carlos Arnaldo Schwantes, Going Places: Transportation Redefines the Twentieth-Century West 152 (2003).

17 Roel Hammerschlag, *Legislating the Highway Act of 1956: Lessons for Climate Change Regulation*, 31 Environs Env't L. & Pol'y J. 59, 68 (2007).

18 Jason Scott Smith, Building New Deal Liberalism: The Political Economy of Public Works, 1933–1956 (2006).

19 Robert A. Caro, The Power Broker: Robert Moses and the Fall of New York (1974).

20 Lee Lacy, *Dwight D. Eisenhower and the Birth of the Interstate Highway System*, Army Sustainment, Mar./Apr. 2018, at 64.

21 *1919 Transcontinental Motor Convoy*, Dwight D. Eisenhower Presidential Libr., www.eisenhowerlibrary.gov/research/online-documents/1919-transcontinental-motor-convoy (last visited June 13, 2025).

22 Mark H. Rose, Interstate: Express Highway Politics, 1941–1956, at 48 (1979).

23 Hammerschlag, *supra* note 17, at 59–72.

24 *Id.* at 69–75.

25 *Id. See also* Zygmunt J. B. Plater et. al, Environmental Law and Policy: Nature, Law, and Society 239 (4th ed. 2010).

26 For a more detailed version of this story, see Hammerschlag, *supra* note 17, at 69–75.

27 President's Advisory Committee on a National Highway Program, a ten Year National Highway Program (1955); *see also* John M. Martin, Jr., *The Proposed Federal Highway Legislation in 1955: A Case Study in the Legislative Process*, 44 Geo L.J. 221, 226 (1956).

28 Federal-Aid Highway Act of 1956, ch. 462, 70 Stat. 374.

29 This story is told in much more depth in Joseph DiMento & Cliff Ellis, Changing Lanes: Visions and Histories of Urban Freeways (2012).

30 Gary T. Schwartz, *Urban Freeways and the Interstate System*, 8 Transp. L.J. 167, 196 (1976).

31 Steven E. Polzin & Daniel Sperling, *Positioning Transit for the 21st Century*, Transfers Mag., Fall 2019, at 9.

32 *Status of the Nation's Highways, Bridges, and Transit Conditions & Performance 23rd Edition: Chapter 3: Travel*, U.S. Dept. Transp. (Oct. 22, 2020), www.fhwa.dot.gov/policy/23cpr/chap3.cfm.

33 *See* DiMento & Ellis, *supra* note 29, at 216–19.

34 *See generally* Mark Baldassare, *Suburban Communities*, 18 Ann. Rev. Sociology 475 (1992); *see also* Christopher W. Wells, Car Country: An Environmental History 123–227 (2013).

35 Franklyn P. Salimbene & William P. Wiggins, *Unending Environmental Injustice: The Legacy of the 1956 Federal-Aid Highway Act*, 53 Env't L. Rep. 10169 (2023).

36 Deborah N. Archer, *"White Men's Roads Through Black Men's Homes": Advancing Racial Equity Through Highway Reconstruction*, 73 VAND. L. REV. 1259, 1265 (2020).

37 *Id.* at 1265 n.19.

38 *Id.* at 1275, 1277.

39 Triangle Improvement Council v. Ritchie, 402 U.S. 497, 502 (1971) (per curiam) (Douglas, J., dissenting, "as often happens with interstate highways, the route selected was through the poor area of town, not through the area where the politically powerful people live.").

40 Gregory C. Pratt et al., *Traffic, Air Pollution, Minority and Socio-Economic Status: Addressing Inequities in Exposure and Risk*, 12 INT. J. ENV'T RSCH. PUB. HEALTH 5355, 5367 (2015); Douglas Houston et al., *Structural Disparities of Urban Traffic in Southern California: Implications for Vehicle-Related Air Pollution Exposure in Minority and High-Poverty Neighborhoods*, 26 J. URBAN AFFS. 535, 580–84 (2004).

41 Ann Carlson, *The Clean Air's Blindspot*, 65 UCLA L. REV. 1036, 1051–56 (2018).

42 *History of Urban and Rural Areas*, U.S. CENSUS BUREAU (Sept. 3, 2024), www.census.gov/about/history/historical-censuses-and-surveys/census-programs-surveys/geography/urban-and-rural-areas.html.

43 W. Walker Hanlon, *Coal Smoke, City Growth, and the Costs of the Industrial Revolution*, 130 ECON. J. 462 (2020).

44 Robert L. Boyd, *A "Migration of Despair": Unemployment, the Search for Work, and Migration to Farms During the Great Depression*, 83 SOC. SCI. Q. 554 (2002); Richard C. Schragger, *Cities, Economic Development, and the Free Trade Constitution*, 94 VA. L. REV. 1091, 1105 (2008).

45 Boyd, *supra* note 44, at 555.

46 Christopher Barrington-Leigh & Adam Millard-Ball, *A Century of Sprawl in the United States*, 110 PNAS 8244 (2017).

47 DANIEL R. MANDELKER, THE ZONING DILEMMA 175 (1971).

48 *See* Christopher Silver, *The Racial Origins of Zoning: Southern Cities from 1910–40*, 6 PLAN. PERSPS. 189, 189 (1991) ("In 1908, Los Angeles adopted the nation's first citywide 'use' zoning ordinance to protect its expanding residential areas from industrial nuisances.").

49 *Id.* at 196.

50 Village of Euclid, Ohio v. Ambler Realty Co., 272 U.S. 365, 386 (1926).

51 *Id.* at 380.

52 *Id.*

53 *Id.* at 388. *See also* Silver, *supra* note 48, at 190.

54 *Village of Euclid*, 272 U.S. at 388.

55 *Zoning and the Law of Nuisance*, 29 FORDHAM L. REV. 749 (1961).

56 Alejandro E. Camacho, *Mustering the Missing Voices: A Collaborative Model for Fostering Equality, Community Involvement and Adaptive Planning in Land Use Decisions—Installment One*, 24 STAN. ENV'T L.J. 3, 13 (2005) (citing JULIAN

C. JUERGENSMEYER & THOMAS E. ROBERS, LAND USE PLANNING AND CONTROL LAW 41 (1998)).

57 Patricia E. Salkin, *From* Euclid *to Growing Smart: The Transformation of the American Local Land Use Ethic into Local Land Use and Environmental Controls*, 20 PACE ENV'T L. REV. 109 (2003).

58 *See* Donald A. Krueckeberg, *The Culture of Planning*, *in* INTRODUCTION TO PLANNING HISTORY IN THE UNITED STATES 1, 3–6 (Donald A. Krueckeberg ed., 1983). Although not all planning professionals shared the same mission, the goals of the early land use planning and zoning movement were fairly explicit: (1) developing a rational, "scientific" order to the urban place environment, *see* Judith E. Innes, *Planning Through Consensus Building*, 62 J. AM. PLAN. ASS'N 460, 461–62 (1996); Krueckeberg, *supra*, at 3; (2) making urban environments more beautiful and livable, *see id.* at 4; (3) facilitating economic prosperity and development, *see* M. CHRISTINE BOYER, DREAMING THE RATIONAL CITY: THE MYTH OF AMERICAN CITY PLANNING 64–65 (1983); and (4) promoting justice, distributive fairness, and social equity in metropolitan areas, *see* Krueckeberg, *supra*, at 6.

59 *See* Camacho, *supra* note 56, at 9.

60 Michael Lewyn, *Campaign of Sabotage: Big Government's War Against Public Transportation*, 26 COLUM. J. ENV'T L. 259, 284 (2001); Paul S. Weiland, *Environment in Context*, 18 UCLA J. ENV'T L. & POL'Y 131, 138 (1999/2000); Lee R. Epstein, *Where Yards Are Wide: Have Land Use Planning and Law Gone Astray?*, 21 WM. & MARY ENV'T L. & POL'Y REV. 345, 357–58 (1997).

61 Village of Euclid, 272 U.S. at 394.

62 Many cities, particularly those in the South, attempted to use zoning to keep people of color out of white neighborhoods. *See* RICHARD ROTHSTEIN, THE COLOR OF LAW 44–45 (2017).

63 *See, e.g.*, Buchanan v. Warley, 245 U.S. 60 (1917) (the Supreme Court unanimously held unconstitutional an ordinance from Louisville, Kentucky prohibiting "colored people" from living in houses in white-majority neighborhoods).

64 Amnon Frenkel & Maya Ashkenazi, *Measuring Urban Sprawl: How Can We Deal With It?*, 35 ENV'T & PLAN. B: PLAN. & DESIGN 56 (2008).

65 Richard S. Chused, Euclid*'s Historical Imagery*, 51 CASE W. RSRV. L. REV. 597, 614 (2001).

66 *See* John Infranca, *Singling out Single-Family Zoning*, 111 GEO. L.J. 659, 722 (2023); JAMES CHARLES SMITH ET AL., PROPERTY: CASES & MATERIALS 799–800 (5th ed. 2022).

67 *See generally* Peter Margulies, *Building Communities of Virtue: Political Theory, Land Use Policy, and the Not in My Backyard Syndrome*, 43 SYRACUSE L. REV. 945 (1992).

68 E.C. YOKLEY, 1 ZONING LAW AND PRACTICE § 3–17 (2024); Christopher Silver, *The Racial Origins of Zoning in American Cities*, *in* URBAN PLANNING AND THE AFRICAN AMERICAN COMMUNITY: IN THE SHADOWS 23, 23–42 (June

Manning Thomas & Marsha Ritzdorf eds., 1997); Jonathan T. Rothwell, *Racial Enclaves and Density Zoning: The Institutionalized Segregation of Racial Minorities in the United States*, 13 AM. L. & ECON. REV. 290, 347–48 (2011).

69 *See generally* JON C. TEAFORD, THE METROPOLITAN REVOLUTION: THE RISE OF POST-URBAN AMERICA (2006) (describing the disappearance of the "single-focus metropolis" and the rise of suburban sprawl in post-WWII United Sates).

70 Christine H. Rossell, *School Desegregation and White Flight*, 90 POL. SCI. Q. 675 (1975/1976).

71 Brown v. Bd. of Educ., 347 U.S. 483 (1954).

72 Wayne Batchis, *Urban Sprawl and the Constitution: Educational Inequality as an Impetus to Low Density Living*, 42 URB. LAW. 95 (2010).

73 Milliken v. Bradley, 418 U.S. 717, 806 (1973) (Marshall, J. dissenting). *See also Education: Coleman on the Griddle*, TIME, Apr. 12, 1976, at 91; ROTHSTEIN, *supra* note 62, at 93–99.

74 Willy E. Rice, *Race, Gender, "Redlining," and the Discriminatory Access to Loans, Credit, and Insurance: An Historical and Empirical Analysis of Consumers Who Sued Lenders and Insurers in Federal and State Courts 1950–1995*, 33 SAN DIEGO L. REV. 583 (1996).

75 ROTHSTEIN, *supra* note 62, at 20–23.

76 *Id.* at 70–75.

77 *Id.* at 64–66.

78 Shelley v. Kraemer, 334 U.S. 1 (1948).

79 ROTHSTEIN, *supra* note 62, at 85–88.

80 *See* BOOZ, ALLEN & HAMILTON INC., VETERANS HOUSING LOAN PROGRAM EVALUATION FINAL REPORT, II-1–II-4 (1990).

81 Samuel Brody, *The Characteristics, Causes, and Consequences of Sprawling Development Patterns in the United States*, 4 NATURE EDUC. KNOWLEDGE 2 (2013).

82 HOWARD FRUMKIN ET AL., URBAN SPRAWL AND PUBLIC HEALTH: DESIGNING, PLANNING, AND BUILDING FOR HEALTHY COMMUNITIES 127–29 (2005).

83 BASUDEB BHATTA, ANALYSIS OF URBAN GROWTH AND SPRAWL FROM REMOTE SENSING DATA 30–31 (2010).

84 Patti Miller, *Health Impacts of Suburban Development Patterns*, DEL. J. PUB. HEALTH, Mar. 2018, at 32.

85 *See generally* T. R. Oke, *Urban Heat Islands*, *in* THE ROUTLEDGE HANDBOOK OF URBAN ECOLOGY 120, 120–30 (Ian Douglas et al. eds., 2011); *see also* Hassan Saeed Khan et al., *Synergies and Exacerbations—Effects of Warmer Weather and Climate Change*, *in* URBAN CLIMATE CHANGE AND HEAT ISLANDS: CHARACTERIZATION, IMPACTS, AND MITIGATION 73 (Mattheos Santamouris & Riccardo Paolini eds., 2022).

86 Angel Hsu et al., *Disproportionate Exposure to Urban Heat Island Intensity Across Major US Cities*, 12 NATURE COMMC'NS. 1, 5–6 (2012); Gary W. Evans & Elyse

Kantrowitz, *Socioeconomic Status and Health: The Potential Role of Environmental Risk Exposure*, 23 ANN. REV. PUB. HEALTH 303, 305–10, 319–20 (2002).

87 WILLIAM D. ROWLEY, THE BUREAU OF RECLAMATION: ORIGINS AND GROWTH TO 1945 6, 99–100 (2006).

88 DONALD C. JACKSON, POLITICS AND DAM SAFETY: THE ST. FRANCIS DAM DISASTER AND THE BOULDER CANYON PROJECT ACT (2010).

89 An Act Regulating the Practice of Civil Engineering, ch. 801, 1929 Cal. Stat. 1645 (1929).

90 16 U.S.C. § 791 *et seq.* (1920).

91 16 U.S.C. § 824d(a)-(b). *See also* Todd S. Aagaard, *Energy-Environment Policy Alignments*, 90 WASH. L. REV. 1517, 1526 (2015).

92 Gifford Pinchot, *Long Struggle for Effective Federal Water Power Legislation*, 14 GEO. WASH. L. REV. 9, 20 (1945–1946).

93 John Franklin Shields, *Federal Power Act*, 73 U. PA. L. REV. 142, 143–46 (1924–1925).

94 *See* FED. POWER COMM'N, FIRST ANNUAL REPORT OF THE FEDERAL POWER COMMISSION (1921); *see also* FED. POWER COMM'N, TWENTIETH ANNUAL REPORT OF THE FEDERAL POWER COMMISSION (1940).

95 Carl J. Bauer, *The Long View of the Water/Energy Nexus: Hydropower's First Century in the U.S.A.*, 60 NAT. RES. J. 173, 177–79 (2020).

96 Dan Tarlock, *Hydro Law and the Future of Hydroelectric Power Generation in the United States*, 65 VAND. L. REV. 1723, 1727 (2012).

97 Bauer, *supra* note 95, at 195–96.

98 *See generally* DENISE FORT & BARRY NELSON, PIPE DREAMS: WATER SUPPLY AND PIPELINE PROJECTS IN THE WEST (2012).

99 In 1941, aqueducts began to divert water to Los Angeles from various streams that flow into Mono Lake in northern California. Michael C. Blumm & Thea Schwartz, *Mono Lake and the Evolving Public Trust in Western Water*, 37 ARIZ. L. REV. 701, 704–06 (1995). This was just one of the early projects diverting water from the Sacramento River.

100 Colorado River Compact, Nov. 24, 1922, 42 Stat. 171. *See also* Jason A. Robison, *The Colorado River Revisited*, 88 U. COLO. L. REV. 475, 511 (2017).

101 Jonathan Thompson, *On Its 100th Birthday, the Colorado River Compact Shows Its Age*, HIGH COUNTRY NEWS (Nov. 11, 2022).

102 Boulder Canyon Project Act of 1928, Pub. L. No. 70–642, 45 Stat. 1057 (authorizing the Hoover Dam project).

103 *Hoover Dam*, BUREAU OF RECLAMATION (Mar. 12, 2015), www.usbr.gov/lc/hooverdam/faqs/damfaqs.html.

104 For a riveting read about California's efforts to redirect its waters along with its share of the Colorado River, see MARC REISNER, CADILLAC DESERT: THE AMERICAN WEST AND ITS DISAPPEARING WATER (1986).

105 *See* National Industrial Recovery Act of 1933, Pub. L. No. 73–67, 48 Stat. 195; *see also* Carl H. Bauer, *Public Works Administration Water Projects in Illinois*, 28 J.

AM. WATER WORKS ASS'N 1022 (1936) (describing the spending, number of projects, and number of working hours provided by the Public Works Administration in its first few years, with a particular focus on projects in Illinois).

106 ROWLEY, *supra* note 87, at 285–302.

107 REISNER, *supra* note 104, at 319.

108 Elizabeth B. Drew, *Dam Outrage: The Story of the Army Engineers*, THE ATLANTIC, Apr. 1970, at 51, 55. Dam projects are frequently held out as quintessential examples of what is known as *logrolling*, legislative approval that is won by conditioning support of projects championed by others. Robert D. Tollison, *Public Choice and Legislation*, 74 VA. L. REV. 339, 352 (1988).

109 ROWLEY, *supra* note 87, at 337–38.

110 *See* TIM PALMER, ENDANGERED RIVERS AND THE CONSERVATION MOVEMENT 64 (2004) (describing how various groups protested, halting the dam plans).

111 *Id.* at 69–75.

112 JAMES LAWRENCE POWELL, DEAD POOL: LAKE POWELL, GLOBAL WARMING, AND THE FUTURE OF WATER IN THE WEST (2008).

113 *See generally* DAVID P. BILLINGTON, ET AL., THE HISTORY OF LARGE FEDERAL DAMS: PLANNING, DESIGN, AND CONSTRUCTION IN THE ERA OF BIG DAMS (2005).

114 DONALD WORSTER, RIVERS OF EMPIRE: WATER, ARIDITY, AND THE GROWTH OF THE AMERICAN WEST 276 (1985).

115 Ryan E. Emanuel & David E. Wilkins, *Breaching Barriers: The Fight for Indigenous Participation in Water Governance*, 12 WATER 2113 (2020).

116 ROWLEY, *supra* note 87, at 380.

117 *Petroleum & Other Liquids: U.S. Field Production of Crude Oil*, U.S. ENERGY INFO. ADMIN. (May 30, 2025), www.eia.gov/dnav/pet/hist/LeafHandler.ashx?n=pet&s=mcrfpus2&f=a.

118 *Natural Gas: U.S. Natural Gas Marketed Production*, U.S. ENERGY INFO. ADMIN. (May 30, 2025), www.eia.gov/dnav/ng/hist/n9050us2a.htm.

119 *See* JOSEPH A. PRATT ET AL., OFFSHORE PIONEERS: BROWN & ROOT AND THE HISTORY OF OFFSHORE OIL AND GAS, 1–14 (1997) (describing the 1930s as a time of exploration of the oceans as a place to drill for oil and gas, particularly through the history of one company, Brown & Root, who experimented with offshore drilling in the Gulf).

120 Exec. Order No. 9,633, 10 Fed. Reg. 12,305 (Sept. 28, 1945) (the "Truman Proclamation").

121 U.N. Conference on the Law of the Sea, *6 Official Records: Fourth Committee (Continental Shelf)*, U.N. Doc. A/Conf.13/42 (Oct. 1958). *See also* Marjorie M. Whiteman, *Conference on the Law of the Sea: Convention on the Continental Shelf*, 52 AM. J. INT'L L. 629 (1958).

122 U.N. Convention on the Law of the Sea, Dec. 10, 1982, 1833 U.N.T.S. 397; *see also* Daniel S. Cheever, *The Politics of the UN Convention on the Law of the Sea*, 37 J.

INT'L AFFS., 247 (1984) (explaining that the United States never signed, even after several other conferences).

123 Lisa Friedman, *The Zombies of the U.S. Tax Code: Why Fossil Fuels Subsidies Seem Impossible to Kill*, N.Y. TIMES (Mar. 15, 2024), www.nytimes.com/2024/03/15/climate/tax-breaks-oil-gas-us.html.

124 Owen L. Anderson, *The Evolution of Oil and Gas Conservation Law and the Rise of Unconventional Hydrocarbon Production*, 61 ARK. L. REV. 231, 241–43 (2015).

125 *Id.* at 243–44.

126 Joint Resolution Consenting to an Interstate Oil Compact to Conserve Oil and Gas, H.R.J. Res. 407, 74th Cong., 49 Stat. 939 (1935).

127 Tara K. Righetti, *The Incidental Environmental Agency*, 20 UTAH L. REV. 685, 697 (2020).

128 J. Leonard Bates, *The Teapot Dome Scandal and the Election of 1924*, 60 AM. HIST. REV. 303 (1955).

129 *Id.* at 17.

130 *See* Richard Lane, *The American Anthropocene: Economic Scarcity and Growth During the Great Acceleration*, 99 GEOFORUM 11 (2019).

131 *See generally* RICHARD RHODES, THE MAKING OF THE ATOMIC BOMB (2012).

132 42 U.S.C. Ch. 23.

133 42 U.S.C. § 2013(d).

134 Pub. L. No. 83–703, 68 Stat. 919 (1954) (current version at 42 U.S.C. § 2011 *et seq.*); *see also* Frank Norton, *Atom Energy and the Atomic Energy Act of 1954*, 27 ROCKY MOUNTAIN. L. REV. 521 (describing differences between the 1946 and 1954 Acts).

135 MARK HOLT, CONG. RSCH. SERV., IF10821, PRICE-ANDERSON ACT: NUCLEAR POWER INDUSTRY LIABILITY LIMITS AND COMPENSATION TO THE PUBLIC AFTER RADIOACTIVE RELEASES (2018).

136 *Reuther Assails A.E.C.; Protests Issuance of Permit for Reactor in Michigan*, N.Y. TIMES, Aug. 30, 1956, at 49.

137 R. P. Allen et al., *Shippingport Atomic Power Station. A Source of Power Plant Aging Information, in* SAFETY ASPECTS OF THE AGEING AND MAINTENANCE OF NUCLEAR POWER PLANTS (International Atomic Energy Agency ed., 1988).

138 Noah D. Lichtenstein, *The Hanford Nuclear Waste Site: A Legacy of Risk, Cost, and Inefficiency*, 44 NAT. RES. J. 809 (2004).

139 FERENC MORTON SZASZ, THE DAY THE SUN ROSE TWICE: THE STORY OF THE TRINITY SITE NUCLEAR EXPLOSION, JULY 16, 1945 131–44 (1984) (detailing the Trinity test in 1945 and its impacts on people, land, and resources); *see also* KENNETH TOMPKINS BAINBRIDGE, TRINITY (1976).

140 Shan Xu & Alicia Dodt, *Nuclear Bomb and Public Health*, 44 J. PUB. HEALTH POL'Y 348 (2023).

141 Douglas Brinkley, Silent Spring Revolution: John F. Kennedy, Rachel Carson, Lyndon Johnson, Richard Nixon, and the Great Environmental Awakening 84–85 (2022).

142 Laura A. Bruno, *The Bequest of the Nuclear Battlefield: Science, Nature, and the Atom Bomb During the First Decade of the Cold War*, 33 Hist. Stud. Physical & Biological Scis. 237, 237 (2003).

143 Victor Margolin, *The United States in World War II: Scientists, Engineers, Designers*, 29 Design Issues 14 (2013).

144 The Imperial Japanese Army and Nazi Germany rarely used chemical warfare against Western combatants, but each used such agents extensively, the Japanese against Asian combatants and the Nazis at Holocaust death camps. *See, e.g.*, Yuki Tanaka, *Poison Gas, the Story Japan Would Like to Forget*, 8 Bull. Atomic Scientists 10, 16–17 (1988); Patrick Coffey, American Arsenal: a century of Waging War 152–54 (2014).

145 Robert Bilott, Exposure: Poisoned Water, Corporate Greed, and One Lawyer's Twenty-Year Battle Against Dupont 57 (2019) (discussing the discovery of Teflon).

146 William M. Tuttle, Jr., *The Birth of an Industry: The Synthetic Rubber 'Mess' in World War II*, 22 Tech. & Culture 35 (1981).

147 Jeffrey L. Meikle, American Plastic: a cultural History 1–2 (1995); Augustin Cerveaux, *Taming the Microworld: DuPont and the Interwar Rise of Fundamental Industrial Research*, 54 Tech. & Culture 262, 271–82 (2013).

148 Edmund Russell, *Nicking the Thin Edge of the Wedge: What History Suggests about the Environmental Law of War*, 24 Va. Env't L.J. 377, 381–82 (2005).

149 Cerveaux, *supra* note 147, at 281–82.

150 Marcela Romero Mosquera, *Banning Plastic Straws: The Beginning of the War Against Plastics*, 9 Env't & Earth L.J. 5, 8 (2019).

151 R. Douglas Hurt, The Problems of Plenty: The American Farmer in the Twentieth Century 40, 95–96 (2002); Michael Pollan, The Omnivore's Dilemma: a natural History of Four Meals 41 (2d ed. 2007).

152 Jason J. Czarnezki, *Everyday Environmentalism: Concerning Consumption*, 41 Env't L. Rep. 10,374, 10,377 (2011).

153 Nicole E. Martinez et al., *Radium Dial Workers: Back to the Future*, 98 Int'l J. Radiation Biology 750 (2022); The Million Person Study of Low-Dose Radiation Health Effects (John D. Boice, Jr. et al. eds., 2025).

154 Laurence Locke, *Adapting Workers' Compensation to the Special Problems of Occupational Disease*, 9 Harv. Env't L. Rev. 249, 258–63 (1985); for early definitions of "occupational disease," *see* Thomas C. Angerstein, *Legal Aspects of Occupational Disease*, 18 Rocky Mountain L. Rev. 240, 256–66 (1946).

155 For a detailed and riveting story of Vogt, and his foil, Norman Borlaug—the father of the Green Revolution, see Charles C. Mann, The Wizard and

THE PROPHET: TWO REMARKABLE SCIENTISTS AND THEIR DUELING VISIONS TO SHAPE TOMORROW'S WORLD (2018).

156 Van S. Katzman, *The Waste of War: Government CERCLA Liability at World War II Facilities*, 79 VA. L. REV. 1191, 1218–19 (1993).

157 Daniel A. Farber, *The BP Blowout and the Social and Environmental Erosion of the Louisiana Coast*, 13 MINN. J.L. SCI. & TECH. 37, 44 (2012).

158 NATIONAL ACADEMY OF SCIENCES, ALLOCATING FEDERAL FUNDS FOR SCIENCE AND TECHNOLOGY (1995).

159 Fukuo Akimoto, *The Birth of 'Land Use Planning' in American Urban Planning*, 24 PLAN. PERSPS. 457 (2009); Barry D. Karl, *Public Administration and American History: A Century of Professionalism*, 36 PUB. ADMIN. REV. 489 (1976).

160 NATIONAL ACADEMY OF SCIENCES, *supra* note 158.

161 Daniel J. Kevles, *The National Science Foundation and the Debate over Postwar Research Policy, 1942–1945: A Political Interpretation of Science—The Endless Frontier*, 68 ISIS 5 (1977).

162 MICHAEL HILTZIK, THE NEW DEAL: A MODERN HISTORY (2011).

163 Reorganization Plan No. 3 of 1946, 11 Fed. Reg. 7,875 (July 20, 1946), 60 Stat. 1097 (forming the BLM).

164 *See* JAMES R. SKILLEN, THE NATION'S LARGEST LANDLORD: THE BUREAU OF LAND MANAGEMENT IN THE AMERICAN WEST 14–37 (2009). The BLM was responsible for "more land than any other federal agency, including 190 million acres in the western United States, 330 million acres in Alaska Territory, and additional subsurface mineral estate." *Id.*

165 5 U.S.C. § 551 *et seq. See generally* George B. Shepherd, *Fierce Compromise: The Administrative Procedure Act Emerges from New Deal Politics*, 90 NW. U. L. REV. 1557 (1996).

166 5 U.S.C. § 706.

167 Mark D. Bauer, *The Licensed Professional Exemption in Consumer Protection: At Odds with Antitrust History and Precedent*, 73 TENN. L. REV. 131, 134, 138 (2006).

168 Elisabeth Keller, *Introductory Comment: A Historical Introduction to the Securities Act of 1933 and the Securities Exchange Act of 1934*, 49 OHIO ST. L.J. 329, 336, 338 (1988).

169 MAURY KLEIN, RAINBOW'S END: THE CRASH OF 1929 25 (2001); Joel Seligman, *The Origins of the Securities and Exchange Commission*, L. QUADRANGLE, Fall 1994, at 46.

170 Seligman, *supra* note 169; Douglas W. Diamond & Philip H. Dybvig, *Bank Runs, Deposit Insurance, and Liquidity*, 91 J. POL. ECON. 401, 404 (1983).

171 Securities Act of 1933, 15 U.S.C. §§ 77a-77aa.

172 Securities Exchange Act of 1934, 15 U.S.C. §§ 78a-78qq.

173 Keller, *supra* note 168, at 349.

174 Charles K. Whitehead, *Risky Business: Portfolio Risk, Institutional Investing, and the Securities Act*, 2021 COLUM. BUS. L. REV. 1396, 1396 (2022).

175 *See* Elizabeth Ann Glass Geltman, *Disclosure of Contingent Environmental Liabilities by Public Companies Under the Federal Securities Laws*, 16 Harv. Env't L. Rev. 129, 133 (1992).
176 *See* G. Edward White, *Tort Reform in the Twentieth Century: An Historical Perspective*, 32 Vill. L. Rev. 1265, 1281 (1987).
177 William Boyd, *Genealogies of Risk: Searching for Safety, 1930s-1970s*, 39 Ecology L.Q. 895, 915 (2012).
178 Cindy A. Schipani, *Infiltration of Enterprise Theory into Environmental Jurisprudence*, 22 J. Corp. L. 599, 619 (1997).
179 Mark Conrad, *Fake News, Personal Attacks, and Ideological Media Run Amok—It is Time for Fairness Doctrine 2.0*, 21 Va. Sports & Ent. L.J. 77, 89 (2022).
180 *Id.*
181 Radio Act of 1927, ch. 169, 44 Stat. 1162; *see* Richard E. Labunski, *May It Rest in Peace: Public Interest and Public Access in the Post-Fairness Doctrine Era*, 11 Hastings Comm. & Ent. L.J. 219 (1988).
182 B. R. Mitchell, International Historical Statistics: The Americas 1750–1988 618 (1993).
183 *See* Communications Act of 1934, Pub. L. No. 73–416, 48 Stat. 1064.
184 Conrad, *supra* note 179, at 90.
185 Naomi Oreskes & Erik M. Conway, Merchants of Doubt 57 (2010).
186 Conrad, *supra* note 179, at 92.
187 *Id.* at 92–93.
188 Ashutosh Bhagwat, *The New Gatekeepers?: Social Media and the "Search for Truth,"* 3 J. Free Speech L. 41, 47 (2023).
189 *Id.*
190 While network television remained relatively uniform, the expansion of talk radio eventually brought more controversial ideas and political influence into the mainstream after the era in the 1960s. Conrad, *supra* note 179, at 104. However, it would not be until nearly a decade after the Modernization Era that the Fairness Doctrine's rules on presenting conflicting views would be further refined. *Id.* at 94; *see* Red Lion Broadcasting Co. v. FCC, 395 U.S. 367 (1969).
191 John D. Leshy, Our Common Ground: a history of America's Public Lands 504–05 (2022).
192 *Id.*
193 *Id.*
194 *Id.* at 359–61.
195 Mineral Leasing Act of 1920, 30 U.S.C. § 181.
196 *See generally* Logan Hovis & Jeremy Mouat, *Miners, Engineers, and the Transformation of Work in the Western Mining Industry, 1880–1930*, 3 Tech. & Culture 429 (1996).
197 The Indian Reorganization Act, Pub. L. No. 73–383, 48 Stat. 984 (1934) (current version at 25 U.S.C. § 5101 *et seq.*).
198 *Id.*

199 Lawrence C. Kelly, *The Indian Reorganization Act: The Dream and the Reality*, 44 PAC. HIST. REV. 291, 293 (1975).

200 *Id.*

201 *See* SAMUEL P. HAYS, CONSERVATION AND THE GOSPEL OF EFFICIENCY: THE PROGRESSIVE CONSERVATION MOVEMENT, 1890–1920 55 (1959).

202 43 U.S.C. §§ 315–316.

203 Hugh E. Kingery, *The Public Grazing Lands*, 43 DENV. L.J. 329 (1966).

204 43 U.S.C. § 315. *See also* Phillip O. Foss, *The Determination of Grazing Fees on Federally-Owned Range Lands*, 41 J. FARM ECON. 535 (1959).

205 *Id.*

206 CHRISTOPHER MCGRORY KLYZA, WHO CONTROLS PUBLIC LANDS? MINING, FORESTRY, AND GRAZING POLICIES, 1870–1990 109–14 (2000).

207 Debra L. Donahue, *Western Grazing: The Capture of Grass, Ground, and Government*, 35 ENV'T L. 721, 752–53 (2005).

208 DAVID LOUTER, WINDSHIELD WILDERNESS: CARS, ROADS, AND NATURE IN WASHINGTON'S NATIONAL PARKS, 85–86 (2009).

209 SETHA M. LOW ET AL., RETHINKING URBAN PARKS: PUBLIC SPACE AND CULTURAL DIVERSITY 41–43 (2009) (discussing disproportionate use of the National Parks system by white Americans).

210 *See* Allan K. Fitzsimmons, *The Impact of Recreational Facilities on National Park Landscapes*, 78 J. GEOGRAPHY 230 (1979).

211 *Id.*

212 LOUTER, *supra* note 208, at 36–37 (describing how Park Service leaders promoted national parks for automobile tourism and the concurrent growth of auto travel in the American middle class).

213 A. S. LEOPOLD ET AL., ADVISORY BOARD ON WILDLIFE MANAGEMENT, WILDLIFE MANAGEMENT IN THE NATIONAL PARKS 13–14 (1963); *see also* CAROLYN MERCHANT, REINVENTING EDEN: THE FATE OF NATURE IN WESTERN CULTURE (2003).

214 Richard J. Ansson, Jr., *Funding Our National Parks in the 21st Century: Will We be Able to Preserve and Protect Our Embattled National Parks?*, 11 FORDHAM ENV'T L.J. 1, 46–51 (1999).

215 Michael C. Blumm, *The Nation's First Forester-in-Chief: The Overlooked Role of FDR and the Environment*, 33 J. LAND USE & ENV'T L. 25, 45 (2017).

216 Act of March 31, 1933, Pub. L. No. 73–5, 48 Stat. 22 (1933).

217 JOHN C. PAIGE, THE CIVILIAN CONSERVATION CORPS AND THE NATIONAL PARK SERVICE, 1933–1942: AN ADMINISTRATIVE HISTORY 1–39 (1985) (discussing the establishment, development, and decline of the Corps).

218 Lincoln L. Davies, *Lessons for an Endangered Movement*, 31 ENV'T L. 229, 279 (2001).

219 NEIL M. MAHER, NATURE'S NEW DEAL: THE CIVILIAN CONSERVATION CORPS AND THE ROOTS OF THE AMERICAN ENVIRONMENTAL MOVEMENT 43 (2007).

220 *Id.* at 3.
221 EUGENE ODUM, FUNDAMENTALS OF ECOLOGY (1953).
222 *Id.*
223 Federal Aid in Wildlife Restoration Act, 16 U.S.C. §§ 669–669i.
224 Act of March 16, 1934, ch. 71, 48 Stat. 451 (codified as amended at 16 U.S.C. § 718 *et seq.*).
225 The Sport Fish Restoration Act, ch. 658, 64 Stat. 430 (1950) (codified as amended at 16 U.S.C. § 777 *et seq.*).
226 Act of February 18, 1929, ch. 257, 45 Stat. 1222 (codified as amended at 16 U.S.C. § 715 *et seq.*).
227 *See* MICHAEL W. GIESE, A FEDERAL FOUNDATION FOR WILDLIFE CONSERVATION: THE EVOLUTION OF THE NATIONAL WILDLIFE REFUGE SYSTEM, 1920–1968 88 (2008).
228 Fish and Wildlife Coordination Act, ch. 55, 48 Stat. 401 (1934) (codified as amended at 16 U.S.C. § 661).
229 Act of August 14, 1946, ch. 965, 60 Stat. 1080 (1946).
230 16 U.S.C. § 662(a).
231 *See* Douglas M. Thompson & Gregory N. Stull, *The Development and Historic Use of Habitat Structures in Channel Restoration in the United States: The Grand Experiment in Fisheries Management*, 56 GÉOGRAPHIE PHYSIQUE ET QUATERNAIRE 45 (2002) (outlining changes in fishing culture, policy, and habitat management in the United States pre-1885 through modern times, including commodification and diet demands in the early 1900s).
232 16 U.S.C. § 668.
233 Shepherd, *supra* note 165, at 1557.
234 Brian Waddell, *Corporate Influence and World War II: Resolving the New Deal Political Stalemate*, 11 J. POL'Y HIST. 223 (1999).
235 Kal Raustiala, *Empire and Extraterritoriality in Twentieth Century America*, 40 SW. L. REV. 605, 611–14 (2011).
236 SARAH CHURCHWELL, BEHOLD, AMERICA: THE ENTANGLED HISTORY OF 'AMERICA FIRST' AND 'THE AMERICAN DREAM' 267 (2018).
237 *See* Raymond R. Tucker, *Smoke Prevention in St. Louis*, 33 INDUS. ENG'G CHEMISTRY 836 (1941); *see also* James M. Lents & William J. Kelly, *Clearing the Air in Los Angeles*, SCI. AM., Oct. 1993, at 32, 32–34.

CHAPTER 4. THE ENVIRONMENTAL ERA

1 Ralph H. Lutts, *Chemical Fallout: Rachel Carson's* Silent Spring, *Radioactive Fallout, and the Environmental Movement*, 9 ENV'T REV. 210, 220–23 (1985).
2 *See* DOUGLAS BRINKLEY, SILENT SPRING REVOLUTION: JOHN F. KENNEDY, RACHEL CARSON, LYNDON JOHNSON, RICHARD NIXON, AND THE GREAT ENVIRONMENTAL AWAKENING (2022); MARK HAMILTON LYTLE, THE GENTLE SUBVERSIVE: RACHEL CARSON, SILENT SPRING, AND THE RISE OF THE ENVIRONMENTAL MOVEMENT (2007).

3 RACHEL CARSON, SILENT SPRING (1962).
4 ASIF A. SIDDIQI, CHALLENGE TO APOLLO: THE SOVIET UNION AND THE SPACE RACE, 1945–1974 (2000).
5 JIM RASENBERGER, THE BRILLIANT DISASTER: JFK, CASTRO, AND AMERICA'S DOOMED INVASION OF CUBA'S BAY OF PIGS (2011).
6 NILS GILMAN, MANDARINS OF THE FUTURE: MODERNIZATION THEORY IN COLD WAR AMERICA (2003).
7 *See* MARK KURLANSKY, 1968: THE YEAR THAT ROCKED THE WORLD (2005); PETER B. LEVY, THE GREAT UPRISING: RACE RIOTS IN URBAN AMERICA DURING THE 1960S 153–54 (2018).
8 *See generally* ROBERT BLAIR KAISER, "R.F.K. MUST DIE!" A HISTORY OF THE ROBERT KENNEDY ASSASSINATION AND ITS AFTERMATH (1st ed. 1970).
9 16 U.S.C. § 459c; 16 U.S.C. § 459d; 16 U.S.C. § 459b.
10 *See, e.g.*, Lynn White, Jr., *The Historical Roots of Our Ecologic Crisis*, 155 SCI. 1203 (1967); Garrett Hardin, *The Tragedy of the Commons*, 162 SCI. 1243 (1968); Fred P. Bosselman & A. Dan Tarlock, *The Influence of Ecological Science on American Law: An Introduction Symposium on the Ecology and the Law*, 69 CHI.-KENT L. REV. 847 (1993–1994).
11 *See, e.g.*, Scenic Hudson Pres. Conf. v. Fed. Power Comm'n, 354 F.2d 608 (2d Cir. 1965); United States v. Republic Steel Corp., 362 U.S. 482 (1960); United States v. Standard Oil Co. 384 U.S. 224 (1966).
12 *See, e.g.*, Mulford-Carrell Resources Act of 1967, ch. 1545, 1967 Cal. Stat. 3680.
13 *See generally* ROBERT POOLE, EARTHRISE: HOW MAN FIRST SAW THE EARTH (2008).
14 CAROL E. STEINHART & JOHN S. STEINHART, BLOWOUT: A CASE STUDY OF THE SANTA BARBARA OIL SPILL (1972).
15 Teresa Sabol Spezio, *The Santa Barbara Oil Spill and Its Effect on United States Environmental Policy*, 10 SUSTAINABILITY 2750, 3 (2018).
16 *See generally* Harvey Molotch & Marilyn Lester, *Accidental News: The Great Oil Spill as Local Occurrence and National Event*, 81 AM. J. SOCIOLOGY 235 (1975); Teresa Sabol Pezio, *The Santa Barbara Oil Spill and Its Effect on United States Environmental Policy*, 10 SUSTAINABILITY 2750 (2018).
17 Adam Rome, *The Genius of Earth Day*, 15 ENV'T HIST. 194 (2010).
18 Michael McCloskey, *Wilderness Act of 1964: Its Background and Meaning*, 45 OR. L. REV. 288, 297–98 (1966).
19 Terry Bracy & Ellen Wheeler, *Stewart Udall: Renaissance Man*, 1 ARIZ. J. ENV'T L. & POL'Y 3 (2010).
20 Thomas G. Smith, *John Kennedy, Stewart Udall, and New Frontier Conservation*, 64 PAC. HIST. REV. 329, 360 (1995).
21 *See* Peter A. Appel, *Wilderness and the Courts*, 29 STAN. ENV'T L.J. 62, 92 (2010).
22 Alejandro E. Camacho, *Assisted Migration: Redefining Nature and Natural Resource Law Under Climate Change*, 27 YALE J. ON REG. 171, 212–13 (2010).

23 *See* Martin Nie & Christopher Barns, *The Fiftieth Anniversary of the Wilderness Act: The Next Chapter in Wilderness Designation, Politics, and Management*, 5 ARIZ. J. ENV'T L. & POL'Y 237, 247 (2014).

24 16 U.S.C. § 1131(c).

25 Michael McCloskey, *The Meaning of the Multiple Use-Sustained Yield Act of 1964*, 41 OR. L. REV. 49, 52 (1961).

26 CHRISTOPHER MCGRORY KLYZA, WHO CONTROLS PUBLIC LANDS?: MINING, FORESTRY, AND GRAZING POLICIES, 1870–1990 40 (2000).

27 *National Wilderness Preservation Act: Hearings on S. 1176 Before the S. Comm. on Interior and Insular Affairs*, 85th Cong. 329 (1957) (statement of W. Howard Gray, Chairman, American Mining Company).

28 *National Wilderness Preservation Act: Hearings on S. 174 Before the Comm. on Interior and Insular Affairs*, 87th Cong. 368–69 (1961).

29 Kenneth D. Hubbard, et al., *Wilderness Act's Impact on Mining Activities: Policy Versus Practice*, 76 DENV. U.L. REV. 591, 600 (1998). Note, however, this compromised turned out to be a hollow victory for mining interests because of the practical and regulatory challenges of developing valid claims in such areas. *Id.*

30 16 U.S.C. § 1131.

31 Endangered American Wilderness Act of 1978, Pub. L. No. 95–237, 92 Stat. 40.

32 *See The Wilderness Act*, THE WILDERNESS SOC'Y, www.wilderness.org/articles/article/wilderness-act (last visited June 13, 2025).

33 *See, e.g.*, Louise Mendel, *The Consequences for Wilderness Conservation in the Development of the National Park System in Tasmania, Australia.* 40 AUSTRALIAN GEOGRAPHICAL STUD. 71–83 (2002); Emily Wakild, *Acts of Courage, Acts of Culture: The Wilderness Act and Latin America.* 19 ENV'T HIST. 728 (2014).

34 16 U.S.C. § 1271.

35 *See* Sandra Zellmer, *Wilderness, Water, and Climate Change*, 42 ENV'T L. 313, 361–63 (2012).

36 43 U.S.C. §§ 1631–1641.

37 Miranda Strong, *Alaska National Interest Lands Conservation Act Compliance & Nonsubsistence Areas: How Can Alaska Thaw Out Rural & Alaska Native Subsistence Rights*, 30 ALASKA L. REV. 71, 75 n.36 (2013).

38 54 U.S.C. §§ 300101–320303.

39 *Id.* § 3021; *id.* § 3041.

40 Federal Coal Mine Health and Safety Act of 1969, Pub. L. No. 91–173, 83 Stat. 742.

41 30 U.S.C. § 1201 *et seq.*

42 30 U.S.C. § 1251 *et seq.*

43 16 U.S.C. §§ 528, 529, 531(a).

44 Tony Arjo, *Watershed and Quality Protection in National Forest Management*, 41 HASTINGS L.J. 1111, 1114 (1990).

45 16 U.S.C. §§ 528–532.

46 Charles F. Wilkinson & H. Michael Anderson, *Land and Resource Planning in the National Forests*, 64 OR. L. REV. 1, 371–73 (1985).

47 43 U.S.C. § 1701 *et seq.*

48 Roger Flynn, *Daybreak on the Land: The Coming of Age of the Federal Land Policy and Management Act of 1976*, 29 Vt. L. Rev. 815, 817–18 (2005).

49 *See* Richard N. L. Andrews, Managing the Environment, Managing Ourselves: a history of American Environmental Policy 136–39 (2020).

50 16 U.S.C. §§ 460k–460k-4.

51 16 U.S.C. §§ 668dd–668ee.

52 16 U.S.C. § 668dd(a)(1).

53 Land and Water Conservation Fund Act of 1965, Pub. L. No. 88–578, 78 Stat. 897.

54 Carol Hardy Vincent, Cong. Rsch. Serv., RL33531, Land and Water Conservation Fund: Overview, Funding History, and Issues (2019).

55 *Id.*

56 16 U.S.C. §§ 1451–1466.

57 16 U.S.C. §§ 1801–1803.

58 Daniel R. Mandelker & Thea A. Sherry, *The National Coastal Zone Management Act of 1972*, 7 Urb. L. Ann. 119, 122 (1974).

59 *Id.*

60 16 U.S.C. § 1451(i).

61 *Id.* § 1455(d).

62 16 U.S.C. §§ 2401–2413.

63 *See generally* Antarctic Conservation Act of 1978, 95 Pub. L. No. 541, 92 Stat. 2048.

64 Scenic Hudson Pres. Conf. v. Fed. Power Comm'n, 354 F.2d 608 (2d Cir. 1965).

65 William M. Goodman, *Scenic Hudson Revisited: The Substantial Evidence Test and Judicial Review of Agency Environmental Findings*, 2 Ecology L.Q. 837 (1972).

66 U.S. Const. art. III, § 2, cl. 1.

67 *Scenic Hudson Pres. Conf. v. Fed. Power Comm'n*, 354 F.2d at 616.

68 Skip Card, *Scenic Standing: The 40th Anniversary of* Scenic Hudson *and the Birth of Environmental Litigation*, 77 N.Y. State Bar J., 10 (2005).

69 *Id.*

70 Cary Coglianese, *Social Movements, Law, and Society: The Institutionalization of the Environmental Movement*, 150 U. Pa. L. Rev. 85, 92–94 (2001).

71 Nina M. Hart & Linda Tsang, Cong. Rsch. Serv., IF11932, National Environmental Policy Act: Judicial Review and Remedies (2021).

72 Brigham Daniels et al., *Reconsidering NEPA*, 96 Ind. L.J. 865, 870 (2021).

73 John Hart, *The National Environmental Policy Act and the Battle for Control of Environmental Policy*, 31 J. Pol'y Hist. 464, 472 (2019).

74 42 U.S.C. § 4332; *see also* Daniels et al., *supra* note 72, at 885.

75 *See* Terence T. Finn, Conflict and Compromise: Congress Makes a Law, The Passage of the National Environmental Policy Act (Nov. 16, 1972) (Ph.D. dissertation, Georgetown University) (ProQuest).

76 *See* Daniels et al., *supra* note 72, at 870–71.

77 Sam Kalen, *The Devolution of NEPA: How the APA Transformed the Nation's Environmental Policy*, 33 WM. & MARY ENV'T L. & POL'Y REV. 483, 484 (2009).

78 Calvert Cliffs' Coordinating Comm., Inc. v. U.S. Atomic Energy Comm'n, 449 F.2d 1109 (D.C. Cir. 1971).

79 42 U.S.C. 4331(c).

80 Winter v. Natural Res. Def. Council, Inc., 555 U.S. 7 (2008); Robertson v. Methow Valley Citizens Council, 490 U.S. 332 (1989); Vermont Yankee Nuclear Power Corp. v. Natural Res. Def. Council, Inc., 435 U.S. 519, 558 (1978).

81 *See, e.g.*, Matthew J. Lindstrom, *Procedures Without Purpose: The Withering away of the National Environmental Policy Act's Substantive Law*, 20 J. LAND, RES., & ENV'T L. 245 (2000). Several state environmental impact assessment laws, such as the California Environmental Quality Act (Cal. Pub. Res. Code §§ 21000–21177 (2016)) or New York's State Environmental Quality Review Act (N.Y. Env't Conserv. L. §§ 8–0101 to 8–0117 (2016)) have incorporated substantive implementation requirements that state or local agencies mitigate environmental harm. *See* Philip Weinberg, *It's Time to Put NEPA Back on Course*, 3 N.Y.U ENVTL L.J. 99, 110–12 (1994).

82 CHARLES H. ECCLESTON, NEPA AND ENVIRONMENTAL PLANNING: TOOLS, TECHNIQUES, AND APPROACHES FOR PRACTITIONERS (2008).

83 GEORGE CAMERON COGGINS & ROBERT L. GLICKSMAN, PUBLIC NATURAL RESOURCES LAW § 17:40 (2d ed. 2013).

84 Martin V. Melosi, *Energy and Environment in the United States: The Era of Fossil Fuels*, 11 ENV'T REV. 167, 173 (1987). For a detailed account, see STEINHART & STEINHART, *supra* note 14.

85 *See generally* Molotch & Lester, *supra* note 16; *see also generally* Pezio, *supra* note 16.

86 Water Quality Improvement Act of 1970, 33 U.S.C. § 1161 *et seq.*, now part of the Federal Water Pollution Control Act (Clean Water Act), 33 U.S.C. § 466 *et seq.*

87 Thomas J. Wagner, *The Oil Pollution Act of 1990: An Analysis*, 21 J. MAR. L. & COM. 569, 570–71 (1990).

88 Joseph F. Zimmerman, *National-State Relations: Cooperative Federalism in the Twentieth Century*, 31 PUBLIUS: J. FEDERALISM 15 (2001).

89 ALEJANDRO E. CAMACHO & ROBERT L. GLICKSMAN, REORGANIZING GOVERNMENT: A FUNCTIONAL AND DIMENSIONAL FRAMEWORK 81–87 (2019).

90 Barton H. Thompson, Jr., *The Continuing Innovations of Citizen Enforcement*, 2000 U. ILL. L. REV. 185 (2000).

91 Clean Air Act Amendments of 1977, Pub. L. No. 95–95, 91 Stat. 685 (codified in scattered sections of 42 U.S.C. §§ 7401–7642).

92 Clean Water Act of 1977, Pub. L. No. 95–217, 9 Stat. 1566 (codified at 33 U.S.C. §§ 1251–1376).

93 OTIS L. GRAHAM, JR., ENVIRONMENTAL POLITICS AND POLICY, 1960S–1990S 27–28 (2000); Samuel Hays, *Clean Air: From the 1970 Act to the 1977 Amendments*, 17 DUQ. L. REV. 33, 45 (1977).

94 *See, e.g.*, GERALD R. FORD, PUBLIC PAPERS OF THE PRESIDENTS OF THE UNITED STATES, GERALD R. FORD, 1976–1977 451 (1977); ANDREWS, *supra* note 49, at 239.

95 William L. Andreen, *The Evolution of Water Pollution Control in the United States—State, Local, and Federal Efforts, 1789–1972: Part II*, 22 STAN. ENV'T L.J. 215, 245–46 (2003).

96 Adam D. Orford, *The Clean Air Act of 1963: Postwar Environmental Politics and the Debate over Federal Power*, 27 HASTINGS ENV'T L.J. 1, 3–5 (2021).

97 Water Quality Act of 1965, Pub. L. No. 89–234, § 5, 79 Stat. 903, 907–09.

98 Solid Waste Disposal Act, Pub. L. No. 89–272, 79 Stat. 997 (1965).

99 Robert Martin & Lloyd Symington, *A Guide to the Air Quality Act of 1967*, 33 L. & CONTEMP. PROBS. 239, 245–55 (1968).

100 Motor Vehicle Air Pollution Control Act of 1965, Pub. L. No. 89–272, 79 Stat. 992.

101 Howard H. Baker, Jr., *U.S. Environmentalism, Comity, and the Clean Air Act*, *in* CLEANING AMERICA'S AIR: PROGRESS AND CHALLENGES 7 (David C. Brill ed., 2005).

102 Presidential Statement About the National Environmental Policy Act of 1969, 6 WEEKLY COMP. PRES. DOC. 11 (Jan. 5, 1970).

103 Richard M. Nixon, President, United States, Annual Message to the Congress on the State of the Union (Jan. 22, 1970), www.presidency.ucsb.edu/documents/annual-message-the-congress-the-state-the-union-2.

104 Richard M. Nixon, President, Special Message to the Congress on Environmental Quality (Feb. 10, 1970), https://www.presidency.ucsb.edu/node/240088.

105 *See generally* JOHN C. ESPOSITO, VANISHING AIR: THE RALPH NADER STUDY REPORT ON AIR POLLUTION (1970).

106 Brigham Daniels, Andrew P. Follett & Joshua Davis, *The Making of the Clean Air Act*, 71 HASTINGS L.J. 901, 933 n.220.

107 Fred P. Graham, *Court Allows City to Sue Car Makers on Pollution*, N.Y. TIMES, Sept. 9, 1970, 1.

108 *Id.*

109 Gladwin Hill, *Decree Settles Auto Smog Suit*, N.Y. TIMES, Oct. 29, 1969, 28.

110 115 CONG. REC. 24035–24036 (1969) (statement of Rep. George Brown, "Congressmen Urge Open Trial in Smog Control Antitrust Case"); Letter from Ralph Nader to Hon. Richard W. McLaren, Assistant Attorney General, Antitrust Division, U.S. Department of Justice, Washington, D.C. (1969).

111 California Air Resources Act of 1967, Pub. L. No. 90–148, 81 Stat. 485.

112 Michael E. Kraft, *US Environmental Policy and Politics: From the 1960s to the 1990s*, 12 J. POL'Y HIST. 17, 26 (2000).

113 Interview with Tom Jorling, former Minority Counsel, U.S. Senate Comm. on Pub. Works, in Saranac Lake, New York (Sept. 21, 2018).

114 *Id.*

115 Gaylord Nelson, *Earth Day '70: What It Meant*, EPA J., Apr. 1980, at 6.

116 Roger Eardley-Pryor, *Earth Day at 50: Memories from Sierra Club Oral Histories*, Berkeley Libr. (Apr. 11, 2020), https://update.lib.berkeley.edu/2020/04/11/earth-day-at-50-memories-from-sierra-club-oral-histories/.

117 *Id.*

118 Daniels et al., *supra* note 72, at 942.

119 *Cf.* Richard L. Revesz & Jack Lienke, Struggling for Air: Power Plants and the "War on Coal" 3 (2016).

120 Clean Air Act of 1970, Pub. L. No. 91–604, 84 Stat. 1676, 1690 (1970) (codified at 42 U.S.C.S. § 7521(b)(1)(A)).

121 *Id.* at 1713 (codified at 42 U.S.C.S. § 7411).

122 *Id.*

123 *Id.* at 1680 (codified at 42 U.S.C.S. § 7413).

124 At the time, the president had the ability to reconfigure the federal bureaucracy through an executive order that Congress could only stop by calling a vote and rejecting the proposal. *See* Reorganization Plan No. 3 of 1970, 35 Fed. Reg. 15,623 (Oct. 6, 1970), 84 Stat. 2086 (1970).

125 Brigham Daniels & Andrew P. Follett, *Building Credibility: Lessons from the Leadership of William Ruckelshaus*, 50 Env't L. Rep. 10238, 10238 (2020).

126 Daniels et al., *supra* note 72, at 913.

127 Nixon Tape 255–33, recording date, June 9, 1971.

128 Nixon Tape 508, recording date, June 2, 1971.

129 Water Pollution Control Act, Pub Law No. 80–845, 62 Stat. 1155 (1948).

130 An Act to extend and strengthen the Water Pollution Control Act, Pub. L. No. 84–660, 70 Stat. 498 (1956).

131 Water Quality Act of 1965, Pub. L. No. 89–234, § 5, 79 Stat. 903, 907–09.

132 N. William Hines, *History of the 1972 Clean Water Act: The Story behind how the 1972 Act Became the Capstone on a Decade of Extraordinary Environmental Reform*, 4 Geo. Wash. J. Energy & Env't L. 80 (2013).

133 33 U.S.C. § 407.

134 United States v. Republic Steel Corp., 362 U.S. 482 (1960); United States v. Standard Oil Co., 384 U.S. 224 (1966).

135 Kalur v. Resor, 335 F. Supp. 1, 12–15 (D.D.C. 1971).

136 33 U.S.C. §§ 1311(b)(1), 1342, 1362(14).

137 David Stradling & Richard Stradling, Perceptions of the Burning River: Deindustrialization and Cleveland's Cuyahoga River, 13 Env't Hist. 515 (2008).

138 *Id.*

139 33 U.S.C. § 1344. *See* Hines, *supra* note 132, at 80.

140 Susan Dudley Gold, Clean Air and Clean Water Acts 19–21 (2012).

141 *Id.* at 27.

142 Nixon Tape, 772–15, recording date, Sept. 7, 1972.

143 E. W. Kenworthy, *President Vetoes Clean Water Bill*, N.Y. TIMES, Oct. 18, 1972, at 20.

144 The President's Veto Message to the Senate Returning the Federal Water Pollution Control Act Amendments of 1972 Without His Approval, 8 WEEKLY COMP. PRES. DOC. 1531–33 (Oct. 17, 1970) [hereinafter Nixon CWA Veto].

145 *See* Andreen, *supra* note 95, at 238, 285–86.

146 John W. Dean III, *Watergate: What Was It?*, 51 HASTINGS L.J. 609, 609 (1999).

147 *Id.* at 646.

148 *Id.* at 619.

149 John B. Heppes & Eric J. McFadden, *The Convention on International Trade in Endangered Species of Wild Fauna and Flora: Improving the Prospects for Preserving Our Biological Heritage*, 5 B.U. INT'L L.J. 229, 229 (1987).

150 *List of Contracting Parties*, CITES.ORG, https://cites.org/eng/disc/parties/chronolo.php (last visited June 16, 2023).

151 93 CONG. REC. 11837 (1973).

152 *Id.*

153 *Id.*

154 Alejandro E. Camacho et al., *Assessing State Laws and Resources for Endangered Species Protection*, 47 ENV'T L. REP. 10837, 10837 (2017).

155 *See generally* ZYGMUNT J. B. PLATER, THE SNAIL DARTER AND THE DAM: HOW PORK-BARREL POLITICS ENDANGERED A LITTLE FISH AND KILLED A RIVER (2013).

156 Stacy Nagel, *The Taking of the Delhi Sands Flower-Loving Fly: A Commerce Clause Challenge to the Application of Section 9(a)(1) of the Endangered Species Act: National Ass'n of Home Builders v. Babbitt*, 5 MO. ENV'T L. & POL'Y REV. 143 (1997).

157 Omar N. White, *The Endangered Species Acts Precarious Perch: A Constitutional Analysis Under the Commerce Clause and the Treaty Power*, 27 ECOLOGY L.Q. 215, 222 (2000).

158 Presidential Statement on Signing the Endangered Species Act of 1973, 10 WEEKLY COMP. PRES. DOC. 2 (Dec. 28, 1973).

159 16 U.S.C. § 1538.

160 *Id.*

161 16 U.S.C. § 1536(a).

162 Tennessee Valley Auth. v. Hill, 437 U.S. 153 (1978).

163 *Id.*

164 16 U.S.C. § 1533(a)(1), (d); Hill v. Tennessee Valley Auth., 419 F. Supp. 753, 760 (E.D. Tenn. 1976), *rev'd*, 549 F.2d 1064 (6th Cir. 1977), *aff'd*, 437 U.S. 153.

165 16 U.S.C. § 1533; *Tennessee Valley*, 437 U.S. at 154.

166 16 U.S.C. §§ 1361–1362, 1371–1389, 1401–1407, 1411–1418, 1421–1421h, 1423–1423h.

167 16 U.S.C. § 1331 *et seq.*

168 16 U.S.C. § 1333(a).

169 16 U.S.C. §§ 2901–2911.

170 Cristobal S. Berry-Cabán, *DDT and* Silent Spring: *Fifty Years After*, 19 J. MIL. & VETERANS HEALTH 19, 21 (2011).

171 CARSON, *supra* note 3.

172 U.S. ENVTL. PROTECTION AGENCY, DDT, A REVIEW OF SCIENTIFIC AND ECONOMIC ASPECTS OF THE DECISION TO BAN ITS USE AS A PESTICIDE 251–56 (1975) [hereinafter EPA DDT REVIEW].

173 Elena Conis, *Debating the Health Effects of DDT: Thomas Jukes, Charles Wurster, and the Fate of an Environmental Pollutant*, 125 PUB. HEALTH REPORTS 337 (2010).

174 Monsanto Corp., *The Desolate Year*, MONSANTO MAG., Oct. 1962, at 4.

175 EPA DDT REVIEW, *supra* note 172, 251–56.

176 15 U.S.C. § 1453.

177 15 U.S.C. § 1454.

178 PUBLIC HEALTH SERVICE, PROTECTING THE HEALTH OF EIGHTY MILLION AMERICANS (1966).

179 29 U.S.C. § 651 *et seq.*

180 29 U.S.C. § 653.

181 29 U.S.C. § 658. In 1977, the federal government finally banned use of lead-based paint in all residential and public properties. *CPSC Announces Final Ban on Lead-Containing Paint*, U.S. CONSUMER PROD. SAFETY COMM'N, www.cpsc.gov/Recalls/1977/cpsc-announces-final-ban-on-lead-containing-paint (last visited June 14, 2025) (discussing Sept. 2, 1977 ban on lead-containing paint).

182 *Federal Insecticide, Fungicide, and Rodenticide Act (FIFRA) and Federal Facilities*, U.S. ENVTL. PROTECTION AGENCY (Jan. 31, 2025), www.epa.gov/enforcement/federal-insecticide-fungicide-and-rodenticide-act-fifra-and-federal-facilities.

183 7 U.S.C.A. § 136a.

184 7 U.S.C. § 136 *et seq.*

185 CHRISTINA M. VALENTE & WILLIAM D. VALENTE, INTRODUCTION TO ENVIRONMENTAL LAW AND POLICY: PROTECTING THE ENVIRONMENT THROUGH LAW 91–94 (1995).

186 15 U.S.C. § 2601 *et seq.*

187 *Id.*

188 U.S. ENVTL. PROTECTION AGENCY, SUMMARY OF THE TOXIC SUBSTANCES CONTROL ACT, LAWS & REGULATIONS (Sept. 9, 2024), www.epa.gov/laws-regulations/summary-toxic-substances-control-act.

189 *See* U.S. ENVTL. PROTECTION AGENCY ARCHIVE, NEW LAW TO CONTROL HAZARDOUS WASTES, END OPEN DUMPING, PROMOTE CONSERVATION OF RESOURCES (Aug. 11, 2016), www.epa.gov/archive/epa/aboutepa/new-law-control-hazardous-wastes-end-open-dumping-promote-conservation-resources.html (reposting an EPA press release from Dec. 13, 1976 about RCRA).

190 49 U.S.C. § 5101 *et seq.*

191 42 U.S.C. § 6901 *et seq.*

192 Roger W. Andersen, *The Resource Conservation and Recovery Act of 1976: Closing the Gap*, 1978 WIS. L. REV. 633, 651 (1978).

193 *Id.* at 646.

194 Theodore Baurer, *Love Canal: Common Law Approaches to a Modern Tragedy*, 11 ENV'T L. 133, 135 (1980).

195 *Id.*

196 *Id.*

197 *Id.* at 136.

198 U.S. ENVTL. PROTECTION AGENCY, SUPERFUND HISTORY (Nov. 25, 2024), www.epa.gov/superfund/superfund-history.

199 Edkardt C. Beck, *The Love Canal Tragedy*, EPA J., Jan. 1979, at 16, 17–18; JENNIFER REED, LOVE CANAL 46 (2002).

200 *See, e.g.*, SUPERFUND HISTORY, *supra* note 198.

201 Donald G. Vicneil, Jr., *Toxic Waste Fund Sought in Congress*, N.Y. TIMES, June 10, 1979, at 51.

202 42 U.S.C. § 9601 *et seq.*

203 Martha L. Judy & Katherine N. Probst, *Superfund at 30*, 11 VT. J. ENV'T L. 191, 195 (2009).

204 Comprehensive Environmental Response, Compensation, and Liability Act, 42 U.S.C. § 9604.

205 *Id.*

206 *Id.* § 9621.

207 Robert V. Percival et al., *CERCLA in a Global Context*, 41 SW. L. REV. 727, 727 (2012).

208 Joseph G. Theis, *Wetlands Loss and Agriculture: The Failed Federal Regulation of Farming Activities Under Section 404 of the Clean Water Act*, 9 PACE ENV'T L. REV. 1, 28–29 (1991).

209 Jason Scott Johnston, *Climate Change Confusion and the Supreme Court: The Misguided Regulation of Greenhouse Gas Emissions Under the Clean Air Act*, 84 NOTRE DAME L. REV. 1, 18–20 (2008).

210 G. VIALETTO ET AL., GREENHOUSE GAS INDICATORS: A HELPFUL TOOL FOR POLICY MAKING IN THE GREENHOUSE EFFECT ERA, WIT TRANSACTIONS ON ECOLOGY AND THE ENVIRONMENT 1 (1970).

211 *See* H. Doremus & J. E. Pagel, *Why Listing May Be Forever: Perspectives on Delisting Under the U.S. Endangered Species Act*, 15 CONSERVATION BIOLOGY, 1258, 1263 (2001).

212 Jeff McNeely, *Invasive Species: A Costly Catastrophe for Native Biodiversity*, 1 LAND USE & WATER RES. RSCH. 1 (2001).

213 Shubhra Gupta & Kapil Gupta, *Bioaccumulation of Pesticides and Its Impact on Biological Systems*, *in* PESTICIDES IN CROP PRODUCTION: PHYSIOLOGICAL AND BIOCHEMICAL ACTION 55, 55–67 (Srivastava et al. eds., 2020).

214 *Policy on Wildlife*, WASH. POST, Oct. 7, 1974, at A24.

215 Fish and Wildlife Conservation Act, Pub. L. No. 96–366, 94 Stat. 1322 (1980) (codified at 16 U.S.C. § 2901 *et seq.*).
216 *Id.* at Stat. 1325–1329 (current version at 16 U.S.C. §§ 2905–2908).
217 Davina Kari Kaile, *Evolution of Wildlife Legislation in the United States: An Analysis of the Legal Efforts to Protect Endangered Species and the Prospects for the Future*, 5 GEO. INT'L ENV'T L. REV. 441, 445–46 (1992).
218 *See, e.g.*, Joseph M. Callahan, *New Controls Could Mean Auto Industry's Death*, AUTO. INDUS., Oct. 15, 1970, at 17; WALTER KAISER, CLEAN AIR ACT AND AMERICAN AUTOMOBILE INDUSTRY 31, 33 (2003).
219 Nixon CWA Veto, *supra* note 144, at 1531–33.
220 Meir Rinde, *Richard Nixon and the Rise of American Environmentalism: How a Republican President Ushered in the EPA*, SCI. HIST. INST. MUSEUM & LIBR. (June 2, 2017).
221 *See generally* John Brooks Flippen, *Containing the Urban Sprawl: The Nixon Administration's Land Use Policy*, 26 PRESIDENTIAL STUD. Q. 197 (1996).
222 Joseph A. Califano, *What Was Really Great About the Great Society*, 31 WASH. MONTHLY 13, 13–20 (1999).
223 Michael Fisher, *Environmental Racism Claims Brought Under Title VI of the Civil Rights Act*, 25 ENV'T L. 285 303–09 (1995).
224 42 U.S.C. § 2000d.
225 JAMES LESTER, ENVIRONMENTAL INJUSTICE IN THE US: MYTHS AND REALITIES 1 (2018).
226 Robert D. Bullard & Glenn S. Johnson, *Environmentalism and Public Policy: Environmental Justice: Grassroots Activism and Its Impact on Public Policy Decision Making*, 56 J. SOC. ISSUES 555, 574 (2000).
227 EILEEN MCGURTY, TRANSFORMING ENVIRONMENTALISM: WARREN COUNTY, PCBS, AND THE ORIGINS OF ENVIRONMENTAL JUSTICE 1–21 (2009).
228 Bean v. Sw. Waste Mgmt. Corp., 482 F. Supp. 673, 680 (S.D. Tex. 1979).
229 Michael Corbett, *Oil Shock of 1973–74*, FED. RSRV. HIST. (Nov. 22, 2013), www.federalreservehistory.org/essays/oil-shock-of-1973-74.
230 MEG JACOBS, PANIC AT THE PUMP: THE ENERGY CRISIS AND THE TRANSFORMATION OF AMERICAN POLITICS IN THE 1970S 82–84 (2016).
231 Energy Policy and Conservation Act, Pub. L. No. 94–163, 89 Stat. 871 (1975) (codified at 42 U.S.C. § 6201 *et seq.*).
232 Pub. L. No. 94–163, 89 Stat. 881 (1975) (codified at 42 U.S.C. § 6231).
233 Laura R. Hall, *The Evolution of CAFE Standards: Fuel Economy Regulation Enters Its Second Act*, 39 TRANSP. L.J. 1 (2011).
234 *Statutory Rules and Authorities*, U.S. Dep't of Energy, www.energy.gov/eere/buildings/statutory-rules-and-authorities (last visited June 14, 2025).
235 Pub. L. No. 94–163, 89 Stat. 890 (1975) (codified at 42 U.S.C. § 6246).
236 Trans-Alaska Pipeline Authorization Act, Pub. L. No. 93-153, 87 Stat. 576 (1973).

237 National Energy Conservation Policy Act, Pub. L. No. 95–619, 91 Stat. 3206 (1978) (codified at 42 U.S.C. § 8201 *et seq.*).

238 *Id.* §§ 3213–3214, 3224–3228.

239 Pub. L. No. 95–617, 92 Stat. 3117 (1978).

240 16 U.S.C. § 824a-3.

241 William Boyd & Ann E. Carlson, *Accidents of Federalism: Ratemaking and Policy Innovation in Public Utility Law*, 63 UCLA L. REV. 810, 842 (2016).

242 Rena I. Steinzor, *Unfunded Environmental Mandates and the "New (New) Federalism": Devolution, Revolution, or Reform*, 81 MINN. L. REV. 97, 182–84 (1996).

243 *Id.* at 130–48.

244 42 U.S.C. § 7410.

245 *Id.* § 7661c.

246 Safe Drinking Water Act, 42 U.S.C. §§ 300f–300j-27 (2023).

247 *Id.* § 300f.

248 *Id.* § 300g-3.

249 ELENA H. HUMPHRIES & MARY TIEMANN, CONG. RSCH. SERV., RL31243, SAFE DRINKING WATER ACT (SDWA): A SUMMARY OF THE ACT AND ITS MAJOR REQUIREMENTS (2021).

250 Ridgway M. Hall, Jr., *The Clean Water Act of 1977*, 11 NAT. RES. LAW. 343, 345 (1978).

251 Rosemary O'Leary, *The Courts and the EPA: The Amazing "Flannery Decision,"* 5 NAT. RES. & ENV'T 18, 18–55 (1990).

252 Federal Water Pollution Control Act, Pub. L. No. 95–217, 91 Stat. 1566 (1977) (codified at 33 U.S.C. § 1251).

253 33 U.S.C. § 1344 (g-m).

254 *Id.* § 1344(f).

255 Johanna H. Wald & Elizabeth H. Temkin, *The Sagebrush Rebellion: The West Against Itself—Again*, 2 UCLA J. ENV'T L. & POL'Y 187, 187–88 (1981).

256 Robert L. Fischman & Jeremiah I. Williamson, *The Story of* Kleppe v. New Mexico*: The Sagebrush Rebellion as Un-Cooperative Federalism*, 83 U. COLO. L. REV. 123 (2011).

257 *See* Gaylord Nelson, *Earth Day '70: What It Meant*, 6 EPA J. 38 (1980).

258 HENRY DAVID THOREAU, CIVIL DISOBEDIENCE (1849).

259 MARTIN LUTHER KING JR., LETTER FROM A BIRMINGHAM JAIL (1963).

260 EDWARD ABBEY, THE MONKEY WRENCH GANG (1975).

261 REX WEYLER, GREENPEACE: HOW A GROUP OF ECOLOGISTS, JOURNALISTS, AND VISIONARIES CHANGED THE WORLD (2015) (providing an insider and celebratory view of Greenpeace's agenda and accomplishments).

262 *See* Eric R. Pogue, *The Catastrophe Model of Risk Regulation and the Regulatory Legacy of Three Mile Island and Love Canal*, 15 PENN ST. ENV'T L. REV. 463, 464 (2007).

CHAPTER 5. THE CONTESTED ERA

1 *See* Daniel A. Farber, *The Conservative as Environmentalist: From Goldwater and the Early Reagan to the 21st Century*, 59 ARIZ. L. REV. 1005, 1034–35 (2017) ("Reagan revamped his approach when the initial anti-environmental initiatives ran into trouble. In the end, he accepted a considerable number of new protections for the environment. He went along with significant environmental legislation from Congress, toughening regulation of hazardous waste and requiring public disclosures of the use and discharge of toxic chemicals. He signed numerous wilderness bills, which designated more than ten million acres of wilderness, despite his administration often opposing the bills prior to passage. During the Reagan years, 'Congress did not roll back a single substantive statutory protection, and in 1984 and 1986 it expanded the protections afforded by two hazardous waste control and cleanup statutes.' Congress also passed the Commercial Motor Vehicle Safety Act in 1986 and the Rail Safety Improvement Act in 1988.") (internal quotes omitted).

2 *See id.* at 1032.

3 Philip Arestis & Mike Marshall, *The New Right and the US Economy in the 1980s: An Assessment of the Economic Record of the Reagan Administration*, 4 INT'L REV. APPLIED ECON. 45, 47 (1990).

4 *See id.* at 1033; R. McGreggor Cawkley & William Chaloupka, *James Watt and the Environmentalists: A Clash of Ideologies*, 14 WILLIAM POL'Y STUD. J. 244, 250 (2002).

5 Brady Dennis & Chris Mooney, *Neil Gorsuch's Mother Once Ran the EPA. It Didn't Go Well*, WASH. POST, Feb. 1, 2017.

6 *Id.*

7 Philip Shabecoff, *New Environmental Chief Vows to Lift Regulatory 'Overburden'*, N.Y. TIMES, June 21, 1981.

8 *See* Craig N. Oren, *When Must EPA Set Ambient Air Quality Standards—Looking Back at NRDC v. Train*, 30 UCLA J. ENV'T L. & POL'Y 157, 179–80 (2012); Joel A. Mintz, *EPA Enforcement of CERCLA: Historical Overview and Recent Trends*, 41 SW. L. REV. 645 (2012).

9 Scott Tong & Grace Tatter, *Permanent Capture: What a Decades-Old Scandal at the EPA Tell[s] Us About Power in Washington Today*, WBUR, HERE AND NOW, Sept. 16, 2022.

10 Dennis & Mooney, *supra* note 5.

11 Jacob Darwin Hamblin, *Ronald Reagan's Environmental Legacy*, *in* A COMPANION TO RONALD REAGAN (A. L. Johns ed., 2015).

12 R. McGreggor Cawley & William Chaloupka, *James Watt and the Environmentalists: A Clash of Ideologies*, 14 POL'Y STUD. J. 244 (1985).

13 Mead Gruver, *James Watt, Sharp-Tongued and Pro-Development Interior Secretary Under Reagan, Dies at 85*, AP PRESS, June 9, 2023.

14 *Id.*

15 Michael E. Kraft & Norman J. Vig, *Environmental Policy in the Reagan Presidency*, 99 Pol. Sci. Q. 415, 429 (1984).

16 Philip Shabecoff, *House Panel Finds Watt in Contempt*, N.Y. Times, Feb. 26, 1982, at A1.

17 Kraft & Vig, *supra* note 15, at 438.

18 Letter accepting the resignation of Anne M. Burford as Administrator of the Environmental Protection Agency, 1983 Pub. Papers 370 (Mar. 9, 1983). Burford's view of her story can be found in Anne Burford & John Greenya, Are You Tough Enough? (1986).

19 *See* Statement on the Resignation of James G. Watt as Secretary of the Interior, 1983 Pub. Papers 1438 (Oct. 9, 1983). Watt gives his side of the story in James G. Watt & Doug Wead, Courage of a Conservative (1985).

20 James Watt pled guilty years later to withholding information from a Federal grand jury following an investigation of influence-peddling at the Department of Housing and Urban Development. *See* Lou Cannon, President Reagan: The Role of a Lifetime (2000).

21 *See* David M. Shafie, Presidential Administration & the Environment: Executive Leadership in the Age of Gridlock 5 (2014).

22 *See* Sophie Lecheler & Jana Laura Egelhofer, *Disinformation, Misinformation, and Fake News: Understanding the Supply Side*, *in* Knowledge Resistance in High-Choice Information Environments 69, 74 (Jesper Strömbäck et al. eds., 2022).

23 *See, e.g.*, Christopher Hare & Keith T. Poole, *The Polarization of Contemporary American Politics*, 46 Polity 411, 411 (2014).

24 Rachel Kleinfeld, *The Rise of Political Violence in the United States*, 32 J. Democracy 160, 161 (2021).

25 Fiscal Responsibility Act of 2023, Pub. L. No. 118–5, 137 Stat. 10 (2023).

26 Shafie, *supra* note 23.

27 For example, there was a longstanding split among federal courts regarding the extent of liability for hazardous waste generators under the Comprehensive Environmental Response, Compensation, and Liability Act (CERCLA) that was only resolved after three decades. Burlington Northern & Santa Fe Ry. v. United States, 556 U.S. 599, 608 (2009).

28 *See* Shafie, *supra* note 23, at 5.

29 *See, e.g.*, *id.* at 3.

30 *See id.* at 4–10.

31 Exec. Order No. 13,792, 82 Fed. Reg. 20,429 (2017). *See also* John Yoo & Todd Gaziano, *Presidential Authority to Revoke or Reduce National Monument Designations*, 35 Yale J. on Regul. 617 (2018).

32 Proclamation No. 10285, 86 Fed. Reg. 57,321, 57,331 (Oct. 15, 2021) (restoring and expanding the Bears Ears National Monument); Proclamation No. 10286, 86 Fed. Reg. 57,335, 57,344–45 (Oct. 15, 2021).

33 Exec. Order No. 14,148, 90 Fed. Reg. 8237 (Jan. 28, 2025); Exec. Order No. 14,154, 90 Fed. Reg. 8353 (Jan. 29, 2025).

34 Exec. Order No. 14,154, 90 Fed. Reg. 8353 (Jan. 29, 2025); Interim Final Rule, 90 Fed. Reg. 10,611 (Feb. 25, 2025). *See also, e.g.,* Department of Energy, Revision of National Environmental Policy Act Implementing Processes, 90 Fed. Reg. 29676 (July 3, 2025).

35 SHAFIE, *supra* note 23, at 405.

36 Newt Gingrich et. al., *Contract with America: The Bold Plan by Rep. Newt Gingrich, Rep. Dick Armey, and the House Republicans to Change the Nation* (1994).

37 John D. Leshy, *The Babbitt Legacy at the Department of the Interior: A Preliminary View*, 31 ENV'T L. 199, 204 (2001); Robert L. Glicksman & Stephen B. Chapman, *Regulatory Reform and (Breach of) the Contract with America: Improving Environmental Policy or Destroying Environmental Protection*, 5 KAN. J.L. & PUB. POL'Y 9, 14–16 (1995).

38 Leshy, *supra* note 39, at 204–08.

39 Alejandro E. Camacho, *Can Regulation Evolve: Lessons from a Study in Maladaptive Management*, 55 UCLA L. REV. 293, 312–13 n.108 (2007).

40 MATHA F. LEE, EARTH FIRST!: ENVIRONMENTAL APOCALYPSE (1995) (providing a history of the first years of Earth First!).

41 *See, e.g.*, Healthy Forests Restoration Act of 2003, Pub. L. No. 108–48; Presidential Memo, A 21st Century Strategy for America's Great Outdoors, 75 Fed. Reg. 20,767 (Apr. 16, 2010); Exec. Off. of the Pres., The President's Climate Action Plan (2013); Clean Power Plan, Carbon Pollution Emission Guidelines for Existing Stationary Sources: Electric Utility Generating Units, 80 Fed. Reg. 64,662 (Oct. 23, 2015).

42 Neal Devins & Lawrence Baum, *Split Definitive: How Party Polarization Turned the Supreme Court into a Partisan Court*, 1 SUP. CT. REV. 301, 303 (2016).

43 Jessica Hejny, *The Trump Administration and Environmental Policy: Reagan Redux?*, 8(2) J. ENV'T STUD. & SCI. 197, 204–05 (2018).

44 *Id.* at 206; *see also generally*, Dena P. Adler, *U.S. Climate Change Litigation in the Age of Trump: Year Two*, SABIN CENTER FOR CLIMATE CHANGE LAW, COLUMBIA LAW SCHOOL, 2019.

45 Inflation Reduction Act, H.R. 5376, 117th Cong. (2022) White House, Inflation Reduction Act Guidebook 5 (2d ed. 2023).

46 Alexa St. John, *What Trump's Budget Cuts Could Mean for the Environment*, AP NEWS (May 2, 2025).

47 *See, e.g.*, Just Security, Litigation Tracker: Legal Challenges to Trump Administration Actions, www.justsecurity.org.

48 Julian E. Barnes and Catie Edmondson, *Trump Tramples Congress's Power, With Little Challenge from G.O.P.*, N.Y. TIMES (Sept. 7, 2025).

49 Jan Wolfe and Nate Raymond, *Judges Vexed By Supreme Court 'Shadow Docket' Rulings In Trump Cases*, REUTERS (Sept. 10, 2025).

50 *See* JOANNA M. BURKHARDT, COMBATTING FAKE NEWS IN THE DIGITAL AGE 5, 8 (2017).

51 Douglas Blanks Hindman & Kenneth Wiegand, *The Big Three's Prime-Time Decline: A Technological and Social Context*, 52 J. Broadcasting & Electronic Media 119, 119 (2008) ("In 1980, more than 90% of television viewers were tuned in to one of . . . three networks during prime time.").

52 *See* Lili Levi, *Social Media and the Press*, 90 N.C. L. Rev. 1531, 1545 (2012).

53 David A. Logan, *All Monica, All of the Time: The 24-Hour News Cycle and the Proof of Culpability in Libel Actions*, 23 U. Ark. Little Rock L. Rev. 201, 202 (2000).

54 *See, e.g.*, Howard Rosenberg, *'Baghdad': When CNN was the News*, L.A. Times, Dec. 6, 2002.

55 *See* Bill Kovach & Tom Rosenstiel, Warp Speed: America in the Age of Mixed Media 5–7 (1999); Paul Gronke & Timothy E. Cook, *Disdaining the Media: The American Public's Changing Attitudes Toward the News*, 24 Pol. Comm. 259, 260–61 (2007).

56 *See* Craig R. Smith, *The Campaign to Repeal the Fairness Doctrine*, 2 Rhetoric & Pub. Aff. 481, 481 (1999).

57 *In re Complaint of Syracuse Peace Council Against Television Station WTVH Syracuse, New York*, 2 FCC Rcd 5043 (1987).

58 *See In re Repeal or Modification of the Personal Attack and Political Editorial Rules*, 15 FCC Rcd 20697 (2000) (rescinding provisions granting the subject of an editorial or personal attack an opportunity to reply).

59 *See In re Amendment of Parts 1, 73 and 76 of the Commission's Rules*, 26 FCC Rcd 11422 (2011).

60 *See* Levi, *supra* note 54, at 1547.

61 Steven Waldman & the Working Grp. on Info. Needs of Cmtys., FCC, The Information Needs of Communities: The Changing Media Landscape in a Broadband Age 10, 105–06 (2011).

62 *See* Paul Sagan & Tom Leighton, *The Internet & the Future of News*, 139 Dædalus 119, 119 (2010).

63 *See* Waldman et al., *supra* note 63, at 118–19.

64 Burkhardt, *supra* note 52, at 7–8 (2017).

65 *See* Russell L. Weaver, *Remedies for "Disinformation,"* 55 U. Pac. L. Rev. 185, 188–89 (2024).

66 *See* Burkhardt, *supra* note 52, at 7.

67 Waldman et al., *supra* note 63, at 117.

68 *See* Amy Kristin Sanders & Rachael L. Jones, *Clicks at Any Cost: Why Regulation Won't Upend the Economics of Fake News*, 2 Bus. Entrepreneurship & Tax L. Rev. 339, 356 (2018).

69 Waldman et al., *supra* note 63, at 134.

70 *See* Jeffrey S. Pollak et al., *From Beepers to Smartphones: Challenges in Applying Title III to Modern Communication Technology*, 69 DOJ J. Fed. L. & Prac. 141, 149 (2021).

71 *See* Levi, *supra* note 54, at 1556.

72 *See* Gail Ehrlich, *Fighting Misinformation: How New Laws Might Help*, 93 N.Y. St. B.J. 16, 17 (2021).

73 Russell L. Weaver, *Free Speech in an Internet Era*, 58 U. Louisville L. Rev. 325, 346–47 (2020).

74 Ehrlich, *supra* note 74, at 17.

75 *See generally* Haydn Washington & John Cook, Climate Change Denial: Heads in the Sand (2011).

76 Russell L. Weaver, *Fake News (& Deep Fakes) and Democratic Discourse*, 24 J. Tech. L. & Pol'y 35, 38 (2021).

77 Russell L. Weaver, *Fake News (& Deep Fakes) and Democratic Discourse*, 24 J. Tech. L. & Pol'y 35, 38 (2021).

78 *See* Aaron M. McCright & Riley E. Dunlap, *Challenging Global Warming as a Social Problem: An Analysis of the Conservative Movement's Counter-Claims*, 47 Soc. Problems 499 (2000).

79 *See* Robert J. Brulle, *Institutionalizing Delay: Foundation Funding and the Creation of U.S. Climate Change Counter-Movement Organizations*, 122 Climate Change 681 (2014); Geoffrey Supran & Namoi Oreskes, Assessing ExxonMobil's Climate Change Communications (1977–2014), 12 Envtl. Res. Letters 084019 (2017).

80 Executive Order, Ending Taxpayer Subsidization of Biased Media (May 1, 2025), www.whitehouse.gov/presidential-actions/2025/05/ending-taxpayer-subsidization-of-biased-media/.

81 Dan Garisto, *How Trump is Following Project 2025's Radical Roadmap to Defund Science*, Nature, Mar. 27, 2025.

82 Makiya Seminera, *A Look at the Universities with Federal Funding Targeted by the Trump Administration*, AP News (Apr. 15, 2025).

83 Alyson C. Flournoy, *Beyond the "Spotted Owl Problem": Learning from the Old-Growth Controversy*, 17 Harv. Env't L. Rev. 261 (1993).

84 Daniel R. Dinger, *Throwing Canis Lupus to the Wolves:* United States v. McKittrick *and the Existence of the Yellowstone and Central Idaho Experimental Wolf Populations Under a Flawed Provision of the Endangered Species Act*, 2000 BYU L. Rev. 377 (2000).

85 Michael C. Blumm et al., *Practiced at the Art of Deception: The Failure of Columbia Basin Recovery Under the Endangered Species Act*, 36 Env'l L. 709 (2006).

86 *Endangered Species Act Amendments of 1982*, Pub. L. No. 97–304, § 6, 96 Stat. 1411, 1422 (1982).

87 Camacho, *supra* note 41, at 303–04.

88 *Id.* at 308.

89 The "No Surprises" program was announced in August 1994 by Secretary Babbitt and Secretary of Commerce Ron Brown. *Administration's New Assurance Policy Tells Landowners: 'No Surprises' in Endangered Species Planning*, Office of the Secretary, U.S. Dep't of the Interior (Aug. 11, 1994). In 1998, the U.S. Fish and

Wildlife Service codified the program. Habitat Conservation Plan Assurances ("No Surprises") Rule, 63 Fed. Reg. 8,859 (Feb. 23, 1998).

90 Holly Doremus, *Adaptive Management, the Endangered Species Act, and the Institutional Challenges of "New Age" Environmental Protection*, 41 WASHBURN L.J. 50, 51 (2001); J. B. Ruhl, *Who Needs Congress? An Agenda for Administrative Reform of the Endangered Species Act*, 6 N.Y.U. ENV'T L.J. 367 (1998).

91 *See* 16 U.S.C. § 1531(b) (2006); John Leshy, *The Babbitt Legacy at the Department of the Interior: A Preliminary View*, 31 ENV'T L. 199, 204–14 (2001).

92 Michael Russell, *The Endangered Species Act and the Conflict with Modern Economic and Development Interests*, 22 J. NAT. RES. & ENV'T L. 139, 139 (2008).

93 *See* Shi-Ling Hsu, *The Potential and the Pitfalls of Habitat Conservation Planning Under the Endangered Species Act*, 29 ENV'T L. REP. 10592. 10595 (1999) (explaining that some environmental advocacy groups saw the HCP innovation and program as a form of agency capture by loggers and developers of FWS).

94 *See* John C. Kunich, *Preserving the Womb of the Unknown Species with Hotspots Legislation*, 52 HASTINGS L.J. 1149, 1173–74 (2001).

95 Zachary Bray, *The Hidden Rise of 'Efficient' (De)Listing*, 73 MD. L. REV. 389, 452–53 (2014).

96 Endangered and Threatened Wildlife and Plants; Regulations for Listing Species and Designating Critical Habitat, 84 Fed. Reg. 44,753, 45,020, 45,024–26, 45,034–35 (Aug. 27, 2019) (to be codified at 50 C.F.R. 424).

97 Endangered and Threatened Wildlife and Plants; Regulations for Interagency Cooperation, 89 Fed. Reg. 24,268 (Apr. 4, 2024); Endangered and Threatened Wildlife and Plants; Listing Endangered and Threatened Species and Designating Critical Habitat, 89 Fed. Reg. 24,300 (Apr. 5, 2024).

98 *See* Press Release, U.S. House of Representatives Nat. Res. Comm. Democrats, Grijalva Statement on Biden Administration Action to Finalize Endangered Species Act Rules (Mar. 28, 2024), https://democrats-naturalresources.house.gov/media/press-releases/grijalva-statement-on-biden-administration-action-to-finalize-endangered-species-act-rules.

99 *Babbitt v. Sweet Home Chapter of Communities for a Great Oregon*. 515 U.S. 687 (1995).

100 Rescinding the Definition of "Harm" Under the Endangered Species Act, 90 Fed. Reg. 16,104 (Apr. 17, 2025).

101 State Energy & Environmental Impact Center, *Sixteen AGs Commented to Oppose Proposed Rule to Weaken Endangered Species Act Protections* (May 19, 2025).

102 *See* J. B. Ruhl, *Climate Change and the Endangered Species Act: Building Bridges to the No-Analog Future*, 88 B.U. L. REV. 1 (2008); Alejandro E. Camacho, *De- and Re-Constructing Public Governance for Biodiversity Conservation*, 73 VAND. L. REV. 1585–1641 (2020).

103 Alan C. Miller, *Longtime Foes Cleared Air for Clean Air Act*, L.A. TIMES, May 25, 1990, at B3. Waxman explains how the Clean Air Act Amendments got across the line and why it matters in The Honorable Henry A. Waxman, *An Overview of the Clean Air Act Amendments of 1990*, 21 ENVTL. L. 1721 (1991).

104 Doyle McManus, Tougher than a Boiled Owl, L.A. TIMES, Feb. 2, 2014, at A22.

105 Clean Air Act Amendments of 1990, Pub. L. No. 101–549, 104 Stat. 2399 (1990).

106 Clean Air Act Amendments of 1990, Pub. L. No. 101–549, 104 Stat. 2399 (1990).

107 Clean Air Act Amendments of 1990 Title VI—Stratospheric Ozone Protection, Pub. L. No. 101–549, 104 Stat. 2648 (1990).

108 *See* Montreal Protocol on Substances that Deplete the Ozone Layer, Sept. 16, 1987, 26 I.L.M. 2541 (entered into force Jan. 1, 1989).

109 Pamela Wexler, *Protecting the Global Atmosphere: Beyond the Montreal Protocol*, 14 MD J. INT'L L. & TRADE 1, 9 (1990).

110 Duncan Brack, *Monitoring the Montreal Protocol*, *in* VERIFICATION YEARBOOK (Trevor Findlay ed., 2003); Marco Gonzalez et al., *The Montreal Protocol: How Today's Successes Offer a Pathway to the Future*, 5 J. ENV'T STUD. AND SCI. 122, 124 (2015).

111 *Id.* at 124.

112 Jasmine Abdel-khalik, *Prescriptive Treaties in Global Warming: Applying the Factors Leading to the Montreal Protocol*, 22 MICH. J. INT'L L. 489, 511–18 (2001) (discussing effects and incentives in the Montreal Agreement for developing nations and industry innovation).

113 Amendment to Montreal Protocol ("Kigali Amendment") at III, S. Treaty Doc. 117–1, 117th Cong. (2021).

114 Almost two hundred nations have bound themselves by the Montreal Protocol. FACT SHEET: Nearly 200 Countries Reach a Global Deal to Phase Down Potent Greenhouse Gases and Avoid up to 0.5°C of Warming, Obama White House Archives (Oct. 15, 2016), https://obamawhitehouse.archives.gov/the-press-office/2016/10/15/fact-sheet-nearly-200-countries-reach-global-deal-phase-down-potent.

115 *See* Richard McKenzie et al., *Success of Montreal Protocol Demonstrated by Comparing High-Quality UV Measurements with "World Avoided" Calculations from Two Chemistry-Climate Models*, 9 SCI. REPORTS 12332 (2019).

116 *Montreal Protocol Emerges as a Powerful Climate Treaty*, NATIONAL OCEANIC AND ATMOSPHERIC ADMINISTRATION (Jan. 11, 2023), www.noaa.gov/news-release/montreal-protocol-emerges-as-powerful-climate-treaty.

117 *See* Clean Air Act Amendments of 1990, Pub. L. No. 101–549, 104 Stat. 2399 (1990); U.S. ENVTL. PROTECTION AGENCY, 1990 CLEAN AIR ACT AMENDMENT SUMMARY: TITLE VI (1990), www.epa.gov/clean-air-act-overview/1990-clean-air-act-amendment-summary-title-iv.

118 Paul L. Joskow & Richard Schmalensee, *The Political Economy of Market-Based Environmental Policy: The US Acid Rain Program*, 41 J.L. & ECON. 37, 40 (1998); Ronald P. Jackson, Jr., *Extending the Success of the Acid Rain Provisions of the Clean Air Act: An Analysis of the Clear Skies Initiative and Other Proposed Legislative and Regulatory Schemes to Curb Multi-Pollutant Emissions from Fossil Fueled Electric Generating Plants*, 12 U. BALT. J. ENV'T L. 91, 93 (2005).

119 Gabriel Chan et al., *The SO2 Allowance-Trading System and The Clean Air Act Amendments of 1990: Reflections on 20 Years of Policy Innovation*, 65 NAT'L TAX J. 419, 421–23 (2012).

120 Jackson, Jr., *supra* note 121.

121 *See generally* U.S. ENVTL. PROTECTION AGENCY, CLEAN AIR MARKETS DIV., CLEARING THE AIR, THE FACTS ABOUT CAPPING AND TRADING EMISSIONS (May 2002); Gabriel Chan et al., *supra* note 122, at 447.

122 *See, e.g.*, Lesley K. McAllister, *The Overallocation Problem in Cap-and-Trade: Moving Toward Stringency*, 34 COLUM. J. ENV'T L. 395, 437–39 (2009); Steven Ferrey, *Auctioning the Building Blocks of Life: Carbon Auction, the Law, and Global Warming*, 23 NOTRE DAME J.L. ETHICS & PUB. POL'Y 317, 366 (2009); Antonio Bento et al., *On the Importance of Baseline Setting in Carbon Offsets Markets*, 137 CLIMATIC CHANGE 625, 625 (2016).

123 North Carolina v. EPA, 531 F.3d 896 531 F.3d 896 (D.C. Cir. 2008). For a full history of this trading market, see Richard Schmalensee & Robert N. Stavins, *The SO2 Allowance Trading System: The Ironic History of a Grand Policy Experiment*, 27 J. ECON. PERSPS 103 (2012).

124 *See* MATTHEW C. NISBET & EZRA MARKOWITZ, STRATEGIC SCIENCE COMMUNICATION ON ENVIRONMENTAL ISSUES 2 (2016).

125 U.S. ENVTL. PROTECTION AGENCY, VOLKSWAGEN NOTICE OF VIOLATION, CLEAN AIR ACT (Sept. 18, 2015), www.epa.gov/sites/default/files/2015-10/documents/vw-nov-caa-09-18-15.pdf.

126 U.S. ENVTL. PROTECTION AGENCY, VOLKSWAGEN CLEAN AIR ACT CIVIL SETTLEMENT (March 11, 2025), www.epa.gov/enforcement/volkswagen-clean-air-act-civil-settlement.

127 *Id.*

128 Steven Barrett et al., *Impact of the Volkswagen Emissions Control Defeat Device on US Public Health*, 10 ENVT'L RES. LETTERS 114005, 114008 (2015). *See also* Cary Coglianese & Jennifer Nash, *The Law of the Test: Performance-Based Regulation and Diesel Emissions Control*, 34 YALE J. ON REG. 33, 33–51 (2017).

129 *See* Daniel S. Greenbaum, *The Clean Air Act: Substantial Successes and the Challenges Ahead*, 15(3) ANNALS AM. THORAC. SOC. 296 (2018).

130 Susan Solomon et al., *Irreversible Climate Change due to Carbon Dioxide Emissions*, 106 PROC. NAT'L ACAD. SCIS. 1704, 1709 (2009).

131 G. A. Res. 43/53 (Dec. 6, 1988). *See also* Noami Oreskes, *The Scientific Consensus on Climate Change*, 306 SCI. 1686 (2004); Cinnamon Carlarne, *Climate Change—The New "Superwhale" in the Room: International Whaling and Climate Change Politics—Too Much in Common?*, 80 S. CAL. L. REV. 753, 766 (2007).

132 Intergovernmental Negot. Comm. for a Framework Convention on Climate Change, Rep. on the Work of the Second Part of Its Fifth Session, Held at New York from 30 April to 9 May 1992, at 9, U.N. Doc. A/AC.237/18 (Part II) (1992).

133 For a historical overview of the development of international climate negotiations up through the United States' agreement to join the Paris Climate Accord, see *United Nations Framework Convention on Climate Change, Timeline*, https://unfccc.int/timeline/.

134 Kyoto Protocol to the United Nations Framework Convention on Climate Change, Dec. 10, 1997, 2303 U.N.T.S. 162 (entered into force Feb. 16, 2005).

135 Michael Hopkin, *Kyoto Protocol Comes into Force*, NATURE (Feb. 16, 2005).

136 S. Res. 98, 105th Cong. (1997).

137 Donald A. Brown, *The U.S. Performance in Achieving Its 1992 Earth Summit Global Warming Commitments*, 32 ENV'T REP. 10741 (2002).

138 Cinnamon P. Carlarne, *U.S. Climate Change Law: A Decade of Flux and an Uncertain Future*, 69 AM. U. L. REV. 387, 398–99 (2019).

139 *See* Albert Gore, *The Turning Point: New Hope for the Climate*, 18 ROLLING STONE, June 18, 2014.

140 *Climate Action Summit 2019—Morning Session*, United Nations (Sept. 23, 2019), www.youtube.com/watch?v=haewHZ8ubKA; *Transcript: Greta Thunberg's Speech at the U.N. Climate Action Summit*, NPR (Sept. 23, 2019), www.npr.org/2019/09/23/763452863/transcript-greta-thunbergs-speech-at-the-u-n-climate-action-summit.

141 Vicki Arroyo, *Keynote Address: A Brief History of U.S. Climate Policy and a Call to Action*, 34 MD. J. INT'L L. 1, 4 (2019).

142 *See* Paris Agreement to the United Nations Framework Convention on Climate Change, Dec. 12, 2015, T.I.A.S. No. 16–1104.

143 Jessica Durney, *Defining the Paris Agreement: A Study of Executive Power and Political Commitments*, 11 CARBON & CLIMATE L. REV. 234, 235 (2017).

144 UNITED NATIONS, REPORT OF THE CONFERENCE OF THE PARTIES SERVING AS THE MEETING OF THE PARTIES TO THE PARIS AGREEMENT ON ITS FIFTH SESSION, HELD IN THE UNITED ARAB EMIRATES FROM 30 NOVEMBER TO 13 DECEMBER 2023 2–21 (2024).

145 The White House, Climate Change and President Obama's Action Plan (2015), Obama White House Archives, https://obamawhitehouse.archives.gov/president-obama-climate-action-plan. *See also* Brigham Daniels, *Why Stop Grazing the Climate Commons?*, 13 MICH. J. ENVTL. & ADMIN. L. 88, 107–113 (2023) (providing historical background surrounding the Paris Accord and the United States' role in creating it and lifting it up).

146 *See* President Trump Announces U.S. Withdrawal from the Paris Climate Accord, Trump White House Archives (June 1, 2017), https://trumpwhitehouse.archives.gov/articles/president-trump-announces-u-s-withdrawal-paris-climate-accord/ (claiming that the Paris Accord "Undermines U.S. Competitiveness and Jobs"); *President Trump Announces Withdrawal from Paris Agreement*, SABIN CENTER FOR CLIMATE CHANGE LAW, COLUMBIA LAW SCHOOL, https://climate.law.columbia.edu/content/president-trump-announces-withdrawal-paris-agreement-0; Brigham Daniels, *Come Hell and High Water: Climate Change Policy in the Age of Trump*, 13 FIU L. REV. 65 (2018) (providing an overview of Trump's first term and the actions taken to walk back U.S. climate commitments).

147 *See* Paris Climate Agreement, (Jan. 20, 2021), https://bidenwhitehouse.archives.gov/briefing-room/statements-releases/2021/01/20/paris-climate-agreement/.

148 Exec. Order No. 14,162, 90 Fed. Reg. 8,455 (Jan. 30, 2025).

149 State of California, California Releases World's First Plan to Achieve Net Zero Carbon Pollution, California Governor (Nov. 16, 2022), www.gov.ca.gov/2022/11/16/california-releases-worlds-first-plan-to-achieve-net-zero-carbon-pollution/; California Governor's Office of Emergency Services, California Adaptation Planning Guide (June 2020), www.caloes.ca.gov/wp-content/uploads/Hazard-Mitigation/Documents/CA-Adaptation-Planning-Guide-FINAL-June-2020-Accessible.pdf; *The New England States' Frameworks for Reducing Greenhouse Gas Emissions Continue to Evolve*, ISO NEWSWIRE (Jan. 19, 2021), https://isonewswire.com/2021/01/19/the-new-england-states-frameworks-for-reducing-greenhouse-gas-emissions-continue-to-evolve/.

150 CONG. RSCH. SERV., IF10479, THE ENERGY CREDIT OR ENERGY INVESTMENT TAX CREDIT (updated Apr. 23, 2021).

151 *Yale Experts Explain Climate Lawsuits*, YALE SUSTAINABILITY (Aug. 16, 2023), https://sustainability.yale.edu/explainers/yale-experts-explain-climate-lawsuits; *People of the State of California v. Big Oil*, California Governor (Sept. 16, 2023), www.gov.ca.gov/2023/09/16/people-of-the-state-of-california-v-big-oil/.

152 *See* Stephen M. Johnson, *From Climate Change and Hurricanes to Ecological Nuisances: Common Law Remedies for Public Law Failures?*, 27 GA. ST. U. L. REV. 565 (2011).

153 American Elec. Power Co., Inc. v. Connecticut, 564 U.S. 410, 131 S. Ct. 2527 (2011).

154 *See also* BP PLC v. Mayor & City Council of Baltimore, 141 S. Ct. 1532 (2021); City of New York v. Chevron Corp., 993 F.3d 881 (2d Cir. 2021); County of San Mateo v. Chevron Corp., 32 F.4th 733 (9th Cir. 2022); City of Hoboken v. Chevron Corp., 45 F.4th 699 (3d Cir. 2022); City of Oakland v. BP PLC, 696 F.3d 895 (9th Cir. 2020); Mayor and City Council of Baltimore v. BP PLC, 31 F.4th 178 (4th Cir. 2022); Native Village of Kivalina v. ExxonMobil Corp., 696 F.3d 849 (9th Cir. 2012); Rhode Island v. Shell Oil Products Co., 35 F.4th 44 (1st Cir. 2022).

155 Aisha I. Saad, *Attribution for Climate Torts*, 64 B.C. L. REV. 867 (2023).

156 Massachusetts v. EPA., 549 U.S. 497 (2007).

157 *Id.* at 500 ("Because greenhouse gases fit well within the Act's capacious definition of 'air pollutant,' EPA has statutory authority to regulate emission of such gases from new motor vehicles.").

158 Peter Marcus Kristensen, *After Abdication: America Debates the Future of Global Leadership*, 2 CHINESE POL. SCI. REV. 550 (2017); Zhang Hai-Bin et al., *U.S. Withdrawal from the Paris Agreement: Reasons, Impacts, and China's Response*, 8 ADVANCES IN CLIMATE CHANGE RSCH. 220, 222 (2017).

159 Endangerment and Cause or Contribute Findings for Greenhouse Gases Under Section 202(a) of the Clean Air Act; Final Rule, 74 Fed. Reg. 66,496 (Dec. 15, 2009); 2017 and Later Model Year Light-Duty Vehicle Greenhouse Gas Emissions and Corporate Average Fuel Economy Standards, 77 Fed. Reg. 62,624 (Oct. 15, 2022).

160 *See* Cathy Milbourn, U.S. Envtl. Protection Agency, dot, epa propose the Nation's First Greenhouse Gas and Fuel Efficiency Standards for Trucks and Buses (Oct. 25, 2010), www.epa.gov/archive/epapages/newsroom_archive/newsreleases/9b3706622f4ac560852577c7005ea140.html.

161 Cathy Milbourn, U.S. Envtl. Protection Agency, epa proposes First Carbon Pollution Standard for Future Power Plants (Mar. 27, 2012), www.epa.gov/archive/epapages/newsroom_archive/newsreleases/9b4e8033d7e641d9852579ce005ae957.html.

162 Proposed Rule: Carbon Pollution Emission Guidelines for Existing Stationary Sources: Electric Utility Generating Units, 79 Fed. Reg. 34,830 (June 18, 2014); Final Rule: Carbon Pollution Emission Guidelines for Existing Stationary Sources: Electric Utility Generating Units, 80 Fed. Reg. 6,4661 (Oct. 23, 2015).

163 Final Rule: Repeal of the Clean Power Plan; Emission Guidelines for Greenhouse Gas Emissions from Existing Electric Utility Generating Units; Revisions to Emission Guidelines Implementing Regulations, 84 Fed. Reg. 32,520 (July 8, 2019).

164 Withdrawal of Waiver; Final Rule: The Safer Affordable Fuel-Efficient (SAFE) Vehicle Rules Part One: One National Program, 84 Fed. Reg. 51,310 (Sept. 27, 2019).

165 Exec. Order No. 14,008, 86 Fed. Reg. 7,619 (Feb. 1, 2021).

166 FACT SHEET: Biden–Harris Administration Strengthens the Federal Government's Resilience to Climate Change Impacts, (Oct. 6, 2022), https://bidenwhitehouse.archives.gov/briefing-room/statements-releases/2022/10/06/fact-sheet-biden-harris-administration-strengthens-the-federal-governments-resilience-to-climate-change-impacts/. In 2023, the administration also introduced a holistic National Climate Resilience Framework offering robust objectives for domestic climate policy. *See* National Climate Resilience Framework, (Sept. 28, 2023), https://bidenwhitehouse.archives.gov/wp-content/uploads/2023/09/National-Climate-Resilience-Framework-FINAL.pdf.

167 Notice of Decision: California State Motor Vehicle Control Standards; Advanced Clean Car Program; Reconsideration of a Previous Withdrawal of a Waiver of Preemption; Notice of Decision, 87 Fed. Reg. 14,332 (Mar. 14, 2022).

168 West Virginia v. EPA, 597 U.S. 697, 731 (2022).

169 Pub. L. No. 117–58 (2021).

170 Pub. L. No. 117–169 (2022).

171 U.S. Envtl. Protection Agency, Summary of Inflation Reduction Act Provisions Related to Renewable Energy (Oct. 5, 2023), www.epa.gov/green-power-markets/summary-inflation-reduction-act-provisions-related-renewable-energy. *See also* Cinnamon P. Carlarne, *The Acceleration of Climate Creep: The Court Crashes, Congress Surges*, 52 Env't L. Rep. 10778 (2022).

172 Greg Dotson & Dustin J. Maghamfar, *The Clean Air Act Amendments of 2022: Clean Air, Climate Change, and the Inflation Reduction Act*, 53 Env't L. Rep.

10017, 10018 (2023). *See also* Cinnamon P. Carlarne, *The Acceleration of Climate Creep: The Court Crashes, Congress Surges*, 52 ENV'T L. REP. 10778 (2022).

173 *See* Exec. Order No. 14,154, Unleashing American Energy, 90 Fed. Reg. 8,353 (Jan. 29, 2025).

174 *See, e.g.*, Exec. Order No. 14,154, Unleashing American Energy, 90 Fed. Reg. 8,353 (Jan. 29, 2025); *Woonasquatucket River Watershed Council v. U.S. Dep't of Agric.*, No. 1:25-cv-00097 (D.R.I. Apr. 15, 2025) (prelim. injunction) (ordering DOE, EPA, HUD, DOI, and USDA to release already-awarded IRA/IIJA funds).

175 Benjamin Storrow & Jean Chemnick, *How Trump Gutted Climate Policy in 30 Days*, E&E NEWS (Feb. 20, 2025).

176 One Big Beautiful Bill Act (Pub. L. No. 119-21).

177 90 Fed. Reg. 36,288 (Aug. 1, 2025).

178 Michael Phillis and Seth Borenstein, *National Academy of Sciences Rebuffs Trump EPA's Effort to Undo Regulations Fighting Climate Change*, AP (Sept. 17, 2025).

179 *See* Brett McDonnell et al., *Green Boardrooms?*, 53 CONN. L. REV. 335 (2021); Brigham Daniels, *Why Stop Grazing the Climate Commons?*, 13 MICH. J. ENV'T & ADMIN. L. 88, 116–121 (2023).

180 Ann Sanson & Ann Sanson, *Children and Youth in the Climate Crisis*, 45 BJPSYCH BULLETIN 205 (2021).

181 See Gregory R. Nosek, The Fossil Fuel Industry's Push to Target Climate Protesters in the U.S., 37 PACE ENVTL. L. REV. 54, 71, 89, 97 (2020); Nick Crockett, The Rise of Critical Infrastructure Protest Legislation and Its Implications for Radical Climate Activism, 33 COLO. ENV'T L.J. 408, 410 (2022) ("This legislative protection of the extraction industry has manifested in a recent wave of critical infrastructure protest laws being rapidly enacted in states around the country. These laws, which have proliferated across the nation since the first introduction in 2017, seek to harshly criminalize protests around and interference with pipelines and oil and gas facilities").

182 James Everett Katz, *US Energy Policy Impact of the Reagan Administration*, ENERGY POL'Y 122, 135–45 (1984).

183 Armin Rosencranz, *U.S. Climate Change Policy Under G. W. Bush*, 32 GOLDEN GATE U. L. REV. 479 (2002).

184 American Energy Dominance: Bad for Bureaucrats, Great for Our Country, Trump White House Archives (July 29, 2020), https://trumpwhitehouse.archives.gov/articles/president-trump-is-restoring-american-energy-dominance/.

185 White House, Declaring a National Energy Emergency, WhiteHouse.gov (Jan. 20, 2025), www.whitehouse.gov/presidential-actions/2025/01/declaring-a-national-energy-emergency/.

186 *See, e.g.*, Press Release, Obama White House Archives, Off. of the Press Sec'y, Remarks by the President on Energy, Obama White House Archives (Mar. 15, 2012), https://obamawhitehouse.archives.gov/the-press-office/2012/03/15/remarks-president-energy; Press Release, ConocoPhillips Co., ConocoPhillips Welcomes Record of Decision on the Willow Project (Mar. 23, 2023), www

.conocophillips.com/news-media/story/conocophillips-welcomes-record-of-decision-on-the-willow-project/ (acknowledging the Biden administration's approval of the Willow Project, "estimated to produce 180,000 barrels of oil per day at its peak").

187 John T. Shaw, Richard G. Lugar: Stateman of the Senate 73–93 (2012).

188 *See* Brock Ternes et al., *Grassroots Resistance to Energy Project Encroachment: Analyzing Environmental Mobilization Against the Keystone XL Pipeline*, 16 J. Civ. Soc'y 44–60 (2020); Danielle Quichocho & Burton St. John, *The Standing Rock Water Protests Against the Dakota Access Pipeline: Addressing Environmental Degradation Through Indigenous Political Ecology as the "Trickster Science," in* Communicating Climate Change, 135–50 (Juita-Elena (Wie) Yusaf & Burton St. John eds., 2022).

189 *See* Matthew Gravlin, *To Forsake Becoming: Indigenous Ontologies, Land Defense, and the Resistance at Standing Rock*, 1 Agoriad 1.7 (2024).

190 Juliet Grable, *A New Hope for Shutting down the Dakota Access Pipeline*, Sierra Club (Nov. 14, 2023), www.sierraclub.org/sierra/new-hope-shutting-down-dakota-access-pipeline.

191 On his first day in office, President Biden rescinded the Keystone XL permit, effectively killing the project. Exec. Order No. 13,990 of Jan. 20, 2021, 86 Fed. Reg. 7,037, 7,040 (2021).

192 Act of December 22, 2017, Pub. L. No. 115–97 Title II § 20001 Oil and Gas Program, 131 Stat. 2054,.

193 Alaska National Interest Lands Conservation Act, Pub. L. No. 96–487 § 1002, 94 Stat. 2371, 2449 (Dec. 2, 1980).

194 Laura B. Comay et al., Cong. Rsch. Serv., RL33872, Arctic National Wildlife Refuge (ANWR): An Overview (2025).

195 *See* James I. Crowley, *In the Wake of the* Exxon Valdez*: Charting the Course of Pilotage Regulation*, 22 J. Mar. L. & Com. 165 (1991); Elizabeth R. Millard, *Anatomy of an Oil Spill: The* Exxon Valdez *and the Oil Pollution Act of 1990*, 18 Seton Hall Legis. J. 331 (1993).

196 *See* Stephen Haycox, *"Fetched Up": Unlearned Lessons from the* Exxon Valdez, 99 J. Am. Hist. 219, 227 (2012).

197 *See* Oil Pollution Act, Pub. L. No. 101–380, 104 Stat. 484 (1990); Inho Kim, *Ten Years After the Enactment of the Oil Pollution Act of 1990: A Success or a Failure*, 26 Marine Pol'y 197 (2002).

198 *See* Oil Pollution Act, Pub. L. No. 101–380, 104 Stat. 484 (1990).

199 *See* Oil Pollution Act, Pub. L. No. 101–380, 104 Stat. 484, 573 (1990).

200 *See* Oil Pollution Act, Pub. L. No. 101–380, 104 Stat. 484, 529–30 (1990).

201 *See* Haycox, *supra* note 199, at 228.

202 Melissa K. Merry, Framing Environmental Disaster: Environmental Advocacy and the Deepwater Horizon Oil Spill 1 (1st ed., 2014); Remarks by the President to the Nation on the BP Oil Spill, Obama White

House Archives (June 15, 2010), https://obamawhitehouse.archives.gov/the-press-office/remarks-president-nation-bp-oil-spill.

203 Samuel Issacharoff & D. Theodore Rave, *The BP Oil Spill Settlement and the Paradox of Public Litigation*, 74 LA. L. REV. 397, 398 (2014).

204 *See* US Labor Department Provides $27 Million to Help Workers Displaced by Oil Spill in Gulf of Mexico, Occupational Safety and Health Administration (June 30, 2010), https://www.dol.gov/newsroom/releases/eta/eta20100630-0; Tom Zeller, *Drill Ban Means Hard Times for Rig Workers*, N.Y. TIMES (June 18, 2010).

205 *See* Arthur De Vany & W. David Walls, *Open Access and the Emergence of a Competitive Natural Gas Market*, 12 CONTEMP. ECON. POL'Y 77 (1994).

206 *See* Richard Kerr, *Natural Gas from Shale Bursts onto the Scene*, 328 SCI. 1624, 1625 (2010); Lauren Karam, *Fracking Across the Globe: The Debate in the United States and Europe and the Role of Federal, State, and Local Regulations*, 41 SUFFOLK TRANSNAT'L L. REV. 173, 176 (2018).

207 For an explanation of the development of fracking policies in the United States, see Charles Davis, *Shaping State Fracking Policies in the United States: An Analysis of Who, What, and How*, 49 STATE AND LOCAL GOVERNMENT REV. 140 (2017).

208 Blake Watson, *Hydraulic Fracturing and Tort Litigation: A Survey of Landowner Lawsuits*, 31 PROB. & PROP. 10 (2017).

209 *Id.* at 11.

210 *See* Sorell E. Negro, *Fracking Wars: Federal, State and Local Conflicts over the Regulation of Natural Gas Activities*, 35 ZONING & PLAN. L. REP. 1–16 (2012).

211 Barbara Warner & Jennifer Shapiro, *Fractured, Fragmented Federalism: A Study in Fracking Regulatory Policy*, 43 PUBLIUS 474, 485 (2013).

212 *Id.* at 483.

213 For further discussion, see, for example, Davis, *supra* note 210.

214 *See* Standards of Performance for New, Reconstructed, and Modified Sources and Emissions Guidelines for Existing Sources: Oil and Natural Gas Sector Climate Review, 89 Fed. Reg. 16,820 (Mar. 8, 2024) (to be codified at 40 C.F.R. pt. 60).

215 *See* Trevor House et al., *Can Coal Make a Comeback?*, COLUM. CTR. ON GLOB. ENERGY POL'Y 5 (2017).

216 *See id.*

217 *See* Presidential Executive Order on Promoting Energy Independence and Economic Growth, Trump White House Archives (Mar. 28, 2017), https://trumpwhitehouse.archives.gov/presidential-actions/presidential-executive-order-promoting-energy-independence-economic-growth/; Exec. Order No. 14,261, 90 Fed. Reg. 15,517 (2025) (emphasizing the coal industry as a national priority and removing all federal barriers hindering coal production).

218 LYNN J. CUNNINGHAM &, CLAIRE M. JORDAN, CONG. RSCH SERV., R40913, RENEWABLE ENERGY AND ENERGY EFFICIENCY INCENTIVES: A SUMMARY OF FEDERAL PROGRAMS (2023); DAVID TIMMONS ET AL., THE ECONOMICS OF RENEWABLE ENERGY 52 (2014).

219 *What is U.S. Electricity Generation by Energy Source?*, United States Energy Information Administration (2022) (In 2021, of the energy generated by U.S. facilities, "[a]bout 61% of this electricity generation was from fossil fuels—coal, natural gas, petroleum, and other gases. About 19% was from nuclear energy, and about 20% was from renewable energy sources."), www.eia.gov/tools/faqs/faq.php?id=427&t=3.

220 Thomas Tran & Amanda Smith, *Evaluation of Renewable Energy Technologies and Their Potential for Technical Integration and Cost-Effective Use Within the U.S. Energy Sector*, 80 Renewable & Sustainable Energy Rev. 1372, 1373 (2017).

221 U.S. Envtl. Protection Agency, Computer Manufacturers Launch Program to Introduce Energy-Efficient Personal Computers (June 17, 1992),. Note that the Energy Star program started with computers and displays. For a history of the Energy Star program, visit www.energystar.gov/about/history/major-milestones.

222 ENERGY STAR International Partners, ENERGY STAR, www.energystar.gov/partner_resources/international_partners.

223 Energy Policy Act of 1992, H.R. 776, 102d Cong. (1992).

224 Energy Policy Act of 2005, H.R. 6, 109th Cong. (2005).

225 Robert W. Adler, *The Decline and (Possible) Renewal of Aspiration in the Clean Water Act*, 88 Wash. L. Rev. 759, 777 (2013).

226 *A Look back at the Birth of the Clean Water Act*, Living On Earth (Dec. 28, 2012), www.loe.org/shows/segments.html?programID=12-P13-00052&segmentID=1.

227 Statement on Signing the Safe Drinking Water Act Amendments of 1986, Ronald Reagan Presidential Library (June 19, 1986), www.reaganlibrary.gov/archives/speech/statement-signing-safe-drinking-water-act-amendments-1986.

228 Safe Drinking Water Act Amendments of 1986, S. 124, 99th Cong. (1986).

229 U.S. Environmental Protection Agency, President Clinton Signs Legislation to Ensure Americans Safe Drinking Water (Aug. 6, 1996), https://www.epa.gov/archive/epa/aboutepa/president-clinton-signs-legislation-ensure-americans-safe-drinking-water.html.

230 Safe Drinking Water Act Amendments of 1996, S. 1316, 104th Cong. (1996).

231 James Salzman, Drinking Water: a history 139–56 (2017).

232 Adler, *supra* note 228, at 777.

233 *See* Jan Laitos & Heidi Ruckriegle, *The Clean Water Act and the Challenge of Agricultural Pollution*, 37 Vt. L. Rev. 1033, 1036 (2013).

234 *See* Robert Glicksman & Matthew Batzel, *Science, Politics, Law, and the Arc of the Clean Water Act: The Role of Assumptions in the Adoption of a Pollution Control Landmark*, 32 Wash. U. J.L. & Pol'y 99 (2010); Robin Rotman & Ashley Hollis, *Control of Nonpoint Source Pollution Under the Clean Water Act*, 37 Nat. Res. & Env't 8 (2022).

235 Water Quality Act of 1987, H.R. 1, 100th Cong. (1987).

236 U.S. Envtl. Protection Agency, Clean Water Action Plan (Oct. 15, 2009), www.epa.gov/sites/default/files/documents/actionplan101409

.pdf; *See* Robin Kundis Craig, *Local or National? The Increasing Federalization of Nonpoint Source Pollution Regulation*, J. ENV'T L. & LITIG. 15, 179 (2000).

237 Water Pollution Control Act Amendments of 1972, 33 U.S.C. § 1362(7) ("The term 'navigable waters' means the waters of the United States, including the territorial seas"); *see* Jeffrey Miller, *Plain Meaning, Precedent, and Metaphysics: Interpreting the "Navigable Waters" Element of the Clean Water Act Offense*, 45 ENV'T L. REP. NEWS & ANALYSIS (2015).

238 *See* Rotman & Hollis, *supra* note 237, at 11.

239 Gina McCarthy & Jo-Ellen Darcy, Reasons We Need the Clean Water Rule, Obama White House Archives (May 27, 2015), https://obamawhitehouse.archives.gov/blog/2015/05/27/reasons-we-need-clean-water-rule; Final Rule: Clean Water Rule: Definition of "Waters of the United States," 80 Fed. Reg. 37,054 (June 29, 2015).

240 Proposed Rule: Definition of "Waters of the United States"—Recodification of Pre-Existing Rules, 82 Fed. Reg. 34,899 (June 27, 2017).

241 Final Rule: Definition of "Waters of the United States"—Recodification of Pre-Existing Rules, 84 Fed. Reg. 56,626 (Oct. 22, 2019).

242 The Navigable Waters Protection Rule: Definition of "Waters of the United States," 85 Fed. Reg. 22,250 (Apr. 21, 2020).

243 U.S. ENVTL. PROTECTION AGENCY, REVISING THE DEFINITION OF "WATERS OF THE UNITED STATES," www.epa.gov/wotus/revising-definition-waters-united-states.

244 Proposed Rule: Revised Definition of "Waters of the United States," 86 Fed. Reg. 69,372 (Dec. 7, 2021).

245 *See* Rotman & Hollis, *supra* note 237, at 8.

246 Sackett v. EPA, 598 U.S. 651, 143 S. Ct. 1322, 1325 (2023).

247 *Id.* at 1325.

248 33 C.F.R. 328.3; *see also* Revised Definition of "Waters of the United States"; conforming, 60 Fed. Reg. at 61,966.

249 Amended Complaint, Texas v. EPA, No. 3:23-CV-00017 (S.D. Tex. Nov. 13, 2023).

250 Cale Jaffe, *Sackett and the Unraveling of Federal Environmental Law*, 53 ENV'T L. REP. 10,801 (2023).

251 For a riveting history of the early shaping of the environmental justice movement, see Jedediah Purdy, *The Long Environmental Justice Movement*, 44 ECOLOGY L.Q. 809 (2018).

252 Clifford Villa, *Remaking Environmental Justice*, 66 LOY. L. REV. 469 (2020).

253 GENERAL ACCOUNTING OFFICE, SITING OF HAZARDOUS WASTE LANDFILLS AND THEIR CORRELATION WITH RACIAL AND ECONOMIC STATUS OF SURROUNDING COMMUNITIES (1983).

254 UNITED CHURCH OF CHRIST COMMISSION FOR RACIAL JUSTICE, TOXIC WASTES AND RACE IN THE UNITED STATES: A NATIONAL REPORT ON THE RACIAL AND SOCIO-ECONOMIC CHARACTERISTICS OF COMMUNITIES WITH HAZARDOUS WASTE SITES (1987); ROBERT BULLARD, ET. AL.,

TOXIC WASTES AND RACE AT TWENTY: 1987–2007: GRASSROOTS STRUGGLES TO DISMANTLE ENVIRONMENTAL RACISM IN THE UNITED STATES (2007).

255 *See* Dollie Burwell & Luke Cole, *Environmental Justice Comes Full Circle: Warren County Before and After*, 1 GOLDEN GATE U. ENV'T L.J. 9 (2007); Andrea Simpson, *Public Hazard, Personal Peril: The Impact of Non-Governmental Organizations in the Environmental Justice Movement*, 18 RICH. J.L. & PUB. INT. 515, 522 (2015).

256 *See* Burwell & Cole, *supra* note 258.

257 *See id.*

258 EPA, ENVIRONMENTAL EQUITY: REDUCING RISK FOR ALL COMMUNITIES (1992).

259 Exec. Order No. 12,898, 59 Fed. Reg. 7,629 (Feb. 16, 1994), www.archives.gov/files/federal-register/executive-orders/pdf/12898.pdf.

260 *See* Burwell & Cole, *supra* note 258; Villa, *supra* note 255; Simpson, *supra* note 258; Tendai Chitewere, *Equity in Sustainable Communities: Exploring Tools from Environmental Justice and Political Ecology*, 50 NAT. RES. J. 315 (2009).

261 Stephen M. Johnson, *NEPA and SEPA's in the Quest for Environmental Justice*, 30 LOY. L.A. L. REV. 565 (1997).

262 White House, Fact Sheet: A Year Advancing Environmental Justice, WhiteHouse.gov (Jan. 26, 2022), https://bidenwhitehouse.archives.gov/briefing-room/statements-releases/2022/01/26/fact-sheet-a-year-advancing-environmental-justice/.

263 *See* White House, Justice 40 (2020), WhiteHouse.gov, https://bidenwhitehouse.archives.gov/environmentaljustice/justice40/.

264 Exec. Order No. 14,008, *supra* note 168.

265 U.S. DEPT. OF JUSTICE OFFICE OF THE ATTORNEY GENERAL, ACTIONS TO ADVANCE ENVIRONMENTAL JUSTICE (May 5, 2022), www.justice.gov/media/1221536/dl?inline=. *See* U.S. DEPT. OF JUSTICE OFFICE OF THE ASSOCIATE ATTORNEY GENERAL, COMPREHENSIVE ENVIRONMENTAL JUSTICE ENFORCEMENT STRATEGY (May 5, 2022), www.justice.gov/d9/pages/attachments/2022/05/05/02._asg_strategy_memorandum.pdf.

266 *See* Will McNamara, et al., *Seeking energy equity through energy storage*, 35 ELECTRICITY J., 107,063 (2022).

267 Exec. Order No. 14,096, 88 Fed. Reg. 25,251, 25,253 (Apr. 21, 2023).

268 Press Release, U.S. Envtl. Protection Agency, Biden–Harris Administration Announces $2 Billion to Fund Environmental and Climate Justice Community Change Grants as Part of Investing in America Agenda (Nov. 21, 2023), www.epa.gov/newsreleases/biden-harris-administration-announces-2-billion-fund-environmental-and-climate-justice.

269 Exec. Order No. 14,151, 90 Fed. Reg. 8,339 (Jan. 29, 2025).

270 Amudalat Ajasa, *EPA to Fire or Reassign more than 450 Staffers Working on Environmental Justice, DEI*, WASH. POST, Apr. 22, 2025.

271 Mining Law of 1872, 30 U.S.C. § 22 *et seq.* (1872); Tyler Weidlich, *The Mining Law Continuum: Is There a Contemporary Prospect for Reform?*, 44 Brandeis L.J. 951 (2006).

272 Taylor Grazing Act of 1934, 73d Cong., 43 U.S.C. ch. 8A § 315 *et seq.* (1934).

273 Raymond Rasker, *A New Look at Old Vista: The Economic Role of Environmental Quality in Western Public Lands*, 65 U. Colo. L. Rev. 369 (1994).

274 Weidlich, *supra* note 274, at 977–78.

275 *See* Randall Wilson, America's Public Lands: From Yellowstone to Smokey Bear and Beyond 281 (2d ed. 2020).

276 *Id.* at 223.

277 *See* Sandra Zellmer, *The Changing Nature of Private Rights to Federal Resources*, 1 Rocky Mtn. Min. L. Found. Spec. Inst. 5 (2017); Sandra Zellmer, *Mitigating Malheur's Misfortunes: The Public Interest in The Public's Public Lands*, 31 Geo. Env't L. Rev. 509 (2019).

278 *See* Cristopher Klapperich, *The New Frontier of Environmental Preservation: The Antiquities Act*, 58 Santa Clara L. Rev. 189 (2018).

279 William Clinton, *Proclamation 6920—Establishment of the Grand Staircase–Escalante National Monument*, Administration of William J. Clinton, 1996 (Sept. 18, 1996), www.govinfo.gov/content/pkg/WCPD-1996-09-23/pdf/WCPD-1996-09-23-Pg1788.pdf.

280 *See* Wilson, *supra* note 278.

281 Presidential Proclamation Modifying the Grand Staircase–Escalante National Monument, Trump White House Archives (Dec. 4, 2017), https://trumpwhitehouse.archives.gov/presidential-actions/presidential-proclamation-modifying-grand-staircase-escalante-national-monument/; Presidential Proclamation Modifying the Bears Ears National Monument, Trump White House Archives (Dec. 4, 2017), https://trumpwhitehouse.archives.gov/presidential-actions/presidential-proclamation-modifying-bears-ears-national-monument/. *See also* John Ruple, *The Trump Administration and Lessons Not Learned from Prior National Monument Modifications*, 43 Harv. Env't L. Rev. 1, 5 (2019).

282 *See* A Proclamation on Grand Staircase–Escalante National Monument, WhiteHouse.gov (Oct. 8, 2017), www.whitehouse.gov/briefing-room/presidential-actions/2021/10/08/a-proclamation-on-grand-staircase-escalante-national-monument/; A Proclamation on Bears Ears National Monument, WhiteHouse.gov (Oct. 8, 2017), www.whitehouse.gov/briefing-room/presidential-actions/2021/10/08/a-proclamation-on-bears-ears-national-monument/.

283 *See* A Proclamation on Establishment of the Baaj Nwaavjo I'tah Kukveni–Ancestral Footprints of the Grand Canyon National Monument, WhiteHouse.gov (Aug. 8, 2023), https://bidenwhitehouse.archives.gov/briefing-room/presidential-actions/2023/08/08/a-proclamation-on-establishment-of-the-baaj-nwaavjo-itah-kukveni-ancestral-footprints-of-the-grand-canyon-national-monument/.

284 Exec. Order No. 14,008, *supra* note 168, at 7,627.

285 Dep't. of Justice, Office of Legal Counsel, "Revocation of Prior Monument Designation" (May 27, 2025), https://www.justice.gov/olc/media/1403101/dl.

286 U.S. Envtl. Protection Agency, Superfund History (updated Nov. 25, 2024), www.epa.gov/superfund/superfund-history.

287 Dennis & Mooney, *supra* note 5.

288 Kristin M. Carter, *Superfund Amendments and Reauthorization Act of 1986: Limiting Judicial Review to the Administrative Record in Cost Recovery Actions by the EPA*, 74 Cornell L. Rev. 1152, 1157 (1988–1989).

289 42 U.S.C. § 9611(a).

290 42 U.S.C. § 9621(b)(1).

291 42 U.S.C. § 9613(k)(2)(B).

292 Anne Slaughter Andrew, *Brownfield Redevelopment: A State-Led Reform of Superfund Liability*, 10 Nat. Res. & Env't 27, 30 (1996).

293 U.S. Envtl. Protection Agency, Brownfields Program Accomplishments, https://www.epa.gov/brownfields/accomplishments.

294 Martina E. Cartwright, *Superfund: It's No Longer Super and It Isn't Much of a Fund*, 18 Tulane Env't L.J. 299, 315 (2005).

295 U.S. Gov't Accountability Off., gao-15-812, Superfund: Trends in Federal Funding and Cleanup of epa's Nonfederal National Priorities List Sites 16 (2015).

296 U.S. Envtl. Protection Agency, Superfund: National Priorities List (2024), www.epa.gov/superfund/superfund-national-priorities-list-npl.

297 Publ. L. No. 117–58 (2021).

298 Pub L. No. 117–169 (2022).

299 *See, e.g.*, U.S. Envtl. Protection Agency, Superfund Environmental Justice Best Practices, United States (2023), https://semspub.epa.gov/work/HQ/100003346.pdf.

300 Cong. Rsch. Serv., R41039, Comprehensive Environmental Response, Compensation, and Liability Act: a summary of Superfund Cleanup Authorities and Related Provisions of the Act (2012).

301 Nuclear Waste Policy Act, Pub. L. No. 97–245, 96 Stat. 2201 (codified in H.R. 3809) (1983). *See also Remarks on Signing the Nuclear Waste Policy Act of 1982*, 1983 Pub. Papers 21 (Jan. 7, 1983).

302 *See id.* at Title I—Disposal and Storage of High-Level Radioactive Waste, Spent Nuclear Fuel, and Low-Level Radioactive Waste.

303 *See id.* at Title II—Research, Development, and Demonstration Regarding Disposal of High-Level Radioactive Waste and Spent Nuclear Fuel.

304 Department of Defense and Full-Year Continuing Appropriations Act, Pub. L. No. 112–10 (2011).

305 U.S. Gov't Accountability Off., gao-11–229, Commercial Nuclear Waste: Effects of a Termination of the Yucca Mountain Repository Program and Lessons Learned (2011).

306 Hazardous and Solid Waste Amendments of 1984, Pub. L. No. 98–616, 98 Stat. 3221 (1984) (Section 221 of the Act covers "Small Quantity Generator Waste.").

307 *Id.*

308 Emergency Planning and Community Right-to-Know, 42 U.S.C. § 11001 *et seq.* (1986).

309 *See id.*

310 *See* U.S. ENVTL. PROTECTION AGENCY, TOXICS RELEASE INVENTORY (TRI) PROGRAM, www.epa.gov/toxics-release-inventory-tri-program/what-toxics-release-inventory.

311 Safe Drinking Water and Toxic Enforcement Act of 1986 (Proposition 65), Cal. Health and Safety Code § 25249.5 *et seq.* (1986).

312 *See* Cal. Health & Safety Code § 25249.6.

313 *See, e.g.*, David B. Fischer, *Proposition 65 Warnings at 30—Time for a Different Approach*, 11 J. BUS. & TECH. L. 131, 145 (2016); Bradley C. Karkkainen, *Information-Forcing Environmental Regulation*, 33 FLA. ST. U. L. REV. 861, 872 (2006); Clifford Rechtschaffen, *The Warning Game: Evaluating Warnings under California's Proposition 65*, 23 ECOLOGY L.Q. 303, 306–07 (1996).

314 Food Quality Protection Act of 1996, Pub. L. No. 104–170, 110 Stat. 1489 (1996).

315 *See id.*

316 Global Food Security Act of 2016, Pub. L. No. 114–196, 130 Stat. 675 (2016).

317 Frank R. Lautenberg Chemical Safety for the 21st Century Act, Pub. L. No. 114–182, 130 Stat. 448 (2016).

318 *See id.*; U.S. ENVTL. PROTECTION AGENCY, THE FRANK LAUTENBERG CHEMICAL SAFETY FOR THE 21ST CENTURY ACT, www.epa.gov/assessing-and-managing-chemicals-under-tsca/frank-r-lautenberg-chemical-safety-21st-century-act.

319 15 U.S.C. § 2601 *et seq.* (1976).

320 Swati D. G. Rayasam et al., *Toxic Substances Control Act (TSCA) Implementation: How the Amended Law Has Failed to Protect Vulnerable Populations from Toxic Chemicals in the United States*, 56 ENV'T SCI. & TECH. 11969, 11970 (2022).

321 *Id.*

CONCLUSION

1 *See* chap. 1.

2 Of the public lands, substantial amounts of land have been set aside as national forests (193 million acres), wildlife refuges (89 million acres), and national parks (80 million acres). CAROL HARDY VINCENT ET AL., CONG. RSCH. SERV., R42346, FEDERAL LAND OWNERSHIP: OVERVIEW AND DATA (2020). Over 111 million of acres managed by federal agencies are designated as federal wilderness and protected from further extractive disturbance. *Three Key Environmental Victories from This Year*, ENVIRONMENT AMERICA (June 28, 2024), https://environmentamerica.org.

3 *Listed Species Summary (Boxscore)*, U.S. FISH & WILDLIFE SERVICE, https://ecos.fws.gov (last visited Mar. 23, 2019).

4 S. Res. 516, 118th Cong. (2023).

5 J. Michael Scott et al., *By the Numbers*, *in* THE ENDANGERED SPECIES ACT AT THIRTY 16, 31 (Dale D. Goble et al. eds., 2006).

6 *Delisted Species*, U.S. FISH & WILDLIFE SERVICE, https://ecos.fws.gov (last visited Mar. 27, 2019).

7 *Has the Endangered Species Act Saved 'Very Few' Plants and Animals?*, WASH. POST, Aug. 16, 2019.

8 *The Ridiculously Stupid Reason the US Is Letting Animals Spiral Toward Oblivion*, VOX (Dec. 18, 2023).

9 *The Endangered Species Act is Criticized for Its Costs. But It Generates More than $1 Trillion a Year*, TIME, July 25, 2018.

10 *See, e.g.*, Mark W. Davis, *Air Quality in the United States*, *in* ENVIRONMENTAL ISSUES TODAY: CHOICES AND CHALLENGES 53 (Robert J. Duffy & Susan M. Opp eds., 2020).

11 E. Donald Elliott, *A Critical Assessment of the EPA's Air Program at Fifty and A Suggestion for How It Might Do Even Better*, 70 CASE W. RSRV. L. REV. 895 (2020).

12 JUTTA BRUNNEE, ACID RAIN AND OZONE LAYER DEPLETION: INTERNATIONAL LAW AND REGULATION (1988).

13 Simon Mui & Amanda Levin, *Clearing the Air: The Benefits of the Clean Air Act*, NATURAL RESOURCES DEFENSE COUNCIL (May 5, 2020), www.nrdc.org (identifying Clean Air Act benefits in 2020 of "up to 370,000 avoided premature deaths, 189,000 fewer hospital admissions for cardiac and respiratory illnesses, and net economic benefits of up to $3.8 trillion for the U.S. economy").

14 Kara Manke, *Clean Water Act Dramatically Cut Pollution in U.S. Waterways*, BERKELEY NEWS, Oct. 8, 2018.

15 Final Rule, Asbestos Part 1; Chrysotile Asbestos; Regulation of Certain Conditions of Use Under the Toxic Substances Control Act (TSCA), 89 Fed. Reg. 21,970 (Mar. 28, 2024).

16 Environmental Law Institute, *NEPA Success Stories: Celebrating 40 Years of Transparency and Open Government* 3 (2010); Robert L. Glicksman & Alejandro E. Camacho, *The Trump Card: Tarnishing Planning, Democracy, and the Environment*, 50 ENV'T L. REP. 10281, 10281–82 (2020).

17 Daniel R. Mandelker, *Melding State Environmental Policy Acts with Land-Use Planning and Regulations*, 49 LAND USE L. & ZONING DIG. 3 (1997).

18 Neil Craik, *The Duty to Cooperate in the Customary Law of Environmental Impact Assessment*, 69 INT'L & COMPAR. L.Q. 239 (2020).

19 Yusuf Khan, *U.S. Renewable Power Growth Is Setting New Records on the Back of Federal Support*, WALL ST. J., Feb. 21, 2024. A record 31 gigawatts (GW) of solar energy capacity was installed in the United States in 2023, a roughly 55 percent increase from 2022 installations and substantially more than the previous record

in 2021. Lori Bird & Joseph Womble, *State of US Clean Energy Transition: Recent Progress, and What Comes Next*, World Resources Institute (Feb. 7, 2024), www.wri.org.

20 *Lazard's Levelized Cost of Energy Analysis*, LAZARD (Apr. 12, 2023), https://www.lazard.com/research-insights/2023-levelized-cost-of-energyplus/.

21 *See, e.g.*, *Vermont Commits to 100% Renewable Electricity*, ENVIRONMENT AMERICA (June 17, 2024), https://environmentamerica.org (describing Vermont law that commits to 100 percent renewable electricity by 2030 and New York law deploying clean energy home rebates).

22 PURPA § 3(4), 16 U.S.C. § 2602(4).

23 *See* Roberta F. Mann & Tracey M. Roberts, *The Long and Winding Road: The Inflation Reduction Act's Energy and Environmental Tax Credits*, 70 NAT'L TAX J. 223, 243–49 (2025) (explaining incentives across different sectors of the economy).

24 *See, e.g.*, Joseph P. Tomain, *"Our Generation's Sputnik Moment": Regulating Energy Innovation*, 31 UTAH ENV'T L. REV. 389, 397 (2011). The nature, timing, and scope of those physical changes and how they will interact with one another remain uncertain. Climate change may generate feedback loops which exacerbate physical changes already occurring. *See* Martin Heimann & Markus Reichstein, *Terrestrial Ecosystem Carbon Dynamics and Climate Feedbacks*, 451 NATURE 289 (2008); Robin Kundis Craig, *Stationarity Is Dead'—Long Live Transformation; Five Principles for Climate Change Adaptation Law*, 34 HARV. ENV'T L. REV. 9, 15 (2010).

25 Intergovernmental Panel on Climate Change, *Climate Change 2014 Synthesis Report: Summary for Policymakers* 6–8 (2014); U.S. Global Change Research Program, GLOBAL CLIMATE CHANGE IMPACTS IN THE UNITED STATES 9 (Susan J. Hassol et al. eds., 2009).

26 *See generally* CLIMATE ENGINEERING AND THE LAW: REGULATION AND LIABILITY FOR SOLAR RADIATION MANAGEMENT AND CARBON DIOXIDE REMOVAL (Michael B. Gerrard & Tracy Hester eds., 2018); Jay Michaelson, *Geoengineering: A Climate Change Manhattan Project*, 17 STAN. ENV'T L.J. 73 (1998).

27 *See, e.g.*, ENGINEERING THE CLIMATE: THE ETHICS OF SOLAR RADIATION MANAGEMENT (Christopher J. Preston ed., 2012); Joshua B. Horton, *Geoengineering and the Myth of Unilateralism: Pressures and Prospects for International Cooperation*, 4 STAN. J.L., SCI. & POL'Y 56 (2011).

28 *See, e.g.*, International Union for Conservation of Nature, *Synthetic Biology and Its Implications for Biodiversity Conservation* (2019); ALBERT C. LIN, PROMETHEUS REIMAGINED: TECHNOLOGY, ENVIRONMENT, AND LAW IN THE TWENTY-FIRST CENTURY (2017).

29 Alejandro E. Camacho, *Going the Way of the Dodo: De-extinction, Dualisms, and Reframing Conservation*, 92 WASH. U. L. REV. 849 (2015).

30 Amy L. Stein, *Artificial Intelligence and Climate Change*, 37 YALE J. ON REGUL. 890, 917–18 (2020).

31 Shaolei Ren & Adam Wierman, *The Uneven Distribution of AI's Environmental Impacts*, HARV. BUS. REV. (July 15, 2024), https://hbr.org.

32 *See* California Government Operations Agency, *State of California: Benefits and Risks of Generative Artificial Intelligence Report* 16 (2023) ("GenAI tools may enable bad actors to design, synthesize, or acquire dangerous chemical, biological, radiological, or nuclear (CBRN) weapons.").

33 *See, e.g.*, CHRISTOPHER H. FOREMAN, THE PROMISE AND PERIL OF ENVIRONMENTAL JUSTICE (2011).

34 *See* chap. 5.

35 *See* DANIEL FARBER, ECO-PRAGMATISM: MAKING SENSIBLE ENVIRONMENTAL DECISIONS IN AN UNCERTAIN WORLD (1999); View article page _quoteCITE David Manuel-Navarrete, *A Power, Realism, and the Ideal of Human Emancipation in a Climate of Change*, 1 WIRES CLIMATE CHANGE 765.

36 For a general overview of how nuisance law has adapted to address environmental challenges, see Michael C. Blumm, *A Dozen Landmark Nuisance Cases and Their Environmental Significance*, 62 ARIZ. L. REV. 403 (2020). For a more specific discussion about the potential of nuisance law to adapt to address a particular challenge, see, for example, Connor J. Fraser, *Note: The Public Plastic Nuisance: Life in Plastic, Not So Fantastic*, 98 N.Y.U. L. REV. 2055 (2023); Jack Wold-McGimsey, *Note: Climate Change and Modern State Common Law Nuisance and Trespass Tort Claims*, 94 U. COLO. L. REV. 815 (2023).

37 Nicholas Bryner, *The Once and Future Clean Air Act: Impacts of the Inflation Reduction Act on EPA's Regulatory Authority*, 65 B.C. L. Rev. 1, 1–41 (2024) (discussing history of Clean Air Act legal challenges related to climate change); J. B. Ruhl, *Climate Change and the Endangered Species Act: Building Bridges to the No-Analog Future*, 88 B.U. L. Rev. 1 (2008) (discussing challenges of applying the ESA to the problem of climate change).

38 Gregory N. Mandel & Gary E. Marchant, *The Living Regulatory Challenges of Synthetic Biology*, 100 IOWA L. REV. 155 (2014) (reviewing the reach of various environmental laws to regulate synthetic biology).

39 Alejandro E. Camacho & Robert L. Glicksman, *Legal Adaptive Capacity: How Program Goals and Processes Shape Federal Land Adaptation to Climate Change*, 87 U. COLO. L. REV. 711 (2016).

40 *See, e.g.*, CORRIE E. CLARK, ET. AL, CONG. RSCH. SERV., R46947, U.S. CLIMATE CHANGE POLICY (2021) (providing an overview of bills and actions taken and proposed at the federal level); Brigham Daniels, *Why Stop Grazing the Climate Commons?*, 13 MICH. J. ENV'T & ADMIN. L. 88 (2023) (providing an overview of meaningful climate actions at various levels of governance); Jonathan B. Wiener, *Think Globally, Act Globally: The Limits of Local Climate Policies*, 155 U. PA. L. REV. 1961 (2007) (discussing and critiquing local climate action).

41 Alejandro E. Camacho, *Adapting Governance to Climate Change: Managing Uncertainty Through a Learning Infrastructure*, 59 EMORY L.J. 1 (2009).

42 *See, e.g.*, Safe Drinking Water Act, § 300g-1(b)(3)(A)(i) (requiring the EPA to apply the "best available, peer-reviewed science"); Toxic Substances Control Act, 15 U.S.C. § 2625(h) (requiring the "best available science"); Endangered Species Act, 16 U.S.C. § 1533(b) (requiring reliance on "best scientific and commercial data available").

43 Camacho, *supra* note 41; Dave Huitema et al., *The Governance of Adaptation: Choices, Reasons, and Effects*, 21 ECOLOGY & SOC'Y 37 (2016).

44 *See, e.g.*, United States Administrative Procedure Act § 6, 5 U.S.C. §§ 551–559; 5 U.S.C. §§ 701–706.

45 *See, e.g.*, Craig R. Allen et al., *Adaptive Management for a Turbulent Future*, 92 J. ENV'T MGMT. 1339, 1343 (2011).

46 Robin Craig & J. B. Ruhl, *Designing Administrative Law for Adaptive Management*, 67 VAND. L. REV. 1, 4–5 (2014); Alejandro E. Camacho, *Transforming the Means and Ends of Natural Resource Management*, 89 N.C. L. Rev. 1405, 1414.

47 *See, e.g.*, Eric Biber, *The Problem of Environmental Monitoring*, 83 U. COLO. L. REV. 1, 34–52 (2011); Management Systems International, *An Independent Evaluation of the Effectiveness of the U.S. Fish and Wildlife Service's National Wildlife Refuge System* 20 (2008).

48 *See, e.g.*, J. B. Ruhl & Robert L. Fischman, *Adaptive Management in the Courts*, 95 MINN. L. REV. 424, 429 (2010) (stating that the adaptive management framework relies on "iterative cycles of goal determination, model building, performance standard setting, outcome monitoring, and standard recalibration").

49 Camacho, *supra* note 41, 76.

50 ALEJANDRO E. CAMACHO & ROBERT L. GLICKSMAN, REORGANIZING GOVERNMENT: A FUNCTIONAL AND DIMENSIONAL FRAMEWORK 221 (2019).

51 Cary Coglianese, *Deploying Machine Learning for a Sustainable Future*, *in* A BETTER PLANET: FORTY BIG IDEAS FOR A SUSTAINABLE FUTURE 200, 203 (Daniel C. Esty ed., 2019); *see also* M. Hino et al., *Machine Learning for Environmental Monitoring*, 1 NAT. SUSTAINABILITY 583 (2018).

52 Coglianese, *supra* note 50, 206.

53 *See, e.g.*, Alejandro E. Camacho & Nicholas J. Marantz, *Beyond Preemption, Toward Metropolitan Governance*, 39 STAN. ENV'T L.J. 125, 131 (2020) (describing provincial and local control over land use in the United States).

54 Alejandro E. Camacho, *In the Anthropocene: Adaptive Law, Ecological Health, and Biotechnologies*, 15 LAW, INNOVATION & TECH. 280 (2023).

55 *See, e.g.*, Robert L. Glicksman, *From Cooperative to Inoperative Federalism: The Perverse Mutation of Environmental Law and Policy*, 41 WAKE FOREST L. REV. 719, 747 (2006).

56 CAMACHO & GLICKSMAN, *supra* note 50.

57 *Id.* at 81–87.

58 *Id.*

59 *Id.*

60 *Id.* at 197–205.
61 *Id.* at 217–26.
62 *See* chap. 2.
63 *See* chap. 4.
64 *See* chap. 2.
65 *See* chap. 4.
66 *See* chap. 4.
67 *See* chap. 2.
68 *See* chap. 5.
69 *See, e.g.*, THOMAS O. MCGARITY, FREEDOM TO HARM: THE LASTING LEGACY OF THE LAISSEZ FAIRE REVIVAL (2013).
70 *See, e.g.*, Henry A. Giroux, *The Terror of Neoliberalism: Rethinking the Significance of Cultural Politics*, 32 COLL. LIT. 1, 2 (2005).
71 *See* chap. 4.
72 *See, e.g.*, Harvey M. Jacobs, *The Anti-Environmental "Wise Use" Movement in America*, 47 LAND USE LAW & ZONING DIGEST 3, 3–5 (1995) (discussing the wise-use movement); Maxwell T. Boykoff, *Consensus and Contrarianism on Climate Change*, 6 MÈTODE SCI. STUD. J. 89, 92–93 (2015); Spencer Sunshine & Chip Berlet, *Rural Rage: Right-Wing Populism and Patriot Movement in the United States*, *in* AUTHORITARIAN POPULISM AND THE RURAL WORLD 120, 128–34, 138–39 (Ian Scoones et al. ed., 2021).
73 *See, e.g.*, NAOMI ORESKES & ERIK M. CONWAY, MERCHANTS OF DOUBT: HOW A HANDFUL OF SCIENTISTS OBSCURED THE TRUTH ON ISSUES FROM TOBACCO SMOKE TO GLOBAL WARMING (2010); Charles N. Herrick & Dale Jamieson, *Junk Science and Environmental Policy: Obscuring Public Debate with Misleading Discourse*, 21 PHIL. & PUB. POL'Y Q. 11 (2001); Jeremy Levy et al., *Science and the Politics of Misinformation*, *in* THE ROUTLEDGE COMPANION TO MEDIA DISINFORMATION AND POPULISM 231, 231–39 (Howard Tumber & Silvio Waisbord eds., 2021).
74 *See generally* Derrick A. Bell, Jr., *Brown v. Board of Education and the Interest-Convergence Dilemma*, 93 HARV. L. REV. 518 (1980) (defining "interest convergence" as the principle that social change occurs for disenfranchised groups or perspectives when their interests align with those of more powerful majorities).
75 *See* chap. 2.
76 *See* Marianne Engelman Lado & Kenneth Rumelt, *Pipeline Struggles: Case Studies in Ground Up Lawyering*, 45 HARV. ENVTL. L. REV. 377 (2021) ("One of the most important lessons from each case study is that the courts alone are likely unable to drive systemic change. In the DAPL case, success has largely come from the community-driven social movement, which compelled the Obama Administration to reevaluate the Army Corps's actions under NEPA.").
77 *See e.g.*, Ben Kenward & Cameron Brick, *Large-Scale Disruptive Activism Strengthened Environmental Attitudes in the United Kingdom*, 2 GLOB. ENVTL. PSYCH. e11079, 25 (2024); RIK SCARCE, ECO-WARRIORS: UNDERSTANDING THE

Radical Environmental Movement 6 (Routledge updated ed. 2016). ("The tree sitters' presence, like that of the wolf activists, sometimes delays cutting until a judge can hear a request for an injunction. In other instances, the radicals offer extreme proposals for wilderness areas and the like that make those of mainstream environmental groups, such as the Sierra Club, Wilderness Society, and the National Wildlife Federation, look more reasonable").

78 Recognizing the duty of the Federal Government to create a Green New Deal, H.R. Res. 109, 116th Cong. (2019).

79 *See* chap. 5.

80 *See* Gilad Abiri, *Public Constitutional AI*, 59 Ga, L. Rev. 601, 669 (2025); Camacho, *supra* note 54, at 305; Camacho, *supra* note 41, at 16.

81 *See* Debra J. Davidson et al., *Just Don't Call It Climate Change: Climate-Skeptic Farmer Adoption of Climate-Mitigative Practices*, 14 Envtl. Res. Lett. 034015, 2 (2019).

82 Elizabeth Fisher, *EU Environmental Law and Legal Imagination*, *in* The Evolution of EU Law 847 (Paul Craig & Gráinne de Búrca eds., 3d ed. 2021).

83 *Id.* at 853.

84 *See* chap. 2.

85 *See* chap. 2.

86 *See* chap. 4.

87 H. Res. 109, 116th Cong. (2019).

88 *See, e.g.*, New York Constitution, Art. I, §19 (2022); Montana Constitution, Art. IX, § 1 (2025). *See also Held v. Montana*, 2024 MT 353 (2024) (holding state law limitations on considering greenhouse gas emissions when assessing oil and gas permit applications violated the state constitution's right to "a clean and healthful environment in Montana for present and future generations").

89 *See, e.g., Universal Declaration of the Rights of Mother Earth, International Rights of Nature Tribunal*, https://www.rightsofnaturetribunal.org/wp-content/uploads/2018/04/ENG-Universal-Declaration-of-the-Rights-of-Mother-Earth.pdf (last visited Sept. 29, 2025). *See also* Christopher D. Stone, *Should Trees Have Standing?–Towards Legal Rights for Natural Objects*, 45 S. Cal. L. Rev. 450 (1972).

90 *See, e.g.*, John Borrows, *Indigenous Law and Climate Change*, in Law in a Changing World 36 (Jutta Brunnée et al., eds., 2025); Elizabeth Kronk Warner & Jensen Lillquist, *Laboratories of the Future: Tribes and Rights of Nature*, 111 Cal L. Rev. 325, 328 (2023).

91 *See* The Red Nation, The Red Deal: Indigenous Action to Save Our Earth (2021); Nick Estes, Our History Is the Future: Standing Rock Versus the Dakota Access Pipeline and the Long Tradition of Indigenous Resistance (2019).

92 Richard J. Lazarus, *Super Wicked Problems and Climate Change: Restraining the Present to Liberate the Future*, 94 Cornell L. Rev. 1153, 1158 (2009).

93 Camacho, *supra* note 29, 897–902.

94 *See* chap. 1.
95 *See* chap. 4.
96 Dan Garisto, *How Trump is Following Project 2025's Radical Roadmap to Defund Science*, NATURE, Mar. 27, 2025.
97 *See* Richard L. Revesz, *Federalism and Environmental Regulation: A Public Choice Analysis*, 115 HARV. L. REV. 553, 585–88 (2001).
98 Bruce R. Huber, *How Did RGGI Do It? Political Economy and Emissions Auctions*, 40 ECOLOGY L.Q. 59 (2013); Sharmila L. Murthy, *States and Cities as 'Norm Sustainers': A Role for Subnational Actors in the Paris Agreement on Climate Change*, 37 VA. ENV'T L.J. 1 (2019).
99 Roderick Nash, *The American Invention of National Parks*, 22 AM. Q. 726 (1970). For a comparative discussion about parks around the planet, see NATIONAL PARKS BEYOND THE NATION: GLOBAL PERSPECTIVES ON "AMERICA'S BEST IDEA" (Adrian Howkins et al. eds., 2016).
100 Tseming Yang, *NEPA's Conquest of the World*, 37 NAT. RES. & ENV'T 1 (2023).
101 CAMACHO & GLICKSMAN, *supra* note 50, at 234–39.
102 DR. MARTIN LUTHER KING, JR., WHERE DO WE GO FROM HERE: CHAOS OR COMMUNITY? 12 (1967).
103 Dr. Martin Luther King, Jr., *Remaining Awake Through a Great Revolution*, Speech at the National Cathedral (Mar. 31, 1968).
104 *See* chap. 4.

INDEX

Page numbers in italics indicate photos

ABOUT THE AUTHORS

ALEJANDRO E. CAMACHO is a Professor of Law at the University of California, Los Angeles. His award-winning scholarship explores the evolution of legal goals, processes, and institutions, particularly in the context of environmental, natural resources, and land use law.

BRIGHAM DANIELS is Professor of Law and Co-Director of the Wallace Stegner Center for Land, Resources, and the Environment at the University of Utah, S. J. Quinney College of Law, as well directing the Stegner Center's Great Salt Lake Project. His scholarship focuses on common pool resource management, legal innovations needed to save Great Salt Lake, and environmental legal history.